The Editor and Translator

Dorothy Gilbert has served on the faculties of the University of California at Davis, Mills College, Merritt College, and the California State University, East Bay; since retiring from the California State University, she has taught in the Fall Program for Freshmen at the University of California, Berkeley. In addition, she has long been secretary of the West Coast branch of PEN, the writers' international advocacy organization. Her publications include a verse translation of Chrétien de Troyes' *Erec et Enide*, the first known Arthurian romance; verse translations of Old French fabliaux and Old English heroic poetry; original poetry in *The New Yorker, The Nation, The Iowa Review, PEN Southern Lights Anthology*, the online publications *Persimmon Tree* and *Tattoo Highway*, and numerous other journals. She has also published science fiction. Her reviews and articles have appeared in *Women's Studies, Translation Review*, and elsewhere.

Norton Critical Editions
Ancient, Classical, and Medieval Eras

For a complete list of Norton Critical Editions, visit
wwnorton.com/nortoncriticals

A NORTON CRITICAL EDITION

MARIE DE FRANCE
POETRY

NEW TRANSLATIONS
BACKGROUNDS AND CONTEXTS
CRITICISM

Translated and Edited by
DOROTHY GILBERT

W. W. NORTON & COMPANY · *New York* · *London*

W. W. Norton & Company has been independent since its founding in 1923, when William Warder Norton and Mary D. Herter Norton first published lectures delivered at the People's Institute, the adult education division of New York City's Cooper Union. The firm soon expanded its program beyond the Institute, publishing books by celebrated academics from America and abroad. By midcentury, the two major pillars of Norton's publishing program—trade books and college texts—were firmly established. In the 1950s, the Norton family transferred control of the company to its employees, and today—with a staff of more than four hundred and a comparable number of trade, college, and professional titles published each year—W. W. Norton & Company stands as the largest and oldest publishing house owned wholly by its employees.

Production manager: Vanessa Nuttry

Library of Congress Cataloging-in-Publication Data

Marie, de France, active 12th century.
   [Works. Selections. English.]
   Marie de France : poetry, new translations, backgrounds and contexts, criticism / translated and edited by Dorothy Gilbert.
       pages cm. — (A Norton critical edition)
   Includes bibliographical references.
   Translated from the Old French, with two lais also included in the original Old French.
   ISBN 978-0-393-93268-3 (pbk.)

   1. Marie, de France, active 12th century—Translations into English.
   2. Marie, de France, active 12th century—Criticism and interpretation.
   I. Gilbert, Dorothy, 1936- editor, translator.   II. Title.
   PQ1494.A3G55 2015
   841'.1—dc23

                                                          2015010079

W. W. Norton & Company, Inc., 500 Fifth Avenue, New York, NY 10110
wwnorton.com

W. W. Norton & Company Ltd., 15 Carlisle Street, London W1D 3BS

2   3   4   5   6   7   8   9   0

for my family

ki tant estes pruz e curteis,
a ki tute joie s'encline
E en ki quoer tuz biens racine—

—Marie de France, Dedication, Prologue to the *Lais,* 44–46

Contents

Backgrounds and Contexts

Preface

Virtually all we know about Marie de France we know, or deduce, from the internal evidence of her works. She is, as Howard Bloch has shown us, "anonymous"—but so vibrant that in effect she is not anonymous at all. External evidence, though, presents a challenge: it is not only scarce, but in Catholic France in the late twelfth century—the time period where we can safely place this writer—there were a number of prominent women named Marie who might be candidates for the historic personage behind the literary presence who exists for us. In her own time (1180), Denis Piramus mentions a Dame Marie who composed "*lais* in verse that are not at all true" (vv.37–38) but which were extremely popular, delighted in by both men and women who never tired of hearing them repeated; the title "Marie de France" did not exist for her until Claude Fauchet bestowed it on her in 1581. That is about as far as historical identification goes. Attempts have been made to establish our poet as the abbess of Shaftesbury, the illegitimate half-sister of Henry II of England; as the abbess of Reading; the countess of Boulogne; or Marie de Meulan, a daughter of one of the great nobles of Burgundy. Her dedication of the *Lais* to a most "noble king" is assumed by most scholars to be addressed to Henry II, though other monarchs, such as Philip Augustus of France, have occasionally been suggested. Whoever Marie was, she was fluent in Latin, French, and quite likely English. She had at least a passing acquaintance with Norman and Breton; words in those languages appear, emphasized, in several of her *Lais*. She knew her Ovid; she knew her *clergie*, the Latin inheritance of learned discourse down through the centuries of the Christian Church; she had a great store of popular tales that had existed in many parts of Europe for centuries before her time (many have lived on since, some plainly or possibly because of her). And she most certainly knew the practice of *courtoisie*, or *fin' amors*—courtliness, refined love between men and women—that was the fashion in the aristocratic society of her age.

But within these works is a most distinctive, individual voice, and one hears its strength and vigor early. In the Prologue to the *Lais* is, immediately, the voice of a conscious artist who has cast about for a work to translate from Latin into French and believes that so much has been done in that field that there is no individual distinction in doing it; therefore, she has chosen *lais* that she has heard and, to preserve their memory, has set them down in poetry, working "far into a sleepless night" (l.42). In the Prologue to the *lai* "Guigemar," she responds with vigorous indignation to the "vicious cowardly curs" (*malveis chien coart*, 1.13) who envy her renown and slander her; but they are within their rights, she says, if they wish to be that sort of people. Throughout the *Lais,* and in the often individual morals she draws in her *Fables,* one can sense a distinct voice, as one can in *Saint Patrick's Purgatory* (the *Espurgatoire Seint Patriz*), where she expresses a desire to make the story available to the common people (secular people who don't read Latin). In the *Fables,* when she might refer to Jupiter as her sources do, or to the "scippend"—English for the "Shaper" or Creator"—she prefers the feminine form—"sepande," the goddess, Nature.

In the past, there has been some debate over whether these three works were by the same poet; currently, most scholars believe that they have one voice. Since 2004 debate has arisen around the argument by June Hall McCash that a fourth work, *La Vie seinte Audree,* is by Marie. Much of the language and perspective in this work resembles Marie's established *oeuvre* in a highly suggestive way; I have not, at present, followed the number of distinguished critics who have definitely assigned Marie this work. For reasons of space, I have included only the three established works; an edition and translation of *La Vie seinte Audree* is available. (See the bibliography to this volume.)

The present book contains, along with my verse translations of Marie's established three works, a "Contexts" section and a small collection of "Criticism." Known sources for Marie are few, but in the "Contexts" section are some obvious and famous ones: Ovid's love poetry, Petronius's naughty story of the "Woman Who Hanged Her Husband's Body" (or "The Widow of Ephesus"), and some Fables of Babrius and Phaedrus, part of the fable tradition available to Marie. The Middle English "Launfal" and "Lay le Freine" are essentially translations from her work. The charming Middle English debate poem *The Owl and the Nightingale* (ca. 1200), an excerpt of which I have translated into modern English, refers to Marie's "Laüstic," her sad story of the nightingale. Other works included, such as Child Ballad #62, "Fair Annie," the Boccaccio tale of ever-patient Griselda, or Chaucer's "Merchant's Tale," from *The Canterbury Tales* (where, of course, Chaucer also retold Boccaccio's Griselda story in "The Clerk's Tale"), may not be directly influenced by Marie de France; they are retellings of much-loved stories that she used well before they did, or themes and plots that she used, that seem to have been hugely enjoyed in much of European culture for centuries and surely had an existence in oral culture long before they were written down. Chaucer's "Tale of Sir Thopas" is included here because it is a hilarious parody of the medieval fairy story so loved that it was told to (a ridiculous) death: the story of a knight who in some wilderness finds a most compliant fairy mistress and enjoys ebullient sex and various other gifts from her. I have also included a selection from the tongue-in-cheek twelfth-century treatise *The Art of Courtly Love* (*De arte honeste amandi*) by Andreas Capellanus (André the Chaplain), which purports to be a guide for those refined souls at various levels of the aristocracy who are seeking love. And I have included some lore on the ancient theme of the man-wolf—Marie's troubled, decent "Bisclavret"—a prevalent theme in Western culture from Ovid and the New Testament to the popular literature and film of the present. On another note, this book contains an excerpt from Marie's source for the *Saint Patrick's Purgatory*, the Latin treatise *Tractatus de Purgatorio Sanctii Patricii*, by the monk H. of Saltrey[1] (translated by Jean-Michel Picard); and accounts by Bede (English, seventh century) and the Irishman Tnugdal (1149) of an afterlife of torture and anguish for sinners who were at least spared Hell (though not by much; many of the punishments described are as bad as anything in Dante, who was well aware of this kind of literature).

Reasons of space have prevented me from including as many critical discussions of Marie as I would have liked. In any case, it is impossible to do justice to all the significant and valuable criticism of Marie; the body of commentary has often been described as "vast" or "huge" and is accounted for in four distinguished and invaluable annotated bibliographies by Glyn S. Burgess (see the Selected Bibliography in this volume). In the last thirty years or so, investigations and discussions of Marie—a writer whose themes are so various, whose range of subject matter is so wide—have truly burgeoned. I include a few short passages of early commentary, by the eighteenth-century historians Thomas Warton and Thomas Tyrwhitt; the Abbé Gervais de la Rue (1800); the dismissive and patronizing reference by the major nineteenth-century French critic Joseph Bedier; and a brief discussion of imagery by Leo Spitzer. Denis Piramus, Marie's contemporary, is included in later discussion. From modern criticism I include observations by R. Howard Bloch, who in his distinguished book *The Anonymous Marie de*

---

1. I follow Jacques Le Goff in *The Birth of Purgatory* (trans. Arthur Goldhammer) in referring to "H. of Saltrey" rather than "Henry" or "Henricus." Le Goff states that Matthew Paris, in the thirteenth century, expanded the "H." to "Henry," "for no good reason." See p. 193 of *The Birth of Purgatory* or p. 393 of this Norton Critical Edition, where the relevant passage is excerpted.

France refers to Marie as "the Joyce of the twelfth century," "among the most self-conscious, sophisticated, complicated, obscure, tricky, and disturbing figures of her time" (19). E. A. Francis's early article (1939) on how "Lanval" demonstrates that Marie knew well the practice of English law in her time is also included; also here are Jill Mann's magisterial comments on beast literature in medieval Britain and the complex view of society shown in Marie's *Fables* and, very differently, in her *Lais*. Last, I include excerpts from Jacques Le Goff's celebrated volume *The Birth of Purgatory*, with its forceful account of how the need for the institution of Purgatory arose— probably established by 1170—and its very useful discussions of Otherworld Journeys such as those included in the present volume.

As a translator, I sought the quick, fluid, turn-on-a-dime quality of Marie's octosyllabic couplets. I translated line by line, so that my versions are exactly the length of hers and each line corresponds to one of hers. Since I write in English, I do use iambic tetrameter; the stresses of English demand it, and to ignore or suppress that or set it aside means that the lines do not "bounce" right. I freely took advantage of modern rhyming practice in English, where half-rhyme, or slant rhyme, is used much of the time, perhaps to good advantage, since octosyllabics can have what George Saintsbury called a "fatal fluency," and too many exact rhymes in many such short lines can create an off-putting "chime of rhyme all the time." I trust I have been able to make some approximation of Marie's supple style, which can carry so many different emotional qualities and which employs so beautifully the elegant cages of sound— "sound that bounds around"—this kind of verse offers.

My copy text for the *Lais* is Jean Rychner's *Les Lais de Marie de France* in the series *Les Classiques de Moyen Age*, edited by Mario Roques (Librarie Honoré Champion, 1966). I have also consulted the well-known edition *Marie de France: Lais*, edited by A. Ewert (Basil Blackwell, 1944). Both are based on the most authoritative manuscript of the *Lais*, BL MS Harley 978. For the *Fables* I have consulted Karl Warnke's *Die Fabeln der Marie de France* (Halle: Niemeyer, 1898) and a compact disc supplied by the British Library of MS Harley 978. For Marie's *Espurgatoire de seinte Patriz*, I have consulted the edition of Karl Warnke, *Das Buch vom Espurgatoire S. Patrice der Marie de France und Seine Quelle* (Halle, 1938; Geneve: Slatkine Reprints, 1976), which is based on BN fr.22407, folios 102r –122v. For the Middle English *The Owl and the Nightingale*, my copy text is Eric Gerald Stanley's excellent edition (Thomas Nelson, 1960); I was also able to consult the fine, much-praised more recent edition by Neil Cartlidge (University of Exeter Press, 2001).

I feel the deepest gratitude to those luminous and generous spirits whose assistance has made this work possible. The late Charles

Muscatine vetted several of my translations of the *Lais*, and he was unfailingly astute, encouraging, enthusiastic, and gallant. Joseph J. Duggan similarly vetted two of the *Lais* for me most rigorously and helpfully, before the demands of his own magisterial work on the *Chanson de Roland* claimed him; he was glad to help with any cruxes or interpretations I found perplexing. Sandra M. Gilbert gave me careful and most valuable readings of all translations with advice on poetic practice. The poet and translator Anne Winters was also helpful. The poet-translators Chana Bloch, Dan Bellm, and Peter Dale Scott gave some valuable pointers about the *Fables*. I also warmly thank my writer friends Mimi Albert, Maria Espinosa, and Judith Stephens. The staff at the Bibliothèque Nationale and the Bibliothèque de l'Arsenal in Paris were most helpful in enabling me to examine original manuscripts or facsimiles of them. As above, the British Library supplied me with a compact disc of MS Harley 978, the most authoritative manuscript of the *Lais*; it contains all of them together with the *Fables*. The Gardner Library of the University of California at Berkeley and the Graduate Theological Union Library of Berkeley provided invaluable materials and assistance. E. Arnon and Sanjeev Sood gave much invaluable help with manuscript preparation; Judith and Jay Piper were essential in assisting me with computer exigencies. I am deeply grateful to my Norton editor, Carol Bemis, for her warm and astute support and her near-infinite patience; to her most perspicacious and resourceful assistants, Thea Goodrich and Rachel Goodman; to our invaluable copy editor Katharine Ings, and to other colleagues who assisted in the preparation of this book. All errors and infelicities in this work are mine.

On a personal note, I must also warmly thank my friend Ann Abbott, who frequently offered me the use of her home inside Yosemite National Park, where I translated many hundreds of Marie's lines as I looked out into the forest of giant ponderosas and incense cedars. The support of my family has been beyond all price.

The Poetry of
MARIE DE FRANCE

The Lais

TRANSLATIONS

Prologue

WHOM God has given intelligence
and the great gift of eloquence
must not conceal these, or keep still,
4 but share and show them with good will.
When much is heard of some good thing,
then comes its first fine flowering;
when many more have praise to give,
8 these blossoms flourish, spread and thrive.
Among the ancients, custom was—
Priscian can testify to this—[1]
that in their books they made obscure
12 much that they wrote; this would ensure
that wise folk of another day,
needing to know what these texts say,
could gloss these works, and with their sense
16 give all the more intelligence.
Savants and scholars were aware
that in their strivings, more and more
they sensed the works' great subtlety
20 increasingly, as time went by.
And thus, too, they knew how to guard
from error in time afterward.
He who would keep from vice and sin
24 must some great arduous work begin;
struggle and study, strive to know,
and doing so avoid much woe,
free from great suffering and regret.

---

1. Ewert's note (163). "Priscianus [was] a Latin grammarian of the sixth century. Marie here refers to the beginning of his *Institutiones* (text in Keil *Grammatici Latini* II, i)." Burgess and Busby add (138), "Marie's reference may be to his best known work, the *Institutiones Grammaticae*, but could be to his remarks in his *Prae-exercitamina.*"

3

28   Thus I began to give some thought
      to telling some good story, that
      taken from Latin, I would put
      into French; but then I would win
32   no glory there; so much is done!
      I thought of *lais* that I had heard
      and did not doubt; I felt assured
      that these first writers who began
36   these *lais*, who told them, made them known,
      wished, for remembrance, to record
      adventures, stories, they had heard.
      I too have heard them; I do not
40   wish them abandoned, lost, forgot.
      Thus I made rhymes and poetry
      late into night-time, wakefully!

      To honor you, most noble King,[2]
44   courtly and skilled in everything,[3]
      to whom all joy makes obeisance,
      in whose heart roots all excellence,
      to gather *lais* I undertook,
48   to rhyme, make, tell; this was my work.
      I in my heart thought this I'd do,
      fair Sire: present this work to you.
      If it should please you to receive
52   my gift, for all the days I live
      I shall be joyful; you shall give
      great happiness. Do not believe

2. Most probably this is Henry II, who reigned over England from 1154–1189 and also held lands in much of France. Some scholars believe that Marie was his illegitimate half-sister, the abbess of Shaftesbury.

3. Marie says in her original that she does not wish to neglect or forget the stories she has heard; one can say that she fears that they will die out of common knowledge and be lost and therefore she feels a duty to rescue them.
   The word I have translated "skilled" is *pruz* (sometimes spelled *preux*), often translated "brave" or "worthy." It is a necessary quality of the chivalrous male, the knight, just as he must also be *curteis*, or "courtly." Alternative translations might be the following: "Courtly, worthy in everything," which sounds metrically awkward to my ear. I was also very tempted to use the word "wise," since a worthy king had better be a wise one, and good judgment is implicit in the brave knight, in his readiness to act: "Courtly and wise in everything." I have settled on "skilled" (following the suggestion mentioned below) since it seems to me to carry out the sense of "worthy" and to also echo and reinforce the idea of *curteis* as "courtly" or "refined, courteous" and also be applicable in a military sense, referring to courage.
   Professsor Joseph J. Duggan, of the French and Comparative Literature Departments at UC Berkeley, wrote to me after looking at my translation: "I too have struggled with *preux* and finally translated it as "skilled" and "accomplished" since it signifies excellence in whatever is one's occupation. Thus a monk who is *preux* is learned and pious, a *preude femme* is chaste (whence Eng. *prude*), and a vassal who is *preux* is brave, battle-worthy, and a good counselor."

me proud, presumptuous; but hear
56   as I begin my tales; give ear.

Guigemar

Who treats of good material
must suffer when it's not told well.
Good seigneurs, listen to Marie,
4   who in her time takes seriously[1]
her duty, not neglecting it.
People should praise the one whose wit
earns good repute; but often when
8   in some land there exists a man
or woman of a great renown,
those envious of the work they've done
speak villainy, intending thus
12   by abuse to do business.
Such folk are vicious, cowardly curs,
biting maliciously. Their slurs
will never stop me; slanderers,
16   false and vindictive posturers,
Oh, let them try such calumny!
It is their right to slander me!

These stories, that I know are true,
20   from which the Breton poets drew
their *lais*, I'll briefly tell to you.
After these words, what I will do
is show you an adventure, one
24   from Little Brittany, and known
as an event in ancient days.
Writings, old texts, say thus, and *lais*.[2]

Hoilas was king, then, heretofore:
28   often at peace, often at war.
And this king had a vassal, one

1. The original, *en sun tens* ("in her time") is generally thought to mean "given her opportunity" (i.e., she does not neglect her obligations). See the Introduction to Burgess and Busby's Penguin Classics edition (9) and R. Howard Bloch's introductory chapter to his study *The Anonymous Marie de France* (12). It can also have the meaning of "in her time, in her age." I think both meanings are intended, with the first the dominant one.
2. Marie distinguishes among three kinds of narrative: the *aventure*, which is purported to take place in history; the *lai*, or tale, which is what the Bretons composed; and the *conte*, which is what she herself is telling. First comes the "adventure," which she says really happened; then the *lai* that the Bretons made of it; and, finally, her version, the *conte* she derived from the Breton *lai*.

who was the baron of Lïun;[3]
this man was called Oridials.
32 Much in the confidence, he was,
of Hoilas; a brave knight and true.
By his wife he had children, two,
a boy, and lovely girl, as well—
36 named Noguent, this demoiselle.
Her brother was named Guigemar;
in that realm none was handsomer!
A marvel was his mother's love,
40 and great respect his father gave.
When they could bear such offering
they sent him out to serve the king.
There, this astute and brave young man
44 was greatly loved by everyone.
After a time, he reached the stage
of understanding, came of age,
and the king dubbed him splendidly
48 with all the arms he wished; then he
made his departure, left the court;
so many gifts he handed out!
Flanders he sought, to make his fame;
52 there's always war there. In Lorraine,
in Burgundy, or in Anjou,
the Southeast, Gascon regions, too,
no man could find, try as he might,
56 the equal of this fine young knight.

In one way, Nature, though, did err:
for love this young man had no care.
Under sweet heaven, no demoiselle
60 nor dame, noble and beautiful,
would not, if he had sought her love,
been happy to acceptance give!
Many dames sought him, often; never
64 did one awake in him the lover.
Any observing him could see
he had no thought of an *amie*;[4]
stranger perceived him, as did friend
68 as loving men, and surely damned.

---

3. This place is Léon, in Finisterre, on the Breton coast facing England.
4. *Ami/amie* is French for "friend"; in medieval courtly usage it means "sweetheart, lover."
It could also be used as an address in situations of flirtation or gallantry.

Now when his fame was in full bloom
this baron made a visit home
to see his lord, to see his father,
72   his sister, his devoted mother,
all of whom longed for his return.
With them he made a long sojourn;
I think it was a month, entire.

76   To hunt: now, that was his desire.
His knights he summoned, and his hunters,
the night before; called out his beaters,
then in the morning started out,
80   for dearly he enjoyed this sport.
For a great stag they gathered there;
the dogs were loosed. And Guigemar
had all his huntsmen ride before.
84   He lingered, dallying in the rear.
A servant bore his dog, his bow;[5]
his quiver, and his knife also,
for, given opportunity,
88   he'd aim before the deer could flee.

Then, in a thicket's thickest part,
he saw a hind, with fawn. Her coat[6]
was all pure white, and on her head
92   a stag's fine antlers branched and spread.
The brachet barked; she bounded out—
he took his bow, he drew his shot!
—and struck her forehead. She went down[7]
96   instantly, crumpled on the ground.
The arrow bounced, and then flew back
toward Guigemar again, and struck
clear through his thigh, and grazed his horse

---

5. Ewert's note (166): "*berseretz* as a subst. normally means 'hunting dog'; and it is a fact
   that certain hunting dogs were carried to the chase; but it appears from the examples
   cited by Tobler-Lammasch, *Altfr. Wb*, that it also denoted some part of the huntsman's
   equipment, most probably the quiver, as in the present instance." In my translation
   I have opted for both the quiver and the dog. See also Rychner, 241.
6. White animals are frequently associated with the supernatural in medieval tales. Cf.
   Chrétien de Troyes' *Erec et Enide*, where Arthur and his courtiers hunt a white stag and
   the hero is set out on his adventures, in love and prowess, as a consequence. Marie's
   animal is clearly hermaphroditic; it is a hind (doe) with its young but possesses a stag's
   signature antlers.
7. The word *esclot* is glossed in Ewert as "hoof." Rychner, while saying that "sabot" is a
   common translation, says that it is the forehead of the animal, citing evidence from sev-
   eral other scholars, and commenting that the ricochet is more plausible if it is the hind's
   forehead being described, the hoof being a bit low down! (Rychner, 241). I follow Rych-
   ner and Burgess and Busby in using "forehead."

100   so that he slipped and fell, perforce,
      spread out upon a grassy spot
      next to the white hind he'd just shot.

      The hind, who was in agony
104   from her great wound, spoke sorrowfully
      words of lament, out of her pain:
      "Alas, my death wound! I am slain.
      You, vassal! You, who wounded me,
108   this is to be your destiny.
      No medicine of any sort,
      no kindly herb, no soothing root,
      physician, potion, shall be yours.
112   Never shall you know any cures
      of the deep wound there in your thigh
      till you meet her whose injury
      is her great suffering for your love.
116   The pain and anguish she shall have
      —greater than ever woman has known—
      shall wound you, too, and be your own.
      Many shall marvel, and be aghast—
120   lovers present, and lovers past,
      lovers who will love by and by.
      Now go: leave me in peace to die."

      Guigemar saw now, with dismay,
124   he had a serious injury,
      and he considered where to go,
      where, in what region, one would know
      to cure the damage in his thigh.
128   He would not languish here and die.
      He knew, he said, he'd never seen
      ever, a lady who had been
      one he could seek in love, for sure—
132   or one whose sorrow he could cure.

      He called his servant to his side.
      "Friend!" he said, "Quickly, go! Due speed!
      Bring my companions back to me,
136   I wish to speak to them, urgently."

      The squire spurred off, the knight remained,
      his pain acute; much he complained.
      He tore his shirt in strips. He bound
140   a bandage of them on his wound.

Then he mounted and rode away,
to distance himself speedily.
He did not wish his men to come
144   galloping back to hinder him.

There was a green path through the wood.
He followed it until it led
into a clearing. From this plain
148   he saw a cliff and a mountain.
Below, a stream ran, formed a river
running straight down to deeper water,
making a harbor. There lay by
152   a ship, just one; he could descry
one sail. Well fitted to depart
this vessel was; inside and out
caulked so no joint was visible.
156   The fittings, pegs and deck-rails, all
were of the blackest ebony.
No gold more rich beneath the sky!
The sail was silken, and when full,
160   playing the wind, how beautiful!

The knight felt great anxiety.
About this wild locality
he'd never heard, from any talk,
164   this was a place where ships could dock.
Forward he rode, got off his horse,
embarked. He felt his pain's full force,
but thought to find some men on board.
168   Surely there were some, standing guard.
But he saw no one; they were gone.
In the ship's midst he happened on
a bed, made in the fashion
172   of Solomon;[8] posts, sides, all done,
cut, carved, engraved, with gold inlay,
and cypress and white ivory.
Silk cloth with woven gold was spread
176   —a splendid quilt—upon the bed.
Other bedclothes I could not price,
the pillow, though—I'll tell you this—

8. I.e., in richly chased, carved metal. Opulent and costly furnishings and fabrics came to
be associated in the Middle Ages with Solomon and his magnificence and wealth, which,
along with his wisdom, was proverbial. Cf. The Song of Songs, Cap. III, vv. 9–10, Vul-
gate, which, Abercrombie has pointed out (*Modern Language Review*, XXX, 353), has a
description of a bed or litter made by Solomon that closely resembles this passage.

whoever laid his head down there
180 would never, ever have white hair.
The sable spread had purple lining
of Alexandrian designing;
two golden candelabras shone
184 at the ship's prow; the lesser one
still a great treasure, of great price.
Candles illumined all the place.
He marveled. He could not resist;
188 he lay down on the bed, to rest,
his wound continually hurt him so.
Then he got up again, to go,
but he could not! Now he could see
192 the ship was on the wide, high sea!
With him it swiftly moved, with ease,
making good time in a mild breeze.
There was no way that he could leave!
196 Much he began to fear and grieve.
No wonder that he felt dismay—
his wound, worse, gave him agony.
This falling out he must endure.
200 He prayed to God to give him cure,
give him safe port, if such could be,
and save him from mortality.
He lay and slept. Unknown to him
204 the very worst had come and gone,
and before evening he would come
to where his cure awaited him,
an ancient town, the principal
208 town of its realm, the capital.

This city's lord was of great age,
and he was joined in marriage
to a fine dame of high degree,
212 wise, noble, skilled in courtesy.
Madly jealous the husband was
and by his nature, covetous,
suspicious, as old men will be,
216 wild at the thought of cuckoldry.
Such is old coots' perversity!
He did not guard her carelessly.
A garden lay just by the keep
220 set with enclosures high and steep,
walls of green marble all around,

oh, formidably stout and sound!
It had one entrance, one sole way,
224 and that was guarded night and day.
Then on the other side, the sea
made an effective boundary,
for none could enter or go out
228 unless they did so with a boat
should need arise within the keep.
Inside these walls so stout and steep
the lord, to keep his wife secure,
232 had made a chamber; lovelier
room, under heaven, has never been.
A chapel was in front; and then
the room, its paintings. On the wall,
236 Venus, goddess of love, with all
her traits portrayed; how lovers must
serve loyally, and live their trust.
That book of Ovid, where he tells
240 how lovers must restrain themselves,[9]
was being cast in a fierce fire,
and divine Venus, in her ire
was calling excommunicate
244 all who had read or followed it.
Here the lord's wife was prisoner.
She'd a young girl to wait on her,
thus was the husband generous.
248 Noble, and well brought up, she was,
the lord's own niece, his sister's daughter.
Much the two women loved each other.
And always, when the lord was gone,
252 the niece was there till his return.
Man or woman there was none
who could have entered, or have flown
such walls. A hoary, elderly
256 priest held in charge the postern key.
His lower members were long lost;
this was the reason for his trust.
He said God's Service, this old priest;
260 and served the lady her repast.

---

9. Ovid (Publius Ovidius Naso, 43 B.C.E.–17 C.E.) wrote the *Remedia Amoris*, or *Cures for Love*, a mock recantation of his earlier *Ars Amatoria*, or *Art of Love*, in addition to other love poems and the great *Metamorphoses*. The *Ars Amatoria* is a mock-didactic work on the arts of seduction and intrigue. Ovid's works were enormously influential in the Middle Ages and the Renaissance. See note on p. 243 of this Norton Critical Edition; also pp. 269–75, for examples of Ovid's love poetry.

Early that very afternoon
the dame had to the garden gone;
after her meal she slept, and then
264 wanted diversion. She looked down,
she and her maiden, toward the shore,
saw how the ship was rising there,
climbing the waves, and rapidly
268 sailing toward port. She could not see
that someone steered. Anxiety
rose in her, and she wished to flee—
small wonder! In her fear, she blushed
272 deeply; into her face blood rushed.

But the young girl, intelligent
and with a bolder temperament,
comforted and assured her. Then,
276 wasting no time, they hurried down,
and the girl tossed her coat off. Now,
boarding the ship, so beautiful,
she saw no living thing, apart
280 from the one man, the sleeping knight.
She stood still, looking down. The color
of the man' face, the awful pallor,
convinced her he was dead; and she
284 went to her lady hastily,
reporting truly what she'd seen,
lamenting much the poor dead man.

"We'll see to this!" the lady said.
288 "We'll bury him, if he is dead,
our priest will help us. If I see
that he's alive, he'll speak to me."
They went together, all due speed:
292 this time the lady took the lead,
the girl held back. She boarded, stood
quite motionless, before the bed,
looking down at the chevalier.
296 Deeply his beauty saddened her,
his lovely body, his young life
over so soon, filled her with grief.
Over his breast she put her hand;
300 the warmth, the healthy heart she found,
under his ribs the beat was strong.
The knight, who'd been asleep so long
awoke and saw her. Full of joy

304   he greeted her delightedly;
       he'd come to shore, that much was clear.
       Pensive and tearful, she made cheer,
       however, and polite reply.
308   And then she asked him how and why
       he'd come, he'd happened on this shore.
       Was he an exile? From a war?

          "No, lady, not at all," said he.
312   "But if it pleases you, I'll say
       truthfully, how I came here, not
       concealing from you any part.
       I am from Little Brittany.
316   I hunted in the woods today.
       I found a white hind, drew my shot;
       the arrow bounded back, and hit
       my thigh. Here is the wound, you see.
320   I think there is no remedy,
       ever. The hind, in pain and grief
       cursed me, swore I'd find no relief
       from my own pain, ever, till I found
324   a damsel who could cure my wound.
       Who knows where such a girl might be!
       But when I heard my destiny
       I left the forest speedily.
328   I found the harbor; I could see
       the ship. I boarded it, fool me!
       It took me off on the wide sea.
       I have no notion where I am,
332   or by what name this town is known.
       For God's sake, lovely lady, say,
       Help me! I beg of you! Which way,
       in what direction, must I go?
336   Sailing's a skill I do not know!"

          She said, "Fair sire, most willingly
       I'll help, and do it easily.
       My husband rules this town, this ground;
340   he's lord of all the country round.
       He's wealthy, of high lineage;
       but he is much advanced in age,
       wild in his crazy jealousy.
344   For honor's sake, he's prisoned me
       within these walls; no liberty
       for me! There's just one entranceway;

an old priest guards it, guards the gate.
348 May hell's flames take him, hell's own hate!
Day and night I am shut in here,
never to leave. I do not dare
unless with his consent, to stir.
352 Or I can serve my old *seigneur*!
My chapel and my room you see,
and my dear maid who lives with me.
Now, if it pleases you to stay
356 until you've strength to go your way,
willingly we shall shelter you
and do what service we can do."
    The wounded man, when he had heard,
360 thanked her with a most gracious word;
yes, he would stay with them, he said.
He sat up then; he rose from bed;
the women, struggling, aided him.
364 The lady led him to the room.
They laid him on the maiden's bed;
behind a curtain he was hid,
well tucked under a canopy
368 meant for the young girl's privacy.
In golden bowls, water was brought
to wash his thigh-wound, clean it out;
cloth of white linen, fine and good,
372 the ladies used to wash the blood,
tightly they wound the bandage there;
they did it with much tender care!
And when the evening meal was brought
376 the maiden ate less, just a bit,
so that the guest could fill his plate.
Oh, very well he drank and ate!

    But Love, that ambusher, had found
380 the man; had struck, a mortal wound.
The injury was so profound
he lost all thought of native land.
No pain he felt now in his thigh,
384 but the new anguish made him sigh,
and of the girl he made request
she let him be, to sleep and rest.
She went away, left him alone;
388 once he dismissed her, she was gone.
Sent from her post, she sought her dame,
the lady, warmed by the same flame

as Guigemar, lit by the fire
392 of incandescent, fierce desire!
      Still by himself, the chevalier,
pensive, full of despair and fear,
did not yet fathom why he grieved;
396 certainly Guigemar perceived
that if the lady worked no cure
his death was imminent and sure.

      "Alas!" he said. "What shall I do?
400 I'll go to her. I'll beg; I'll sue
for mercy, pity; ask that she
help a poor wretched man like me.
If she refuses then to grant
404 my prayers, is proud and arrogant,
then of my sorrow I must die,
or languish, ill, indefinitely."

      Again, he sighed. After a bit
408 there came to him another thought,
that he must suffer and endure;
there was no other way, no cure.
All night he lay awake and pined,
412 he sighed, and struggled in his mind,
seeing again all he had seen—
her speech, her beauty and her mien;
her lovely mouth, her sparkling eyes
416 stirred in his heart sweet agonies.
Just to himself, inaudibly
he—almost!—called her his *amie*!
If he'd suspected half her thought,
420 how Love likewise distressed her heart,
he'd have felt joy, it's my belief,
some consolation, some relief
from all that agony and dolor
424 that robbed his countenance of color.

      If his love pangs made him distraught,
she could not boast advantage, but
before the daybreak and the light
428 she rose. She had not slept all night,
and desperately complained. For sure
Amor it was that tortured her.
Her maiden, though—astute and keen—
432 quickly saw, from the lady's mien

she'd fallen for the chevalier
who was their guest, sojourning there,
resting and hoping for a cure.
436 She did not know if he loved her.
    The lady went to chapel; then
the girl slipped in to see the man.
She sat herself down by his bed.
440 At that he spoke to her, and said:
    "Friend, where has my lady gone?
Why did she rise before the dawn?"
Then he was silent; sighed. And she
444 spoke to him expeditiously.
    "Ha, sire, you are in love, I see!
Fair sire, beware of secrecy
kept too long! You've a chance to have
448 place in my lady's heart, and love.
He who would win my lady's heart
must hold her always in his thought.
Steadfast and faithful to each other—
452 that's the right way, lover to lover!
Courage! You are a handsome knight
and she is beautiful."
                      At that
he spoke. "I feel that spark ignite!
456 If I've no help, some rotten plight
will find me, and this tale will end
wretchedly. Counsel me, dear friend,
what shall I do, then, with this love?"
460   She, with the natural sweetness of
her nature, gave the chevalier
comforting words, to reassure,
with all her skills, the wretched knight.
464 She was most graceful and adroit.
    The lady, coming back from mass,
was mindful, too, of politesse
and duty, for the sick man's sake.
468 Had he slept well? Or lain awake?
Her passion had not gone away.
The maiden called to her to say,
go to the chevalier! Oh, go!
472 There they could at their leisure show
what moved each heart, what drove each will;
turn it to fortune, good or ill.
    She greeted him; he greeted her.
476 And there they were, both wild with fear.

How could he ask such favors, dare!
Here on strange soil, a foreigner,
his terror of her was acute.
480 What if she loathed, despised, his suit?
But he who hides infirmity
cannot expect recovery.
Love is the secret wound within;
484 outside, perhaps not seen or known.
It's Nature's gift, to be a lover—
how the wound lasts! Perhaps forever?
There are those jesting chevaliers
488 one knows of, boorish courtiers,
trying, seducing everyone!
And then they boast of what they've done.
This is not love, but travesty—
492 It's wickedness and lechery.
One who is able to discover
a loyal love, must serve that lover
loyally and devotedly.
496   Guigemar loved so desperately,
instantly he must find relief
or live a life of barren grief.
Love gave courage to Guigemar:
500   And thus he spoke his will to her.
"Oh, lady, for your sake I die!
My heart is full of misery.
You could cure me; if you do not,
504 a wretched death will be my lot.
Oh, fair one, I must have your love!
Do not reject what you can save!"
When she had heard this heartfelt try
508 she gave the seemly, right reply
and answered, laughing. "This request,
friend, is too hasty! Much too fast
for me to think of granting it.
512 I'm not accustomed to such thought!"

"Oh, lady, mercy, for God's sake!
Do not be vexed at what I speak.
We know how fickle, worldly dames
516 make a vocation of their games,
teasing, denying in a guise
that makes them seem a dearer prize
—and less corrupted! But the wise,
520 true, worthy lady never tries

such folly! If she likes the man,
she'll not be proud or cruel to him,
but love him, and enjoy his love.
524   Before it's known, heard, spoken of,
what profit's theirs, what good, dear friend!
Fair one, this argument must end!"
     The truth of what he had to say
528   seemed to her plain. Without delay
she granted all he asked of her.
He kissed her. Henceforth Guigemar
was at his ease. They lay together,
532   kissing, embracing, lover to lover.
May they achieve most happily
the rest, that comes so naturally!

     From what I'm told, then Guigemar
536   lived a year and a half with her
deliciously, in joy content.
But Fortune, ever vigilant,
turns her great wheel as time goes by;
540   one's crushed beneath, and one's thrust high.
So these two, turn and turn about:
oh, soon enough they were found out.
     Very early one summer day,
544   side by side the lovers lay,
beautiful lady and young man.
She kissed his mouth, his face; spoke then:
     "Fair sweet friend, my fearful heart
548   tells me I'll lose you, that we'll part,
we'll be discovered. If you die,
I wish to die too. If you fly,
you'll find another love, while I
552   will stay here in great misery."
     "Oh, never say so, dearest love!
Peace and joy I can never have
with someone else, some former dear.
556   Of such a thing, oh, have no fear!"
     "Then, friend, give me a surety.
Oblige me; hand your shirt to me.
Here in the tail I'll make a knot.
560   I give you leave, no matter what,
to love whoever can undo
this knot that I will make for you."
     To comfort her, he gave the shirt.
564   She made the knot, of such a sort,

no woman could untie this knot
unless she used a knife, and cut.
She gave the shirt back, and then he
568 asked, in his turn, a surety
and a like gesture. She must make
a belt, a ceinture; she must take—
around her naked flesh must wind—
572 this belt, and thus her loins must bind.
He who undid the buckle, not
by breaking or by severing it,
him she must love, said Guigemar.
576 He kissed her, and they said no more.

      That very day, as things turned out,
they were discovered, found, seen, caught,
by a sly chamberlain the lord
580 had sent, who wished to have a word
there with the lady, speak with her.
He found he could not enter there,
and through a window saw the pair.
584 Then he indeed had news to share!
The lord, when he had heard it all,
had never been so miserable.
Of trusted henchmen he took three,
588 went to the chamber instantly,
and the stout trusties broke the door.
Inside he soon found Guigemar.
The lord commanded, wild with fury,
592 the knight must die, and in a hurry.
Up to his feet got Guigemar.
It was not in him to feel fear.
A large fir log lay close at hand;
596 it functioned as a clothing stand
for hanging garments. Guigemar
seized it; he meant the grief of war
for anyone who dared come close.
600 He would have maimed them all, God knows.
      The lord gave him a vicious stare,
then asked: who was he, then, and where
his people and his place of birth?
604 And, he demanded, how on earth
had he contrived to enter here?
All of the story Guigemar
told; how the lady had him stay,
608 recounted all the destiny

that with the wounded hind he found,
and of the ship, and his own wound,
caught, at the mercy of the lord.
612   The lord did not believe a word,
but, if true story, and ship found,
to sea the man would go; if drowned,
what satisfaction! If he lived,
616   truly, the lord said, he'd be grieved.

With this assurance, Guigemar
was given full escort to the shore.
There he was placed aboard the boat,
620   and toward his home was set afloat.

The ship set out at once. The knight,
sighing and weeping at his plight,
over his lost love made lament.
624   He prayed to God omnipotent
To bring swift death, a speedy end,
and that he never come to land,
since never again he was to have
628   what meant more to him than to live.
Such was his wretchedness and pain
when the ship reached to port again,
where first he found it, lying by;
632   close, it was, to his own country.
He came to land, soon as he could.
A youth whom he had taught, had bred,
was following a chevalier,
636   leading by hand a destrier.[1]
He recognized the youth, called out,
and the squire noticed him. At that
he knew his lord, slid to his feet,
640   invited him to mount and sit.
Knight followed squire; away they went;
friends found them and were jubilant.

Loved and much honored in his land,
644   Guigemar lived in a profound
pensiveness. Many women wished
for his regard and interest.
He spurned them all, and he would never

---

1. A warhorse, a charger. A very powerful and very expensive mount, it was when not being
   ridden led by a squire or knight *a destre*, or with the right hand.

648 for sweet love or for riches, ever
consider any lady but
she who could take apart the knot.
The news spread all through Brittany,
652 and girls and ladies all must try,
be she who got that knot undone.
Oh, how they tried! But no one won.

    But now I wish to speak of her
656 so dearly loved by Guigemar.
She was imprisoned. By the word
—counsel—one baron gave her lord,
in a dark marble tower she sat;
660 her days were hell, nights worse than that.
None on earth could begin to say
how great her pain and misery,
the anguish, grief, profound dolor
664 the lady suffered in that tower.
Two years and more, I do believe,
she felt no joy; could only grieve,
mourn for her lover over and over:
668 "Ill fate, that we two saw each other,
ever! I'd rather quickly die
than suffer here interminably!
Friend, if I could escape, and be
672 down where they made you put to sea,
I'd drown myself!" At that, heartsore,
she rose and went to try the door.
No bolt there was, or key or lock!
676 And she went out. And by some luck
no one was there to hinder her.
She went to shore. The ship was there.
It was attached just to that rock
680 she'd meant to drown by; there, its dock.
She saw; she climbed aboard. Her thought
was only of the notion that
Guigemar drowned here, at this site.
684 Then she could not stand on her feet.
She wished to go to the vessel's side,
slip over it, and down she'd slide;
enough, her anguish; farewell, pain.
688 But now the ship sailed off again.

    To Brittany, to port, it went,
beneath a keep, a valiant

strong castle, where the baron who
692   held it was called Meriadu.[2]
With his neighbor he was at war;
he'd got up very early, for
he wished to send his people out
696   delivering harm to all they fought.
At his window, the view he got
was of the ship now in the port,
and from his steps he started down
700   calling his chamberlain to come,
and to the ship they went in haste.
Up the ladder the two men raced,
finding at once the lovely lady,
704   strange in her beauty, like a fairy.
He seized her cloak, this Meriadu;
they led her to the keep, these two.
Oh, he was happy with his find!
708   Her beauty was of such a kind
it seemed past nature; he could tell
her lineage was high as well.
    And so he fell in love, this lord;
712   no woman could be more adored.
One sister had this Meriadu;
a beautiful young woman, who
in the dame's chamber waited on her,
716   serving her with grace and honor,
fitting her out in splendid dress.
Pensive she stayed, in deep distress.
Often the lord came by; he sought
720   to speak with her, for with true heart
he loved her, wooed her; she cared not.
    At length she showed to him the belt.
No man could be her love, but he,
724   the very one, who could untie
the belt, not breaking it. He heard,
and in great anger spoke this word:
    "I know a tale that's similar.
728   In this land there's a chevalier
—distinguished!—who in just this way
will not accept a wife, and he

2. In Rychner's edition this Celtic name takes varying forms; most of the time it appears
as Meriadu but sometimes Meriaduc (line 841) or Meriadus (lines 745, 788, 804, 846).
Often the variation seems to be for convenience in making rhyme. I have used Meriadu
consistently throughout to avoid possible confusion. The name appears elsewhere in
medieval literature with a Celtic background with variant spellings (e.g., in the *Cheva-
lier as deus espees*).

wears a shirt that has got a knot
732   on the right flap, that can't be got[3]
loose, but with knife or scissors. But,
I swear it's you who made that knot!"
     She sighed, gasped, at this angry word,
736   and almost fainted. Then the lord
took her up in his arms; he cut
the laces of her fine *bliaut*.[4]
The belt he tried hard to undo;
740   This prize was not for Meriadu.
Then every chevalier who dwelt
in that land came to try the belt.

     For a long time, thus matters went.
744   Then was proclaimed a tournament
by Meriadu, and this event
as yet another blow was meant,
against his foe. He summoned there
748   knights; he knew well that Guigemar
would come, expecting a reward
for a friend's service to a lord,
and would not fail him in his need,
752   but help Meriadu to succeed.
     Splendid in gear rode Guigemar,
leading a hundred knights and more.
Inside his keep the warrior
756   sheltered his friend with great honor,
his sister sent, as welcomer.
Two knights made sure that she prepare,
attire herself, and then appear
760   leading the dame he held so dear.
     The sister followed this request;
most splendidly and richly dressed,
hand in hand the two ladies came.
764   Still sad and pensive was the dame.
Then she heard the name, Guigemar!
and the floor gave way under her.
If the sister had not been there,
768   she would have fallen on that floor.

---

3. In Marie's time both men and women of all social classes wore long undershirts, often
of white linen, known in France as *chemises*. A woman's *chemise* was of floor length; a
man's was shorter and might be tucked into *braies* or trousers.
4. A tunic with long, full sleeves worn by women of Marie's period. It was fastened by
lacings at the back and sides. It covered the chemise or undergarment that had a
long, full, pleated skirt and a *chainse*, a long dress of linen or hemp with long tight
sleeves.

Guigemar rose to greet the two;
saw her; regarded her, and knew
her beauty, recognized her mien.
772   Back he stepped, shrank at what he'd seen.
"Is this, he said, "my sweet *amie*,
my hope, my heart, my life, I see?
My lovely friend, who so loved me?
776   Who brought her here? And where has she
come from? This is ridiculous of me—
I know it cannot possibly
be she; women look much the same,
780   often, and I've disturbed my brain
for naught. But the resemblance! Oh,
since it has made me tremble so,
and sigh—Oh, I must speak to her!"
784   Up to her went the chevalier,
kissed her, requested her to sit;
no word he spoke to her, no whit
except that she sit down by him.
788   Meriadu watched the two of them,
ill pleased. Chagrin he felt, regret,
and laughing, at his friend called out:
"Sire," he said, "if it pleases you,
792   this damsel will try to undo[5]
that shirt of yours, the famous knot—
See if she's capable or not!"
Guigemar said, "I'll do just that!"
796   He called a chamberlain to get
the shirt, one who took care of it,
told him to bring that shirt—with knot!
He brought it to the dame; but she
800   could not begin; failed, utterly.
Most certainly she knew that knot,
but her distress and pain were great;
deeply she longed to try; she cared;
804   she would have done it if she'd dared.
Meriadu was well aware;
his anguish more than he could bear.
"Lady," he said, "proceed now. Try.
808   See if this knot you can untie."
When he had given this command,
she took the shirt flap in her hand

5. Elsewhere in the poem the lady is referred to as a "dame"; Meriadu thinks of her as a
pucelle (pronounced "putzelle"), a maiden.

and she undid it easily.
812 Guigemar was amazed to see;
For sure he knew his lady, but
he couldn't fully credit what
he'd seen, and thus he spoke to her:
816 "Sweetheart! *Amie!* Oh, sweet creature,
tell me the truth! Is it you, really?
I beg of you, show me your body,
that belt you wore for me, that band."
820 On her hips, each, he put a hand,
where, without doubt, he found the belt.
     "Fair one," he said, "what fortune, what
great luck it is I've found you here!
824 Who brought you to this place, my dear?"
     She told him of her dreadful trial,
her anguish and her sadness while
she was in prison; how she got
828 out of doors, managed to get out,
free of her cell, came to the shore.
She planned to drown; the ship came there;
she went aboard; then it came here;
832 she was held by this chevalier.
With honor—much—he guarded her,
but always pressing for amour.
Joy would be theirs again, made new—
836 "Friend, take me away with you!"
     Up to his feet rose Guigemar;
"Seigneurs," he said, "now hear me! Hear!
I've found my fair sweet friend, my lover
840 whom I believed I'd lost forever.
Now I entreat of Meriadu,
Mercy! Give me my sweetheart true!
I swear I will be his liegeman for
844 two years, or three; also my more
than hundred knights will be his, too."
     This the response of Meriadu:
"My handsome friend, Sir Guigemar,
848 I am not that harassed by war,
or that distressed by my campaign!
Sir, you negotiate in vain.
I found her. I shall have her, too.
852 To hold her I'll make war on you!"
     Instantly, at this show of force
Guigemar had his men take horse.

To Meriadu he made *defi*;[6]
856   parting in grief from his *amie*.
In the town there was not one knight
come for the tourney and the fight,
who did not follow Guigemar,
860   pledging his loyalty in war.
Where he goes, they go, everywhere—
shame to him who fails Guigemar!
     Night fell. They'd reached the castle, though,
864   The keep, of Meriadu's foe.
The baron lodged them, jubilant
at this unlooked for good event
if Guigemar was now his friend
868   he knew the war was at an end.
     The next day they rose up and got
there at the hostel, fitted out.
All through the town, what noise they made!
872   —Guigemar riding in the lead.
They tried to take the castle, but
it was too strong, and they could not.
Guigemar then besieged the town
876   and would not leave till it was won.
His crowd of followers had grown
so great, he starved the foes within.
He seized the castle and destroyed
880   it all, and killed the lord inside;
with great joy led away his lover.
Now all his sufferings were over.

From this to which you've given ear
884   was made the *lai* of Guigemar.[7]
It is performed with harp and rote:[8]
Graceful and good to hear, the note.

Equitan

Men of such great nobility,
the Bretons, men of Brittany!

---

6. In making a formal *defi*, a knight renounced and negated his obligations as a vassal and could legally attack another knight or the overlord he had renounced, without being liable for accusations of treason.
7. In other words, Marie somewhat disingenuously claims to be telling the *original* tale, from which a more artful *lai* was later made.
8. Burgess and Busby say that the rote was "a harp of five strings, rather like a zither" (127). Curt Sachs, in *The History of Musical Instruments* (252), says that it—the *rotta*—could

They were wont, through their worthiness,
4   their noble minds, their courtliness,
to invent *lais*, when they had heard
of wonders, dangers, that occurred
to various people. Memory
8   was thus preserved, and did not die.
Such an old *lai* I've heard; this one
must not slip to oblivion.
It is of Nauns' lord, Equitan:[1]
12   King; Justice; a most courtly man.

King Equitan's renown was great.
Much loved he was, throughout his state.
Much he loved dalliance, *druerie*,[2]
16   such pleasures maintained chivalry.
They show to life indifference
who in love lack *mesure*, good sense;
Such is love's own *mesure*, however,[3]
20   that reason soon forsakes a lover.
Equitan had a seneschal[4]
—brave, loyal—a fine knight withal.
Over the king's land he stood guard
24   and justice he administered.[5]
Never, except in waging war
did a necessity occur
to keep the king from sport, but rather
28   he preferred hawking by a river.

The seneschal had a wife, through whom
much harm, to the whole realm, would come.

---

be small or large, could have anywhere from seven to ten to seventeen strings and was derived from a triangular *psalterium*. Gottfried von Strassburg, in his *Tristan*, describes two of these *rottas*, one small, one large enough to conceal a small dog inside it.

1. Scholars disagree on the location of Nauns. Some manuscript evidence suggests that it is the city of Nantes in Brittany; another MS suggests that the word is "nains," or dwarf, and thus that Equitan was a king of a dwarf nation. The name "Equitan" may refer to horsemanship.
2. Courtly love; it can also mean a love token. "*Drue*" means "sweetheart" or "mistress."
3. Marie here puns on two meanings of *mesure*, an Anglo-Norman word: 1) a sense of proportion; wisdom, good judgment, appropriate behavior; 2) the nature of a phenomenon or a person, as in modern English, "He took the man's *mesure* accurately." The first concept is a seminal one in Marie's poetry; cf., for instance, the *lai* "Les Deus Amanz." This passage for some critics suggests that she takes a dim view of the Provençal concept of *amour courtois* (see Ewert's edition, notes, p. 169).
4. Steward or bailiff in a great lord's, or a king's, establishment. He could represent the lord in the feudal courts, in the management of his estate, and in the superintending of great festivals and other domestic matters. Royal seneschals could become high officers of state or have high military responsibilities.
5. In this line and the ones immediately following it is already evident that the seneschal has taken on much of the king's role (*jostise* and administrator) and his responsibilities;

She was exquisite, beautiful,
32 her breeding elegant as well,
a lovely form, a lovely body—
Nature had here made special study!
Her mouth was sweet, her face was fair,
36 Her nose well set, her eyes were vair,[6]
Oh, in that realm she had no peer!
Often the king heard praise of her,
often sent salutations there,
40 and of his wealth, some little share.
Sight unseen, he desired her; sought
speech with her, giving it his best thought.
Privately, with intent to hunt,[7]
44 off to the countryside he went
where lived the seneschal, he knew.
The wife was at the castle too.
The king lodged there that night; then sought
48 when he returned from hunting sport
sufficient chance to speak with her;
his fine traits show, fine feelings share.
He found her full of winsome grace,
52 lovely of figure and of face,
courtly, sagacious, witty too.
Now he was of Love's retinue!
For him the arrow had been drawn
56 and made its wound; he was far gone.
His heart was pierced, the harm was done,
Sense and good judgment lost and flown.
For her sake he became oppressed,
60 Pensive and downcast; a sad guest.
Love held him fast, in every sense,
incapable of all defense.
At night he had no rest; so caught,
64 chastised himself for his great fault.
"Alas," he said, "what destiny
drew me to come to this country?
Thanks to this woman I have seen

---

soon the king will seek a role properly belonging to the seneschal. A useful discussion
of this matter is in Hanning and Ferrante's edition and translation, *The Lais of Marie
de France*, (New York: Dutton, 1978), 71ff.

6. Bright, gleaming, shining; sparkling, shimmering. "Vair" was a popular adjective for
   praising a woman's eyes; also, in descriptions of squirrel fur, it meant variegated grey and
   white; of a horse's coat, dappled. Both the fur and the dappled horse were highly prized.
7. The hunt often served in literature of this period as a metaphor for the erotic chase (as
   it has since!). See E. J. Mickel, "A Reconsideration of the *Lais* of Marie de France," *Spec-
   ulum* 46 (1971): 39–65, for implications of the hunting metaphor in "Equitan."

68 my heart is battered, bruised with pain,
my body shakes. Oh, I believe
I have no choice here but to love,
but it is wrong to love her thus!
72 She is my seneschal's own spouse!
I should guard his love faithfully,
as I would have him do for me.
If by some craft he were aware,
76 he'd be much grieved by this affair.
but it would be much worse if she
drove me mad, did me injury.
And what a tragedy, what shame
80 if she did not know love, this dame!
Can one be courtly lady, ever,
if one does not know love and lover?
There is no mortal under heaven
84 who would not profit if she loved him.
The husband, if he heard of it,
should not distress himself one bit—
he can't hold her exclusively!
88 I'll share with him most happily!"

He sighed then, after saying that,
and then he lay absorbed in thought.
Presently he spoke out: "Oh, why
92 suffer strife and anxiety!
I don't yet know, have not known, ever,
if she will have me for her lover;
immediately I must discover—
96 does she, too, wish for me to have her?
Then all this torment will be gone.
God! Why does day delay so long!
I cannot sleep, I cannot rest—
100 since I lay down, what hours have passed!"

He stayed awake till day; the wait
had been extremely difficult.
He rose, to hunt; but soon he found
104 that he preferred to turn around.
Weary, he said he was, and worn.
He sought his chamber and lay down.
His host, sad and solicitous,
108 had no idea what thing it was
disturbed his guest, brought on his fever:
his own wife caused this heat and shiver.

He sent her to him, to beguile
112 and soothe the king some little while.
The king revealed his heart to her.
She must know, he was at death's door.
Hers was the power to give him health,
116 Hers was the power to cause his death.

"Sire," she said to her would-be lover,
"give me some respite, by your favor!
This is the first time you have ever
120 spoken thus! Let me think this over!
You are king; your nobility
is great; my wealth and my degree
much less. You should not seek out me
124 for courtly love and *druerie*.
Were I to grant you your desire,
I do not doubt, I know, fair sire,
too soon you'd leave me; you would tire,
128 do me an injury most dire.
Were it to come about, this love—
were I to grant you what you crave—
there would be no equality
132 between us in this *druerie*.
Since, mighty king, it's through your hands
my sire has title to his lands,
you would expect, I do believe,
136 to have like mastery in love.
Unequal love is of no worth.
A poor man, loyal, of low birth,
is better, if he's wise and brave.
140 There's greater joy in such a love
Than that of king or prince, who may
have in his heart no loyalty.
To love someone of high noblesse
144 when one's own claims are so much less
is to doubt all and live in fear.
The great man will believe, for sure,
that none can take from him what he
148 loves by his right of seigneurie!"
Equitan spoke at once to her.
"Mercy, madame! Oh, say no more!
This is not courtly, not refined!
152 It's commerce, that the bourgeois mind
employs, for wealth, fiefs, property,
working his game deceitfully!

On earth no woman, wise, well-bred,
156   courtly and noble-spirited,
who knows her love's great value well,
who is not fickle, changeable—
although her mantle may be all
160   she owns, a rich prince in his hall
should take his utmost pains to give
this lady a true, loyal love.
Those who are fickle, fancy free,
164   those lovers who try trickery,
are mocked to shame, and tricked in turn.
Often it's seen; such people earn
—small wonder!—what they labored for:
168   their just reward, and nothing more.
Sweet, I surrender! Think of me
not as your king, but your *ami*;
accept me as your man, I pray.
172   I give you my assurance; say,
swear, I will serve you faithfully.
Oh, sweetheart, do not let me die!
I shall be servant, you, great lady;
176   I, suppliant; you, proud and haughty!"
        After the king had spoken all,
beseeched her to be merciful,
she made a pledge to him, this lady:
180   her love she granted, and her body.
        They exchanged rings, and plighted troth;
each to each, these two swore an oath,
they kept it well, true lovers both.
184   Later it was to be their death.

        This love affair, so passionate,
lasted long; no one knew of it.
Those times they wished to meet, to speak,
188   seek secretly what lovers seek,
the king gave out instructions, said
that privately he would be bled.[8]
The doors were shut tight, every one;
192   Could there be anywhere a man

8. Most illnesses were thought to be the result of an imbalance of the four humors—
blood, phlegm, yellow bile (choler) and black bile (melancholy)—in the body. Someone
could be bled when actually ill, or blood could be taken from the body and examined by
a physician to detect an imbalance or counter a suspected one. Since humors were
generated in different parts of the body, one could be bled in the area that appeared to
be overproducing or creating the problem.

so bold, he'd come into that room
unless the king invited him?
Meanwhile, the seneschal held court:
196 heard suits, complaints, the people brought.

     So very long was this romance
no other woman stood a chance.
The king had no desire to marry,
200 refused all counsel, and all query;
his people took this very hard;
so much, his lady love got word
repeatedly, and now she feared
204 she'd lose him, from the talk she heard.
Now when they spoke, and she'd the chance
to express her exuberance,
kissing, embracing him with joy,
208 playing with him delightedly,
she wept and grieved most bitterly.
Her royal lover asked her: Why?
What did such sorrow signify?
212   "Sire, it is for our love I cry,"
the lady said. "Our love, no less,
drives me to this profound distress.
You'll take a wife eventually,
216 a princess; you'll abandon me!
I've heard much talk! I know, I see—
Alas, what will become of me!
For you, I die; I cannot live;
220 no comfort's left me but the grave."
     The king replied, most lovingly:
"Oh, have no fear, my sweet *amie*!
Surely I'll take no wife, or ever
224 abandon you for other lover.
Know this for truth; you must believe,
love, if your husband weren't alive,
you'd be queen! No one, if he died,
228 could make me turn our vow aside!"
     The lady thanked him, and professed
much gratitude. At her behest
he gave assurances that never
232 would he desert her for another.
The bargain: hastily she would
see to it that her lord was dead.
Oh, it was easy, could be fast—
236 but her royal lover must assist.

He said that he would do her will
—wisdom or folly, good or ill—
if it lay in his power; he would
240   speed her intent, do all she said.
    "Sire," she said, "here is what you do.
Go hunting, if it pleases you,
where I live, in our countryside,
244   our forest; and then lodge inside
my husband's castle. There, be bled;
bathe[9] on the third day, afterward.
My husband will be bled then, too,
248   and after he will bathe with you.
Say to him—don't neglect to say—
that you desire his company.
I'll make sure that the baths are hot
252   and that two bathing tubs are brought;
so boiling hot will be his bath
no man, no creature drawing breath
could escape scalding, searing death—
256   that he'll find, sitting in that bath!
When he's well cooked, he's scalded well,
summon your men, and his, to tell,
to give out evidence, that he
260   met death in his bath, suddenly."
And the king granted it, agreed
to all her wishes, all she said.

Three months went by, perhaps—or less—
264   when the king came there, to the chase.
He thought, for health, he should be bled;
the seneschal should too, he said.
He wished to bathe on the third day;
268   the seneschal said: "Certainly!"
"You will bathe," said the king, "with me."
The seneschal said: "I agree."

---

9. Contrary to modern misconceptions, bathing was very popular in the Middle Ages, a custom carried over from the Romans. After 1300, firewood was scarce and baths became too expensive for any except aristocrats, but they frequently bathed socially, in groups of ladies, or men and women bathed together. Friends bathed together. As noted: "Hot water, sometimes with herbs, perfume, or rose petals, was brought to a lord in his bedchamber, and poured into a tub shaped like a half barrel and containing a stool, so the occupant could sit and soak long" (www.godecookery.com). Sometimes people dressed elaborately above the navel, with fancy headdresses and jewelry, and feasted and listened to music in their baths. See also Georges Duby, who writes in *A History of Private Life*, "Among the dominant classes, at least, cleanliness was much prized," and adds, "A hot bath was an obligatory prelude to the amorous games described in the fabliaux." Hanning and Ferrante, however (*The Lais*, 67), present a different perspective in a footnote to l. 246: "Baths were taken much less frequently in the Middle Ages than now and would normally be planned in advance."

The lady had the baths made hot;
272 two tubs she sent for and she got;
right by the bed was placed each vat.
This was the plan so well thought out.
The boiling water now was brought
276 all for the husband's benefit.

He'd just got up, this worthy man;
outside, for pleasure, he had gone.
The wife went to the king, just then;
280 he took her, held her close to him.
On her lord's bed the lovers lay
and passed the time in sport and play:
there, mingled, all at one, were they.
284 A tub stood near; for privacy
a guard was set, to be secure:
a servant girl outside the door.
But now the seneschal came back
288 hurriedly; where the girl stood, struck
so violent, so strong a knock
the door sprang open at the shock.
His king, his wife, lay in that place
292 entwined in passionate embrace.

The king saw him, too; instantly,
trying to hide his villainy,
he leaped into the boiling vat
296 all naked, landing with both feet.
Of the great risk he took no care;
boiling and scalding, he died there.
Thus his great evil was his grief;
300 the prey he sought was sound and safe.
The seneschal for certain, guessed
how fate had led his royal guest;
his wife he seized on instantly;
304 headfirst into the bath went she.
Both lovers died a dreadful death—
the king first, then she, in the bath.

If for the right you truly care,
308 take note of this example here:
he who seeks harm to other men
finds it turns back on him again.
This tale all came out as I say.
312 The Bretons made of it a *lai*
of Equitan and of his death,
and that of his loved lady, both.

Le Fresne

Of Le Fresne[1] I'll tell the *lai*
from the old tale that's known to me.

In Brittany, in former years,
4   there lived two neighbor chevaliers,
important, prosperous, wealthy men,
for worth and valor both well known.
Close by, in one locality
8   they lived, each with his own lady.
One lady became pregnant; when
her term was up, her time had come,
she bore two children. This event
12 made her lord happy—jubilant!
In his great joy and his delight
he sent word to his neighbor knight
his wife had borne two sons, a sign!
16 Such increased vigor in his line!
One son he wanted to present
to his good neighbor, and he meant
to give the child his neighbor's name.

20   The rich knight sat at dinner. Came
the messenger, who on his knees
before the high dais, spoke his piece.
The knight gave thanks to God, and then
24 a handsome horse gave to the man.
The knight's wife, dining by his side,
laughed at the news, though. Full of pride,
haughty, deceitful, envious,
28 a slanderer, she spoke up thus,

---

1. The word *fresne* means "ash tree." There is a Middle English version, 402 lines long, known as *Lay Le Freine*, that exists in the fourteenth-century Auchinleck MS W 4, 1 of the Advocates' Library, Edinburgh (see pp. 294–99). The story is not thought to be original with Marie. A number of ballads exist that tell a similar story in Scottish, Danish, Dutch, Icelandic, German, and Swedish. The Griselda story in Boccaccio's *Decameron* and Chaucer's *Canterbury Tales* ("The Clerk's Tale") has similarities but is not thought to have been derived from Marie's work. Ewert believes that Marie got the story from "Breton intermediaries," but it is not Breton in origin. For further commentary and sources, see Ewert, 169–70.

When Charles Muscatine read this translation, he asked me whether I thought Fresne should be pronounced with one syllable or two. He heard one; I have difficulty pronouncing it as anything but two. The modern French equivalent, *frêne*, is of course one; the Middle English *freine* is two if final *e* is pronounced. But I note that in Rychner's edition of "Le Fresne" Marie seems to count it as two syllables, e.g., in lines 167, 172, 229–30. *Codre*, on the other hand, is sometimes one syllable, as in line 335 and the crucial lines 337–40 (though I think line 338 may be iffy).

rashly and foolishly, before
all of the household serving her:
"So help me God, I marvel that
32 this worthy sire could have a thought
so to announce this way his shame
and great dishonor to his name.
His lady has two sons! Abased,
36 both he and she; oh so disgraced!
We know what is at work in this!
It never, ever was the case
or will be, on this whole wide earth
40 that in one pregnancy, one birth
two babes are born. This case just shows
two men have labored in the cause!"[2]
She got a look from her seigneur,
44 and harsh was his reproach to her:
"Dame," he said, "leave this well alone!
You must not speak of this again.
The truth is that this lady's been
48 of fine repute; her worth's well known!"
The people present in the hall
heard all, and they remembered all;
enough was said and told to be
52 gossip throughout all Brittany.
The mother, hated savagely
was shamed, disgraced, in misery.
The women all, who heard this talk
56 despised her, poor and wealthy folk.
The messenger who brought the word
told the whole story to his lord.
Again, repeatedly, he heard,
60 grieved, wondered what to do. Then, toward
his wife he too felt hate, disgust,
suspicion, utter lack of trust.
He kept her close in custody;
64 not her just fate in any way.

The lady who had so reviled
this one became, that year, with child;
with two babes, twins, it soon turned out!

---

2. Ewert in his edition comments (170): "The idea of twins as a sign of adultery, though
condemned by enlightened opinion, had wide currency in the Middle Ages and finds
expression in various forms of literature. It was not unknown in Antiquity (Aristotle,
Pliny, etc.) and still survives among certain primitive races (see Wärnke-Köhler, pp. cxi–
cxxi, and Hertz, pp. 403–04)."

68 Thus was her neighbor's vengeance brought
about. She carried them to term
and bore two girls, in much alarm,
regret and grief. Greatly distraught,
72 to herself she cried out this thought:
   "Alas, what shall I do? I'll never
recover worth and honor, ever.
I'll be disgraced now, certainly;
76 when my lord hears this news of me
—he, and each single relative—
none of them ever will believe
I'm virtuous. I have maligned,
80 judged myself; slandered womankind.
Did I not say, it's never been,
no instance ever has been seen
of children, two babes born together,
84 but, for sure, two men knew their mother?
Now *I* have two! Oh, I can see
the worst fate has befallen me!
Who demeans other folk, and lies,
88 little thinks she will pay the price,
and one can slander and disgrace
someone far worthier of praise.
I must protect myself from shame;
92 murder one child, to shield my name:
better to hope God will forgive
than be dishonored while I live."
   The women in the room with her
96 comforted her, and said, for sure
they'd not permit *that*! Up they spoke:
to murder someone is no joke!
The lady had a maid; this one
100 of free, distinguished origin.[3]
For a long time she'd watched and nourished
this young girl, whom she loved and cherished.
This maiden heard her lady cry,
104 grieve and lament so bitterly;

---

3. The original line reads, "*Ki mut esteit de franche orine.*" Other translators (Burgess and Busby, Hanning and Ferrante) have used the English "noble" for "*franche*," and my original line was "of very noble origin." Certainly that is one of the meanings given in *The Anglo-Norman Dictionary*. However, Charles Muscatine thought my choice too exalted for a servant and believed the woman more probably descended from a class of freedmen. That made sense to me, and the *Dictionary* does give "freeman, freewoman" as meanings for "*franche*." But the woman's position is important enough so that the word "distinguished" may be warranted. As with the English word "free," the history of the word "franche" is most interesting and seems to connote either nobility of blood, nobility of spirit or soul, or freedom from bondage, an enfranchised person.

and herself anguished, full of grief,
went to give comfort and relief.
   "Lady," she said, "no matter! Leave
108 off all this sorrow! Do not grieve.
All shall be well. One child, give me;
you shall be free of it, I'll see
to that. You shall not live in shame;
112 you'll never see the child again.
To church I shall deliver her;
Safe and sound I shall bring her where
Some worthy man shall find her there;
116 God willing, take and nurture her."
   All this the lady heard her say,
and promised her, in her great joy,
that if she did this service, she
120 would be rewarded handsomely.
In a fine linen wrap, they wound
the lovely baby; all around
a striped brocade placed over that;
124 a gift the lady's husband brought
from Constantinople, where he'd been;
never was one more splendid seen!
Tied with a lace, the lady's own,
128 a large ring graced the baby's arm.
Of finest gold it was, an ounce,
and in its center, a jagonce.[4]
The band was all inscribed, all round.
132 Whoever it might be who found
this girl-child, they would surely see
she was of noble family.

   The maiden took the child. She went
136 out of the room with the infant.
   Evening and dark were coming on,
and night fell as she left the town.
She found a big road, followed it;
140 it led into the forest's heart.
Within the woods she found her way;
with the child, came out straightaway,
never abandoning the road.
144 Some distance to the right she heard
dogs bark and chickens crow; the sound

---

4. A gem. Rychner says it is the "hyacinthe" or jacinth, a yellow or orange stone (306); Ewert
says it is a ruby (203).

told her a town could there be found.
Quickly she went, she followed where
148 the noise of dogs broke in the air,
and came into the city, which
was, she saw, beautiful and rich.
There was an abbey in this town,
152 a splendidly appointed one,
and surely there were nuns inside;
an abbess was their head and guide.
The young girl saw the abbey towers,
156 the walls, the bell that told the hours,
and hastily she came right up;
before the door she made a stop,
and then she placed the infant there.
160 And on her knees she said a prayer,
humbly she spoke her orison;
    "God, by your holy Name, great one,
if it's your pleasure, Lord on high,
164 protect this child! Don't let her die!"
    She finished; stood up, looked around
behind her, where at once she found
a huge ash-tree. Backward she glanced
168 into its dense depths, many-branched.
Four forks made clefts in the great spread.
It had been planted there for shade.
Babe in her arms, she hurried over
172 and in[5] the ash-tree's shadow-cover
she placed the child and said A Dieu,
entrusted her to God the true.
That task performed, she went back home
176 and told her mistress what she'd done.

The abbey had a porter; he
opened up, customarily
the church's outer door, so there
180 people could enter in, to hear
the service. Early in the night
he'd risen, candles, lamps to light,
sound the bells, open up the door.
184 He saw the rich clothes lying there

---

5. MS H has "desuz," and both Rychner and Ewert have "desus" here. Ewert glosses the
word as "beneath, below, under" in some contexts and "on, thereon" in others (198).
Rychner insists in his note that while the MS H "desuz" suggests that the young girl
placed the baby under the tree, in fact the baby was placed *on* the tree, among the
branches, "dans l'embranchement du frêne" (250).

in the tree's cleft; some thief, he thought,
had left them lying there like that.
Nothing else caught his eye, but he,
188   Fast as he could, went to the tree,
felt the clothes, felt the infant there.
To God he offered thanks and prayer,
and, not to leave the child alone,
192   took her and went back to his home.
There, living at his house, this porter
had with him his own widowed daughter
and her small cradled child, still at
196   the breast. The good man gave a shout:
"Get up, get up!" he said to her;
"Light the fire, light the candles! Here
I've got a baby! Found her stuck
200   up in the ash-tree, in the fork!
Give her the breast, give her some milk,
Warm her, bathe her, let the child suck!"
The daughter did as she was bid;
204   lit the fire, just as he had said,
warmed the child, bathed her well, gave suck,
offered the foundling breast and milk.
The ring on the child's arm, she found;
208   the rich brocade, too, wrapped around
the body; she well understood
this was a child of noble blood.
Next day, church services were done;
212   the abbess out the door had come;
the porter went to speak to her.
His story he was keen to share
about the child's discovery;
216   The abbess gave command, that he
bring her the foundling, just as found;
child, ring, and rich brocade wrapped round.
The porter went home to his house,
220   willingly brought the child back thus,
before the abbess brought the baby.
She gave the child intent, close study,
then said she'd raise her; she'd receive
224   the girl as niece, as relative.
The porter she forbade to say
a word; bound him to secrecy.
She herself would the nurturer be;
228   the child found in the great ash tree

was named Le Fresne; she was known
as Le Fresne by everyone.[6]

    The lady's niece she then became;
232 an act kept secret a long time.
And there within the abbey wall
she was brought up, this demoiselle.
She reached the age when Nature's will
236 is to make young girls beautiful.
None matched her, in all Brittany,
in beauty or in courtesy.
Noble she clearly was, well raised,
240 well spoken, full of poise and grace.
All who laid eyes upon her, gazed
and loved, and all with highest praise.

    At Dol lived a fine nobleman;[7]
244 there's never been a better one!
I'll tell his name; this lord was known
in all that country as Gurun.
Talk of this maiden reached his ear,
248 and he began to fancy her.
He took part in a tournament;
returning, by the abbey went
and asked to meet the demoiselle.
252 The abbess brought her. He marked well
her beauty, how well raised she was—
wise, cultivated, courteous—
he would be in sad plight, he thought,
256 if this girl's love could not be got.
But how to win her? He could not
see, if he came there often, what
could keep her aunt from finding out.
260 He'd lose sight of her then, no doubt!
    Then he saw how to win his case.
The abbey lands he would increase;
from his own holdings he'd give much,
264 so that the abbey could enrich
itself forever. Then he'd have

---

6. Ewert (170) cites other examples of foundlings who are given the name of the place where they have been found and comments: "We have here an unmistakable trait of popular legend."
7. Dol, located in upper Brittany. There was an archbishopric there at one point, but it was dissolved in 1199. That does not necessarily give the story a date.

a lord's rights to sojourn or live
as part of that community;[8]
268   he gave of his wealth generously—
but his intent in this largesse
was not his sins' forgiveness!

Often he visited, and there
272   saw the young woman, spoke with her.
So much he prayed, begged, promised, that
finally she granted what he sought.
One day, when he felt sure of her,
276   He thus addressed the girl: "My dear,
fair one! At last it's come to be;
you have now made me your *ami*.
Come away! Come with me and live!
280   You know, I'm sure—I do believe—
if your aunt ever did perceive
that we are lovers, how she'd grieve!
If you were pregnant, in her house,
284   she'd be incensed, and furious!
If you have faith in what I say,
Come with me now! Oh, come away!
I'll never fail you, or betray—
288   I'll provide for you splendidly."
Because she loved him passionately
the girl consented eagerly,
together with her love she fled,
292   and to his castle she was led.
Her ring and rich brocade she brought
for they might serve her well, she thought.
The abbess had returned these things,
296   and told her all the happenings
that led to her discovery—
a baby tucked in an ash tree.
Whoever sent her to the abbey
300   sent ring, brocade, and tiny baby.
That was all; there was nothing else.
The abbess raised her as her niece.
So with great care the girl had laid
304   in a box, ring and fine brocade.
Now in her flight she brought this coffer,
never forgotten, carried with her.

8. "A lord's rights," line 267, *retur,* line 265 in the original, refers to the lord's right in law
to seek shelter or refuge in the house of a vassal.

The knight who took the girl away
308 cherished her, loved her ardently
as did his household, servants all;
not one but loved her, great and small,
and honored her. Her noble ways
312 and her refinement, won much praise.

He lived with her a while, this man.
But then his landed knights began
reproaching him vociferously.
316 Often they came to him to say
Find a good, noble wife! Be wed,
and of this mistress, be well rid!
They would be jubilant, they said,
320 if he would have an heir, who would
title and lands of his inherit.
Shame it was now, no act of merit
that with this concubine he whiled
324 his time, and had no wife or child.
He would not have their fealty,
they would not serve him more, if he
refused their counsel. So the lord
328 granted their wishes, and concurred.
He'd take a wife. That measure won,
Now they must search out, locate one.
"Sire," they said, "there lives close to here
332 a worthy man, in rank your peer.
He has a daughter. She's his heir.
Plenty of land will come with her!
Named La Codre,[9] this demoiselle;
336 none in this land's more beautiful.
Without Le Fresne—sent away—
you'll have La Codre, and much joy;
La Codre will make tasty nuts;
340 Le Fresne, none; she bears no fruits.
Let us ask for this maid; we'll sue.
God willing, she will marry you."

The vassals made their suit, and won;
344 all sides consented; it was done.
Alas! What pity it fell out

---

9. "The hazel tree." The word is of either gender in Old French but is normally "La Codre," the feminine form.

these worthies never knew nor thought
what story lurked in this affair;
348 it was twin sisters they had here!
Le Fresne now was made to hide;
the other twin became the bride.
Le Fresne, when she knew, did not
352 show rage or sorrow at her lot;
but served her lord with grace and humor;
his vassals, too, she served with honor.
Friends of the household, of the castle,
356 —chevalier, servant, valet, vassal—
their grief was something marvelous.
They loved her, and they feared her loss.

The chosen wedding day had come;
360 friends had been summoned by the groom.
And the Archbishop, he appeared,
for he was vassal to this lord.
It was this prelate led the bride,
364 the mother with her, by her side.
The other girl the mother feared,
for she was still loved by the lord,
and might do her own daughter harm;
368 she'd power to influence the groom.
Resolved the mother: she'd eject
the girl; her son-in-law elect
must find her some good man to wed;
372 then they'd be rid of her, she said.

It was a sumptuous wedding, full
of merriment and festival.
Le Fresne saw the bedchamber;
376 nothing that she had witnessed there
appeared to grieve her, or upset
or anger her, but all about
the bride, she served with diligence,
380 showing much skill and competence.
All of the folk who saw her do it
marveled much at her grace and spirit.
The mother watched her, saw her merit,
384 in her heart prized and loved her for it.
She thought—she said!—if she had known
what grace was here, what manners shown,
even for her own child, she'd never
388 have taken from her lord and lover.

That night, to fit out and prepare
the marriage bed for the new pair,
Le Fresne went; soon as she took
392 off from her shoulders her good cloak[1]
and called the chamberlains, to show
the manner and the protocol
to follow, made her lord's wish known.
396 Oh, she had often seen it done!
　　When they'd prepared the bed, they'd set
over it all a coverlet;
the sheets were made of old dress-stuff,
400 she saw; this was not good enough,
not good at all, she strongly felt,
and she felt sadness in her heart,
went to the chest, took her brocade
404 and on her lord's bed it was laid.
She did this deed to honor him:
soon the Archbishop was to come,
to give the blessing, ring the bell;
408 to him this holy office fell.[2]
The room was empty now. Inside
the mother duly led the bride;
she would install her in the bed,
412 have her undress, as custom said.
And there she saw the brocade spread.
So fine a one she never had
laid eyes on, but the one she'd given
416 to the child she'd renounced and hidden.
Instantly memory and thought
caused her to shudder in her heart.
She called a chamberlain. "Please, say,
420 —by your faith, do this thing for me!—
where was it found, this fine brocade?"
　　"Lady, I'll tell you that," he said.
"The demoiselle—she offered it.
424 She threw it on the coverlet,
the spread, which seemed no good to her.
The brocade's hers, I'm pretty sure."
　　The lady called Le Fresne there;
428 Le Fresne came at once to her.
Before her, she removed her cloak,

---

1. Fresne is a servant and as such would remove her cloak as a sign of respect when talk-
ing to a member of the nobility.
2. The blessing of the marriage bed was, as Ewert points out, "a universal custom in France in
the Middle Ages"; also in England and Germany. It is referred to in Chrétien de Troyes and in
Chaucer; see, for instance, Chrétien's *Erec and Enide* (lines 2023–24) and *Cligés* (3330–31).

and to the girl the mother spoke:
"Fair friend, say frankly: speak your mind,
432 hide nothing. Child, where did you find
that lovely silk? How did it come
into your hands? Where is it from?"
    Le Fresne answered right away:
436 "My aunt, who brought me up, lady,
—an abbess—gave the silk to me.
She bade me keep it carefully.
Whoever wished me nourished, sent
440 it, and a ring, saved by my aunt."
    "Fair one, this ring; oh, may I see?"
    "Yes, dame; a pleasure that will be!"
The girl obliged; the ring was brought;
444 The lady closely studied it.
For sure she recognized it; both
it and the lovely figured cloth.
No more she doubted; she was sure
448 it was her daughter standing there.
All heard her say—no secrecy!—
"You are my daughter, *bele amie!*"
Emotion seized her, and she fell
452 backward, slipped in a fainting spell,
but then recovered, rose and stood
and hastily sent for her lord.
    He came at once, in great alarm.
456 Soon as he came into the room
she threw herself down at his feet
with a hug tight and desperate,
beseeching pardon of her lord.
460 Of this affair he had not heard.
    "Lady," he said, "what's this strange word?
Between us two is only good.
Whatever's wrong, I pardon you.
464 Tell me your wish! Speak, lady, do!"
    "Sire, since you have pardoned me,
if you will listen, I will say.
Once, in great boorish nastiness,
468 I wronged our neighbor. I confess,
of her two children I spoke ill.
I slandered my own self as well,
for truly, when I was with child,
472 I bore twin girls. One I concealed,
abandoned. To a church I had
her carried, with our silk brocade,

also a ring you gave to me,
476 when first we spoke, in courtesy.
The truth I can no longer hide;
both I've found, ring and fine brocade.
Our daughter, whom I thus concealed
480 —and through my folly lost our child—
she is here! She's the demoiselle
so wise and brave and beautiful
who's been so loved by this good knight
484 who wed her sister just tonight!"
    Her lord said, "What great news is this!
Never have I known happiness
like this. Our daughter has been found!
488 God granted that we not compound
this sin, twin it, and suffer more.
Daughter," the seigneur said, "come here!"
    Hearing this story come to light
492 filled the young woman with delight.
The father did not stay, but went
to find his son-in-law, and sent
for the Archbishop; these he'd tell
496 the whole adventure as it fell.
He told; as for the chevalier,
never had he been happier,
and the Archbishop counseled that
500 things be left as they were that night;
bride and groom, next day, by decree
he would declare unjoined and free.
This was next day agreed upon;
504 the marriage voided and undone.
    After, the knight wed his *amie*;
her father gave the bride away
to this good man, a mark of love;
508 half his inheritance he gave!
Both parents saw the two unite;
the other girl too, as was right.
When they returned to their domain,
512 they took La Codre home with them.
There, richly, she was given away,
She too was married, splendidly.

    When this adventure was well known,
516 the story told of what had been,
a *lai* was made, *Le Fresne*, for
that was the name the lady bore.

Bisclavret[†]

   Quant des lais faire m'entremet,
   Ne voil ublier *Bisclavret*;
   Bisclavret ad nun en bretan;
4 *Garwaf* l'apelent li Norman.

   Jadis le poeit hum oïr
   E sovent suleit avenir,
   Hume plusur garval devindrent
8 E es boscages meisun tindrent.
   Garvalf, ceo cest beste salvage;
   Tant cum il est in cele rage,
   Hummes devure, grant mal feit,
12 Es granz forez converse e vait.
   Cest afere les ore ester;
   Del Bisclavret vus voil cunter.

   En Bretaine maneit uns ber;
16 Merveille l'ai oï loër;
   Beaus chevaliers e bons esteit

---

† From Jean Rychner, ed., *Les Lais de Marie de France*, Les Classiques Français du Moyen Age, ed. Mario Roques (Paris: Librairie Honoré Champion, 1966), 61–71. Note that there is variation in spelling: Rychner follows the orthography of, mainly, BL MS 978 (H), a mid-thirteenth-century document. The twelfth-century poet and the scribes subsequently recording her work lived before orthography was standardized, and their Anglo-Norman-French dialect differed considerably from modern French.

Bisclavret[1]

In crafting lays, I won't forget
—I mustn't—that of Bisclavret;
Bisclavret: so named in Breton;
4 But *Garwaf* in the Norman tongue.[2]

One used to hear, in times gone by
—it often happened, actually—
men became werewolves, many men,
8 and in the forest made their den.
A werewolf is a savage beast;
in his blood-rage, he makes a feast
of men, devours them, does great harms,
12 and in vast forests lives and roams.
Well, for now, let us leave all that;
I want to speak of Bisclavret.

In Brittany there lived a lord
16 —wondrous, the praise of him I've heard—
a good knight, handsome, known to be

---

1. Lycanthropy—belief in werewolves—was an intensely popular belief in the Middle Ages, and it figures frequently in folklore and also in literature: *lais*, romances, fabliaux and beast fables. Versions of this story appear as early as in Roman works by Pliny (*Natural History*) and Petronius (*The Satyricon*). Marie's story may well have contributed to later versions in the thirteenth and fourteenth centuries, such as the *Roman de Reynart le Contrefait*, where the hero is called Bisclarel and the king is Arthur.

   In their version of the *Lais*, Robert Hanning and Joan Ferrante comment: "In Marie's hands, the story of the man compelled by fortune (*aventure*) to spend part of his existence as a beast of prey in the forest becomes a parable about the forces of bestiality that exist within human nature and how they should (and should not) be transcended. None of the *lais* is more deeply concerned with the fragility of social existence, given the battle within men and women between their higher and baser impulses, but Bisclavret is also concerned with the human capacity to manifest nobility even under the most trying conditions, and thus to transcend the animal part of our nature and garner the hardwon benefits of civilization" (*The Lais of Marie de France*, 101).

2. Ewert derives the name *bisclavret* from the Breton *bleis lauaret*, "speaking wolf" (*Marie de France, Lais*, 172). Jean Rychner, in his perhaps even more authoritative edition, mentions as well an alternative opinion, in which the form *bisclavret* may derive from *bisc lavret*, which suggests a wolf in pants or breeches, a different human characteristic. *Garwaf* (with other variant spellings in the manuscripts) is, Rychner thinks, probably scribal misspelling of the normal words *garolf* or *garou*(*s*), which ultimately derive from earlier words (Old English, Franconian, Latin) meaning "man-wolf" (*Les Lais de Marie de France*, 252).

   I follow Rychner in using the capital "B" in "Bisclavret" when the creature is referred to by his proper name (e.g., "I want to speak of Bisclavret" [line 14]). When he is referred to as a creature (e.g., "the bisclavret" [line 223]), I follow Rychner in using the lower-case initial "b." Ewert capitalizes the word throughout, with the exception of line 63, where the husband confesses to his wife, "Dame, I become a bisclavret." The capitalization and proper name for me imply man's estate (though of course animals can have proper names); Ewert's choice suggests that he regards the creature as a man throughout, except in this confession of animality to his subsequently horrified wife.

E noblement se cunteneit.
De sun seinur esteit privez
20   E de tuz veisins amez.
Femme ot espusé mut vailant
E ki mut feseit beu semblant.
Il amot li e ele lui,
24   Mes d'une chose ert grant ennui,
Qu'en la semeine le perdeit
Treis jurs entiers, qu'el ne saveit
U deveneit ne u alout;
28   Ne nus de soens nient n'en sout.
Une feiz esteit repeiriez,
A sa meisun, joius e liez;
Demandé li ad e enquis;
32   "Sire," fet el, "beaus duz amis,
Une chose vuz demandasse
Mut volentiers, si jeo osasse,
Mes jeo criem tant vostre curut
36   Que nule rien tant ne redut."
    Quant il l'oï, si l'acola,
Vers lui la traist, si la beisa.
    "Dame," fet il, "car demandez!
40   Ja cele chose ne querrez,
Si jo le sai, ne la vus die."
    "Par fei," fet ele, "or sui garie!
Sire, jeo sui en tel esfrei
44   Les jurs quant vus partez de mei,
El cuer en ai mut grant dolur
E de vus perdre tel poür,
Si jeo n'en ai hastif cunfort,
48   Bien tost en puis aveir la mort.
Kar me dites u vus alez,
U vus estes, u conversez!
Mun escïent que vus amez,
52   E si si est, vus meserrez."
    "Dame," fet il, "pur Deu merci!
Mal m'en vendra si jol vus di,
Kar de m'amur vus partirai;
56   E mei meïsmes en perdrai."
    Quant la dame l'ad entendu,
Ne l'ad neent en gab tenu:
Suventefeiz li demanda,
60   Tant le blandi e losenga,
Que s'aventure li cunta;
Nule chose ne li cela.

all that makes for nobility.
Prized, he was, much, by his liege lord;
20 by all his neighbors was adored.
He'd wed a wife, a worthy soul,
most elegant and beautiful;
he loved her, and she loved him, too.
24 One thing she found most vexing, though.
During the week he'd disappear
for three whole days, she knew not where;
what happened to him, where he went.
28 His household, too, was ignorant.
He returned home again one day;
high-spirited and happy. She
straightway proceeded to inquire:
32 "My fair sweet friend," she said, "fair sire,
if I just dared, I'd ask of you
a thing I dearly wish to know,
except that I'm so full of fear
36 of your great anger, husband dear."
When he had heard this, he embraced her,
drew her to him, clasped and kissed her.
"Lady," he said, "come, ask away!
40 Nothing you wish, dear, certainly
I will not tell you, that I know."
"Faith!" she said, "you have cured me so!
But I have such anxiety,
44 sire, on those days you part from me,
my heart is full of pain. I fear
so much that I will lose you, dear.
Oh, reassure me, hastily!
48 If you do not, I soon will die.
Tell me, dear husband; tell me, pray,
What do you do? Where do you stay?
It seems to me you've found another!
52 You wrong me, if you have a lover!"
"Lady," he said, "have mercy, do!
I'll have much harm in telling you.
I'd lose your love, if I should tell
56 and be lost to myself, as well."
Now when the wife was thus addressed,
it seemed to her to be no jest.
Oftimes she begged, with all her skill,
60 coaxing and flattering, until
at last he told her all he did,
the tale entire; kept nothing hid.

"Dame, jeo devienc bisclavret.

64 En cele grant forest me met,
Al plus espés de la gaudine,
S'il vif de preie e de ravine."
Quant il li avait tut cunté,

68 Enquis li ad e demaundé
S'il se despuille u vet vestuz.
    "Dame," fet il, "jeo vois tuz nuz."
"Di mei, pur Deu, u sunt vos dras?

72 "Dame, ceo ne dirai jeo pas,
Kar si jes eüsse perduz
E de ceo feusse aparceüz,
Bisclavret sereie a tuz jurs.

76 Ja nen avreie mes sucurs
De si k'il me fussent rendu.
Pur ceo ne voil k'il seit seü.
    "Sire," la dame li respunt,

80 "Jeo vus eim plus que tut le mund!
Nel me devez nïent celer,
Ne mei de nule rien duter:
Ne semblereit pas amistié!

84 Qu'ai jeo forfait? Pur queil pechié
Me dutez vus de nule rien?
Dites le mei, si ferez bien!
Tant l'anguissa, tant le suzprist,

88 Ne pout el faire, si li dist.
    "Dame," fet il, "delez cel bois,
Lez le chemin par unt jeo vois,
Une vielz chapele i esteit,

92 Ki mentefeiz grant bien me feit;
La est la piere cruose e lee,
Suz un bussun, dedenz cavee;
Mes dras i met, suz le buissun,

96 Tant que jeo revienc a meisun."
    La dame oï cele merveille,
De poür fu tute vermeille.
De l'aventure s'esfrea.

100 En maint endreit se purpensa
Cum ele s'en puïst partir:
Ne voleit mes lez lui gisir.

    Un chevalier de la cuntree,

104 Ki lungement l'aveit amee
E mut preiee e mut requise

"Dame, I become a bisclavret.
64 in the great forest I'm afoot,
in deepest woods, near thickest trees,
and live on prey I track and seize."
When he had told the whole affair,
68 she persevered; she asked him where
his clothes were; was he naked there?
"Lady," he said, "I go all bare."
"Tell me, for God's sake, where you put
your clothes!"
72   "Oh, I'll not tell you that:
I would be lost, you must believe,
if it were seen just how I live.
Bisclavret would I be, forever;
76 never could I be helped then, never,
till I got back my clothes, my own;
that's why their cache must not be known."
"Sire," said his lady in reply,
80 "more than all earth I love you. Why
hide, why have secrets in your life?
Why, why mistrust your own dear wife?
That does not seem a loving thought.
84 What have I done? What sin, what fault
has caused your fear, in any way?
You must be fair! You have to say!"
So she harassed and harried him
88 So much, he finally gave in.
"Lady," he said, "just by the wood,
just where I enter, by the road,
there's an old chapel. Now, this place
92 has often brought me help and grace.
There is a stone there, in the brush,
hollow and wide, beneath a bush.
In brush and under bush, I store
96 my clothes, till I head home once more."
The lady was amazed to hear:
She blushed deep red, from her pure fear.
Terror, she felt, at this strange tale.
100 She thought what means she could avail
herself of how to leave this man.
She could not lie with him again.

In these parts lived a chevalier
104 who had long been in love with her.
Much did he pray and sue, and give

E mut duré en sun servise,
Ele ne l'aveit unc amé
108 Ne de s'amur aseüré
Celui manda par sun message,
Si li descovri sun curage:
"Amis," fet ele, "seiez liez!
112 Ceo dunt vus estes travaillez
Vus otri jeo sanz nul respit;
Ja n'i avrez nul cuntredit.
M'amur e mon cors vus otrei:
116 Vostre drue fetes de mei!"
       Cil l'en merci bonement
E la fiance de li prent,
E el le met par serement.
120 Pui li cunta cumfaitement
Ses sire ala e k'il devint.
Tute la veie ke il tint
Vers la forest li enseigna;
124 Pur sa despuille l'enveia.
       Issi fu Bisclavret trahiz
E par sa femme maubailiz.
Pur ceo qu'hum le perdeit sovent,
128 Quidouent tuit communalment
Que dunc s'en fust del tut alez.
Asez fu quis e demandez,
Mes n'en porent mie trover;
132 Si lur estuit lessier ester.
La dame ad cil dunc espusee
Que lungement aveit amee.

       Issi remest un an entier,
136 Tant que li reis ala chacier.
A la forest ala tut dreit,
La u li bisclavret esteit.
Quant li chien furent descuplé,
140 Le bisclavret unt encuntré
A li cururent tute jur

largesse in service to his love;[3]
she had not loved him, nor had she
108 granted him any surety
that she, too, loved; but now she sent
this knight the news of her intent.
"Friend," she wrote him," rejoice, and know
112 that for which you have suffered so,
I grant you now without delay;
I'll not hold back in any way.
My body and my love I grant;
116 make me your mistress, if you want!"
Kindly he thanked her, and her troth
accepted; she received his oath.
She told her lover how her lord
120 went to the wood, and what he did,
what he became, once he was there.
She told in detail how and where
to find the road and clothing cache;
124 and then she sent him for the stash.
Thus was Bisclavret trapped for life;
ruined, betrayed, by his own wife.[4]
Because his absences were known,
128 people assumed he'd really gone,
this time, for good. They searched around,
enough, but he could not be found,
for all their inquiries. At last
132 everyone let the matter rest.
The lady wed the chevalier
who'd been so long in love with her.

A whole year, after this event,
136 thus passed. The king went out to hunt,
went to the forest straightaway,
there where the bisclavret now lay.
The hunting dogs were now unleashed
140 and soon they found the changeling beast.
All day they flung themselves at him,

---

3. In other words, the chevalier, doing service to his lady love in the courtly mode, was performing acts of generosity—largesse—in honor of her, hoping to exalt his spirit, be worthy of her, and earn her approval and her love.
4. Hanning and Ferrante observe that the wife's betrayal and the stealing of the werewolf's clothing are "reciprocal metaphors; both embody a loss of that civilizing force in life— symbolized at the surface level by apparel, at a deeper level by the love relationship— which saves humanity from perpetual servitude to its lower, amoral impulses, and allows it to engage in the satisfying social relationships enumerated in Marie's opening statement about the protagonist" (103).

E li chien e li veneür,
Tant que pur poi ne l'eurent pris
144 E tut deciré e maumis.
Des que il ad li rei choisi,
Vers li curut quere merci.
Il l'aveit pris par sun estrié
148 La jambe li baise e le pié.
Li reis le vit, grant poür ad;
Ses cumpainuns tuz apelad:
     "Seignurs," fet il, "avant venez!
152 Ceste merveillë esgardez,
Cum ceste beste s'humilie!
Ele ad sen d'hume, merci crie.
Chaciez mei tuz chiens ariere,
156 Si gardez que hum ne la fiere!
Ceste beste ad entente e sen.
Espleitiez vus! Alum nus en!
A la beste durrai ma pes,
160 Kar jeo ne chacerai hui mes."

     Li reis s'en est turnez a tant.
Li bisclavret le vet siwant;
Mut se tint pres, n'en vout partir
164 Il n'ad cure de lui guerpir.
Li reis l'enmeine en sun chastel.
Mut en fu liez, mut li est bel,
Kar unke mes tel n'ot veü.
168 A grant merveille l'ot tenu
E mut le tient a grant chierté.
A tuz les suens ad comaundé
Que sur s'amur le gardent bien
172 E ne li mesfacent de rien,
Ne par nul d'eus ne seit feruz;
Bien seit abevreiz e peüz.
Cil le garderent voluntiers.
176 Tuz jurs entre les chevaliers
E pres del rei s'alout cuchier.
N'i ad celui ki ne l'ad chier,
Tant esteit francs e deboneire;

all day pursued, both dogs and men;
they almost had him. Now they'd rend
144 and tear him; now he'd meet his end.
His eye, distinguishing, could see
the king; to beg his clemency
he seized the royal stirrup, put
148 a kiss upon the leg and foot.
The king, observing, felt great fear.
Calling his men, he cried, "Come here!"
"Lords!" he said, "Come and look at this!
152 See what a marvel is this kiss,
this humble, gracious gesturing!
That's a man's mind; it begs the king
for mercy. Now, drive back the hounds!
156 See that none strike or give it wounds.
This beast has mind; it has intent.
Come, hurry up! It's time we went.
I'll give protection for this beast.
160 And for today, the hunt has ceased."[5]

    The king had turned around, at that;
following him, the bisclavret
close by; he would not lose the king,
164 abandon him, for anything.
The king then led the beast, to bring
it to the castle, marvelling,
rejoicing at it, for he'd never,
168 seen such a wondrous creature, ever.
He loved the wolf and held it dear
and he charged every follower
that, for his love, they guard it well
172 and not mistreat the animal.
No one must strike it; and, he'd said,
it must be watered and well fed.
Gladly his men now guarded it.
176 Among the knights, the bisclavret
now lived, and slept close by the king;
everyone loved it, cherishing
its noble bearing and its charm.

5. Cf. the famous story of Actaeon as told by the Roman poet Ovid in his *Metamorphoses*,
an immensely popular and influential work in the Middle Ages and the Renaissance. In
that tale the unfortunate hunter Actaeon happens to see—by *aventure*, as Marie would
say—the goddess Diana bathing naked, which enrages her; she turns him into a stag,
and he is mauled to death by his hounds. He has a human mind in a stag's body but no
opportunity to prove it and thus be recognized as human and saved. This story would
certainly have been well known to Marie and her original audience, and the knowledge
might well have added suspense to Marie's episode.

180 Unques ne volt a rien mesfeire.
     U ke li reis deüst errer,
     Il n'out cure de desevrer;
     Ensemble od lui tuz jurs alout;
184 Bien s'aparceit que il l'amout.

       Oëz aprés cument avint!
     A une curt ke li reis tint
     Tuz les baruns aveit mandez,
188 Ceus ke furent de lui chasez,
     Pur aidier sa feste a tenir
     E lui plus beal faire servir.
     Le chevaliers i est alez
192 Richement e bien aturnez,
     Ki la femme de Bisclavret ot.
     Il ne saveit ne ne quidot
     Qu'il le deüst trover si pres!
196 Si tost com il vint al paleis
     E li bisclavret l'aperceut,
     De plein esleis vers lui curut;
     As denz le prist, vers lui le trait.
200 Ja li eüst mut grant leid fait,
     Ne fust le reis ki l'apela,
     D'une verge le manaça.
     Deus feiz le vout mordre le jur!
204 Mut s'esmerveillent li plusur,
     Kar unkes tel semblant ne fist
     Vers nul hume ke il veïst.
     Ceo dient tuit par la meisun
208 K'il ne fet mie sans reisun:
     Mesfeit il ad, coment que seit,
     Kar voluntiers se vengereit.
       A cele feiz remest issi,
212 Tant ke la feste departi
     E li barun unt pris cungié,
     A lur meisun sunt repeirié.
     Alez s'en est li chevaliers
216 Mien escïent tut as premiers,
     Que li bisclavret asailli.
     N'est merveille s'il le haï!

       Ne fu puis gueres lungement,
220 Ceo m'est avis, si cum j'entent,
     Qu'a la forest ala li reis,
     Ki tant fu sages e curteis,

180 It never wanted to do harm,
and where the king might walk or ride,
there it must be, just at his side,
wherever he might go or move;
184 so well it showed its loyal love.

What happened after that? Now, hear.
The king held court; he had appear
all barons, vassals; gave commands
188 to all who held from him their lands,
to help a festival take place,
serving with elegance and grace.
Among those chevaliers was he
192 —so richly dressed, so splendidly!—
who'd wed the wife of Bisclavret.
Little he knew or thought just yet
that he would find his foe so near!
196 Soon as he came, this chevalier,
to court, and Bisclavret could see
the man, he ran up furiously,
sank in his teeth, and dragged him close.
200 Many the injuries and woes
he would have suffered, but the king
called out commands, while brandishing
his staff. The beast rushed, twice, that day,
204 to bite the man; all felt dismay,
for none had seen the beast display
toward anyone, in any way,
such viciousness. There must be reason,
208 the household said, for him to seize on
the knight, who must have done him wrong;
the wish for vengeance seemed so strong.
And so they let the matter rest
212 till the conclusion of the feast.
The barons took their leave, each one,
each to his castle and his home.
All my good judgment counsels me
216 he who was first to leave was he
set upon by the bisclavret.
Small wonder the beast had such hate!

Not too long after this occurred
220 —such is my thought, so I have heard—
into the forest went the king
—so noble and so wise a being—

U li bisclavret fu trovez;
224   E il i est od lui alez.
La nuit, quant il s'en repeira,
En la cuntree herberga.
La femme bisclavret le sot.
228   Avenantment s'appareilot;
El demain vait al rei parler,
Riche present le fait porter.
Quant Bisclavret la veit venir,
232   Nuls hum nel poit retenir:
Vers li curut cum enragiez.
Oiez cum il est bien vengiez:
Le neis li esracha del vis!
236   Que li peüst il faire pis?
De tutes parz l'unt manacié,
Ja l'eüssent tut depescié,
Quant uns sages hum dist al rei:
240   "Sire, fet il, entent a mei!
Ceste beste ad esté od vus;
N'i ad ore celui de nus
Ki ne l'eit veü lungement
244   E pres de lui alé sovent:
Unke mes humme ne tucha
Ne felunie ne mustra,
Fors a la dame qu'ici vei.
248   Par cele fei ke jeo vus dei,
Aukun curuz ad il vers li,
E vers sun seigneur autresi.
Ceo est la femme al chevalier
252   Que taunt suliez aveir chier,
Ki lung tens ad esté perduz,
Ne seümes qu'est devenuz.
Kar metez la dame en destreit,
256   S'aucune chose vus direit
Pur quei ceste beste la heit.
Fetes li dire s'el le seit!
Meinte merveille avum veüe,
260   Ki en Bretaigne est avenue."
Li reis ad sun cunseil creü:
Le chevalier ad retenu,
D'autre part la dame ad prise
264   E en mut grant destresce mise.
Tant par destresce e par poür
Tut la cunta de sun seignur;
Coment ele l'avait trahi

where he'd first found the bisclavret.
224 The animal was with him yet.
The night of this return, the king
took, in this countryside, lodging.
And this the wife of Bisclavret
228 well knew. Dressed fetchingly, she set
out to have speech with him next day;
rich gifts were part of her display.
Bisclavret saw her come. No man
232 had strength to hold him as he ran
up to his wife in rage and fury.
Hear of his vengeance! Hear the story!
He tore her nose off, then and there.
236 What worse could he have done to her?
From all sides now, and full of threat
men ran and would have killed him, but
a wise man expeditiously
240 spoke to the king. "Listen to me!
He's been with you, this animal;
there is not one man of us all
who has not, long since, had to see
244 and travel with him, frequently,
and he has harmed no one, not once
shown viciousness nor violence
save just now, as you saw him do.
248 And by the faith I owe to you,
he has some bitter quarrel with her
and with her husband, her seigneur.
She was wife to that chevalier
252 whom you so prized, and held so dear,
who disappeared some time ago.
What happened, no one seems to know.
Put her to torture. She may state
256 something, this dame, to indicate
why the beast feels for her such hate.
Force her to speak! She'll tell it straight.
We've all known marvels, chanced to see
260 strange events, here in Brittany."
    The King thought this advice was fair;
and he detained the chevalier.
The lady, too, he held; and she
264 he put to pain and agony.
Part out of pain, part out of fear,
she made her former lord's case clear:
how she had managed to betray

268   E sa despoille li toli,
      L'aventure qu'il li cunta,
      E que devint e u ala;
      Puis que ses dras li ot toluz;
272   Ne fud en sun païs veüz.
      Tres bien quidot e bien creeit
      Que la beste Bisclavret seit.
        Li reis demande la despoille;
276   U bel li seit u pas nel voille,
      Ariere la fet aporter,
      Al bisclavret la fist doner.

        Quant il l'urent devant lui mise,
280   Ne s'en prist garde en nule guise.
      Li produm le rei apela,
      Cil ki primes le cunseilla:
      "Sire, ne fetes mie bien!
284   Cist nel fereit pur nule rien,
      Que devant vus ses dras reveste
      Ne mut la semblance de beste.
      Ne savez mie que ceo munte:
288   Mut durement en ad grant hunte!
      En tes chambres le fai mener
      E la despoille od lui porter;
      Une grant piece l'i laissums.
292   S'il devient hum, bien le verums."
        Li reis meïsmes le mena
      E tuz les hus sur lui ferma.
      Al chief de piece i est alez,
296   Deus baruns ad od lui menez.
      En la chambrë entrent tuit trei;
      Sur le demeine lit al rei
      Truevent dormant le chevalier.
300   Li reis le curut enbracier;
      Plus de cent feiz l'acole e baise.
        Si tost cum il pot aveir aise,
      Tute sa tere li rendi;
304   Plus li duna ke jeo ne di.
      La femme ad del païs ostee

268 her lord, and take his clothes away;
the story he had told to her,
what he became, and how, and where;
and how, when once his clothes were gone
272 —stolen—he was not seen again.
She gave her theory and her thought:
Surely this beast was Bisclavret.
These spoils, these clothes, the king demanded;
276 whether she would or no, commanded
that she go back and find them, get
and give them to the bisclavret.

When they were put in front of him
280 he didn't seem to notice them.
The king's wise man spoke up once more
—the one who'd counselled him before—
"Fair sire, this will not do at all!
284 We can't expect this animal,
in front of you, sire, to get dressed
and change his semblance of a beast.
You don't grasp what this means, my king!
288 —or see his shame and suffering.
Into your room have led this beast;
with him, his clothes. Let him get dressed;
For quite some time, leave him alone.
292 If he's a man, that is soon known!"[6]
The king himself led the bisclavret;
and on him all the doors were shut.
They waited. And then finally
296 two barons, with the king, all three,
entered. What a discovery!
There on the king's bed, they could see
asleep, the knight. How the king ran
300 up to the bed, to embrace his man,
kiss him, a hundred times and more!
Quickly he acted to restore
his lands, as soon as possible;
304 more he bestowed than I can tell.
His wife was banished. She was chased

6. The need for privacy can be seen, as Hanning and Ferrante suggest, as a sign of regaining the virtue of modesty and also of human dignity and propriety (104). But it is also true that in many ancient and medieval stories of the supernatural, the change from supernatural creature to human and vice versa, the crossing of the border between human reality and something else, can be shrouded and obscure. The most famous example is probably in *The Odyssey*, where Odysseus, after years of wandering in fantastic lands, is ferried home in a magic ship and put on shore in Ithaca, fast asleep all the while.

E chaciee de la cuntree.
Cil s'en alat ensemble od li
308 Pur ki sun seignur ot trahi.

Enfanz en ad asez eü;
Puis unt esté bien cuneü
E del semblant e del visage:
312 Plusurs des femmes del lignage,
C'est veritez, senz nes sunt neies
E sovent ierent esnasees.

L'aventure k'avez oïe
316 Veraie fu, n'en dutez mie.
De Bisclavret fu fez li lais
Pur remembrance a tuz dis mais.

out of the country, and disgraced,
and chased out, travelling with her,
308   her mate and co-conspirator.

Quite a few children had this dame,
who in their way achieved some fame
for looks, for a distinctive face;
312   numbers of women of her race
—it's true—were born without a nose.
Noseless they lived, the story goes.

And this same story you have heard
316   truly occurred; don't doubt my word.
I made this *lai* of Bisclavret
so no one, ever, will forget.

Lanval

The story of another *lai*,
just as it happened, I will say.
It's of a young, most noble man;
4   he was called Lanval in Breton.
    At Carlisle there was sojourning
Arthur, the valiant, courtly King;
Scottish and Pictish peoples laid
8   waste all that land, in war and raid.
Down into Logres[1] they would come
and often they did cruel harm.
The King was there at Pentecost,
12   lodging there for that summer feast,
Gifts to his barons and his counts
he gave, in great munificence.
And to those of the Table Round
16   —no greater band on earth!—good land,
and wives to wed, he gave them all,
save for one man, who'd served him well,
Lanval. The King forgot this man;
20   none put in a good word for him.
    For his great valor, his largesse,
his manly beauty, his prowess,
he was much envied by most men;
24   they made a show of loving him.
But if he'd met with some mischance,
No day would that be for laments!
A king's son, of high lineage,
28   he was far from his heritage!
Though of King Arthur's house, he had
spent all his money and his good,
for Arthur gave him not a thing,
32   and he asked nothing of the King.
Lanval was much disturbed by now,
pensive, he was, and sorrowful.
Be not dismayed, lords, at the thought
36   that such a man would be distraught,
foreigner in a foreign place—
where to find help, protection, grace?

---

1. An ancient name for England. Ewert, citing Zimmer, refers to it (in a note on "Eliduc")
as "the old designation for the middle and southern part of Britain and for England as
a whole" (186).

This chevalier of whom I tell,
40 who'd served King Arthur long and well,
mounted one day his destrier[2]
for pleasure, and relief from care.
He mounted, and rode out of town,
44 came to a meadow all alone,
by a swift stream got down, to see
his horse was trembling terribly.
Unsaddling it, he let it go
48 roll in the field, as horses do.
Folding his cloak beneath his head
he lay down, made the field his bed
still pensive, deep in his malaise.
52 Nothing, it seemed, could bring him ease.
      He lay there thus, heartsick, heartsore,
and down along the river's shore
he saw two girls approaching; never
56 had he seen fairer women, ever!
Splendidly, richly, they were dressed,
in garments closely, tightly laced,
bliauts of dark silk[3] with the laces,
60 and oh, how beautiful their faces!
Two golden bowls the elder bore,
of splendid workmanship, and pure;
it's true; pure gold each lovely bowl;
64 the younger woman bore a towel.[4]
They were advancing straightaway
just up to where the young knight lay.
Now courteous Lanval rose to greet
68 the women, got up to his feet.
First they saluted the young man;
and then their message gave to him.

---

2. A charger, or warhorse. It was a powerful and very expensive mount, ordinarily used for combat rather than pleasure riding.
3. *Purpre* in the original. Rychner defines it as a silken material, originally Oriental and originally of no particular color (312). Ewert defines it as "silken fabric (not necessarily purple or crimson in color)" but elsewhere, in line 475, he defines it as "scarlet" (211). *The Anglo-Norman Dictionary*, however, defines it as "purple; purple cloth; the purple; rich silken cloth" (online edition). *Bliauts*: long, close-fitting tunics, with long, full sleeves. Under the *bliaut*, in Marie's period, was ordinarily worn two other garments. The *chemise* was worn next to the skin; it had a long, full, pleated skirt. Over the chemise was worn a *chainse*, a garment made of linen or hemp with long tight sleeves and a skirt so long it might trail on the ground. The *chainse* might show just a bit above the *bliaut* at the neck and below the hem. See Chrétien de Troyes, *Erec and Enide,* trans. Gilbert, n. 256; Urban Ticknor Holmes, *Daily Living in the Twelfth Century,* 163–64.
4. The considerate custom of offering two basins for the purpose of ablutions appears also in the medieval *Alexander* romance (Ewert 173–74 and others).

"Sir Lanval, our own demoiselle,[5]
72   so worthy, wise and beautiful,
has sent us here to find you thus;
she bids you come to her with us.
We shall conduct you safely there,
76   for the pavilion is quite near."
   With the girls went the chevalier,
but of his horse he took no care,
he left it grazing while he went.
80   The damsels led him to a tent,
splendidly set, magnificent.
Not Semiramis,[6] opulent
and at the zenith of her power,
84   her wealth, her wisdom in full flower,
nor that Octavian, great Rome's lord,[7]
could that door—its right flap!—afford.
On top, a golden eagle sat.
88   I do not know the worth of it,
nor of the tent ropes or the poles
that gave support to all the walls.
No king exists beneath the sky
92   who could afford all, possibly.
   In the tent lay the demoiselle;
the lily, the new rose as well,
that in the summertime appear—
96   Oh, she was so much lovelier!
She lay upon a gorgeous bed;
—worth a great castle was the spread—
and her chemise[8] was all she wore.
100   Her body so well formed, so fair!
A costly cloak, of ermine fur,
and Alexandrine silk, she wore;[9]
from the heat it protected her.
104   Her side, though, was revealed and bare.[1]

---

5. A young lady, an unmarried woman of gentle birth (English "damsel").
6. A mythical Assyrian queen, wife of Ninus, founder of Nineveh, whom she succeeded as ruler. Famed for her beauty, wisdom, and voluptuousness, she was said to have built Babylon and its hanging gardens, founded certain other ancient cities, conquered Egypt, and unsuccessfully attacked India.
7. Caesar Augustus (63 B.C.E.–C.E. 14), the first Roman emperor. In medieval stories he is often portrayed as enormously wealthy.
8. See note to line 59. An undergarment with a long, full, pleated skirt, it was ordinarily worn under a *chainse*, a long dress with very tight sleeves. Over that was worn the tunic or *bliaut*, with long, full sleeves.
9. As with Octavian, the wealth of Alexander and of Julius Caesar was proverbial.
1. Some readers have seen a contradiction or at least a confusion in this description in which the *pucele* lies only in her chemise (line 98) but a few lines down is described having an ermine fur cloak pulled over her to shield her from the heat (lines 101–103).

Face, neck and breast bare too, and white
as hawthorn bloom, as delicate.
    Into the tent then, Lanval came;
108 the lovely girl called out to him.
He sat down, just beside the bed.
    "Lanval, fair friend," the damsel said,
"I've come for you. I've come from far,
112 I've left my land, to seek you here.
If you are courtly, wise and brave,
joy beyond measure you shall have,
greater than emperors or kings—
116 for I love you above all things."
    He saw her beauty; felt within
the spark ignite, the glow begin
to set his heart alight, to spread,
120 and with due courtesy, he said:
    "Fair one: if you should wish to give
to me such joy, to give your love,
I know of nothing you might ask
124 I would not honor as my task
if it lay in my power at all—
though good, or evil, might befall.
I will do all that you require;
128 forsake all those I might desire,
and never seek to part from you—
this, above all, I wish to do!"
    When the girl heard him thus declare
132 so forcefully his love for her,
her love, her body, she gave, both.
Lanval was now on the right path!
    After, she had a boon to give:
136 anything he might wish to have
was his to hold and to possess;
should he bestow great gifts, largesse,
she would find a sufficiency.
140 This was a pleasant place to be;
the more he lavished, more he gave,
more gold and silver would he have!
    "Friend," she said, "I admonish you—
144 command! beseech! In all you do,

As Marie says, . . . *En sa chemise senglement. / Mut ot le cors bien fait e gent / Un chier mantel de blanc hermine, / Couvert de purpre alexandrine, / Ot pur le chaut sur li geté; / Tut ot descovert le costé, / Le vis, le col, e la peitrine . . .* The fur cloak protects her, presumably covers her, but perhaps not completely? Or one can see her bare side and her bare face, neck and breast, presumably from the side or perhaps through her supernatural abilities.

tell our sweet secret to no one.
Here is my warning, all and sum.
Betray us, and you lose your lover;
148   I shall be lost to you for ever.
Lost to your sight; lost, our amours;
my body never pleasure yours."
      He would obey her, Lanval said,
152   her command he well understood.
      He lay beside her on the bed;
here was a lodging sweet and good!
He lay by her all afternoon,
156   nearly till evening came on,
and would have lingered if he could
and if she had more stay allowed.
      She said, "You must get up, sweet friend.
160   Even this time must have an end.
Go away, now! Here I shall stay,
but listen: I have this to say:
when you may wish for us to speak,
164   there's no place you may know or seek
where one may meet with one's *amie*
without reproach or calumny
that I shall not seek out as well,
168   to be with you, to do your will.
We shall be seen there by no other,
none hear the words we speak together."
      Full of deep joy at what she said,
172   he kissed her, then got out of bed.
Those who had led him to the tent
now gave him clothes most elegant.
Thus dressed anew, beneath the sky
176   No man was handsomer than he!
      Lanval was neither boor nor fool;
they brought him water and a towel;
he washed and dried his hands. That done,
180   they brought a supper to the man.
His love and he took this repast—
who could refuse so fine a feast!
Served it was with great courtesy,
184   which he accepted happily.
Many and fine the dishes were,
all pleasing to the chevalier,
for often his *amie* he kissed,
188   and he embraced and held her fast.
When they had finished every course,

the damsels led him to his horse,
saddled up expeditiously:
192   there too, he found great courtesy!
     He took his leave, got on his mount;
off to the city then he went.
Often he looked back; for our knight
196   Lanval felt great dismay and fright.
Shaken by all these strange events,
disturbed, depressed in heart and sense,
amazed, he could not trust his thought.
200   Had it all truly been, or not?

     Home again, at his hostelry,
he saw his men—dressed splendidly!
That night he was a lavish host:
204   where his wealth came from, no one guessed.
If in that town a chevalier
needed a lodging, he came there;
Lanval would see to it; he'd come,
208   and splendidly be waited on.
Lanval gave gifts to chevaliers;
and Lanval ransomed prisoners;
jongleurs he dressed in fineries;
212   and many were his honorees!
Foreigner, intimate, they all
had gifts from generous Lanval.
Great was his joy and his delight;
216   at times by day, at times by night,
often she came, his sweet *amie*,
to do his will most happily.

     That year, I understand, quite soon
220   after the feast of good Saint John,[2]
a group, perhaps, of thirty knights,
met for amusement and delights
within a garden, very near
224   a tower where stayed Queen Guinevere.
Among these chevaliers, Gawain;[3]
his cousin, handsome Sir Yvain.[4]

---

2. The Feast of St. John is Midsummer Day, June 24.
3. Gawain, the son of King Lot, is Arthur's nephew. In many Arthurian tales he is the finest of Arthur's knights and a model of perfect chivalry and *courtoisie*. In Malory his character becomes corrupted.
4. There are three Arthurian knights known as Yvain (there is some evidence that they may actually be the same person), but this man is undoubtedly Yvain the Valiant (*li preuz*). In Geoffrey of Monmouth, as well as in Marie's work, he is Gawain's (or Walwain's) cousin.

Gawain, that noble, valiant man,
228 who was so loved by everyone,
spoke out: "God, seigneurs! We do wrong
to Lanval, our companion,
so courtly and so generous;
232 his sire is rich, illustrious,
a king! We should have brought Lanval!"
At that the knights turned, and they all
went off to Lanval's lodging; there
236 begged and convinced the chevalier.
At a carved window chanced to lean,
looking about and down, the queen;
three ladies were attending her.
240 She noticed the King's household there;
She knew and recognized Lanval.
She made occasion then to call
one of her ladies to go find
244 the fairest damsels, most refined,
they'd join her in the garden there,
and frolic where the knights all were.
More than thirty she brought with her
248 descending with her down the stair.
The knights, delighted with the meeting,
gave all the women joyful greeting,
taking them by the hands; their speech
252 lacked no refinement, each to each.
Lanval, though, stood alone, apart,
impatient, tumult in his heart,
he longed for his *amie* so much—
256 to kiss her, hold her, know her touch—
how poor, how small, all other joy
with his own pleasure not nearby!
But the queen saw the lone young lover,
260 and lost no time, but hurried over
sat down beside him, spoke his name,
unburdened all her heart to him.
"Dear Lanval," said Queen Guinevere,[5]
264 you are much honored and held dear—

In one of Chrétien de Troyes' best-loved romances (*Yvain*) he is accompanied everywhere by a lion to which he has shown kindness and which assists him in his deeds of derring-do. Yvain is a Breton form of the Welsh name Owein; Owein was the historic son of Urien, a famous prince of the north Britons of the sixth century.

5. Guinevere is not named in Marie's original text; she is always referred to as *la reïne* (i.e., "the queen"). (Likewise Lanval's *amie* is not named, though in Thomas Chestre's Middle English version she is called Tryamor [see pp. 256–57 of this NCE]); many of Marie's characters, especially women characters, are not named.) Since this queen is

you may possess my love entire!
Speak to me! Tell me your desire!
Freely I give you *druerie*;[6]
268   you must rejoice in taking me!"
"Lady," said Lanval, "let me be!"
I care not for your *druerie*.
I've served my king well, kept my faith—
272   I'll never compromise my oath!
No to your love, dame, no's the word—
I will not wrong my sovereign lord!"
At that the queen was furious,
276   and she spoke slander, spoke it thus:
"Lanval," she said, "I know, I sense
you do not care for dalliance;
but it is often rumored, sire,
280   for women you have no desire!
But youths and squires, well-trained young men
You seek out; you disport with them.
Oh, coward! Boor! Unnatural,
284   your service to my lord, Lanval!
He has lost God—I fear it—since
he's known your vicious influence!"[7]
Lanval heard—and with grief intense—
288   but was not slow in his defense.
In fury, though, he spoke such words
he much repented afterwards.
"This calling that you claim I have,
292   Lady, I have no knowledge of;
but I love, and possess the love
of one who should be prized above
all other women whom I've seen;
296   I say this truth to you, my queen,
and you had better understand—
some servant girl she has at hand,
the poorest in her retinue,
300   is, Lady Queen, worth more than you
in beauty—body and in face—
in breeding, virtue, goodness, grace!"
At that the queen abandoned him,
304   and she went weeping to her room.

---

undoubtedly the figure known in Arthurian literature (e.g., the romances of Chrétien de Troyes, who was probably Marie's near contemporary) as Guinevere, I have taken the liberty of supplying her name, especially since it is a very useful one for rhymes.
6. Love, or courtly love; or a love-affair. In other medieval works, it can mean a love token.
7. In other words, Arthur has lost his salvation, is damned, through Lanval's supposed influence.

Great was her grief, rage, wounded pride,
she was so shamed and vilified.
Wretched at heart, she went to bed,
308   never would she get up, she said,
until the king had got redress
for that which caused her such distress.
        The king came riding from the wood,
312   joyful; the sport that day was good!
He went straight to the queen's abode.
She saw him and complained aloud;
"Mercy!" she cried; at his feet fell;
316   she'd been dishonored by Lanval!
Love he'd demanded, *druerie*,
She had refused him, loyally;
he had humiliated her,
320   boasting of an *amie* so fair,
noble, refined and elegant,
even her poorest maidservant,
the lowliest one serving her,
324   was finer than Queen Guinevere.
        Terrible was King Arthur's wrath;
in his great rage he swore an oath,
if in the court this was proved truth,
328   Lanval must hang, or burn to death.
        The king stormed out. He left the room,
he called on barons, three of them,
to summon Lanval; sent them off.
332   Lanval was sorrowful enough;
back to his lodging he had gone.
He knew full well what he had done;
utterly lost was his *amie*—
336   he had revealed their *druerie*!
Alone now in his room, Lanval
was pensive, deeply miserable.
His love he summoned, over and over—
340   there was no answer from his lover.
He sighed, lamented, made complaint;
at times he fell down in a faint;
a hundred times he tried to call,
344   Mercy! Speak to your love Lanval!
He cursed his heart, he cursed his mouth,
a wonder, did not seek his death.
Neither his wailings, shouts and cries,
348   self-lacerations, agonies,
could make his love have mercy, hear,

and to the wretched man appear.
Alas, poor Lanval! What to do?
352   The men of Arthur's retinue
arrived now, with their grave import:
without delay, he must to court.
The summons of the king they bore;
356   he was accused by Guinevere.
He went with them, in misery,
wishing they would just make him die.
Before the king Lanval has come:
360   he stands there pensive, mute, struck dumb,
his bearing shows his great distress.
The king speaks, his rage manifest.
"Vassal, you've done great wrong to me!⁸
364   Disgusting act! Your villainy
traduces, shames me! Vile, obscene,
you slander and abuse the queen!
You boast, then, madly, recklessly,
368   that you've so noble an *amie*
her serving maid is lovelier
and finer than Queen Guinevere!"
Lanval denied he'd said one thing
372   shaming, dishonoring his king.
word for word he denied the scene—
he'd made not trial of the queen.
But then that claim he'd spoken of,
376   he said, was true; he had a love
of whom he'd made, in fact, that boast,
and so she'd gone; his love was lost.
Desolate, he said he'd submit
380   to the decision of the court.
The king was in a tearing rage;
he called all knights in his ménage
to counsel him on protocol;
384   he wished no adverse thoughts at all!
They came at his commandment, whether
they wanted to or not; together
they were assembled. There they weighed
388   judicially, decreed and said
that Lanval needs must have his day

8. The word *vassal* had several meanings. It could commonly be a form of address appro-
priate to a young man of noble rank, either a comrade or someone to whom one must
extend the courtesies of rank. It could also refer to any noble, worthy young man or to
a noble or knight who had sworn fealty to a lord. Here, Arthur uses it in the latter sense,
especially to emphasize his belief that Lanval has betrayed and traduced the bond
between the two of them.

in court, but must pledge faithfully
that he'd attend; give solemn word;
392   present himself before his lord.
The court would be its full size then;
now it was just the household men.
These barons went back to the king,
396   there to announce their reasoning;
the pledges he required, at that.
    Lanval stood, lone and desolate.
With him there were no friends or kin—
400   but bail was offered by Gawain;
his confreres followed, one by one.
The king said, "I'll release this man,
but all each man here holds from me—
404   lands, fiefs—you'll pledge in surety."
    They pledged. No more was to be done.
Lanval was to his lodging gone,
escorted, for the others came,
408   with much chastisement and much blame.
his grief they made reproaches of,
cursing his ludicrous, mad love.
Each day the barons came to call;
412   they wanted to be sure Lanval
ate and drank, did so properly.
They feared he might go mad, or die.

    Then on the designated day
416   the knights all gathered faithfully.
The king and queen were there as well.
The pledge was honored by Lanval.
Many there felt concern and grief;
420   a hundred men, it's my belief,
would have done all within their might
to liberate from trial this knight.
He'd been accused most wrongfully!
424   Now for the verdict. What would be
the finding, and the king's demands?
Now all was in the barons' hands.
All of them were assembled there;
428   many perplexed and saddened for
this foreigner, this noble knight—
with them, he had so hard a plight!
Some wished him harm though, following
432   the wishes of their lord and king.
    Cornwall's Count then addressed the court;

"We have a task; we'll not fall short,
whoever weeps, whoever sings,
436 right must prevail above all things.
The king has charged, before us all,
a vassal I have heard you call
Lanval; charged him with felony,
440 gross misdeed, gross activity,
boasting, it seems, of an *amie*,
infuriating my lady.
The king alone desires to sue.
444 Now by the faith I owe to you,
there should, to speak the truth, not be
for response, a necessity,
save that for one's *seigneur*, one's king,
448 honor is due in everything.
We, with an oath, can bind Lanval,
and the king will excuse us all.
If Lanval can make warranty,
452 and she comes forward, this *amie*,
and it is true—proof can be seen—
this statement that enraged the queen,
then pardon will be his by right,
456 since he did not speak out from spite.
And if he cannot prove his claim,
then we must go and say to him
his service to the king is lost;
460 he must be banished for his boast."

They sent a message to the knight;
they said, announced, that now, by right
he must send for his love to come
464 defend, protect and succor him.
He said this was not possible:
no chance that she would help Lanval!
They returned to the judges' place;
468 no help from Lanval in his case!
King Arthur pressed them to make haste
for the queen's sake. No time to waste!
The verdict was about to come.

472 They saw two damsels riding on
two lovely palfreys ambling near;
the girls were wonderfully fair!
Rich purple taffeta they wore
476 next to their skin, and nothing more.

The knights looked on delightedly!
Gawain, and with him riders three,
went to Lanval, gave him the news,
480   and pointed out the demoiselles.
Full of joy, Gawain begged Lanval—
is one of them your *amie*? Speak! Tell!
But these girls Lanval did not know,
484   where they came from or meant to go.
Still they approached, and still they rode
their palfreys; still in graceful mode
dismounted just before the dais
488   that was King Arthur's honored space.
Their beauty was astonishing.
One said politely to the king:
"Royal sire, make available
492   a chamber, and adorn it well
with silken curtains; for my dame
wishes for lodging in your home."
Arthur obliged; he did this deed,
496   summoned two chevaliers, to lead
the ladies to an upper floor.
For the time being, they said no more.
The king then asked the knights, meanwhile,
500   for judgment, finding, in the trial.
He was incensed, he said to them,
so dilatory they had been.
"Sire," they said, "we debate. We're keen.
504   Thanks to the ladies you have seen
we have not reached a verdict yet.
Now let us all get on with it."
Pensive and anxious, they all met,
508   noisy and brawling and upset.

While their fear hung on them this way
two girls in beautiful array—
Phrygian silk stuff was what they wore,[9]
512   and Spanish mules these damsels bore—
were observed riding by the way.
This gave the vassals all great joy!
Each to each said that these would save
516   Lanval, the worthy and the brave.

---

9. Phrygia was an ancient state located in what is now central Turkey. In Greek legend it
   is associated with the kings Midas and Gordius. It was later conquered by Lydia, the
   Gauls, Pergamum, and Rome.

Up to him now there came Yvain
leading companions after him.
"Sire," he said, "now you must rejoice!
520 For God's love, speak! Give us your voice!
Two demoiselles are coming here,
splendidly dressed and passing fair,
one of them surely your *amie*!"
524 But Lanval replied hastily
neither he knew; all Yvain got:
"I know them not; I love them not."
They arrived now, these demoiselles;
528 before the king, got off their mules.
Many admired them in that place
for form, complexion and for face
and said, more worthy than the queen
532 they were, more than she'd ever been.

The elder, with great courtesy,
spoke wisely, with propriety.
"King, sire, have a chamber ready
536 that can accommodate my lady.
She's on her way to speak to you."
He gave commands to lead the two
where the two others were led before.
540 But of the mules they took no care.
The damsels once provided for
the king gave his commands once more.
The judgment! Now, without delay!
544 Too much was squandered of the day,
and the queen's fury had increased;
she had not broken yet her fast.[1]

They were about to answer, when
548 they could see coming from the town,
upon her horse, a girl. On earth
none had such beauty, none such worth!
A pure white palfrey was her mount;
552 gentle it was and elegant.
Form—neck and head—so beautiful
on earth was no such animal.
Splendid adornments bore this mount;

---

1. The editors Warnke and Rychner (copy text of this translation) give "jeünot" (i.e., "fasted, abstained from food, kept an empty stomach"); Ewert has "atendait," or "waited." Fasting might, for this reader, explain some of the queen's impatience, though not all.

556   under sweet heaven no king nor count
       could ever buy them, have and hold
       unless his lands were pledged or sold.
       Dressed was this damsel in this wise:
560   In a white *chainse* and a chemise[2]
       in two parts laced together, so
       all down her sides the flesh could show.[3]
       Her form was fine, her hips were low,
564   her neck white as a branch in snow,
       brilliant her eyes, her face was white,
       lovely her mouth, nose set just right,
       brown her eyebrows, her forehead fair,
568   her head of curly, quite blonde hair;
       gold thread could not give off such light
       as did her hair in sunbeams bright.
       A mantle of dark silk[4] she wore
572   with the skirts gathered close to her,
       sparrowhawk on her fist she bore,
       following her, a levrier.[5]
       In the town no one, small or great,
576   in childhood or in aged state
       there was, who did not rush to be
       where she rode, where they too could see.
       Her beauty caused no gab, no jokes,
580   but slowly she approached these folks.
       The judges who observed her thus,
       thought her a wonder, marvelous;
       not one of them who looked her way
584   but felt a kindling warmth of joy.

       Barons who loved the knight Lanval
       went to him speedily to tell
       how there was come a demoiselle
588   who, if God pleased, could save him still.
          "Sire—dear companion—here rides one
       who's neither tawny, nor dull brown.[6]

---

2. See note 3, p. 67; note 8, p. 68; note 9, p. 107; and note 3, p. 113.
3. Ewert in his note on this line writes: "According to the testimony of Robert de Blois, who censures it in his *Chastisement des Dames,* it was the fashion to allow the naked skin to show through the laced-up sides of the garment. Other poets describe the fabric itself as transparent" (175).
4. *Purpre* again. See note to line 59; this is "dark" (*bis*) silk, but following the *Anglo-Norman Dictionary* might be seen as purple in color.
5. A greyhound.
6. Dark complexions and black hair were considered unattractive in the Middle Ages. As Ewert writes, "The Middle Ages took their ideas of beauty from the ruling (Germanic) classes, among whom the blond type predominated" (176). See also G. Paris, *Romania* XIX, 316.

In all the world, she's loveliest
592 of all the women who exist!"

That Lanval heard, and raised his head;
He knew her well from what they said,
he gasped, and blood rose to his face.
596 He answered them, and with some haste.
"Faith!" he said, "that is my *amie*!
I do not care who slaughters me
if she shows me no mercy, for
600 all my cure is in seeing her."

Into the palace rode the lady;
none there had ever seen such beauty.
Before the king she stepped down, then
604 she was well seen by everyone.
Dismounted, she let fall her cloak
for better view by all the folk.
The king, so courtly and well bred,
608 rose up to greet her where she stood;
the others honored her as well,
and wished to serve the demoiselle.
When they'd seen all there was to see
612 and praised her beauty fittingly,
she spoke to Arthur in this way,
for she was not inclined to stay.
"King, I have loved thy vassal. See,
616 there he stands; Lanval, it is he!
Here in thy court he stands accused;
Lanval must not be here abused
for what he spoke; thou, King, must know
620 the queen was wrong; it was not so,
he never sought her love at all!
As for the boast made by Lanval,
if his acquittal come through me,
624 let thy good barons set him free!"
King Arthur granted that it must
be as the Court found right and just;
of all the judges, one and all
628 determined to acquit Lanval,
and by their finding he was free.

The lady left, for such as she
not even Arthur could retain,
632 with his fine servants; she was gone.

Before the hall there had been set
a block of stone, dark marble. That
the heavier men could use to mount
636   when to King Arthur's court they went.
Lanval jumped up upon this stone;
when his love out the door had come,
riding her palfrey, up behind
640   leaped Lanval, in a single bound!
With her he went to Avalon
—or so they say, those called Breton—
to an isle, a most lovely one,
644   she carried off this fine young man!
More of Lanval no one has heard;
I cannot tell another word.

Les Deus Amanz

In days gone by, in Normandy,
one heard a story, frequently,
of lovers, youngsters; two who met
4   because of love, their death, their fate.
Of this tale Bretons made a *lai*;
it is called "Deus Amanz," they say.[1]

In truth there is, in Nuestrie,
8   the region we call Normandy,
a wondrous mountain, huge and steep;
up there these youngsters lie in sleep.
Just to the mountain's side was built,
12   after much counsel, care and thought,
a city, by the Pistrians' king.
He wished, in doing such a thing,
to name it for his folk, his own.
16   Pitres[2] is what he called the town.
Still, to this day, the name is known,
still there are houses, still a town;
it's countryside we all know well—
20   the valley of Pitres it's called, still.

1. This *lai* has the most specific setting of those in Marie's collection. On the *Côte* (i.e.,
hill, slope) *des Deux Amants*, just east of the town of Pitre (see note to line 16) there are
still ruins of the twelfth-century *Prieure des Deux Amants*. The legend Marie tells is
one of several about this locality and two lovers; it was evidently invented to explain the
name "Deux Amants" because an older legend had been forgotten, a common occur-
rence in folklore and myth.
2. A castle and town on the Seine, three miles south of Rouen.

The king had one child, beautiful,
a girl most courtly. That was all,
no other daughter, and no son.
24 Greatly he loved and prized this one.
Rich men, and powerful, there were
who would have gladly married her,
but the king would not give his daughter;
28 he could not bear a life without her.
His solace was her company;
she was nearby him night and day,
and by her he was comforted,
32 since by this time the queen was dead.
Many reproached him in their thought;
and his own people, too, found fault.[3]
   When the king heard of all this talk,
36 he felt much sorrow, grief and shock
and he began to contemplate
what sort of scheme he could create
so that no man would seek his daughter.
40 Far and near, for those who sought her,
he spoke out, and he gave command,
that one thing they must understand:
it was decree and fate, that up
44 the mountain, to the very top,
carry her in their arms they must,
and never once must stop to rest.
After that, when this news was known,
48 spread in the country up and down,
attempt was made by several men.
No one succeeded, not a one.
Some made great show of strength, and they
52 actually carried the girl halfway,
but then they'd done all that they could
and there they stopped. So matters stood.
She remained long unmarried, for
56 nobody wished to ask for her.
   In that same land lived a young man
handsome and courtly, a count's son.
He strove by deeds to earn a fame
60 excelling all, a brilliant name;

3. The king's subjects are concerned, even angry, because he does not marry his daughter
to a suitable man and produce heirs, thus ensuring the succession and a secure govern-
ment. (I see no clear inference that the father-daughter relationship is overtly incestu-
ous as in the popular medieval tale *Apollonius of Tyre* and in the versions of it in Gower's
Confessio Amantis and in Shakespeare's *Pericles, Prince of Tyre*.)

he lived much at the king's court; there
he was a frequent sojourner.
He fell in love with the king's daughter,
64   and many were the times he sought her,
addressed her, sued that she would have
mercy, and give to him her love.
Since he was courtly, worthy, brave,
68   much valued by the king, she gave
her love to this young courtier;
humbly he gave his thanks to her.
They spoke together frequently,
72   loving each other loyally,
as secretly as they could do
so no one noticed, no one knew.
Their suffering was grievous, but
76   the young squire kept with him this thought;
better to suffer such travail
than be too hasty and thus fail.
Meanwhile his love was agony.
80   But finally there came a day
when this young man came to his love
—this youth, so handsome, wise and brave—
laid out all his complaint and thought;
84   in anguish he beseeched her, that
they run away together, for
he could not bear it any more.
If he approached her sire, he knew,
88   too well, the king adored her so,
he would not willingly bestow
the girl, unless the youth could go,
girl in his arms, to the high top.
92   After these words, the girl spoke up:
"Friend, I am certain there's no way,
possibly, you can carry me.
Dear one, you're not that strong, that tough!
96   But if together we run off,
my sire will know such rage and grief
little will be left of his life
but anguish. He is dear to me;
100 I love him, and I will not see
him suffer. Make another plan:
I will not listen to this one.
In Salerno, my love, I have
104 a wealthy lady relative;
there, more than thirty years, she's been

using the art of medicine.[4]
She's learned, knows her drugs so well,
108   with herbs and roots she has great skill.
If you are willing, see her! Go,
letters from me you'll have with you.
Explain to her your sad position;
112   much thought she'll give it, this physician,
such letuaries she will give,[5]
such potions you are sure to have
they will restore you altogether
116   and give the strength you need to gather.
When you are back here in our land,
Go to my sire; ask for my hand.
He'll take you for a child, and much
120   he'll say about that contract which
states he will give me to no man
—try as he may, try as he can—
except the one who, without rest
124   carries me to the mountain's crest.
Surrender to him graciously;
for otherwise it cannot be."[6]
The young man listened carefully
128   to the advice of his *amie*;
he thanked his love, and full of joy,
asked for her leave to go his way.
First he went to his country, where
132   with haste, he set out to prepare
rich clothes, rich stuffs, and deniers;[7]
palfreys,[8] and pack mules for these stores,
and from the men he trusted most,
136   he chose the squires he thought were best.
Off to Salerno then he went,
there to consult with his love's aunt.

---

4. The School of Salerno was famous for centuries before Marie's time, and many women, expert in the use of herbal medicines, lived and practiced there. Ewert writes that many prescriptions have been preserved under the title "*mulieres Salernitanae*—particularly recipes for cosmetics" (178).
5. A lectuary, or electuary, is a paste made of a medicinal substance mixed with honey, syrup, or conserve.
6. Lines 125–26 appear in Rychner's edition but not in Ewert or in English translations and editions by Burgess and Busby and by Hanning and Ferrante. Rychner, who generally follows MS H, here substitutes from MS S, remarking that H lacks the two-line passage that appears indispensable: "Ce vers manquent à H, mais paraissent indispensables" (263).
7. This monetary unit was originally the *denarius* of Charlemagne's coinage, which came to be called *denier* in French and "penny" in English. It was the basic coin of Marie's time.
8. The riding horses of the upper classes. A palfrey is sometimes described as a lady's horse, but there are mentions of gentlemen of the period riding them.

He gave the letter from his friend;
140   when she had read it end to end,
she kept him with her in that place
till she knew all about his case.
    Her medicines improved him much,
144   and she gave him a potion, such
that weary, worn as he might be,
burdened, exhausted utterly,
his body all refreshed would be,
148   bones and veins working naturally,
his strength would be once more his own
soon as he drank the potion down.
He put it in a vessel and
152   then he returned to his own land.[9]
    He returned to his home, this boy,
full of great happiness and joy.
He did not stay long, but sought soon
156   the king, and now he asked his boon:
give him the girl! And he would take
the damsel straight up to the peak.
The king did not, at all, say no;
160   he thought it a great folly, though,
for someone of so young an age.
Worthy men, brave, experienced, sage,
had made this climb, tried for the top,
164   but failed and had to give it up.
    The king then named the day and time;
commanded all to see the climb,
vassals and friends, all he could find
168   and summon. None must stay behind.
To see his daughter, see her squire
tempt his fate so for his desire
and bear her to the mountain top,
172   people from everywhere showed up.
    The girl prepared. She did her best,
she starved, she suffered, did a fast,
to make her body lighter, thinner,
176   and help her brave young man to win her.

    That day, when all were gathered there,
the youth came first to this affair,
his potion not forgotten then!

---

9. I follow Rychner in reversing lines 151 and 152.

180 Into a meadow, near the Seine,
     into the huge crowd by the water
     the king came, leading his fair daughter
     in her chemise,[1] no other cover.
184 He took her in his arms, her lover;
     the flask that held the drug, he gave her,
     knowing full well she'd do this favor,
     not fail him now. Into her hand
188 he put the potion. In the end
     it will do little good, I fear;
     Our youth lacked judgment and *mesure*.[2]
        With her he swiftly climbed, until
192 the halfway point. He was so full
     of joy in her, he clean forgot
     the drug. She sensed he was worn out.
     "Friend," she said, "drink your medicine!
196 I know that you are wearing down.
     Drink and restore your vigor, dear!"
        But the youth stoutly answered her:
     "Fair one, I feel my heart's great strength.
200 While I can walk three paces' length
     I will not drink, not take the time
     to stop but go on with the climb.
     These people would so scream and shout
204 and deafen me, I have no doubt,
     they would distract me utterly!
     No stopping at this spot for me!"
        Two-thirds of the way he'd mastered well.
208 But, near collapse, he almost fell.
     Often she pleaded with the man;
     "Oh, sweetheart, drink your medicine!"
     He did not wish to hear or heed
212 her, so great was his pain and need.
        Then, gravely ill, he reached the top.
     He fell there, and could not get up,
     and from his body burst his heart.
216 She saw her lover lie stretched out

1. The shirtlike undergarment worn next to the skin (sometimes called "sherte" in medi-
   eval English; see Chaucer, *Troilus and Criseyde*, IV, 96). It was not ordinarily consid-
   ered sufficient for wear in public. For compelling reasons several women characters in
   Marie's *lais* do appear in public in their chemises (cf. "Yönec").
2. *Mesure*, or a sense of proportion of the right action or degree of action at the right time
   and place, is a cardinal virtue in all of Marie's works; she seems at times to value it
   above other virtues more representative of conventional morality. *Desmesure*, the oppo-
   site, is surely the theme of this story; the two concepts figure in a number of twelfth-
   century works of literature, for example the *Chanson de Roland*.

and thought he'd fainted. By his side
she sat upon her knees, and tried
to make him take his drink at last.
220 His time for talk with her was past;
there the youth died, as I have said.
A great shriek, when she saw him dead,
escaped her; she threw far and wide
224 the vessel with the drink inside.
The mountain was well soaked with it,
and it was of great benefit
to all the countryside around.
228 Many fine plants have there been found
whose roots drank vigor from that peak.

It's of the girl I now must speak.
When she knew she had lost her lover,
232 she felt a grief known by no other,
ever. She lay down by his side,
stretched out, and held him close beside
her body. Oft she kissed his mouth,
236 his eyes. Her heart broke for the youth,
and there she died, this demoiselle,
so worthy, wise and beautiful.
The king and waiting folk below
240 saw they did not return, and so
climbed after them. When they were found,
the king fell fainting on the ground.
He showed, when he could speak at last,
244 deep sorrow, as did all the rest.
Three days they stayed there at the top.
A marble tomb was ordered up
for the two youngsters' resting place.
248 Because folk there gave good advice
there, since that time, the two have lain.
The other folk climbed down again.

To honor these two loving friends
252 the mountain is called "Deus Amanz."
This tale fell out just as I say;
of it the Bretons made a lay.

Yönec[†]

Puis que des lais ai comencié,
Ja n'iert pur mun travail laissié;
Les aventures que j'en sai,
4   Tut par rime les cunterai.
En pensé ai e en talent
Que d'Iwenec vus die avant
Dunt il fu nez, e de sun pere
8   Cum il vint primes a sa mere.
Cil ki engendra Yvvenec
Aveit a nun Muldumarec.

En Bretaingne maneit jadis
12   Uns riches hum, vielz e antis;
De Carwent fu avouez
E del païs sire clamez.
La citez siet sur Duëlas;
16   Jadis i ot de nes trespas.
Mut fu trespassez en eage.
Pur ceo k'il ot bon heritage,
Femme prist pur enfanz aveir,
20   Ki aprés lui fuissent si heir.

De haute gent fu la pucele,
Sage, curteise e forment bele,
Ki al riche hume fu donee;
24   Pur sa beauté l'ad mut amee.
De ceo ke ele iert bele e gente,
En li garder mist mut s'entente;
Dedenz sa tur l'ad enserreie
28   En une grant chambre pavee.

---

†   From Jean Rychner, ed., *Les Lais de Marie de France*, Les Classiques Français du Moyen Age, ed. Mario Roques (Paris: Librairie Honoré Champion, 1966), 102–119.

Yönec

Since I've begun these lays, I'll not
cease when their work is difficult;
adventures, stories, known to me,
4   I'll put, all, in rhymed poetry.
First my desire and my intent
concerns Yönec,[1] and I want
to tell his birth, and how his father
8   before him, first came to his mother.
The man who fathered Yönec
had for his name Muldumarec.[2]

In Brittany, in times gone by,
12   there lived a rich man, elderly
—extremely—known as the seigneur
of Carẅent,[3] and honored there.
The city sits on Duelas,
16   where vessels, at one time, could pass.
Though this man was advanced in age
because of his good heritage
he took a wife; he hoped to breed,
20   and heirs would follow in his stead.

This young girl was of high estate,
courtly and wise; her beauty great;
for this rich man, a fine award.
24   He loved her loveliness, this lord.
Her beauty and nobility
made him guard her most carefully;
he'd shut her in his tower; her home
28   in that high place, a well-paved room.

1. The name is pronounced "Ee oh neck." In Marie's original French the name is given as "Iwenec" in line 6 and "Yvvenec" in line 9; the existing manuscripts of the poem give several other variations of the name. It is thought to be derived from Old Celtic "Esugenus," or "descendant of Esus, god of thunder" (See Ewert's edition of Marie's *Lais,* Notes, 179).
2. Manuscript evidence (according to Ewert) suggests that the *lai* was once named after the father, not the son (Notes, 179).
3. Pronounced "Car u went," with three syllables, as is evident in the meter of Marie's original lines.
   Ewert comments here (179): "Various attempts have been made to identify the scene of the lay. It would appear that, at least at one stage, the scene was laid in S. Wales [not Brittany, as Marie says in line 11] and that *Carẅent* may be identified with Caerwent, the old Venta Silurum, which view would find support in the identification of *Karliun* with Caerleon [in Wales]. *Duelas* may be the name formerly given to the stream on which Caerwent lies."

Il ot une sue serur,
Veille ert e vedve, sanz seignur;
Ensemble od la dame l'ad mise
32 Pur li tenir mieuz en justise.
Autres femmes i ot, ceo crei,
En une autre chambre par sei,
Mes ja la dame n'i parlast,
36 Si la vielle nel comandast.
Issi la tint plus de set anz.
Unques entre eus n'eurent enfanz
Ne fors de cele tur n'eissi,
40 Ne pur parent ne pur ami.
Quant li sires s'alot cuchier,
N'i ot chamberlenc ne huissier
Ki en la chambre osast entrer
44 Ne devant lui cirge alumer.
Mut ert la dame en grant tristur,
Od lermes, od suspir e plur;
Sa beauté pert en teu mesure
48 Cume cele ki n'en ad cure.
De sei meïsme mieuz vousist
Que morz hastive la preisist.

Ceo fu el meis d'avril entrant,
52 Quant cil oisel meinent lur chant.
Li sires fu matin levez;
D'aler en bois s'est aturnez.
La vielle ad fete lever sus
56 E aprés lui fermer les hus.
Cele ad fet sun comandement.
Li sires s'en vet od sa gent.
La vielle portot sun psautier,
60 U ele voleit verseiller.

La dame, em plur e en esveil,
Choisi la clarté del soleil.
De la vielle est aparceüe
64 Que de la chambre esteit eissue.
Mut se pleineit e suspirot
E en plurant se dementot:
"Lasse, fait ele, mar fui nee!

He had a sister, old and lone,
widowed, with no lord of her own,
whom he'd placed with her in the tower
32 so he'd be surer of his power.
Women there were, I'm sure, that he
placed in a chamber separately;
The young wife never spoke with them
36 Without the leave of this old dame.

   And so passed more than seven years.
No children came. There were no heirs.
Shut in the tower, she could not leave,
40 no, not for friend or relative.
When her lord went to bed with her
no manservant dared enter there;
no porter dared to set alight
44 candles before his lord, at night.[4]
Sadness surrounded her, these years;
weeping and sighing, frequent tears.
She lost her beauty in this way,
48 like one whose will has drained away
completely; she no longer cared.
Quick death she would have much preferred.

   April had come, when birds display
52 their loveliest songs, as is their way.
One morning early, the old lord
made ready to ride to the wood
and the old woman rose, too, for
56 after him she must shut the door.
She had performed her duty then.
The lord went off, with all his men.
The old dame, with her psalter, went
60 off to recite her prayers, and chant.

   Awake, in tears, the lady lay;
she saw the sun's warm clarity,
she saw that the old dame had gone
64 and she herself was left alone.
much she complained then, much she sighed,
made lamentation, moaned and cried.
   "Alas, that I was born, to be

---

4. Note that the room in which the young woman is obliged to lie with her husband, in an
intimacy unfruitful and abhorred by her, is utterly dark (lines 41–44).

68 Mut est dure ma destinee!
    En ceste tur sui en prisun,
    Ja n'en istrai si par mort nun.
    Cist vielz gelus, de quei se crient,
72 Que en si grant prisun me tient?
    Mut par est fous e esbaïz!
    Il crient tuz jurs estre trahiz!
    Jeo ne puis al mustier venir
76 Ne le servise Deu oïr.
    Si jo puïsse od gent parler
    E en deduit od lui aler,
    Jo li mustrasse beu semblant,
80 Tut n'en eüsse jeo talant.
    Maleeit seient mi parent
    E li autre communalment
    Ki a cest gelus me donerent
84 E de sun cors me marïerent!
    A forte corde trai e tir,
    Il ne purrat jamés mûrir!
    Quant il dut estre baptiziez,
88 Si fu el flum d'enfern plungiez:
    Dur sunt li nerf, dures les veines,
    Ki de vif sanc sunt tutes pleines!
      Mut ai sovent oï cunter
92 Que l'em suleit jadis trover
    Aventures en cest païs
    Ki rehaitouent les pensis.
    Chevalier trovoent puceles
96 A lur talent, gentes e beles,
    E dames truvoent amanz
    Beaus e curteis, pruz e vaillanz,
    Si que blasmees n'en esteient
100 Ne nul fors eles nes veeient.
    Si ceo peot estrë e ceo fu,
    Si unc a nul est avenu.
    Deus, ki de tut ad poësté,
104 Il en face ma volenté!"

      Quant ele ot fait sa pleinte issi,
    L'umbre d'un grant oisel choisi
    Par mi une estreite fenestre;
108 Ele ne seit que ceo pout estre.
    En la chambre volant entra;
    Giez ot as piez, ostur sembla,

68 cursed with this dreadful destiny!
    Here in this prison tower I lie,
    never to go out till I die.
    Jealous old man, what's in his mind,
72 demented fool, that I'm confined
    in this great prison! He's afraid,
    constantly, that he'll be betrayed.
    I cannot go to church, nor hear
76 the worship service offered there.
    If I could speak with other folk,
    enjoy their company and talk,
    I'd make some semblance to my sire
80 of liking—far from my desire!
    Cursed be my family, with those,
    hateful, the lot of them, who chose
    to give me to Sir Jealousy
84 and to his carcass marry me!
    It's a strong rope I draw and pull—
    he'll never, never die at all!
    When he was baptized, this old sire,
88 they plunged him in Hell's river of fire—
    hard sinews, veins he has! But good
    blood runs inside them, live and red.
        Many times I've heard stories told
92 how it could be, in days of old,
    in this same land, adventures fell
    to folk, and helped the miserable.
    Knights found young women, beautiful,
96 noble, withal desirable:
    ladies found lovers of great price,
    so handsome, valiant, courteous;
    they were not blamed. And what had been
100 was never known, was never seen.
    If such can be, if such was done,
    such things fell out for anyone,
    God, for whom all is possible,
104 grant it to me! My wish fulfill!"

        Just as she spoke, lamenting so,
    She saw, just by the small window
    a great bird's shadow, stretched across;
108 she had no notion what it was.
    It flew into the room. Bands bound
    each foot; a hawk, it seemed, around

De cinc mues fu u de sis.
112 Il s'est devant la dame asis.
Quant il i ot un poi esté
E ele l'ot bien esgardé,
Chevaliers bels e genz devint.
116 La dame a merveille le tint,
Li sens li remut e frémi,
Grant poür ot, sun chief covri.

Mut fu curteis li chevaliers,
120 Il la areisunat primiers:
"Dame, fet il, n'eiez poür:
Gentil oisel ad en ostur!
Si li segrei vus sunt oscur,
124 Gardez ke seiez a seür,
Si fetes de mei vostre ami!
Pur ceo, fet il, vinc jeo ici.
Jeo vus ai lungement amee
128 E en mun quor mut desiree;
Unkes femme fors vus n'amai
Ne jamés autre n'amerai.
Mes ne poeie a vus venir
132 Ne fors de mun paleis eissir,
Si vus ne m'eüssez requis.
Or puis bien estre vostre amis!"
La dame se raseüra,
136 Sun chief descovri, si parla;
Le chevalier ad respundu
E dit qu'ele en ferat sun dru,
S'en Deu creïst e issi fust
140 Que lur amur estre peüst,
Kar mut esteit de grant beauté:
Unkes nul jur de sun eé
Si bel chevalier n'esgarda
144 Ne jamés si bel ne verra.
"Dame," dit il, "vus dites bien.
Ne vodreie pur nule rien

five or six moultings.[5] Now before
112 the girl, it perched, upon the floor.
When it had rested there a bit
and she had had a look, then it
became a handsome, noble knight.
116 The lady marvelled at the sight,
she trembled, shaken in her blood;
in terror, covered up her head.

Most courteous was the chevalier;
120 It was he who first spoke to her.
"Oh, lady, do not fear me so!
the hawk's a noble bird. Although
its secrets are obscure to you,
124 cherish, trust what you know is true,
and take me for your lover! Dame,
it is for that," he said, "I came.
I have long loved you. I have long
128 held in my heart desire—so strong!
No other woman has been my lover
and I shall never have another.
But I could not come to you in love—
132 out of my palace could not move—
had you yourself not summoned me.
But now I can be your *ami!*"[6]
The girl, encouraged by this talk,
136 uncovered now her head, and spoke,
responding. She would be his love
if he believed in God above;[7]
if so, there was no obstacle,
140 and then their love was possible.
For such was his great beauty, she
had never known that this could be,
or seen such beauty in a man.
144 Surely she never would again.
"Lady," he said, "You've spoken well.
Never, for anything at all,

---

5. Hawks molt—that is, they shed and grow new plumage—every year after the first
year of life.
6. *Ami/amie*, French for "friend," or in courtly usage, "lover." It could also be used as an
address in situations of flirtation or gallantry.
7. Ewert in his edition says, "Supernatural beings are commonly made to seek to prove
themselves Christians by partaking of the sacrament" (179). It does seem that this young,
extremely sheltered and dominated woman shows considerable astuteness in making her
request. She has cursed her family and castigated her husband; this would be a most
opportune time for the devil to make an appearance in the form of an amorous, hand-
some knight. However, this knight is what he claims to be.

Que de mei i ait acheisun,
148 Mescreauncë u suspesçun.
Jeo crei mut bien el Creatur,
Ki nus geta de la tristur
U Adam nus mist, nostre pere,
152 Par le mors de la pumme amere;
Il est e ert e fu tuz jurs
Vie e lumiere as pecheürs.
Si vus de ceo ne me creez,
156 Vostre chapelain demandez,
Dites ke mals vus ad susprise,
Si volez aveir le servise
Que Deus ad el mund establi,
160 Dunt li pecheür sunt gari.
La semblance de vus prendrai,
Le cors Damedeu recevrai,
Ma creance vus dirai tute:
164 Ja mar de ceo serez en dute!"
     El li respunt que bien ad dit.
Delez li s'est cuchiez el lit,
Mes il ne vout a li tuchier
168 Ne d'acoler ne de baisier.
A tant la veille est repeiriee;
La dame trovat esveilliee,
Dist li que tens est de lever:
172 Ses dras li voleit aporter.
     La dame dist qu'ele est malade:
Del chapelain se prenge garde,
Sil face tost a li venir,
176 Kar grant poür ad de murir.
     La vielle dist: "Vus sufferez!
Mis sires est el bois alez;
Nuls n'entrera caënz fors mei."
180 Mut fu la dame en grant esfrei;
Semblant fist qu'ele se pasma.
Cele le vit, mut s'esmaia;
L'us de la chambre ad defermé,
184 Si ad le prestre demandé,
E cil i vint cum plus tost pot:
     Corpus domini aportot.
Li chevaliers l'ad receü,

would I wish any accusation
148 or have your doubt or your suspicion.
I worship most devotedly
our dear Creator. It is he
who saved us from the tragic plight
152 where Adam placed us, with the bite
of the bitter apple. God has been
—will ever be—for us in sin
both light and life. But if you fear
156 me still, summon your chaplain here.
Say you are ill; say that you want
that service and that sacrament
given the world by our dear Lord
160 by which we sinners all are cured.
I will assume your form, receive
the Host; and thus you will perceive
my credo, how I speak it then—
164 never will you have doubts again!"
     And she replied; this was well said.
He lay beside her in the bed;
he did not wish to touch her, though,
168 embrace or kiss her, or make show
of love.
                    On the old dame's return
she saw the young girl lying prone
and told her: time to be astir!
172 She wished to bring her clothes to her.
     The lady said, no, she was sick;
send for the chaplain, and be quick,
he must at once come to her side!
176 Dying, she was, and terrified.
     "Patience, madame!" the old dame said.
"My lord has gone off to the wood;
no one but me can enter here."
180 The lady was now seized by fear;
indeed she seemed to faint away.
The old dame saw, with great dismay,
opened the door, and straightaway
184 called for the priest without delay.
He came as quickly as might be,
Bringing the *corpus Domini*.[8]
     And thus the knight received the Host,

8. The Host; the body of Our Lord, the Eucharist.

188   Le vin del chalice beü.
       Li chapeleins s'en est alez
       E la vielle ad les us fermez.
       La dame gist lez sun ami.
192   Unke si bel cuple ne vi!

       Quant unt asez ris e jué
       E de lur priveté parlé,
       Li chevaliers ad cungié pris:
196   Raler s'en voelt en sun païs.
       Ele le prie ducement
       Que il la reveie sovent.
       "Dame," fet il, "quant vus plerra,
200   Ja l'ure ne trespassera;
       Mes tel mesure en esgardez
       Que nus ne seium encumbrez.
       Ceste vielle nus traïra,
204   E nuit e jur nus gaitera;
       Ele parcevra nostre amur,
       Sil cuntera a sun seignur.
       Si ceo avient cum jeo vus di
208   E nus seium issi trahi,
       Ne m'en puis mie departir"
       Que mei n'en estuce murir.

       Li chevaliers a tant s'en veit;
212   A grant joie s'amie leit.
       El demain lieve tute seine;
       Mut fu haitiee la semeine.
       Sun cors teneit en grant chierté:
216   Tute recovre sa beauté.
       Or li plest plus a surjurner
       Qu'en nul autre deduit aler!
       Sun ami voelt suvent veeir
220   E de lui sun delit aveir;
       Des que sis sires s'en depart,
       E nuit e jur e tost e tart
       Ele l'ad tut a sun pleisir.
224   Or l'en duinst Deus lunges joïr!

       Pur la grant joie u ele fu
       Que suvent puet veeir sun dru,
       Esteit tuz sis semblanz changiez.
228   Sis sire esteit mut veizïez:
       En sun curage s'aparceit

188 the wine, the blood of Jesus Christ;
the priest left. They were as before,
and the old woman closed the door.
Lady and knight lay nestled there;
192 never was such a handsome pair!

They laughed and played awhile. They spoke
of their new love in lovers' talk,
the knight then took his leave, to go
196 back to his land. He said adieu;
softly she begged him to return,
to make another visit soon.
"Lady," he said, "at your request
200 I'll come before an hour has passed;
but you must take great care and thought
that we are not surprised and caught.
The old dame will betray us, pry
204 night and day with her spying eye;
she will find out our love; for sure
she will tell all to the seigneur.
If this should happen as I say
208 and we're discovered in this way
I cannot leave, I cannot fly,
without it happening that I die."

After this speech he went away,
212 leaving his sweetheart in great joy.
Next day she woke up hale and sound,
all week a sweet contentment found,
care and attention gave her body,
216 and she recovered all her beauty.
Now she was glad of her small space;
why seek out joy some other place!
Often she wished to call her love
220 and all their sweet communion have;
soon as her husband went away,
early and late, and night and day
she had her pleasure with her knight;
224 God grant these two a long delight!

Having such bliss and joy, to be
much in her lover's company,
her manner was much changed, and thus
228 her lord, astute and devious,
noticed her heart and spirit, her grace,

Qu'autrement est k'il ne suleit.
Mescreance ad vers sa serur.
232 Il la met a reisun un jur
E dit que mut ad grant merveille
Que la dame si s'appareille,
Demande li que ceo deveit.
236 La vielle dist qu'el ne saveit,
Kar nuls ne pot parler od li
Ne ele n'ot dru ne ami,
Fors tant que sule remaneit
240 Plus volentiers qu'el ne suleit:
De ceo s'esteit aparceüe.
Dune l'ad li sires respundue:
    "Par fei," fet il, "ceo qui jeo bien.
244 Or vus estuet fere une rien:
Al matin, quant jeo erc levez
E vus avrez les hus fermez,
Fetes semblant de fors eissir,
248 Si la lessiez sule gisir,
En un segrei liu vus estez
E si veez e esgardez
Que ceo peot estre e dunt ço vient
252 Ki en si grant joie la tient."
    De cel cunseil sunt departi.
Allas! Cum ierent malbailli
Cil ke l'un veut si agaitier
256 Pur eus traïr e enginnier.!

    Tiers jur aprés, ç oï cunter,
Fet li sires semblant d'errer.
A sa femme ad dit e cunté
260 Que li reis l'ad par brief mandé,
Mes hastivement revendra.
    De la chambre ist e l'us ferma.
Dunc s'esteit la vielle levee,
264 Triers une cortine est alee;
Bien purrat oïr e veeir
Ceo qu'ele cuveite a saveir.
    La dame jut, pas ne dormi,
268 Kar mut desire sun ami.
Venuz i est, pas ne demure,
Ne trespasse terme ne hure.
    Ensemble funt joie mut grant
272 E par parole e par semblant,
De si ke tens fu de lever,

so different from her former ways.
He viewed his sister with suspicion;
232 met her one day for some discussion,
saying it was quite marvellous
how his wife seemed to act and dress.
What did this mean? What was the cause?
236 The old dame did not know, because
Madame spoke not with any other,
she did not have a friend or lover,
it was just that she seemed to be
240 all by herself more willingly.
She too had seen what change there was.
And the old lord responded thus:
     "By faith! I think that's so!" said he.
244 Now you must do a thing for me:
tomorrow morning, when I'm gone,
and you have closed the doors again,
pretend that you yourself have gone
248 and leave her lying there alone.
You find yourself a secret spot;
watch keenly. See that you find out
where this thing comes from, what it is,
252 that brings our dame such joy and bliss."
     They parted, done with this cabal.
Alas! What evil can befall
someone whom spies intend to get
256 entangled in the trap they've set!

     Three days later, so I've heard,
the lord left—or it so appeared.
He told his wife he had a writ;
260 the king commanded him to court,
but swiftly he'd return to her.
     He went; his sister shut the door,
and the old woman rose and hid
264 behind an arras, where she stood.
All she desired to hear and see
she could take in most easily.
     The young wife lay in bed, awake,
268 full of desire and love's sweet ache
for her *ami*, her chevalier;
He came. He did not waste an hour.
     What bliss and joy they made together
272 by speech, by deed, lover to lover!
Then they must rise, and all was done,

Kar dunc li estuveit aler.
Cele le vit, si l'esgarda,
276 Coment il vint e il ala.
De ceo ot ele grant poür
Qu'hume le vit e pus ostur.
     Quant li sires fu repeiriez,
280 Ki gueres n'esteit esluignez,
Cele li ad dit e mustré
Del chevalier la vérité,
E il en est forment pensifs.
284 Des engins faire fu hastifs
A ocire le chevalier.
Broches de fer fist granz furgier
E acerer le chief devant:
288 Suz ciel n'ad rasur plus trenchant!
Quant il les ot apparailliees
E de tutes parz enfurchiees,
Sur la fenestre les ad mises,
292 Bien serreies e bien asises,
Par unt li chevaliers passot,
Quant a la dame repeirot.
Deus, qu'il ne sout la traïsun
296 Que aparaillot le felun!

     El demain a la matinee,
Li sires lieve ainz l'ajurnee
E dit qu'il voet aler chacier.
300 La vielle le vait cunveier,
Pus se recuche pur dormir,
Kar ne poeit le jur choisir.
La dame veille, si atent
304 Celui qu'ele eime lealment,
E dit qu'or purreit bien venir
E estre od li tut a leisir.
Si tost cum el l'ad demandé,
308 N'i ad puis gueres demuré:
En la fenestre vint volant.
Mes les broches furent devant:
L'une le fiert par mi le cors,
312 Li sans vermeilz en sailli fors!
Quant il se sot a mort nafrez,
Desferre sei, enz est entrez.
Devant la dame el lit descent,
316 Que tuit li drap furent sanglent.

and he must go, this magic one.
The old dame saw the whole event,
276   saw how he came and how he went,
and wild with terror in her stalk
saw him first man and then a hawk.
    And when the lord was back again
280   most hastily, as was the plan—
she lost no time, but told her brother
all of the truth about this lover.
    Oh, fiercely anxious was this man!
284   Further traps now, and further plan
he made, to kill the chevalier;
prongs he had made of iron, that were
sharp at the tip and razor-keen;
288   beneath sweet heaven no worse have been.
When these had been prepared, in form
forklike—such tines could do most harm—
there in the window they were set,
292   the tines as close as they could get,
through which the chevalier must fly
when he made tryst with his *amie.*
God! How little suspects the knight
296   his foe's great treachery and spite!

    The day that followed, the old sire
rose before dawn, for his desire,
he said, was to go hunt. He went;
300   the old dame also rose, and sent
him forth, then bedward made her way.
Dark was not her idea of day.
The young dame wakened, rose, to see
304   him whom she loved so loyally;
said he could well come now, and seize
this time; they could be at their ease.
Soon as she'd spoken her request,
308   he came, without delay or rest,
swooping up to the window.
                       But
there were the prongs. One of them cut
straight to the heart; in a great spout
312   his scarlet blood came leaping out.
It was his death wound. When he knew
he struggled free, and came on through.
He sat before her on the bed,
316   all of the bedclothes soaked with blood;

Ele veit le sanc e la plaie,
  Mut anguissusement s'esmaie.
Il li ad dit: "Ma duce amie,
320 Pur vostre amur perc jeo la vie.
Bien le vus dis qu'en avendreit:
Vostre semblanz nus ocireit."

    Quant el l'oï dunc chiet pasmee;
324 Tute fu morte une loëe.
Il la cunforte ducement
E dit que dols n'i vaut nient:
De lui est enceinte d'enfant.
328 Un fiz avra, pruz e vaillant;
Icil la recunforterat.
Yônec numer le ferat.
Il vengerat e lui e li,
332 Il oscirat sun enemi.

    Il ne peot dunc demurer mes,
Kar sa plaie seignot adés;
A grant dolur s'en est partiz.
336 Ele le siut a mut granz criz.
Par une fenestre s'en ist;
C'est merveille k'el ne s'ocist,
Kar bien aveit vint piez de haut
340 Iloec u ele prist le saut!
Ele esteit nue en sa chemise.
A la trace del sanc s'est mise
Ki del chevalier degotot
344 Sur le chemin u ele alot.
Icel sentier errat e tint,
De si qu'a une hoge vint.
En cele hoge ot une entree,
348 De cel sanc fu tute arusee,
Ne pot nïent avant veeir.
Dunc quidot ele bien saveir
Que sis amis entrez i seit:
352 Dedenz se met a grant espleit.
El n'i trovat nule clarté.
Tant ad le dreit chemin erré
Que fors de la hoge est issue

she saw the wound, she saw the flood,
anguished, dismayed, at how he bled.
    He said, "Sweet love, sweet *bele amie*,
320 for my great love of you I die.
I warned you this would come to pass;
your beauty was the death of us."

    Hearing, she fainted and fell down
324 deathlike, a moment, in her swoon.
But he consoled her tenderly;
grief was worth nothing, and, said he,
now she was pregnant. She would have
328 a son, most valiant and most brave;
he would restore her, bring her joy.
Yönec he'd be named, this boy;
he would avenge this treachery
332 and kill their mortal enemy.

    The knight could now no longer stay;
for his wound bled continuously,
and in great pain he left her side.
336 She followed. Dreadfully she cried,
tore through the window, leaped and fell.
Truly it was a miracle
she was not killed; it was a leap
340 of twenty feet, down from the keep.
Naked beneath her shift she went,[9]
followed the trace of blood, the spent
drops of it trickling from the wound
344 there on the road, so quickly found.
She kept straight on that road, until
in front of her she saw a hill,
an entrance in it, still the trace
348 of blood that moistened all the place.
Nothing beyond was visible.
But she was certain, through that hill
her love had gone. The track, the lead,
352 was not too plain. But, with due speed
she entered in that lightless place,
kept the right road, and kept her pace
until she came outside the hill.

---

9. *"Ele esteit nue en sa chemise"*; the chemise was the undergarment worn next to the skin.
It was a sort of loose shirt. See note to line 438 for a fuller account of women's gar-
ments of Marie's time.

356   E en un mut bel pré venue.
     Del sanc trovat l'erbe moilliee,
     Dunc s'est ele mut esmaiee.
     La trace ensiut par mi le pré.
360   Asez près ot une cité.
     De mur fu close tut entur;
     N'i ot mesun, sale ne tur
     Ki ne parust tute d'argent;
364   Mut sunt riche li mandement.
     Devers le burc sunt li mareis
     E les forez e li difeis.
     De l'autre part, vers le dunjun,
368   Curt une ewe tut envirun;
     Ileoc arivoent les nefs,
     Plus i aveit de treis cenz tres.
        La porte aval fu desfermee;
372   La dame est en la vile entree
     Tuz jurs aprés le sanc novel,
     Par mi le bure, desk'al chastel.
     Unkes nuls a li ne parla,
376   Humme ne femme n'i trova.
     El paleis vient al paviment,
     Del sanc le treve tut sanglent:
     En une bele chambre entra,
380   Un chevalier dormant trova;
     Nel cunut pas, si vet avant.
     En une autre chambre plus grant
     Un lit trevë e nïent plus,
384   Un chevalier dormant desus.
     Ele s'en est utre passee,
     En la tierce chambre est entree:
        Le lit sun ami ad trové.
388   Li pecol sunt d'or esmeré;
     Ne sai mie les dras preisier;
     Li cirgë e li chandelier,
     Ki nuit e jur sunt alumé,
392   Valent tut l'or d'une cité.

356   There was a meadow, beautiful,
       its grasses stained with blood, and she
       felt terror, now, increasingly.
       But through this field she went, kept on;
360   nearby, she saw, there was a town.
       On every side there was a wall;
       there was not house, nor tower, nor hall
       that did not seem of silver, all;
364   —places so rich, so wonderful!
       Close to the town, the nearer edge
       were marsh and woods, and field and hedge;
       and on the other side of town,
368   close to the keep, a river ran
       encircling all. Berthed ships lay there;
       three hundred sails and more there were.
          The lower gate lay open wide,
372   and so the lady went inside,
       and still she followed blood, and still
       all through the town she went, until
       she reached the castle. No one there
376   spoke to her, or discovered her.
       In the paved palace hall she found
       blood on the floor and all around.
       She saw a lovely room; went in,
380   and found a knight, asleep, within;
       she knew him not. So, leaving him,
       she went, and found a larger room;
       a bed was in it, nothing more,
384   on it, a sleeping chevalier.
       Out of this second chamber, too,
       she went, and in a third, she knew
       her lover.
                     On a bed with feet
388   of purest gold, he lay. No sheet
       or quilt there I'd attempt to price;
       or chandeliers, that would suffice
       to burn all night, to burn all day;[1]
392   worth a whole city's gold, I'd say.

1. Ewert points out here (179): "The description of Muldumarec as a ruler of some super-
   natural realm which is reached through a hill not far from Caerwent is in contradiction
   with the latter part of the story (346ff.) where his domain is situated on the road from
   Caerwent to Caerleon." He then refers to the scholarly supposition that we have here
   two fused versions of the tale but then comments: "But such contradictions are com-
   mon in fairy tales . . . they are not to be arraigned at the bar of Reason, any more than
   the miraculous leap of the heroine through a window bristling with knife-like prongs
   and and at a height of twenty feet from the ground (337–40)."

Si tost cum ele l'ad veü,
Le chevalier ad cuneü,
Avant alat tute esfreee,
396 Par desus lui cheï pasmee.
Cil la receit ki forment l'aime;
Maleürus sovent se claime.
Quant del pasmer fu trespassee,
400 Il l'ad ducement cunfortee:
    "Bele amie, pur Deu merci,
Alez vus en, fuiez d'ici!
Sempres murai en mi le jur;
404 Ci einz avrat si grant dolur,
Si vus i esteiez trovee,
Mut en serïez turmentee.
Bien iert entre ma gent seü
408 Que m'unt por vostre amur perdu.
Pur vus sui dolenz e pensis."
    La dame li ad dit: "Amis,
Mieuz voil ensemble od vus murir
412 Qu'od mun seignur peine suffrir:
    S'a lui revois, il m'ocira!"
Li chevaliers l'aseüra:
Un anelet li ad baillé,
416 Si li ad dit e enseigné,
Ja tant cum el le gardera,
A sun seignur n'en membera
De nule rien ki fete seit,
420 Ne ne l'en tendrat en destreit.
S'espee li cumande e rent,
Puis la cunjurë e defent
Que ja nuls hum n'en seit saisiz,
424 Mes bien la gart a oés sun fiz.
Quant il serat creüz e granz
E chevaliers pruz e vaillanz,
A une feste u ele irra
428 Sun seigneur e lui amerra.
En une abbeïe vendrunt;
Par une tumbe k'il verrunt
Orrunt renoveler sa mort
432 E cum il fu ocis a tort.

Instantly, in that sumptuous place
she knew her lover, knew his face;
in terror, she came toward him. Then
396   she fainted and fell over him.
He held her, he, so passionate;
often he cried out, cursing Fate.
When she'd made some recovery
400   he comforted her tenderly.
     "For God's sake, though, my *bele amie,*
get out of here! Go, sweetheart, flee!
Soon, love, by daybreak, I shall die.[2]
404   There'll be deep grief, and great outcry;
if you are found, most certainly
you will be done great injury.
My people will know well the cost—
408   that through our love I have been lost.
I'm full of grief for you, and fear!"
     The lady said: "Sweet friend, my dear,
I would much rather die right here
412   than at the hands of my seigneur;
if I return, he'll murder me!"
     The knight spoke reassuringly.
He gave her a small ring, and said
416   to guard it well, and if she did
—he carefully instructed her—
she need not fear, for her seigneur
would not keep what she'd done in mind,
420   nor keep her wretched and confined.
He gave into her hands his sword;
required of her her solemn word
it must not pass to any man
424   but she must keep it for their son.
And when he was of age, and grown,
a valiant knight, his courage known,
she must go to a festival,
428   leading her lord and son as well.
And to an abbey they would come
and in that abbey see a tomb.
There they'd be told a memory
432   of wrongful death and treachery.

---

2. Rychner's edition of the original, here followed, employs two manuscripts, (P) and (Q), which give *en mi*, "in the middle of the day." Ewert's edition, following two other manuscripts, (H) and (S), gives *devant le jur*, i.e., "before the day," i.e., "daybreak." In this particular instance, following Joseph J. Duggan's scholarship, I believe *devant le jour* to be more authoritative.

Ileoc li baillerat s'espeie.
L'aventure li seit cuntee
Cum il fu nez, ki l'engendra:
436   Asez verrunt k'il en fera.
Quant tut li ad dit e mustré
Un chier bliaut li ad doné;
Si li cumandë a vestir,
440   Puis l'ad fete de lui partir.
Ele s'en vet, l'anel enporte
E l'espee ki la cunforte.
A l'eissue de la cité,
444   N'ot pas demie liwe erré,
Quant ele oï les seins suner
E le doel el chastel mener
Por lur seignur ki se mureit.
448   Ele set bien que morz esteit;
    De la dolur que ele en ad
Quatre fiëes se pasmad.
E quant de paumesuns revint,
452   Vers la hoge sa veie tint;
Dedenz entra, utre est passee,
Si s'en reveit en sa cuntree.
    Ensemblement od sun seignur
456   Demurat meint di e meint jur
Que de cel fet ne la retta
Ne ne mesdist ne ne gaba.

    Sis fiz fu nez e bien nuriz
460   E bien gardez e bien cheriz.
Yönec le firent numer.
El regné ne pot hum trover
Si bel, si pruz ne si vaillant,
464   Si large ne si despendant.
    Quant il fu venuz en eé,
A chevalier l'unt adubé.
En l'an meïsme que ceo fu,
468   Oëz cument est avenu:

She'd give the sword up to the son,
tell how he was conceived and born,
who fathered him. What he'd do then
436   they would soon see.
                    The knight had shown
the lady all that must be done.
A rich *bliaut*,[3] a lovely gown
he gave her, said that she must wear;
440   and then he took his leave of her.
        She left then, carrying the ring,
and the sword, deeply comforting.
Out of the gate, out of the town,
444   no more than half a league, she'd gone,
when she could hear the bell, the toll,
and cries inside the castle wall,
for the seigneur, who was no more.
448   He must be dead now, she was sure.
        Grief overcame her. In a swoon,
four times, while walking, she fell down,
then she recovered and went on,
452   back toward the hill and tunnel. Soon
she entered, came on through, and found
herself once more in her own land.
        With her old lord, and free of fear,
456   she lived for many a day and year.
He never shamed her, this old sir,
ridiculed or insulted her.

        The son was born, and lovingly
460   nourished and cherished, watchfully,
named Yönec. And in that land,
that kingdom, no man could be found
so handsome, valiant, brave; withal
464   so generous, so liberal.
        When he was grown, and time was right,
this fine young man was dubbed a knight.
When that was done, that very year
468   something else happened: listen, hear.

3. A long tunic, laced at the sides; it had long, full sleeves. A twelfth-century French woman would usually wear a chemise, a shirt-like, shift-like garment next to her skin (see note to line 341); over the chemise she wore a *chainse* of linen or hemp, a floor-length dress with long, tight, sleeves. The most outer garment was the *bliaut*. To wear only the *chainse* without the *bliaut* was considered insufficient. (See U. T. Holmes, *Daily Living in the Twelfth Century*, 163–64.) This lady wore only her chemise. It was most chivalrous of her lover, dying in agony, to consider her comfort and modesty and give her an outer garment to wear on her journey home.

A la feste seint Aaron,
C'um selebrot a Karlïon
E en plusurs autres citez,
472   Li sire aveit esté mandez
Qu'il i alast od ses amis
A la custume del païs;
Sa femme e sun fiz i menast
476   E richement s'aparaillast.
Issi avint, alé i sunt,
Mes il ne seivent u il vunt.
Ensemble od eus ot un meschin
480   Kis ad menez le dreit chemin,
Tant qu'il viendrent a un chastel;
En tut le mund nen ot plus bel!
Une abbeïe i ot dedenz
484   De mut religïuses genz.
Li vallez les i herberja
Ki a la feste les mena.
En la chambre ki fu l'abbé
488   Bien sunt servi e honuré.
El demain vunt la messe oïr,
Puis s'en voleient departir,
Li abes vet od eus parler,
492   Mut les prie de surjurner:
Si lur musterrat sun dortur,
Sun chapitre, sun refeitur,
E cum il sunt bien herbergié.
496   Li sires lur ad otrié.

Le jur, quant il orent digné,
As officines sunt alé.
El chapitre vindrent avant;
500   Une tumbe troverent grant,
Coverte d'un palie roé,
D'un chier orfreis par mi bendé.
Al chief, as piez e as costez
504   Aveit vint cirges alumez;
D'or fin erent li chandelier,
D'ametiste li encensier

It was the feast of St. Aaron,[4]
which was observed at Caerleon
and many other towns. The lord
472 was summoned, and with due accord
gathered his friends up in a band,
which was the custom of the land.
His wife and son, most richly dressed,
476 accompanied him to the feast.
    And so it was. They set out, though
they had no notion where to go.
A young man they brought with them showed
480 these festal seekers the right road.
They found a castle on their quest—
Surely on earth the loveliest!
Inside the wall an abbey lay
where the devoted work and pray,
485 and there the guide, the young valet
brought all his band to lodge and stay,
and in the room of the Abbé
488 they were served with great courtesy.
    Next morning they heard mass, and then
thought to go on their way again,
but the good Abbé prayed they'd stay;
492 he'd much to show, and much to say.
The sleeping rooms, they'd get to see,
the chapter house, refectory—
since they were lodged so graciously
496 the lord consented readily.
    When they had dined, the following day,
the tour began. And on the way
just by the chapter house, they found
500 a large tomb. Cloth, with stripes, and round
wheel patterns, of a silk brocade,
gold-bordered, on the tomb was laid.
And at the feet, the sides, the head,
504 full twenty candles' light was shed,
the chandeliers were gold, the best,
the censers glowed with amethyst.[5]

---

4. The two famous saints of Caerleon were the two native martyrs, Aaron and Julian, who were killed in the persecutions of the emperor Diocletian (284–305). Ewart writes (180): "Each had his church in Caerleon, that of Aaron serving as the Cathedral of the Archbishop and the metropolitan church of Wales."
5. Marie's original, in a number of manuscripts, has *d'ametiste le encensier* for this line, and it appears in both major editions of her work, Rychner's and Ewert's. It is hard to imagine, however, a censer (unless extremely small) made entirely from a gemstone; it would be too heavy to wield. Professor Duggan prefers the reading in one manuscript, (S),

Dunt il encensouent le jur
508 Cele tumbe par grant honur,
Il unt demandé e enquis
Icels ki erent del païs
De la tumbe ki ele esteit
512 E queils hum fu ki la giseit.
Cil comencierent a plurer
E en plurant a recunter
Que c'iert li mieudre chevaliers
516 E li plus forz e li plus fiers,
Li plus beaus e li plus amez
Ki jamés seit el siecle nez.
De ceste tere ot esté reis,
520 Unques ne fu nuls si curteis.
A Carẅent fu entrepris,
Pur l'amur d'une dame ocis.
"Unques puis n'eümes seignur,
524 Ainz avum atendu meint jur
Un fiz qu'en la dame engendra,
Si cum il dist e cumanda."
Quant la dame oï la novele,
528 A haute voiz sun fiz apele:
"Beaus fiz, fet ele, avez oï
Cum Deus nus ad menez ici?
C'est vostre pere ki ci gist,
532 Que cist villarz a tort ocist.
Or vus cormant e rent s'espee,
Jeo l'ai asez lung tens gardee."
Oiant tuz li ad coneü
536 Qu'il l'engendrat e sis fiz fu;
Cum il suleit venir a li
E cum sis sires le trahi,
La vérité li ad cuntee.
540 Sur la tumbe cheï pasmee;
En la paumeisun devïa,
Unc puis a humme ne parla.
Quant sis fiz veit que morte fu,
544 Sun parastre ad le chief tolu;
De l'espeie ki fu sun pere
Ad dunc vengié lui e sa mere.

---

which has *argent* or silver, a material of which censers are indeed traditionally made.
Given the frequency of the word *ametiste* in other sources, however, we believe that the
silver censer was studded with amethysts, which no doubt gave off a beautiful purple light
as they swung, appropriate homage for the tomb of a beloved prince.

All day they swung, and their perfume
508 honored the ornate, splendid tomb.
The visitors made inquiry
of their kind hosts; who could it be
whose tomb was such an honored place?
512 What man lay in such cherished space?
Those whom they asked, the local folk
began to weep. But still they spoke:
here lay the best of chevaliers,
516 the strongest, proudest, and most fierce,
the handsomest, most loved of men
who in this world was ever born.
And of this country he'd been king—
520 never a courtlier was seen.
At Carwënt his blood was spilled;
love for a lady got him killed.
"Since then we have had no seigneur,
524 no king; but waited many a year
for the son he engendered. Thus
our own dear lord commanded us."

The lady heard. The tale was done.
528 In a strong voice she called her son:
"Fair son," said she, "now have you heard
how God has called us here? This lord
who lies here is your father. He,
532 this greybeard, killed him wrongfully.
Now I entrust to you at last
this sword I've kept for long years past."
For all to hear, she now made known
536 how their seigneur had got a son;
how he was wont to come to her,
how her own lord betrayed them there.
She told the truth to one and all;
540 then in a faint they saw her fall;
and there she died, upon the tomb;
never more spoke to anyone.
When her son knew that she was dead,
544 he took his own stepfather's head.
Thus he avenged, with swordthrust, both
his father's and his mother's death.

Puis ke si fu dunc avenu
548 E par la cité fu sceü,
A grant honur la dame unt prise
E el sarcu posee e mise
Delez le cors de sun ami.
552 Deus lur face bone merci!
Lur seignur firent d'Yönec,
Ainz que il partissent d'ilec.

Cil ki ceste aventure oïrent
556 Lunc tens aprés un lai en firent
De la pitié de la dolur
Que cil suffrirent pur amur.

When this had happened, and was known,
548 and the news spread throughout the town,
with all due honor she was borne
in a fair coffin, to the tomb.
There by her lover she was placed;
552 God give them both sweet peace and rest!
Before they left, with due accord
the folk made Yönec their lord.

Those who this tale of love had heard
556 made it a *lai*, long afterward.
Out of compassion they did so
for lovers' suffering and woe.

Laüstic

There's an adventure, I will say,
of which the Bretons made a *lai*.
Laüstic is the name it's called
4 in its own country, so I'm told.
In French it's "Rossignol," this tale;
in proper English, "Nightingale."
Near St. Malo[1] there was a town
8 that in that region had renown.
There lived two knights, and side by side
their mansions, strong and fortified.[2]
For knightly valor each had fame,
12 and gave their city a good name.
One had a wife, an excellent
lady, wise, courtly, elegant;
a marvel was she, so *soignée*,[3]
16 and groomed with great propriety.[4]
The other of these chevaliers,
a bachelor, was by his peers
well known for prowess, and great valor.
20 With pleasure he did deeds of honor.
Much he tourneyed; with much largesse
gave of what he himself possessed.
He loved his neighbor's wife, and he
24 begged and sued so persistently
and had such qualities, that she
above all, loved him ardently;
partly, for all the good she heard;
28 partly, he lived close by, this lord.
Well these two loved, and prudently,
and with great care and secrecy,
making sure they were not detected,
32 hindered, or noticed, or suspected;
and this they could do easily
because their dwellings lay nearby.

1. A town on the coast of Brittany, facing the Channel Islands and England.
2. These two knights are of the lesser nobility; they do not have castles but fortified mansions in imitation of the castles of the great lords.
3. Modern French: well cared for, well groomed.
4. Glyn S. Burgess comments in *The Lais of Marie de France: Text and Context* (117) that Marie's original here, "A merveille se teneit chiere" (line 15), "although difficult to define precisely, indicates an awareness of personal worth and attention to details of appearance and social behavior." He cites Lucie Polak's "Two Lines from Marie de France's *Laüstic*" in *French Studies* 34 (1980): 257–58, remarking that "Polak sees the notion of holding oneself dear as a courtly virtue akin to *mesure* and *courtoisie*."

Nearby, their mansions and their halls,
36   their keeps, their dungeons. But no walls,
no barrier, except for one,
a great high wall of dark-hued stone.[5]
Still, in her bedroom, when she stood
40   right at the window, then she could
talk to her love, her chevalier,
she speak to him and he to her;
they could toss tokens to each other,
44   throw little gifts, lover to lover.
Nothing displeased them in that place,
they were at ease there, face to face,
except that they could only see—
48   not join in pleasure utterly,
for when he was at home, her lord
had his wife under close, strict guard.
Still they made opportunity;
52   and thus by night and thus by day
they met; they spoke; they found a way
and none who watched could say them nay
when to their windows they would each
56   come, and there speak their loving speech.
    For a long time they loved each other,
until one summer, when the weather
had made the fields and forests green
60   and gardens, orchards, bloom again;
above the flowers, with great joy
small birds sang sweetest melody.[6]
He whose desire for love is strong
64   —no wonder that he heeds their song!
The truth about this knight, I'll tell;
he heard the song; he heard it well;
the lady, too, heard in her place;

5. In line 38 of Marie's original, she mentions "un haut mur de piere bise," in other words, "a high wall of dark-hued stone." That wall is not mentioned again and plays no other part—really no part at all—in the story. It seems to be no sort of barrier to the lovers' sight of each other. To give it a context in the story in English, I have in line 39 added the word "still"; for Marie's lines 39–40, "Des chambres u la dame jut / Quant a la fenestre s'estut," I have supplied "Still, in her bedroom, when she stood / right at the window, where she could" talk to her lover and they could see each other.
6. This passage, praising the season of spring, is a medieval convention or device known as the *reverdie*, or "re-greening"; its most famous instance for English-speaking readers is probably the beginning of the General Prologue of Chaucer's *Canterbury Tales*. The device usually contains mention of flowers beginning to bud and bloom and birds singing, with the suggestion that Nature also prompts human beings to desire and find love and procreate. (Chaucer wittily departs from the love convention and says that spring is the time when "longen folk to goon on pilgrimages" where, he suggests later, they may find adventure, profit or, possibly, love.)

68   thus they could love; court; speak, and gaze.[7]
     When the moon shone, the lady would
     rise often from her husband's bed,
     rise from beside him, while he slept
72   and softly, in her mantle wrapped,
     cautiously to the window go

7. Lines 63–68 have been interpreted somewhat variously by other, highly respected, trans-
lators, which I found understandable. The original—lines 58–68—to give context, read:

> Tant que ceo vint a un este,
> Que bruil e pre sunt reverdi
> E le vergier ierenet fluri;
> Cil oiselet par grant ducur
> Mainent lur joie en sum la flur.
> Ki amur ad a sun talent,
> N'est merveille s'il i entent!
> Del chevalier vus dirai veir;
> Il i entent a sun poeir,
> E la dame de l'autre part,
> E de parler e de regart.

The difficulty of interpretation may lie in that (to paraphrase President Clinton's famous
phrase) it all depends on what "i" is or what it refers to. Burgess and Busby in their Pen-
guin prose translation have

> . . . On the flower-tops the birds sang joyfully and sweetly. If love is on anyone's mind, no
> wonder he turns his attention toward it. I shall tell you the truth about the knight. Both
> he and the lady made the greatest possible effort with their words and with their eyes.

In other words, "i" refers to "love," or "amur." But here is the same passage in Hanning and
Ferrante's free verse translation:

> For a long time they loved each other,
> until one summer
> when the woods and meadows were green
> and the orchards blooming.
> The little birds, with great sweetness,
> were voicing their joy above the flowers.
> It is no wonder if he understands them,
> he who has love to his desire.
> I'll tell you the truth about the knight;
> he listened to them intently
> and to the lady on the other side,
> both with words and looks.

Here "i" seems to refer to birdsong.
  My first thought was that "i" referred to "amur." But the story and the poem seem
more cohesive if it is the birds as well. My initial translation read:

> He who has loving in his thought,
> No wonder he gives in to it!
> I'll tell the truth about this knight;
> He pursued love with all his might . . .

But I decided that the translation in my text was a better choice. I trust that "a sun
poeir" in line 66 is adequately expressed in my solution: "He heard the song; he heard
it well."
  Note that the other translators differ in their interpretation of line 67, Burgess and
Busby emphasizing the couple's joint activity and Hanning and Ferrante emphasizing
the activity of the man. I originally opted for the man as well, writing in lines 67–68,
"with all his will he sought out ways / to love; to court; to speak; to gaze." Charles Mus-
catine, however, wrote to me that "since the more important idea in the plot is the lady's
interest in the birdsong, I'd have preferred that 67–68 gave more emphasis to that; as
is, the translation offers a rather amplified account of the man's response instead." After
heeding Muscatine's advice as best I could, I believe now that I have found a good solu-
tion to the dilemma of lines 67–68.

to see her lover, whom she knew
lived as she did, lived for her sight.
76 She'd stay awake most of the night.
    In gazing thus was their delight,
since nothing more could be their fate.
Such was the case. So often she
80 arose, her husband angrily
demanded of her, frequently,
where did she go, what for, and why?
The lady answered with this word:
84 "My sire: he who has never heard
the nightingale, has not known joy
ever, in all this world. That's why,
that's where. So sweetly I have heard
88 it sing at night, enchanting bird,
so great my longing, my delight,
I cannot close my eyes at night."
    When he had heard her answer thus,
92 he laughed, enraged and furious,
and he resolved that without fail
he would entrap the nightingale.
Now every squire within that house
96 put net or snare or trap to use
throughout the garden. Everywhere,
on hazel, chestnut, lay a snare
or gluey bird-lime. So they got
100 the nightingale; so it was caught.
    When they had tricked and trapped the bird
alive, they brought it to the lord.
Oh, he was happy when they came!
104 Right to the chamber of his dame
he hurried. "Lady, where are you?
Come talk to us, my lady, do!
I've trapped your nightingale, the one
108 that's kept you sleepless for so long.
Now, finally, you'll sleep in peace—
these night excursions now can cease."
    She understood, as he spoke thus,
112 and full of grief, and furious
asked for the bird. But her demands
were vain; in rage, with his two hands
he broke its neck. So this seigneur,
116 spiteful and vicious, like a boor
killed it. He threw the corpse at her.
It fell on her chemise and there

bloodied her breast a little bit.
120 He left the room; at once went out.
　　She gathered up the little body,
weeping vehemently. The lady
cursed those who caught the bird and laid
124 snares, nets, devices, all they made.
What joy was taken, wrenched away!
　　"Alas," she said, "Oh, wretched me!
No more shall I arise at night,
128 go to the window for a sight
of my dear love and find him there.
And one thing I do know for sure:
he'll think me weak and faint of heart.
132 I must act now. Let me take thought.
I'll send my love the nightingale,
make known to him this vicious tale."
　　She found a piece of samite,[8] wrought
136 with gold, and writing worked throughout;
in it she wrapped the little bird.
One of her servants she gave word,
gave him her message, and he went
140 to her *ami*, where it was sent,
So to the chevalier he came
and gave him greetings from his dame,
gave the full message, told the tale,
144 delivered up the nightingale.
When the full story was made known
—he gave it good attention!—
he felt much sorrow. This knight, though,
148 was not a boor, nor was he slow
of sense. A tiny reliquary
he soon had forged, for him to carry:
not iron; not steel; pure gold, with stones
152 most rare and precious, lovely ones;
a lid that was a perfect fit.
The little bird was placed in it,
the vessel sealed. The chevalier
156 carried it with him everywhere.
　　This story, more and more, got known;
it was not secret very long.
Of it the Bretons made their lay;
160 It's called *Laüstic* to this day.

---

8. A heavy silk fabric commonly worked with gold or silver and used in the Middle Ages for cushions and formal clothing.

Milun

Who wishes various tales to tell
must vary forms to do it well,
speak a propos, with reason, sense,
4 for this will please the audience.
Just now I shall begin "Milun;"
revealing, by a brief sermon
just how it happened, how and why
8 this tale was formed and named, this *lai*.

In South Wales he was born, Milun.
From the day he was dubbed, no one
he found, no single chevalier,
12 could knock him off his destrier.
He excelled among chevaliers,
noble and valiant, proud and fierce;
well known he was in Ireland,
16 in Norway, also in Gotland,
in Logres and in Albany[1]
many watched Milun enviously.
Loved for his prowess, though, Milun;
20 and many princes honored him.
    In his same country lived a lord;
I do not know what name he had.
He had a daughter, beautiful,
24 and a most courtly demoiselle.
Much she heard mention of Milun
and she began to love the man.
She sent a messenger; she'd be
28 if it should please him, his *amie*.
This news filled Milun with delight;
he thanked the demoiselle for it,
willingly said he'd be her lover—
32 be true, and never quit her, never!
Quite courtly his response to her.
Rich gifts he gave the messenger,
and great affection promised him.
36   "Now, friend, see to it," said Milun,
"that I may speak with my *amie*,
that we meet with due secrecy.
Carry to her my golden ring;

1. Logres is England; Albany is an old name for Scotland.

40   on my behalf this message bring,
that when it pleases her, then she
send thee here; I'll return with thee."
    The servant took his leave, to tell
44   this message to the demoiselle,
gave her the ring, and said he'd well
performed the task, and done her will.
The girl was overjoyed to hear
48   that love had thus been granted her.

    So in a garden, set nearby
her chamber, in great jollity
of spirit, she kept rendez-vous;
52   Oh, frequently they met, these two!
He came so much,[2] he loved so well,
that she conceived, this demoiselle.
When she perceived she was *enceinte*,
56   she summoned Milun, made her plaint,
and told him what had come to pass;
honor and good name lost, alas,
since she'd engaged in this affair.
60   Judgment on her would be severe:
torture by sword, or she might be
sold into foreign slavery.
The ancients had such customs then,
64   and in that time such things were done.
Milun responded that he would
do what her counsel said he should.
    "Take this child," said she, "at its birth;
68   my married sister lives up north,
up in Northumberland's her home.
She's a rich, wise, and worthy dame.
If in writing you display it,
72   if in words you speak and say it,
this is your sister's child you bring,
a cause of her great suffering,
it will be nurtured well, she'll see,
76   boy, girl, whichever one it be.
And hang around its neck your ring,
also a letter you must bring,
written within, its father's name

2. The double entendre of English "came"—"he came so much"—does not occur in Marie's original or, as far as I know, in Marie's language; I have not found it in the many ribald tales of the period. I have retained it in this translation, thinking the pun consistent with Marie's wit and worldly spirit.

80 and the hard story of its dame.
When the child's big, and fully grown,
and to sufficient age has come
so it can reason understand,
84 letter and ring into its hand
she should give, so it may discover
while it cares for these things, its father."

They kept her counsel thoroughly
88 through the term of her pregnancy
until the damsel's time to bear.
Then an old woman cared for her,
with whom she trusted all she did.
92 This dame concealed all, all she hid,
never gave hint of the affair
by word, by manner or by air.
Beautiful was the damsel's son.
96 Around its neck the ring she hung,
also a pouch of silk; within
the letter, which no one had seen.
She laid all in a cradle; over
100 these treasures tucked a linen cover.
She placed beneath the infant's head
a useful pillow, fine and good;
a coverlet placed over him
104 hemmed all about with marten skin.
All, the old woman gave Milun
who, in the garden, took his son.
He bade his serving-folk that they
108 transport the infant loyally.
Through all the towns upon their way
they seven times stopped on each day
to rest, let the child suck, and then
112 bathe him, put him to bed again.
They took the straightest route, and there
found the dame, gave the child to her.
And she received the child with joy—
116 letter and seal and little boy.
When she discovered who he was
her loving care was marvelous!
Those who had brought the baby boy
120 to their own country went their way.

Out of his country went Milun,
a warrior, hired, to win renown.

Meanwhile his sweetheart was at home.
124   Her sire bestowed her on a man,
a baron of that region, rich
and powerful, his fame worth much.
And when she learned this was her fate
128   past reason she was desolate.
Much she regretted her affair
with Milun, for her deeds felt fear.
She'd borne a child, a serious fault,
132   straightway her lord would know of it.
     "Alas," she said, "what shall I do?
Me, take a lord? Not possible!
No longer virgin, no more maid,
136   I'll all my days be serving maid.
I little knew how things would be;
I thought to marry my *ami*.
We'd have concealed the liason,
140   never heard talk by anyone.
Why live? To die is best for me.
But I am not the least bit free,
all around me are guardians,
144   young ones and old, my chamberlains,
who loathe love, with great enmity,
always, and who love misery.
I am compelled to suffer thus—
148   if only I could die! Alas!"
     The time came; she was given away;
led to her lord upon the day.[3]

     Back to his country came Milun,
152   a pensive and a grieving man.
Great pain he showed, great sorrow felt,
but he took comfort from the thought
that nearby lay the country which
156   was home to her he loved so much.
Milun considered how he could
alert his love, or send her word
that he was, once again, at home
160   without the message being known.
A letter he composed, Milun,
and sealed. He had a much-loved swan;

---

3. The line in the original seems ambiguous. In *sis sires l'en ad amenee*, *sires* could refer either to the father, so keen to marry his daughter off to the baron and lead her to him, or to the baron himself, now her lord. Both choices appear in the work of other translators.

he placed the letter round its throat
164   and in its feathers hid the note.
He called one of his squires to come,
And with this speech instructed him:
    "Change thy clothes; quickly go," said he,
168   "to the *chastel* of my *amie*.
My swan thou shalt transport with thee;
take care that, for a surety,
that maid, manservant, either one
172   present my sweetheart with the swan!"
    He did as he was bid, this man;
at that he left and took the swan.
The route he knew, the straightest road,
176   and came there, quickly as he could,
on his way passing through the town;
now to the main gate he has come.
The porter saw him, called to him:
180   "Hear me, friend," called out Milun's man.
"My occupation, you must know,
is catching birds; that's what I do.
In a field under Caerleon,
184   with my snare, I have caught a swan.
I wish protection, strong and sure;
thus I present the swan to her
so that I not be hindered here,
188   charged and accused, as now I fear."
    To him replied the officer:
"Friend, for sure no one speaks with her.
Nevertheless I will find out
192   if I could locate near, some spot
where I could take you, lead you there.
Then I would let you speak with her."
    The porter went into the hall.
196   He saw two knights there, that was all,
at a large table; seated thus,
they much amused themselves at chess.
The porter came back hastily,
200   and led the man in such a way
that no one saw him in the hall,
noticed or hindered them at all.
Now at the chamber, at his call
204   the door was opened; a *pucelle*[4]

4. A "maid," in most of the English senses. Here, it means a maidservant. In line 135 it obviously means a virgin; in line 136, a maidservant. It can also mean a "maiden, young girl" in a more general sense. Joan of Arc, the Maid of Orleans, is often called *La Pucelle*.

went to her lady, took the swan;
thus was the presentation done.
The lady called her valet, then,
208   And gave instructions to the man;
      "See that my swan here is well fed,
cared for, and has sufficient food."
      "Dame," said the man who'd brought the swan,
212   "this is a gift for you alone,
splendid, and fit for royalty!
How beautiful, how fine, just see!"
He put it in her hands, and she
216   received the present graciously.
      Her fingers felt the head, the throat;
under the feathers felt the note.
She trembled; her blood froze; the swan,
220   the note, she knew, was from Milun.
Some recompense she gave his man;
then he could go, his task was done.
      She was alone now in the room;
224   she called a servant girl to come;
unlaced the letter from the swan;
broke the seal, saw the name "Milun"
right at the top. Oh, certainly
228   she knew the name of her *ami*!
A hundred times she kissed the note,
weeping before speech passed her throat.
There at the top, the text she read,
232   all he confided, all he said,
the great distress and agony
that Milun suffered, night and day:
      "Now it was at her pleasure whether
to kill him, or see him recover
If some device she could discover
whereby they two could speak together
she should write back to him in turn
240   and send the letter with the swan.
First the bird must have care and rest,
then she must starve him, let him fast,
three days; and then around his throat
244   she must attach her answering note,
and let him go; then he would come
flying once more to his first home."[5]

---

5. Robert Hanning and Joan Ferrante astutely observe in their commentary that "the starved
   swan, bringing messages to and from the love-starved pair, becomes a symbol of their

When she had read all that he wrote,
248   and understood all in the note,
she kept the swan; he sojourned there.
Fine food and drink he had from her!
A month, in her chamber, had good care.

252   But now hear more of this affair!
How she found, by her stratagem
parchment and ink, made use of them,
wrote such a letter as he sought,
256   and with a ring sealed up her note.
The swan she then allowed to fast,
and then into the air it cast
with the note, and the famished bird
260   craving and longing for its food
flew hastily, until it came
to its first shelter, its first home.
To the town, to the house, the swan
264   flew; to the feet, then, of Milun.
When he sees it, how joyful he!
He held its wings delightedly,
summoned a steward, so he could
268   give the pet swan its well earned food.
From the swan's neck he took the note,
from end to end read all she wrote;
tokens and greetings in the feathers
272   gave him delights well known to lovers:
"Without him I can know no good,
no joy; his sentiments he should
return, as she'd done, by the swan."
276   Hastily he'll comply, Milun.

Twenty years these two lived this way,
The knight Milun and his *amie*,
always the swan their emissary,
280   no other intermediary.
Thus they would cause the bird to fast,
then let him fly off with his trust.
Then the one who received the bird
284   knew very well to give him food.
Sometimes they met, she and Milun.
No lover's so afflicted, none

---

undernourished relationship that survives on words alone because of Milun's passivity":
The Lais of Marie de France (Dutton, 1978), 179.

so much constrained or so beset
288   they cannot find a way to meet.

The lady who had nursed their son
devoted such attention
he grew of age under her care;
292   and then she dubbed him chevalier.
He was a fine young handsome man!
Letter and ring she gave him then,
explained to him who was his mother,
296   and told the fortunes of his father:
the best, she said, of chevaliers,
how worthy, and how bold and fierce,
no better knight upon this earth
300   for reputation, valor, worth.
And when she had revealed this truth
and he had listened well enough,
his father's prowess and this word
304   made him rejoice at all he heard.
Then to himself he thought and spoke:
"He'll be considered small by folk,
if he was sired by such a man,
308   a chevalier of such renown,
who does not seek a greater fame,
leaving the land from which he came."
Convinced of this necessity,
312   only one night more would he stay,
and took his leave the following day.
The lady then had much to say
of admonitions; those bestowed,
316   she gave him money for the road.
At Southampton he passed straight through,
since over sea he meant to go.
To Barfluet[6] he went straightway,
320   and so he came to Brittany.
He tourneyed there; gave largesse; sought
wealthy men's friendship. When he fought,
and raised his lance in any joust,
324   invariably he came off best.
He loved the poor knights; when he won
riches and prizes, the young man
took the poor in his service; he
328   shared the won wealth most lavishly.

6. Modern Barfleur.

In one land he'd no wish to stay,
but in all countries over sea
he bore with him his fame, his valor,
332   so courtly that he knew much honor.
His prowess, largess, his great fame
at length to his own country came,
that there was from that land a youth
336   who crossed the sea to prove his worth,
whose prowess, generosity,
largesse, were all so great that he,
this famous, nameless chevalier,
340   was called by all the knights "Sans Peer."
     Praise of this fine knight reached Milun,
this man who'd such distinction won,
much Milun suffered, much complained
344   to himself of this knight, so famed.
While he himself set forth on journeys,
bore arms, engaged himself in tourneys,
none, in the country of his birth,
348   must prized, or praised, be, for his worth!
A plan he then resolved upon:
he'd cross the sea, make haste, be gone,
and with this chevalier he'd joust,
352   injure him, harm him, do his worst.
Rage spurred him to pursue this course;
if he could knock the man off horse
he'd finally be disgraced; that done,
356   Milun would then seek out his son,
who from the country was long gone,
his whereabouts and fate unknown.
To his *amie* he made this known;
360   he wished her blessing on this plan.
All his heart's feelings to reveal,
he sent the letter with its seal,
to my best knowledge, by the swan.
364   Her desire she must tell in turn.
When she had heard thus from her lover,
she thanked him greatly for the favor,
since, if their son he could discover,
368   he must leave home, the seas cross over,
find out the fortunes of the boy;
never would she stand in his way.
This message of hers reached Milun;
372   appareled splendidly, he soon
sailed to, then passed through, Normandy;

and traveled on to Brittany.
He cultivated folk, and went
376 seeking out any tournament,
rich lodgings he took frequently,
rewarding service courteously.
    All that one winter, I believe,
380 In that land Milun chose to live;
many good knights chose to retain.
Then, after Easter, once again
it was the time for tournaments,
384 also of wars and violence.[7]
They gathered at Mount Saint Michel,
Normans and Bretons and, as well,
Flemings and French assembled there,
388 but Englishmen were rather rare.
Milun, one of the earliest
came, bold and fierce, upon his quest.
Now the fine chevalier he sought;
392 for certain, people could point out
the region that the knight was from,
his arms, his shield, and so quite soon
they'd shown the warrior to Milun,
396 who now most closely studied him.
Tourniers gathered now; each knight
who wished to joust, soon found a fight;
who wished to search the ranks, could choose
400 soon enough, chance to win or lose,
encounter with an adversary.
    But, let me tell you Milun's story.
He was most valiant in the fray,
404 and he received much praise that day,
but the youth I have told of, he
over all, got *le dernier cri*.[8]
No one could match him, of the rest
408 in tourneying or in a joust.
How he behaved, Milun took note,
how well he spurred, how well he smote,
for all his envy of the knight
412 his skill filled Milun with delight.
He sought the ranks; he met the youth;

---

7. Tournaments and warfare were banned by the Church at certain times of the year,
including Lent, in keeping with the principle of "the truce of God." The ban was some-
times ignored.
8. That is, the youth got the loudest, greatest cry of acclaim from observers and
participants.

there they engaged and jousted, both.
Milun struck so ferociously
416 his foe's lance shattered, truth to say,
but he was not unhorsed; in turn
so hardily he struck Milun
that from his charger he fell down.
420 At that, the young man could discern
under the visor, the white hair,
white beard; his grief was hard to bear!
Milun's horse by the reins he led
424 to him; bestowed it on him; said,
    "Sire, mount up, do! I am distraught,
I'm greatly troubled in my thought
that to a fine man of your age
428 I've dealt such insult, such outrage!"
    Milun leaped on his horse, much pleased;
on the youth's finger recognized
the ring, as he returned the horse,
432 and to the young man he spoke thus:
    "Friend, listen! Say, by God above,
by the Omnipotent's sweet love,
what name is that borne by thy father?
436 What is thy name? Who is thy mother?
I wish to know the truth. I've been,
much, a great traveler; much I've seen,
much sought in countries where I went,
440 battle and war and tournament;
never, by strike of chevalier
did I fall from my destrier.
Thou hast, though, jousting, unhorsed me;
444 wonderfully could I love thee!"
    The other said, "I'll speak to you
about my father—what I know.
In Wales, I think, the man was born,
448 and given there the name Milun.
He loved a rich man's daughter; he
in secrecy engendered me.
Sent to Northumbria, there placed,
452 I was well nourished, taught, and raised!
An aunt of mine there nurtured me,
long kept me in her company,
gave me arms and a destrier,
456 and it was she who sent me here.
I've long lived here. But now I want
to leave; my longing, my intent

is to make voyage over sea
460 to my own country, hastily,
know the condition of my father
and his behavior toward my mother.
I will show him my golden ring
464 and certain tokens I will bring;
that he'll disown me, I've no fear;
but he will love me, hold me dear."
When he spoke thus, Milun, for sure
468 could not sit still and listen more;
quickly he leaped up, seized the skirt
of the youth's hauberk, his mailed shirt;
"My God," he said, "healed is Milun!
472 by my faith, friend, you are my son!
I've searched for thee, I've sought for thee,
this year, my country left for thee."
The youth heard; from his horse leaped down
476 and tenderly he kissed Milun.
Such joyous mien had son and father,
such happy speech made to each other
that other folk who watched nearby
480 wept both for pity and for joy.

The tournament broke up. Milun
left, all impatience; with his son
he greatly longed to speak at leisure,
484 impart to him his plans and pleasure.[9]
They at a hostel spent the night,
in joyousness and in delight,
a goodly crowd of knights was there.
488 Milun could tell his son, and share
how he had come to love his mother,
how she was given, by her father,
to a lord of that region; he,
492 Milun, still loved her, faithfully,
and she him, most devotedly.
And how the swan then came to be
bearer of letters, go-between;
they dared not trust a human being.
The son said, "By my faith, dear father,
I shall bring you and her together!

---

9. This is another ambiguous line, variously translated. In *E qu'il li die sun pleisir, sun plei-sir* may be interpreted as referring to either the father's wishes, pleasure, and plans or to those of the son.

This lord of hers I will dispatch,
500 and see you married! Made a match!"
        They spoke no more of this affair.
      Next day their task was to prepare
      to leave; bid their friends farewell; and then
504 to their own land at last return.
      Hastily they passed over seas,
      fair winds they had, auspicious breeze.
      They met, as they went on their way,
508 riding toward them, a servant boy.
      He was sent by Milun's *amie*,
      and meant to go to Brittany;
      she sent this lad, and a report—
512 but now his journey was cut short!
      A letter, sealed, he gave Milun;
      in speech, he urged the man to come
      quickly to her, he must not tarry!
516 Her lord was dead! Milun must hurry!
      When he had heard this news, Milun
      thought it seemed marvelous to him,
      and he explained all to his son.
520 Delay or hindrance there was none;
      they traveled on until they'd come
      to the dame's castle, to her home.
      In her son she took much delight—
524 a worthy, valiant, noble knight!
      No word they sought from relative;
      no counsel took, of none asked leave,
      but the son brought the two together
528 and gave his mother to his father.
      In happiness and sweetest joy
      they lived from then on, night and day.

        Of their good fortune and their love
532 the ancients made the *lai* above,
      and I, who wrote the story down,
      delighted much to tell this one.

Le Chaitivel

        Desire compels me to recall
      a *lai* that I've heard others tell.
      I'll tell the story of the *lai*
  4   and the town I'll identify

where the tale was conceived and born,
why it was called "The Wretched One."[1]
Others there are, though, who insist,
8   that "The Four Sorrows"[2] suits it best.
    At Nantes there lived, in Brittany,
a lady whose great courtesy,
beauty and breeding were much praised.
12 Most elegantly she'd been raised.
In all that region lived no knight
who'd proved his prowess and his might
who, once he had laid eyes on her,
16 did not adore her, ask for her.
She could not love them all, but then,
how do the kill? Refuse these men?[3]
If in a region, just one man
20 woos all the ladies, every one—
that's safer than if some poor clown
strikes back when lady turns him down.
This lady was the sort who knew
24 that to admirers grace is due;
she may not wish their speech; however
she must not shame or wound them, ever,
but, honoring each would-be lover,
28 cherish, thank, serve, and give due favor.
    This lady whom I'm speaking of,
who was so sought after in love,
whose worth and beauty were so great,
32 busied herself both day and night.
    Four barons lived in Brittany;
none of their names are known to me.
Barely of age, they had, these men
36 beauty superbly masculine,
Chevaliers were they, courteous,
worthy and brave and generous.
Great reputations had all four,
40 and nobles of that region were.
All with this lady were in love,
and to do noble deeds all strove,
each to the limits of his might,
44 to win her love and be her knight.

---

1. I.e., *Le Chaitivel*; see lines 208, 226, 228, 235.
2. I.e, *Les Quatres Dols*; see lines 204, 232.
3. The editor Karl Warnke (*Die Lais der Marie de France*, 1st. ed. Halle: Niemeyer, 1885) has *refuser*, "refuse," in his text; *tuer*, "kill," appears in both Ewert's edition and Rychner's. I have used both, liking the plainness of one and vitality of the other.

Each of them sought her for his own,
suffered all pains that this be done,
and each was sure he was the one,
48 the best, by whom she would be won.
This lady, most intelligent,
reflected much, for her intent
was to search out, for sure discover
52 which man was best to choose for lover.
    But all were of great worthiness;
she could not pick out which was best.
For one, she could not give up three!
56 She showed all kindly courtesy,
tokens of love she gave them, favors,
sent messages to all four lovers,
and each one knew about the others,
60 but to give way he had no powers.[4]
By service, prayerful pleas, each man
believed that he was sure to win.
At any tournament or joust
64 each strove to be the first, the best
in knightly strife, if possible,
and please the lady most of all.
All took the lady as *amie*,
68 all carried tokens, *druerie*,[5]
rings, pennons, sleeves; and in the game
each chevalier cried out her name.
    All four regarded her, each one,
72 as his. Then, Easter come and gone,[6]
before the Breton city, Nantes,
there was a tournament announced.
To make acquaintance of these men,
76 there were from other regions come
Normans and French, on tourney bent,

---

4. There is a crucial difference between Rychner's edition and Ewert's in lines 59–60. Ewert in his note to these lines (183) writes: "*nul nes*=nuls ne s(e)—'the one did not know about the other' (i.e., the others' relations with the lady) 'but none could bring himself to leave' (sc. abandon his suit)." But Rychner (whose edition is my copy text), following Brugger (133, 150), does not see the logic of *mes*, "but," following *ne saveit*, "did not know," but finds *mes* after *le saveit*, "knew it," to have a logical connection "*clair et naturel*." Rychner writes that in other words each lover knows himself to not be alone in his suit, but each of them is unable to succeed in detaching himself (or his desires) from the lady, for all retain hope of triumphing over their rivals. The rest of the story shows as well that the knights recognize themselves and the public knows them as suitors of the same woman [my translation of Rychner's note].
5. Here, *druerie* means "love tokens," but see note on "Lanval," line 267. Often the word means "love," "courtly love," or "a love affair."
6. See note on "Milun," line 384. Tournaments were banned by the Church at certain times of the year, especially Lent.

and knights from Flanders and Brabant;
knights Angevin and Boulognois,
80   or from some nearer neighbor place.
Willingly came each chevalier;
long time had they all sojourned there!
The eve before the tournament
84   a fierce and vicious fight broke out.
The lovers four took arms at that,
and from the city they rode out.
Their knights rode with them, but the four
88   the burden of the fighting bore.
They were known by the other side,
ensigns and shields identified.
Four knights were sent to the assault,
92   two Flemish and two from Hainault,
dressed as if battle to incite,
with no reluctance for a fight.
The lovers saw them riding near;
96   no flight they thought of, felt no fear;
lances lowered, galloping in fury,
each lover chose his adversary.
They struck with hatred, with such force,
100   their enemies were all unhorsed,
for their foes' mounts they took no care,
but let them stray and wander there.
Near the fallen they took their place,
104   and their foes' knights came on apace.
The rescue caused a great melee,
and many sword strikes in the fray.
The lady from a tower looked on;
108   picked out her lovers and their men.
She saw her lovers fight so well,
whom to prize most she could not tell.
     The tournament commenced, and now
112   ranks of men thickened, swelled and grew.
Before the city gates that day,
many the tourneys, much the fray,
so doughty were the lover men,
116   they had the prizes, every one,
battling until, at fall of night,
all must disperse and separate.
     Then, foolishly, they thought to stray
120   far from their knights, and thus to pay,
for three of them met with their death;
much mutilated was the fourth,

wounded in heart and thigh, for thus
124 the lance straight through the body passed.
Sideways, athwart, the foes came on,
and all four lovers fell, undone.
Those who had dealt each mortal wound
128 threw down their shields upon the ground
in sorrow for the accident;
killing had not been their intent.
Shrieks and keenings the dark air rent;
132 never was heard such a lament.
The city folk came pouring out;
they had no fear of those who fought.
To mourn each fallen chevalier
136 two thousand men were gathered there;
their visors they unlaced, to tear
and rend in sorrow, beards and hair;
united, felt the grief, the waste.
140 Upon his shield each man was placed;
into the city they were borne,
were brought to her who'd loved each one.
Soon as she learned the dreadful truth,
144 she fell down fainting on the earth,
and then on her recovery
she spoke the name of each *ami*.
    "Alas," she said, "what shall I do?
148 Never shall I be happy now.
Each of the chevaliers I loved,
each for his own dear self I craved;
among them all, such virtues throve!
152 Me, above everything, they loved.
For their beauty, for their prowess,
for their valor, for their largesse,
I made them all contend for me—
156 could not, for just one, give up three!
Which to mourn most, I cannot know;
I won't feign comfort, hide my woe;
one man is wounded, three are dead;
160 never shall I be comforted.
The dead I loved shall be interred;
and if the living can be cured,
most gladly I shall undertake
164 to find a doctor for his sake."
    To her room she had him carried.
The fallen three who must be buried,
nobly and with great tenderness,

168 richly, she had prepared and dressed.
    To a rich abbey she endowed
    a gift, most splendidly bestowed,
    and there the men were laid to rest.
172 God grant them peace, and mercy blessed!
    Sage doctors she had summoned where
    he lay, the living chevalier,
    wounded, within her chamber, till
176 he could be cured by their great skill.
    She came to see him frequently,
    and comforted him tenderly,
    but much she mourned the other three,
180 lamenting them most grievously.
        One summer day, with supper over,
    the dame spoke with her wounded lover.
    Her dreadful grief weighed on her mind;
184 her head, her face, she had inclined,
    as mournful thoughts came over her.
    And he saw this, her chevalier,
    for certain, saw her pensiveness,
188 said to her, kind and courteous;
        "Lady, you are distressed! Say, why?
    What are you thinking? Speak to me!
    What is this grief that troubles you?
192 Be comforted, and let it go!"
    "Dear friend, my thoughts," the lady said,
    "are of your comrades, who are dead.
    Never has dame of my degree,
196 whatever her sagacity,
    beauty, worth, had four loves at once,
    lost in one day, by evil chance,
    killed, all but one; and wounded, you
200 were in great mortal danger too!
    Because my love for you was great,
    my grief I shall commemorate:
    a *lai* about you I'll compose,
204 I shall call it *Le Quatre Dols.*"
        The chevalier, when he had heard,
    quickly responded with this word.
        "Lady, do make this *lai*," he said;
208 "Call it *Le Chaitivel* instead.
    Let me explain the reason why
    this name is a necessity.
    The others' lives are ended, spent;
212 their spans are done; and with them went

all of the suffering they knew
professing their great love for you.
But I, escaped alive, can see—
216 wretched man, lost in misery—
the one I love most on the earth
come and go, often, back and forth;
morning and night she speaks with me,
220 but there are joys that cannot be,
kissing, embracing; out of reach
all love's good deeds, except for speech.
A hundred times, this agony
224 you've caused me; I would rather die.
Now you must know, now you can tell
why the *lai* is *Le Chaitivel*."
    "In faith," she said, "you do say well;
228 let us call it *Le Chaitivel*."
    Thus it was, this *lai* was begun;
completed, then, performed, made known.
Of its performers, there were those
232 who chose the name *Le Quatre Dols*.
The names are both appropriate,
and both of them the matter fit,
Le Chaitivel's the common one.
236 There is no more, now I am done.
No more I know; no more I've heard;
no more I'll say, not one more word.

Chevrefoil

    Much pleased am I to tell the tale,
the *lai* that folk call *Chevrefoil*.[1]
I shall recount the truth, the sum,
4 why it was made, and how: for whom.

    Folk have told me it, several,
and I've found written tales as well,
of Tristram and the Queen's affairs,
8 what an exalted love was theirs,
from which much sorrow came their way:

---

1. In English, "honeysuckle." Literally it means "Goat-leaf." See note to line 115. In Anglo-Norman of this period the vowel sound in "foil" would be *ay*, and the rhyme with English "tale" would be closer than in modern French.
    The Rychner edition of Marie's *Lais*, my copy text, uses the spelling "Chievrefoil," following MS S; he also consulted MS H, which uses the spelling "Chevrefoil" (Rychner,

how they both perished in one day.
      King Mark was raging, furious,
12   his nephew, Tristram, gave him cause.
      Tristram was banished, for he'd been
      the secret lover of the Queen.
      To his own country he had gone,
16   to Southern Wales, where he was born.
      For a full year was his sojourn,
      in exile; he could not return,
      But then he chose, most recklessly,
20   to risk death and calamity.
      That choice should not astonish you,
      for loyal lovers, steadfast, true,
      are troubled, full of doleful thought,
24   when their great longings are not met.
      So Tristram, pensive, doleful, found
      he must go, leave his home and land.
      Straightway he sought Cornwall again,
28   for it was there he'd find the Queen.
         In the forest he hid, alone,
      for he wished notice by no one.
      Only in evening he stole out,
32   needing a lodging for the night.
      He met some poor folk, peasantry;
      glad of their hospitality
      he asked, what news? The King, what quest
36   did he pursue, what business?
      The King had summoned, so they heard,
      all of the barons, every lord.
      To Tintagel they must repair;
40   Mark desired court to be held there.
      At Pentecost they'd gather, all,[2]
      to meet in joyous festival,
      the Queen among the company.
44   Tristram heard, full of joy and glee,
      for if she took that road, for sure

151–54, n. 231). There are other variations in the manuscripts, e.g., "Chevrefoil" and "Chèvrefeuille," the modern spelling. Ewert's edition, consulting MSS H, S, and N (123–26, n. 161), uses "Chevrefoil," as do the editions/English translations by Hanning and Ferrante (*The Lais of Marie de France*, New York: Dutton, 1978, 190–95) and the Burgess and Busby edition (*The Lais of Marie de France*, London: Penguin Books, 1983, 109–10). To avoid confusion I follow Ewert and the modern editions in English here.

2. In Arthurian stories these holiday festivals were notoriously lavish and expensive and in Chrétien de Troyes' roughly contemporary romance *Yvain* he puns, "A cele fest qui tant coste, / qu'an doit clamer le Pentecost"; "At that most costly feast known as Pentecost" (trans. William Kibler); "At that feast day of plentycost, / which we should call the Pentecost" (trans. Ruth Harwood Cline).

Tristram must catch a sight of her.
The day the King moved house, Tristram
48 was hidden in the woods again.
And on the route that he well knew,
the route the party must pass through,
a hazel branch he cut and split,
52 squared it, and made a staff from it.
When he had pared and smoothed the staff,
he carved his name there with his knife.
The Queen would likely see it there;
56 she would be watching, well aware,
for it had happened once before
such a stick was perceived by her—
her lover's stick she'd recognize
60 when it appeared before her eyes.
He wrote just this, and nothing more;
he had made known to her before
that in that place he lay in wait,
64 long tarrying, in a hopeful state,
to catch a glimpse of her and know
how meeting her was possible;
live he could not, if not with her.
68 The two of them were similar
to honeysuckle, which must find
a hazel, and around it bind;
when it enlaces it all round,
72 both in each other are all wound.
Together they will surely thrive,
but split asunder, they'll not live.
Quick is the hazel tree's demise;
76 quickly the honeysuckle dies.
"So with us never, *belle amie*,[3]
me without you, you without me."
The Queen came riding. As she rode
80 she watched the upward-sloping road.
She saw the staff; perceived it well,
could certainly those letters spell.
Attending chevaliers who led her
84 as they rode on their way together
she told to stop; she gave command;
she wished to rest and would descend.
Her men obeyed; did not say nay!
88 and from her knights she went some way,

3. In English, "fair sweetheart," "fair friend," "beautiful lover."

calling to her her maid Brenguein,
so greatly trusted by the Queen.
A distance, small, along the road,
92   she went; found him within the wood,
who loved her most of any being;
great joy they had, he and the Queen.
He spoke, at leisure; time allowed;
96   she spoke, at pleasure, all she would;
and then she told him how he could
win from his uncle an accord.
Much grieved the King was when he sent
100   Sir Tristram into banishment;
accused he had been, by some other.[4]
They parted then; she left her lover,
but as they separated, both
104   wept much, each of them was so loath.
Back home to Wales Sir Tristram went
until his uncle for him sent.

For all the joy that he had known
108   when Tristram had his lover seen,
and for the words he then wrote down
at the fond urging of the Queen—
to keep those words in memory
112   Tristram, who well knew minstrelsy,
made, for remembrance, a new *lai*;
briefly I name it; let me say,
Gotelef[5] the English call this tale;
116   and the French call it *Chevrefoil*.
Now I've recounted all that's true
about this *lai* I've told to you.

4. In the various versions of the Tristan story, various people reveal the affair between the
   knight and the queen. In the mid-twelfth-century Old French work by Beroul, three
   wicked barons observe Tristan and Yseut the Fair in a "compromising situation" and plot
   to discredit the knight; in Thomas of Britain's *Tristran*, much of which is lost, Brangein
   turns against her mistress and tells the king that she is unfaithful not with Tristran but
   with another man. In Gottfried von Strassburg's Middle High German *Tristan* (ca. 1210),
   King Mark's steward, Marjodoc, at first a close confidant of Tristan, discovers that he
   has slipped away to a tryst with the queen (whom Marjodoc himself secretly desires).
   Marjodoc then suggests rather than states to King Mark that the queen and his nephew
   may be having an affair. Marjodoc next conspires with a dwarf, Melot, who spies on the
   queen in her chamber and discovers the lovers. Then the game is up.
5. I.e., "Goat-leaf." The word is not attested in Middle English. See Ewert's edition; in his
   Notes (184) he suggests that "it may be an *ad hoc* literal rendering of *chevrefoil* made by
   those who propagated the original *lai* and did not exist as an independent word at all."

Eliduc

A Breton *lai*, most ancient,
the story and the argument,
I shall recount, to the extent
4   I know its truth and its intent.

There lived a knight in Brittany,
worthy, brave, skilled in courtesy,
named Eliduc, so I am told;
8   In all his land was none so bold!
A wife he'd wed, most noble, wise,
well-born and of high lineage.
Long had they lived in company,
12   and loved each other loyally.
But then it chanced there came a war,
and he became a soldier there;
he loved a girl; had an affair;
16   a king and queen her parents were.
The girl's name was Guilliadun;
none in her land was fairer, none!
At home, the wife of Eliduc
20   stayed; she was called Guildeluëc.
For these two the *lai*'s named and known;
Guildeluëc and Guilliadun.
It was called Eliduc at first,
24   but is renamed; that's for the best,
for what befell the ladies—they,
their story—constitutes this *lai*.
What I shall tell you concerns that;
28   and you shall hear the truth of it.
    Eliduc had a lord, and he,
who was the King of Brittany,
loved him, held him in high regard;
32   loyally Eliduc served this lord.
When the King traveled, he was ward;
Eliduc had the realm to guard.
For his prowess he was retained;
36   many a benefit he gained.
He could go hunting in the wood;
there was no forester so bold
as to deny him, interfere,
40   or even grouch—no one would dare.
There was much envy of his luck;

—so often this occurs with folk!—
with his lord he became embroiled,
44 slandered, accused, his good name spoiled,
and banished from the court, he was,
but never given formal cause.
Why, Eliduc no inkling had;
48 often he begged his King and lord
to listen to him, hear his case,
not believe slander, false and base;
long he'd served, and devotedly!
52 But the King never made reply.
Hear he would not, nor good believe,
so Eliduc, perforce, must leave.
Back to his house went Eliduc,
56 all his friends summoned; his ill luck
explained to them, how that his liege,
his King, was in a dreadful rage.
    "To the extent I could, I served;
60 Ill favor I have not deserved.
A proverb of our peasants says
that when a plowman is chastised
a lord's love is no fief, no prize.
64 He is most sensible and wise
who loyalty his *seigneur* gives.
and his good neighbors kindly loves."
    In the realm he'd no wish to stay,
68 and, he said, he'd go over sea,
he'd go to Logres, in exile,
and there disport himself awhile.
His wife he'd leave here in this land;
72 to his own men he gave command
that they'd protect her faithfully.
Likewise he made his friends agree.
    This counsel he abided by;
76 equipped himself most splendidly.
His friends were much inclined to grieve,
dejected, as he planned to leave,
Ten knights he took, and thought enough.
80 His lady came to see him off.
She displayed to her lord much grief
and sorrow, like a loving wife,
but was assured by her *seigneur*
84 that he would keep good faith with her.
He took his leave; farewells were said,
then he was launched upon his road.

To sea went he, he crossed, was flown—
88   and then he came to Totnes town.[1]
     Many kings in that country were.
Between them was much strife and war.
In this same realm, near Exeter,
92   There lived a powerful *seigneur*,
aged and ancient; he had years,
but was not blessed, though, with male heirs.
His daughter was of age to wed;
96   he did not wish to give this maid
to a lord who made war on him
laid waste his lands, all round his realm.
In a castle, besieged, he lay;
100 none within was so bold that he
would offer single combat, or
challenge this peer in all-out war.
Eliduc heard of this affair
104 and did not wish to journey more,
for in this place his war he'd found;
he would remain here in this land.
The king who was so much oppressed,
108 suffered so, damaged and distressed
he wished to serve; he would remain
as soldier, in the king's domain.
To the beleaguered king he sent
112 letters explaining his intent.
From his own land he'd traveled far;
he wished to aid him in this war.
He waited on his pleasure; but
116 if the king wished not his support,
he wished safe-conduct from the king;
elsewhere he'd do his soldiering.
     When the king saw his men appear,
120 he felt great love, he held them dear.
He called to him his constable,
ordered that he should quickly go
set up safe-conduct, and prepare
124 to bring this baron safely there,
and prepare hostels, too, where they—
he and his men—could lodge and stay.
Also he would provide and give
128 a month's funds on which they could live.

---

1. On the Devonshire coast in England. Ewert remarks that Totnes is "often named as a
port in the literature of the time" (186).

So, fitted out, the escort went,
and to bring Eliduc was sent.
Great honor had he from the king
132 and a most happy welcoming!
His lodging with a burgess was;
a man most wise and courteous.
His beautiful encurtained room
136 his host gave up and offered him.
The knight was well served; he made sure;
and at his meals provided for
chevaliers in the town who were
140 living there in hard straits, and poor.
Eliduc to his men made clear
none should presume and none should dare
for forty days, while serving there,
144 to accept pay or provender.
    Day three it was, of their sojourn,
a cry was raised throughout the town—
the foe had come, the people said,
148 throughout the countryside was spread.
Now they meant to assail the town,
up to the gates they meant to come.
Eliduc heard the noise, the din,
152 the confused, frightened folk within;
armed himself, did not hesitate,
nor did his men waste time or wait.
Forty knights were there, mounted men,
156 all sojourning within the town,
wounded, some of these chevaliers—
quite a few of them prisoners!
When they saw Eliduc go mount,
160 back to their hostels they all went,
and rode with him out to the gate;
not for a summons did they wait!
    "Sire," they said, "we will go with you,
164 and what you do we too shall do."
    "Much thanks!" said Eliduc. "*Merci!*
Is there one in your company
who knows a narrow pass where we
168 can trap and have our enemy?
If need be, here is where we'll wait,
and if it must be, we can fight,
but we'll do best in this exploit
172 if someone knows an ambush site."
    "By my faith, sire!" one of them said,

"there are some rushes,[2] near this wood,
where there's a straight and narrow way,
176 return route of the enemy.
After the pillaging they'll do
this is the place they must pass through;
disarmed, upon their palfreys, they
180 frequently do return this way.
Thus they tempt Fate upon this path,
openly court a speedy death.
Soon enough we can injure them,
184 and bring them hurt and fatal harm."
    "Friends," said Eliduc in reply,
"I pledge my faith to you, and say
that he who sometimes does not dare
188 to go where he thinks loss is sure
will have small gain; he takes no chance;
and to great fame will not advance.
You're the King's vassals; you should be
192 ready to serve him loyally.
Come then with me where I will go,
and do with me what I will do.
Loyally I assure you all
196 that you shall meet no obstacle
while I have power to aid you there.
If we can win some spoils of war
our reputations will increase
200 because we shamed our enemies."
    Happily they received his pledge
and let him to the woodland's edge;
ambush they laid just by the place,
204 the path their foes must needs re-trace.
Eliduc showed the men; he taught
just how they could set up their plot,
by what devices could incite,
208 heckle and rouse their foes to fight.
    Through the pass came the enemy;
Eliduc led the battle-cry,
calling upon his comrades all,
212 exhorting them, that they do well.
They attacked hard and furiously—
not at all spared, this enemy!

2. The word *ristei*, here translated "rushes," is not attested elsewhere, but Ewert believes
that it may be related to the Old High German *rista*, "flax-thread, hemp," and Provençal
risto, "hemp." Warnke and E. Levi believe the word should be *ruflei*, "thicket of rushes,"
or "bed of reeds" (Ewert, ibid.).

Caught off guard, they were terrified,
216　soon routed, shattered, scattered wide,
　　in a short time were overcome.
　　Their constable had to succumb,
　　taken, with other chevaliers;
220　and squires now held these prisoners.
　　Twenty-five men had Eliduc;
　　thirty knights of the foe they took.
　　Harness they seized, gear, booty, loot,
224　jubilant at the spoils they got.
　　Back they turned, full of happiness,
　　full of their exploit and success.
　　　　The king, up in a tower, looked on,
228　Much he was anxious for his men.
　　Much he complained of Eliduc,
　　whom he now thought, now feared, forsook
　　his knights, abandoning his cause,
232　choosing a path most treasonous.
　　The knights set out upon the road,
　　weighed down with all their loot and load,
　　more of them in the company
236　than had set out originally;
　　he did not recognize his men.
　　Doubt and suspicion rose in him;
　　He ordered that the gates be shut
240　and archers on the walls be got
　　to draw on them, and spears be thrown.
　　None of this needed to be done,
　　for, in advance, the men sent on
244　a squire, who spurring hard, made known
　　how it was the campaign had gone.
　　The hired knight's prowess thus was shown,
　　how it was he had won the day,
248　how he had acted in the fray.
　　Never was such a chevalier!
　　Their constable he'd captured there,
　　and other fighters, twenty-nine;
252　he'd wounded many; many slain.
　　The king, when he heard how this went
　　was wonderfully jubilant.
　　Down from the tower he came, to meet
256　Eliduc; for the knight's great feat
　　thanked him; and Eliduc, at that
　　gave him the captives he had caught,
　　and gave out harnesses and gear;

260 nothing he kept, our chevalier,
     but three fine horses, much admired.
     All he distributed, he shared
     with others, all that was his own;
264 to prisoners, knights; to everyone.

        After this feat I've told you of,
     the king bestowed on him much love,
     for a full year retaining him
268 and all the knights who'd with him come.
     And his allegiance the king took;
     guard of the realm was Eliduc.
        Eliduc was wise, courteous;
272 a fine knight, worthy, generous.
     The king's own daughter heard accounts
     of all his attributes and points;
     she sent her chamberlain, her own,
276 requesting Eliduc to come
     divert himself, and talk with her,
     and with her good acquaintance share.
     Greatly she wondered, so she said,
280 He'd not paid call, not visited.
     Eliduc said he'd gladly come
     and make acquaintance with the dame.
     He mounted on his destrier,
284 and led with him a chevalier,
     to the *pucele*[3] went to talk.
     Before her chamber, Eliduc
     sent on the chamberlain, before,
288 while he delayed and waited there
     until the man returned once more.
     With charming manners, simple cheer,
     refined behavior, Eliduc
292 politely to the princess spoke,
     and much he thanked the demoiselle,
     Guilliadun—so beautiful!—
     for wishing to invite him there
296 to have him come and speak with her.
     She took him by the hand, at that;
     together on a bed they sat.
     And there of many things they spoke;
300 much she regarded Eliduc,
     his face, his body and his mien.

3. A maiden, a young girl. Joan of Arc is known as *La Pucelle.*

Nothing displeasing could be seen;
much she was taken in her heart!
304   Love sent his messenger to start
the summons; she must love him! Now
she sighed; her face grew pale; although
she did not wish to speak of this,
308   for fear he would take it amiss.
Long time they spoke; long was his stay,
then he took leave and went away.
Leave she gave most reluctantly;
312   nevertheless, away went he.
    He returned to his hostelry
sad, full of anxiety;
this beauty troubled him; she had—
316   she, the child of his king and lord!—
spoken with such great gentleness,
sighing with every sweet address.
A great regret it seemed to him
320   he had so long lived in this realm
and hardly seen her. Thus, upset,
he spoke; at once repented it;
what of his wife? His promises?
324   He thought of his assurances
that he'd keep faith with her; he would
loyally act, be true and good.
    The girl, after this interview,
328   longed for the knight to be her *dru*;[4]
no man had so impressed her, ever!
If she could, she would keep him with her.
All night she lay awake, distressed;
332   she did not sleep nor did she rest.
Up she rose the next day and went
over to a window; sent
for her own chamberlain to come;
336   then confessed all her case to him.
    "Faith, my predicament is bad!
I've fallen, fallen hard!" she said.
"I love him, the new warrior,
340   Eliduc, the fine chevalier.
All this night I have had no rest,
or shut my eyes, I'm so distressed.
If to love me he'll pledge his troth,
344   his person and his body both,

---

4. "Lover," or also in the feminine form, *drue*, "sweetheart, mistress."

I'll do his pleasure, all and sum;
great fortune to him thus will come;
he will be king of this country.
348 So wise and courteous is he
that if he will not love me, I
in my great grief will surely die."
When she had spoken all her need,
352 the chamberlain she'd summoned said,
loyally giving her advice—
no one should fault the man for this!—
"Since you love him, my lady, do
356 send for him; have him come to you.
A belt, a ribbon, or a ring
send too; he will like that offering.
If he is happy; if the man
360 rejoices in your summons, then
of his love, dame, you can be sure.
Beneath the sky no emperor,
were you to want his love, would not
364 rejoice, most thankful for his lot."
The demoiselle, when she had heard
all of his counsel, spoke this word:
"From my present, how shall I tell
368 if he desires my love as well?
I've never seen a chevalier
who received such a plea or prayer,
but whether he loved or hated, he
372 would keep a present willingly
if it were sent him. I should be
crushed if he made a jest of me!
However, by his mien we can
376 discover something of the man.
Prepare yourself. Make ready; go."
"I am prepared and ready now."
"Carry with you this golden ring,
380 this belt of mine, too, you must bring.
A thousand times, greet him for me."
The chamberlain went on his way.
She remained, her mood much the same;
384 almost, she called him back again,
but let him leave, and off he went.
Fiercely she started to lament:
"Oh, my poor heart! Oppressed and sore,
388 so taken by this foreigner!
Is he of noble birth and blood?

What if he leaves soon? Oh, I should
remain here crushed and desolate!
392   How foolishly my mind is set!
I spoke to him just yesterday;
now for his love I beg and pray!
I fear he may blame me for this—
396   but thank me, if he's courteous.
The course is set; my message sent;
and if he is indifferent
or worse, I shall know shame and grief;
400   never know joy in all my life."
        While she made vehement lament,
the chamberlain sped, all intent,
due speed he made, to Eliduc.
404   To the knight he in secret spoke,
Said he was sent by the *pucele*,
offered him the gold ring as well,
and gave him, too, the belt to wear.
408   He gave due thanks, the chevalier;
he slipped the gold ring on his hand
and the belt round his body wound;
no further words the young squire spoke,
412   and nothing more said Eliduc,
save that he offered, too, a gift.
It was not taken; the squire left.
        He returned to the demoiselle
416   and found her in her chamber still;
and on behalf of Eliduc
greeted her, thanked her. Then she spoke:
"Come! Conceal nothing! Say, deliver!
420   Does the knight wish to be my lover?"
        The man replied, "This is my thought.
He is no light or fickle sort.
Discreet, wise, courtly, he'll conceal
424   his heart, and much that he may feel.
On your behalf I gave your greeting,
gave him your gifts upon our meeting;
he took your belt and wrapped it round
428   his hips, all tight and snugly wound,
placed your ring on his finger, but
said nothing further after that."
        "But did he take them as *druerie*?[5]

---

5. A love token; it can also mean "love," or "a love affair." See note to line 328; also "Le
   Chaitivel," line 68, and cf. "Lanval," lines 267, 270.

432 If not, I'm betrayed! Woe is me!"
     He said: "In faith, I do not know.
     But listen: this I'll say to you;
     unless he wished you well, he would
436 not take your gifts and hold them good."
     She said, "You speak in mockery.
     I know he holds no hate for me,
     for I have never done him wrong
440 except to have such love, so strong.
     And if he should hate me for that—
     well, he deserves to die for it!
     Never, through you or anyone
444 else, shall I speak to him again;
     directly to him I shall talk,
     myself, reveal to Eliduc
     my love—my anguish and my pain—
448 but I don't know! Will he remain?"
     To her replied her chamberlain:
     "Lady, the king will him retain.
     Eliduc by an oath is bound
452 to loyal service, this year round.
     Time and leisure you shall have
     to speak your pleasure; speak of love."
     When she heard Eliduc would stay,
456 She was ecstatic, wild with joy;
     his plans gave her great happiness.
     Nothing she knew of his distress
     since seeing her, the pain he felt;
460 of joy, delight, he had no thought
     except when he had thoughts of her.
     Keenly he felt discomfiture,
     remembering his promise, how,
464 leaving his wife, he made the vow
     he would love her alone. He felt
     now, how imprisoned was his heart!
     He longed to guard his loyalty,
468 but he could not, at all, get free
     of his love for the demoiselle
     Guilliadun, so beautiful;
     he longed to see her, speak to her,
472 kiss and embrace, pay court to her.
     Her love, though, he must not procure,
     dishonoring himself, for sure;
     to his wife he owed loyalty—

476   to Logres' king owed fealty.[6]
     Eliduc's pain was now so great
    he mounted up—he could not wait
    but, all his comrades summoning,
480   rode to the castle and the king.
    He hoped to see the demoiselle—
    that was his purpose, after all.
     The king had from his supper come
484   and gone into his daughter's room;
    there at chess he began to play
    with a knight come from over sea;[7]
    across the chessboard this man sat
488   to teach the demoiselle the art.[8]
     Eliduc now approached. The king
    with cordial mien, most welcoming,
    seated beside him Eliduc,
492   and to the princess then he spoke:
    "Demoiselle, with this chevalier
    be well acquainted; and be sure
    to honor greatly him. Among
496   five hundred, there's no better one!"
     And when Guilliadun had heard
    this counsel from her sire and lord,
    there was a happy girl, God knows!
500   Calling to Eliduc, she rose;
    far from the others, they sat down.
    Both felt Love's fire ignite and burn;
    she could not speak. She did not dare,
504   nor could he, for he felt such fear,
    except that he gave thanks to her
    for the gift she had sent him, for
    no other gift he held so dear.
508   Then she said to the chevalier
    this pleased her greatly. She had sent
    the ring to him with this intent,
    also the other gift, the belt,
512   for she had given him her heart.
    So much she loved him, *par amour*[9]

---

6. In other words, he must not harm the reputation of the daughter of the man who was now his liege, particularly since the princess was his only heir.
7. Ewert, citing Hertz, suggests that the original *d'utre mer* means "from beyond the sea" or "who had been to the Crusades" (187).
8. As Hanning and Ferrante point out in their translation, chess is often an allegory of the game of love (209).
9. I.e., as lovers love.

she wished to make him her *seigneur*.[1]
If she could not such honor have,
516   this truly she could say; she'd love
no living man, not once, again.
Now, his desires he must make plain!
    "Lady, great gratitude I have,
520   and profound joy, to have your love;
such is the gift of your esteem,
my joy in it must be extreme—
I'll not forget it, that is sure!
524   With the king I must serve one year;
he took my oath and thus I swore.
There is no way I'll leave before
we have conclusion of this war.
528   Then to my country, my own shore
I wish to go, not linger more,
if I have leave from you, my dear."
    The demoiselle made this response:
532   "Dear friend, much thanks to you! I sense
your courtly wisdom; and no doubt
by then you will have given thought
to what you wish to do with me.
536   I love you, trust you utterly."
    At that their troth they pledged, they swore;
on that occasion said no more.
Eliduc to his hostel went
540   joyous at his accomplishment.
He could speak with her frequently;
Between them was much *druerie*.[2]
So fierce his efforts in the war
544   he captured and took prisoner
the lord, the king's chief enemy,
and all the country he set free.
So much esteemed for his prowess,
548   his astute sense and his largesse,
indeed, fate made him prosperous!

    During that term, while he lived thus,
his own liege sought him; sent to him
552   three messengers from his own realm.
Much this lord suffered grief and harm,
ruin in devastating form;

1. That is, her husband.
2. See note to line 431. Here probably both senses are meant.

all of his castles had been lost,
556 all of his country been laid waste;
much he repented, frequently,
Eliduc had gone over sea.
Evil counsel he had received,
560 and evilly had it believed.
Traitors, accusers, who had spoiled
the knight's good name, got him embroiled,
were now exiled, their own names soiled,
564 forever thrown out, damned and foiled.
In his great need and urgency—
with summons, with command, with plea—
the king of his knight's fealty spoke,
568 the homage pledged by Eliduc.
By such a pledge he had agreed
to help his lord in time of need.
   Eliduc heard this news, and he
572 felt great distress for his *amie*;
he loved her painfully, and she
loved him to an extremity.
Between them was no foolery,
576 fickleness, shame, or lechery,
but courting, flirting, loving speech,
and giving presents, each to each.
Such things were all their *druerie*,
580 their loving and loved company.
Her hope, her aim, was that he would
be hers completely if she could
just keep him; such was her belief;
584 She did not know he had a wife.
   "Alas!" he said, "I've done great wrong!
In this land I've stayed far too long!
Woe that I ever saw it! Then
588 I loved this girl, Guilliadun,
the king's own daughter, passionately,
and passionately she loves me.
And now we must be parted, thus;
592 it will be death for one of us,
or both, the ending of us two.
Nevertheless, I have to go;
The king by letter summons me,
596 invokes my oath of fealty;
and my wife claims me in her need.
Now with great care I must proceed:
I can't remain, I dare not stay;

600 at once I have to go away.
If I could marry my *amie*!
But of course Christianity
forbids it. All goes wretchedly;
604 God, parting is such agony!
Whatever blame I must endure,
always I shall do right by her,
honor her wishes, and shall do
608 what her good counsel prompts me to.
Her sire is now at peace; no more,
I think, will he be waging war.
To serve my lord of Brittany
612 I'll seek to leave before the day
my promised term comes to an end—
my service to this king and land.
To my *pucele* I'll speak, I'll go,
616 all my affairs make plain and show;
and her desires she'll surely tell.
If I have power, I'll do her will."

The chevalier did not delay,
620 but to the king went straightaway.
He told the monarch how things stood,
showed him the letter; read it; said
his liege was in distress, and he
624 summoned, and bound by fealty.
The lord of Logres knew, no way
would Eliduc serve out his stay.
Pensive and sorrowful, the King
628 of his own goods made offering.
One third of his inheritance
he yielded up in recompense;
Eliduc must, so much he wooed,
632 eternally feel gratitude.
"Oh, God! At such a time as this,
when my liege is in such distress,
and from such distance summons me,
636 he must command my loyalty.
There is no way I can remain.
Should you my service need again,
I shall return most willingly,
640 bringing great force of knights with me."
His thanks the king was glad to give
and graciously bestowed his leave.
All the possessions of his house

644   the king then offered: copious
     horses, dogs, silver; gold as well,
     silken clothes, fine and beautiful.
     A moderate amount he took,
648   and then, most gracious, Eliduc
     said he much wished to speak, as well,
     if the king pleased, with the *pucele*.
       "That would much please me," the king said.
652   And then he sent a squire ahead
     to open up the chamber door.
     Eliduc went to speak with her.
     She saw him, called out, in the room,
656   six thousand times she greeted him.
     Her thoughts on this affair he sought,
     mentioned his journey briefly, but
     before he could discuss it well,
660   ask, or take leave of, the *pucele*,
     she fainted from her grief and shock,
     lost all her color. Eliduc,
     seeing her turn so pale and faint,
664   began to bitterly lament;
     kissed her mouth, over and over,
     weeping like a tender lover,
     he took her in his arms and held her
668   till from her swoon she could recover.
       "Oh, God," he said, "my sweet *amie*!
     Bear with me; hear what I must say.
     You are my life, my death, and more;
672   you are the comfort I live for.
     For this I counsel took from you;
     and for the troth between us two.
     In my own land I need to be;
676   your father's given leave to me.
     But tell me what most pleases you—
     whatever happens, that I'll do."
       "Oh, take me when you go away
680   since you do not desire to stay!
     Or if not, by my own hand I'll die,
     never know happiness or joy."
       Eliduc gently spoke to her,
684   said much he loved her *par amour*.
       "Fair one, I am by solemn oath
     bound to your sire to keep my troth;
     were I to spirit you away,
688   my bond, my faith, I would betray,

the term of service I have sworn.
Loyal, I swear to you in turn,
if you permit me to depart,
692 and name a day—give it good thought—
when you desire me to come back,
naught on earth will stop Eliduc
while he has life and health. You have
696 my life between your hands, my love."
    Great was her love for him, her trust.
A day she named him, when he must
take her away, must keep the date;
700 now in grief they must separate.
Golden rings they exchanged, these two;
exchanged sweet kisses, *drue* and *dru*;
then to the seashore he went down.
704 Fair was the wind; soon he was gone.
    Eliduc came to Brittany.
His lord was glad, full of great joy,
and likewise all his friends and kin
708 together celebrated him;
above all, his good wife, withal
so worthy, wise and beautiful.
But he was pensive and depressed,
712 Love held him captive and oppressed;
Naught near him, naught that could be seen
aroused his joy or happy mien.
No joy was his, or could be, ever,
716 until once more he saw his lover;
his acts were secret and apart.
His wife saw this with mournful heart,
with no idea of what it meant;
720 and to herself she made lament.
Often she asked him; had he heard,
somehow, from people, some foul word
or her behavior, something wrong,
724 rumor of sin, while he was gone?
Before his people, willingly,
she would defend herself, make plea
if he wished.
          "Dame, I have not heard
728 of your wrongdoing any word,
but where I have been sojourning
I swore, I promised to the king
I would return with all due speed,
732 for of my help he has great need.

If my king were at peace, no more
than a week would I sojourn here.
Hardship I must endure, and pain
736 before I travel there again.
Until I go, in all I see
there is no happiness for me;
I cannot break my faith, my trust."
740 At that she let the matter rest.
    Eliduc served his king; in truth
much was his aid, and of great worth.
Acting on good advice from him
744 the king safeguarded all the realm.
But when the time approached that he
promised to be with his *amie*,
he undertook to make the peace
748 and reconciled his enemies.
Then he prepared for journeying
himself, and those he wished to bring:
two much loved nephews of his own,
752 and also his own chamberlain—
this man, the lovers' confidant,
carried the message the knight sent;
these people only, and his squires.
756 For other folk he had no cares.
All of these people pledged and swore
they would keep secret this affair.

    They put to sea without delay;
760 the other coast reached speedily.
The destination they acquired
where Eliduc was so desired.
Now Eliduc, a crafty man,
764 far from the harbor settled in,
not wishing to be seen or known,
nor recognized by anyone.
Briefing his chamberlain, then, he
768 sent off his man to his *amie*,
telling his love he'd come! was here!
He had kept covenant with her.
When night fell, when the day was done,
772 out of the city she must come;
the chamberlain would go with her
and she meet with her chevalier.
His garments changed, the servant went
776 slowly, on foot, where he was sent;

once in the town, at a fair pace,
he sought the *pucele*'s dwelling-place.
He sought; made inquiries; and then
780 found the place and was sent within.
Saluting her, the chamberlain
said that her love had come again.
Deep in her sorrow and dismay,
784 when she heard what he had to say[3]
with joy she wept, most tenderly,
kissed the man much, delightedly,
and then he said to the *pucele*
788 she must go with him when night fell.
Inside the room, all of that day
they planned their trip and strategy,
and when the dark and night came on
792 they left and stole out from the town,
the young man, the *pucele* with him,
no one else but these two alone.
Of being seen, she had great fear.
796 A garment of fine silk she wore,
with gold embroidered, delicate,
and a short mantle over that.
      A bowshot's distance from the gate,
800 in an enclosed wood, stood in wait
under the hedge, the chevalier,
her lover, who had come for her.
The chamberlain led her to him
804 and he dismounted, kissed her; then
what joy it was at last to meet!
Up on the horse she took her seat,
he mounted, took the reins; with her
808 quickly he sped on toward the shore
at Totnes, where a vessel lay;
they boarded it immediately.
No one was on it but his men;
812 he and his lover Guilliadun.
      The wind was up, the breeze was fair,
and settled weather seemed in store.
Before they could arrive, however,
816 a tempest rose, and savage weather
and a great wind, drove them before,
far from the harbor and the shore.

---

3. I have reversed the order of the sense in lines 783–84. In French they read: "Quant ele ad la novele oïe, Tute murnë e esbaïe."

The tempest broke and split the mast,
820 and the torn sails around them crashed.
To God their urgent prayers they sent,
To Nicholas and Saint Clement,[4]
and to Our Lady, Saint Marie,
824 that through her Son, and his mercy,
they could be saved from death, and come
safely to harbor and to home.
Backward an hour, forward an hour,
828 the troubled coast they search and scour,
shipwreck and death are imminent.[5]
A sailor to his fear gives vent
and shrieks: "What folly do we do!
832 Sire, you have carried here with you
one who will be our death! Oh, never
shall we see our own land, not ever!
A loyal, faithful wife you wed;
836 and now this other you have led
here, against God, and right, and faith,
justice and law! She is our death!
Let us throw her into the sea!
840 We shall come home all speedily!"
      This speech was heard by Eliduc;
near mad with fury at such talk
he said,
            "Foul thing! Son of a whore!
844 Vicious, fell traitor, say no more!
If I had let you do your worst,
you would pay dearly! At great cost!"
      He took her in his arms, to ease
848 as best he could, her miseries,
her seasickness; also, she'd heard

---

4. St. Nicholas (d. 345 C.E.?) is the patron saint of mariners and of merchants and children.
St. Clement (d. 97 C.E.?) was the fourth pope, Clement I, known as Clement of Rome.
Tradition has it that he was martyred, but the oldest sources describing his life do not
mention it.
5. Ewert remarks in his note that "these lines introduce an old popular belief that the pres-
ence of a guilty person on board inevitably brings disaster upon the ship. There are many
literary instances: in the story of Jonah, the *Electra* of Euripides, Wieland's *Oberon*, and
in many ballads (Danish, Norwegian, Swedish, etc.), particularly in the Scottish ballads
'Bonnie Annie' and 'Brown Robyn's Confession' (see Warnke-Kohler, pp. clxx–clxxiv)."
Ewert comments that, while the motif is clearly not exclusively Celtic, "it is popular and
current in Celtic countries and may therefore have come to Marie from the more
primitive-popular 'lais bretons'" (187). Another example is the well-known and beauti-
ful Child Ballad #243, known in England, the United States, and Canada as "The
House Carpenter" or "James Harris, or the Demon Lover," in which a woman abandons
her carpenter husband and her children to flee with her lover. The ship they take sinks,
and the drowned couple see that they are approaching the hills of hell (or the Demon
Lover has enticed the lady to hell).

the furious sailor say the word—
he had a wedded wife, this lover!
852 In his own land he had another.
In a faint she fell, face down,
all drained of color, pale and wan.
And there she lay, still in her swoon;
856 she did not breathe, or come round soon.
He who had brought her thought, in truth,
that she was lying there in death.
Wild with anguish, Eliduc
860 rushed toward the sailor, and he struck
and beat the fellow with an oar
till he lay stretched out on the floor;
took his feet; threw him in the sea;
864 and the waves bore the corpse away.
    He hurled him over, Eliduc;
then right away the helm he took,
steering the ship with such sure hand
868 they reached the harbor and made land.
Safe harbor made, and gangway down,
the anchor in the sea was thrown.
The lady still lay in her swoon
872 as if the life from her had gone.
Eliduc in his agony
wished he could follow her and die.
Now all his comrades he besought,
876 each, for his counsel and his thought,
where he could carry the *pucele*,
since he could not part from her still,
where she could be interred, what place
880 with all great honor, fine service,
what holy ground, what sacred rite;
for she, a princess, had this right.
Bewildered, sad, his comrades all
884 had no advice, and could not tell.
Eliduc now thought deeply; where
could he bring her, and bury her?
His dwelling was close by the sea,
888 by dinnertime reached easily.
Surrounding it a forest lay,
thirty leagues in entirety.
And there a holy hermit stayed;
892 he had a chapel. There he'd prayed
for forty years, and Eliduc
often with this old hermit spoke.

To this man they would carry her;
896   in the chapel his love inter;
then he would offer up some land,
and in that place an abbey found,
a convent have for monks or nuns,
900   or canons; there these holy ones
would for her soul forever pray.
God grant her mercy!
                                    Now, away:
Eliduc had the horses brought,
904   commanded all his men to mount;
he made each swear his lips were sealed;
his affair would not be revealed.
Before him on his palfrey, he
908   bore the body of his *amie*.

They started off, took the straight road,
soon they were entering the wood.
To the chapel they came; called out,
912   knocked on the door and beat on it.
No response did they find at all,
no door was opened to their call.
One man got round, and got within;
916   unlocked the door, and let them in.
Eight days before, the holy one
had perished; he was dead and gone.
Eliduc found there the new tomb;
920   stricken, dismayed, he stood in gloom.
The others wanted now to be
digging the grave of his *amie*,
but he insisted they draw back.
924   "That will not do!" said Eliduc.[6]
First I must the best counsel find
from the realm's men of wisest mind,
how to best glorify this place,
928   abbey or church, with God's good grace.
Before the altar let her lie,
commended to the Deity."
Eliduc ordered sheets be brought;
932   a bed was right away laid out.

---

6. Here again I have reversed the sense of two lines, 922–23. Marie's original lines
921–23 read: "Cil voleient la fosse faire—Mes il fist ariere traire—U il deüst mettre
s'amie."

They laid the *pucele* on the bed
and then they left her there, for dead.
And Eliduc, about to go,
936 believed his grief would kill him, too.
He kissed her eyes, her face; he said,
  "Fair one, may it not please dear God
that ever I bear arms again,
940 live and endure this world of pain!
Grief, evil, that you saw me ever!
Grief that you followed me, sweet lover!
Surely you would have been a queen,
but for your loyal love, so fine,
given to me so faithfully!
My heart is wretched, sweet *amie*!
The day they bury you, sweet soul,
948 I'll be a monk, take gown and cowl,
and every day upon your grave
I shall cry out my grief, my love."
At that he took his leave of her,
952 turned away, closed the chapel door.
  He sent back, at his hostelry,
a message to his wife, that he
was on his way to see her, but
956 distressed and anguished, all worn out.
Full of happiness when she heard,
she made all ready, dressed, prepared
to suitably greet her *seigneur*.
960 But there was little joy for her;
no kindly mien had Eliduc,
no friendly, loving words he spoke;
no one dared speak to him at all.
964 Two days he stayed in his own hall;
he heard Mass in the morning, then
he was gone, on the road again,
off to the woods and the *chapele*,
968 and the still form of the *pucele*.
He found her in her swoon, her death;
no, no recovery, no breath.
But still it seemed miraculous
972 that red and white showed in her face;
she seemed to have her natural color,
except that she was somewhat paler.
Over him his huge anguish swept;
976 He offered prayers for her; he wept;

and when the prayers were finally done
he went home to his hall again.

As Eliduc left church one day,
980 his wife engaged—with ample pay!—
a man to spy on him, and see—
at discreet distance, cautiously!—
what road her lord took. She'd bestow
984 a horse and arms, if he would go
at her command. He took the road,
followed her lord into the wood.
Eliduc never was aware.
988 The young man noticed, though, for sure,
that in that place where the lord went,
were sounds of grief and fierce lament.
Long before Eliduc came out,
992 he had returned, this lady's scout,
and told her all that he had heard
the lamentations of his lord,
how, in the hermitage, he cried.
996 Deeply moved in her heart, she said,
    "Let us immediately go
and search the hermitage, all through.
My sire, I think, is traveling
1000 to court, for conference with the king.
The hermit died some time ago;
my husband loved the man, I know,
but not for him would my *seigneur*
1004 show such great anguish and dolor."
At that time she'd no more to say.

That afternoon, that very day,
Eliduc went to his *seigneur*;
1008 She took the young squire off with her
and to the hermitage was led,
entered the chapel in the wood.
She saw the *pucele* on the bed,
1012 a new-blown rose, so white, so red,
and turning down the coverlet
she saw the body, fair and slight,
the long fair arms, the hands, so white,
1016 the fingers, long, smooth, delicate.
The truth at once she understood;
the deep grief that her husband showed.
    She called to the youth, to speak to her,

1020 and showed to him the marvel there.
     "This woman: is she known to you,
     who like a gem is beautiful?
     She's my lord's mistress, his *amie*,
1024 for whom he grieves so strenuously!
     I marvel not at him, in faith,
     when one so lovely lies in death.
     Either for pity or for love
1028 joy again I shall never have!"
     And she began to weep, at that,
     for the dead girl; weep and regret.
     Before the bed she sat and wept.
1032   Across the floor a weasel leapt;
     beneath the altar it had been;
     over the body it had run.
     The squire had hit it, knocked it down
1036 with a stick, killed it, and had thrown
     the animal upon the floor.
     In just a little time, no more,
     Its mate came running up, to see
1040 the place where its companion lay.
     It circled all around the head
     and then the feet began to prod.
     When it could not arouse its mate
1044 the animal seemed desolate.
     Out of the chapel, to the wood
     it ran, to find what herbs it could,
     then returned; in its mouth a flower
1048 of a most brilliantly red color.
     Back to the chapel, hastily
     it came; approached in such a way
     to put the flower in the mouth
1052 of its dead mate, slain by the youth.
     The dead mate woke up, instantly.
       The lady did not fail to see.
       "Catch it!" she said. "Catch it, I say!
1056 Your stick! It must not get away!"
       He threw, and struck the animal,
     so that it let the flower fall.
     The lady rose; from where it lay
1060 she picked the flower up, hastily,
     and in the mouth of the *pucele*
     put the red bloom, so beautiful.
     A little bit she waited, till
1064 it seemed she breathed, the *demoiselle*.

Then her eyes opened; she awoke.[7]
"God, I have slept so long!" she spoke.
She spoke, and when the lady heard,
1068 most gratefully she thanked Our Lord,
then asked the young girl who she was.
And the girl answered the dame thus:
"Lady, I was in Logres born,
1072 the king's own daughter in that realm.
Much have I loved a chevalier,
Eliduc, a fine warrior.
He led me away, fled with me,
1076 deceived me and sinned grievously.
He had a wife; did not tell me,
hint by his mien, he was not free.
When I heard his wife spoken of,
1080 I fainted out of grief and love.
Wickedly he has left me, lone
in foreign land, forlorn. He's gone,
betrayed me. What is to be done?
1084 A woman's a fool to trust a man."
"Fair one," the lady said, "in truth
no living thing on all this earth
could give your lover any joy;
1088 this know, in all sincerity.
He thinks you dead; in this belief
he lives in torment and in grief.
He came to see you every day;
1092 you lay in faint, it seems to me.
I am his wife. That is the truth;
for him I feel much grief and ruth.
Such was his grief, such his lament,
1096 I had to know just where he went.
I followed him; I found you, live;
what joy to me that you survive!
I will take you and bring you back
1100 To join your lover, Eliduc;

7. See Ewert's note (187): "For this weasel episode there are many parallels in antiquity
and in popular legends; some animal revives its fellow creature or mate by means of
some herb which it fetches and of which man obtains possession and with which he
revives another person. Among Western nations (as in Apollodorus) it is usually a snake;
but in one of the best-known instances, Chaucer's *Dream*, it is a bird. Only in *Eliduc* is
it a weasel; weasels were commonly supposed to have magic properties and for that rea-
son were called 'fairies' in Cornwall. The belief in herbs capable of reviving the dead
was of wide currency among the Ancients, Eastern peoples, etc. See Hertz, pp. 409–12,
and Warnke (Kohler), pp. clxxv–clxxix." Ewert also suggests that, as with the story of
the threatened ship, this material came to Marie from popular Breton *lais*.
    Rychner cites similar material in his note on this passage and mentions in addition
Giraldus Cambrensis and Alexander Neckham (288).

most willingly I set him free.
The blessed veil is best for me."
　　She gave such comfort, spoke so well
1104　that she took with her the *pucele*.

　　The young attendant she prepared
and sent him off to find her lord.
He searched till he found Eliduc
1108　and fittingly to him he spoke;
all the adventure he recounted.
On his horse Eliduc then mounted;
for his comrades he did not wait,
1112　but to his hall rode that same night.
He found there, living, his *amie*,
and thanked his wife most tenderly.
　　Eliduc's joy was of a kind
1116　he'd never known, or had in mind.
Many times he kissed his lover;
tenderly she returned the favor;
what a great joy they made together!
1120　Now his wife, seeing this behavior
approached her husband, face to face;
she wished permission now, and grace
to leave the marriage, to have done,
1124　to serve God and become a nun.
He could bestow on her some land,
and there she would an abbey found.
He'd marry, then, his so loved lover;
1128　it was not right or fair, however,
that he be husband to them both.
The law allows but one such troth!
　　Eliduc gladly, kindly gave
1132　permission to his wife to leave;
all her desires, with gracious heart
he granted; of his land gave part.
Near the castle, a wooded plot—
1136　hermitage, chapel, were at that spot—
she had her convent's plans laid out,
and all its edifices built.
Much land she had; wealth, property;
1140　all her needs met, assuredly.
All was prepared; Guildeluëc
then took the veil. Her vows she took
with thirty nuns; she founded thus
1144　her order, way of life, and house.

Eliduc married his *amie*;
much honor, much festivity,
a splendid service, grand display,
1148 they had upon their wedding day.
They lived together many days
in perfect love and kindly grace.
They gave great alms, they did great good,
1152 until at last they turned to God.
Close by the castle, opposite
the convent side, with care and thought
Eliduc built a church; to it
1156 he gave his land, the greater part,
and all his gold and silver, both.
His men, and other folk of faith
and piety, he brought, to thus
1160 maintain the order and the house.
When all was ready, under way,
He, Eliduc, did not delay
but joined, himself, with full intent
1164 to serve his God Omnipotent.
He offered his beloved spouse
to join his first wife and her house.
Like a sister the former wife
1168 honored her, taught her, in this life
to serve God always, love and praise;
and taught the order and its ways.
Both prayed to God for their dear man
1172 that God give him His benison;
Eliduc for the ladies prayed.
Messages, too, he had conveyed,
to know their news, know how they stood,
1176 and comfort each, give all things good.
Each of them individually strove
to serve God in good faith and love;
and each made a good end, the sign
1180 of mercy from the True Divine!

Of the adventure of these three
ancient Bretons courteously
made a *lai*, to remember it;
1184 a tale that folk should not forget.

FIN

The Fables

TRANSLATIONS

Prologue

Learned and lettered people ought[1]
to devote study, time, and thought
to those whose books and texts are full
4 of sayings, tales, examples, all
composed by the philosophers,
who marked well what came to their ears.
To teach the moral and the good
8 they wrote down proverbs that they heard
so folk who wished their lives to better
could profit by the learned letter.
Fathers they were to all of us!
12 The emperor, old Romulus,[2]
instructed thus his son, and by
his own example taught the boy
how he must be on guard, so that
16 he not be done in by some plot.
Aesop wrote to his master, too—
He knew his man, his mind and view—
fables he'd found; they had been done

---

1. In lines 1–16, Marie is expressing a medieval view of culture known as *clergie*: a view that humans have an obligation to study and learn the great works of the past so that they will not be lost. Knowledge is a divine gift: it makes us human, gives us continuity with history, and enables us to comprehend our universe. Cf. the prologue to the first-known Arthurian romance, Chrétien de Troyes' *Erec et Enide* (ca. 1170), which expresses a similar perspective.
2. Marie here conflates the mythic "emperor" and founder of Rome with a compilation of fables in Latin well known to the Middle Ages. It contains a Prologue in which a Romulus asserts that he has translated the fables there from Greek to Latin for his son Tiberinus (or Tiberius). This collection still exists in many versions and derivations in medieval Latin. The first forty of Marie's fables appear to be based on a branch of this work known as the *Romulus Nilantii*. See Leopold Hervieux, *Les fabulistes latins, depuis le siècle d'Auguste jusqu'à la fin de moyen âge*, 2nd ed., Paris: Firmin-Didot, 1893. Volume I contains discussion and classification of these fables, 293–314; Volume II contains Romulus collections of the fables themselves, 195–761; the *Romulus Nilantii* can be found in II, 653–755. Cited in Spiegel, 17, 263.

20 from Greek into the Latin tongue.
   Some people thought it ludicrous
   he'd waste his mind to labor thus.
   No fable is so foolish, though,
24 that wisdom is not found there, too;
   in the examples you'll soon see
   there's always some philosophy.[3]
   To me, who must compose these rhymes,
28 it happens there are, oftentimes,
   words quite unsuitable at best.
   However, he who did request
   my task, is flower of chivalry,
32 of wisdom and of courtesy.[4]
   When such a man approaches me,
   in no way do I wish to be
   shirker of any pains in store,
36 though some may take me for a boor
   in honoring such a behest.
   And now I shall begin the first[5]
   of fables Aesopus wrote down
40 and to his master passed along.

Fable 1

The Cockerel and the Gem

   I'll tell about a cock, who stood
   upon a dunghill, scratched for food
   as Nature prompts these birds to do;
4 how to hunt meals this cock well knew.
   A precious gem he came across;
   a brilliant stone, he saw it was.[6]
   "I thought," he said, "I'd have the luck
8 to find my dinner in this muck.
   But now, this shiny gem I see;

3. Cf. the proverb found at the beginning of Chrétien's romance *Erec et Enide,* supposedly drawn from peasants' tales, that says that a poor despised thing often turns out to be of great unsuspected value.
4. See the Epilogue, line 9, where Marie refers to a Count William. There were many aristocrats named William in Anglo-Norman society of the time, and identifying this William for certain has thus far proved too difficult a task.
5. Many medieval writers—especially those with any pretense to gentility—excuse or justify themselves when providing ribald or coarse material. Cf. Chaucer in the Prologue to "The Miller's Tale" in *The Canterbury Tales.*
6. Harriet Spiegel points out in the notes to her edition that in the Latin versions of this story the cock finds a pearl (266).

it gets no honor, not by me.
If some rich fellow'd been your fate,
12   he'd fix you up, you'd be ornate!
He'd set you up all bright, in gold;
Oh, he'd enhance your pulchritude!
But my desire is not for thee—[7]
16   no honors will you get from me!"

It's thus with many folk, likewise,
who don't want what's before their eyes;
just as it was with cock and gem,
20   so it's with women and with men;
the good, the true, they little prize,
the worst they seize, the best despise.

Fable 2

The Wolf and the Lamb

This one's about a wolf and lamb
who both drank water from a stream.
The wolf drank at the spring, the source,
4   the lamb down by the water's course.
The wolf spoke; he was furious;
his nature was contrarious.
He spoke in anger to the lamb:
8   "You make great trouble and great harm!"
The lamb responded, "Sire, how so?"
The wolf said, "You don't see? Don't know?
You've stirred the water up enough
12   so I can't drink the filthy stuff.
I should drink first, I think, for I
came here so thirsty, I could die."
The lamb responded, sensibly,
16   "But, sire, you drink upstream from me.
I drink the water you have had."
"You slander me?" the fierce wolf said.
The lamb said, "That's not what I meant!"
20   The wolf: "I know your true intent.
Your father tried this gambit, too,
at this same source—it's nothing new—
six months ago, quite recently."

---

7. Spiegel observes here that the cock "shifts from the formal 'vous' to the colloquial 'tu' as the mockery becomes scorn" (266).

24   "For that," the lamb said," you blame me?
        I wasn't born, I'm sure of that."
          The wolf replied to him, "So what?
        Now, here, *you're* hostile; *you* offend;
28   your crimes must be brought to an end."
        He seized the lamb, and with his teeth
        strangled him fast; that was his death.

          But these are things rich nobles do,
32   sheriffs and judges do it too,
        bestowing justice in their courts.
        They try false cases of all sorts:
        destroy folk with false evidence;
36   give summons; there's no real defense.
        The flesh, the skin, they'll seize upon,
        just as the wolf did to the lamb.

Fable 3

The Mouse and the Frog

        True to my text, I will expound
        upon a mouse's case; she found
        by effort, native wit, and will
4   her home and household in a mill.
        In this instructive tale I'll tell
        one day the mouse sat on her sill;
        she cleaned her whiskers, made them neat,
8   and combed them with her little feet.
        A frog, coincidentally,
        just peradventure, came that way.
        She asked, in mouse-speech, if the mouse
12   was herself mistress of the house,
        for such the mouse tried to appear.
        The frog was all agog to hear
        of her affairs. "Friend Frog," said she,
16   long have I held this seigneurie.[8]
        Under my jurisdiction lie
        all holes, all entrances, nearby.
        I reside here, and day and night
20   play, and do all for my delight.
        Now stay, and lodge one night with me!

8. The estate of a lord or an aristocrat, a *seigneur*.

and I will show you faithfully
that on the grindstone, at your ease,
24 nothing you'll have that can displease.
Flour and seeds galore you'll eat,
left by the peasants from their wheat."
     The frog responded to this plea;
28 both on the stone sat happily,
and a great deal they found to eat
all without hindrance, fear or threat.
The friendly mouse asked if the food
32 was pleasing to the frog, and good—
how was it? "Tell me honestly."
The frog replied, "I will not lie.
The cuisine would be somewhat better
36 with water; it should be much wetter.
If we sat in the meadow's middle
this moment, in a lovely puddle—
there is my home, my residence!
40 Fair friend, let us go there at once.
Such joy and such delight you'll have,
you'll never want, I do believe,
ever, to go back to your mill."
44   She promised all with wit and skill,
deceitful speech and blandishment.
The mouse, poor fool, gave her assent.
Together they went off, these two.
48 The meadow was all soaked with dew,
and the poor mouse, all wetted down,
was terrified that she would drown.
She wanted badly to return,
52 it hardly seemed she could go on.
The frog had led the mouse away
against her will; now, lovingly,
pleadingly, she called, to move her.
56 The two beasts came upon a river.
The mouse had no way to get over;
weeping, she told the frog: "I'll never
get any farther, get across!
60 I don't know how to swim, alas!"
     "Take this thread," said the frog, "and tie
it very firmly round your thigh.[9]
The same thread I'll attach to me,

---

9. The *Anglo-Norman Dictionary* gives the word "ham" for the original *garet*. Other English
versions of the *Fables* use "middle" (Mary Lou Martin 39) and "knees" (Spiegel 39).

64 and we'll cross expeditiously."
         The mouse obeyed, and tied the thread,
    the frog tied her end, as she'd said;
    into the shallow ford they went.
68 But frog, in the deep water, meant
    to kill the mouse, to see her drown,
    and she went plunging, diving down.
    The mouse squeaked, made a dreadful cry,
72 thinking she was about to die.
    A kite, by chance, came flying by,
    and saw the mouse squeak piteously,
    folded his wings, came plunging down,
76 both animals he fastened on,
    by the thread dangled frog and mouse.
    The frog was corpulent, and gross;
    the kite in all his greediness,
80 took the fat frog, and left the mouse.
    He ate the frog, summarily,
    devoured her; but the mouse was free.[1]

    So, crafty felons meet their ends:
84 they never have such love for friends
    that they will honor them, if such
    gestures of love will cost them much;
    and they are full of joy and glee
88 if friends fall for their trickery.
    But often their rapacious game
    turns back on them; they get the same
    torment they planned for other folk.
92 *Their* bodies know the fatal joke!

Fable 4

The Dog and the Sheep

    This tale is of a dog, who was
    a liar, cheat and treacherous,
    who sued a sheep. He had her led
4   before the judge; as plaintiff, said
    that he must have the loaf of bread
    he'd lent to her, that she still had.

---

1. "Only in Marie's account is the mouse free and alive at the end. In the Romulus and other Latin versions the mouse is tied around the neck, not the knees, and the mouse (male) dies" (Spiegel's note, 267).

The sheep denied the whole affair;
8   he had not lent a loaf to her!
The judge said: "Dog, can you produce
witnesses that the Court can use?"
The dog said that he could, all right,
12   two; one the wolf and one the kite.
These witnesses were led forth, both,
and both affirmed by solemn oath
that all the dog had said was true.
16   You know why they agreed, don't you?
They hoped to get some portion, if
the sheep, found guilty, lost her life.
The judge, proceeding in the trial,
20   summoned the sheep; why the denial
he asked her, that she had the bread
the dog had lent her, as he said.
Why lie? This item was so small!
24   Return it, or worse would befall!
The wretched sheep, who had no bread,
was forced to sell her wool instead.
Winter and cold soon had her dead.
28   The dog came; took some wool she'd shed,
the kite came flying for his share,
and then the wolf. They took from her
all of her flesh; they seized on it,
32   for they had long been starved for meat.
No vestige of her life was left;
and, too, her master was bereft.

With this example we can state
36   what many false folk demonstrate.
With lies and tricks of every sort
they drag the poor folk into court;
they get false witnesses to lie,
40   they bribe with poor folks' property.
They don't care how the wretched die;
they only want their slice of pie.

Fable 5

The Dog and the Cheese

There was a dog once, so they say,
who crossed upon a bridge one day;

a cheese he carried in his maw.[2]
4 Halfway across he looked down; saw
a cheese reflected in the water.
In his heart he resolved the matter;
he'd have both cheeses. All agog—
8 Oh, he was covetous, this dog!—
he jumps, mouth open, in the stream.
The cheese falls out, escaping him.
Shadow there is; shadow he sees;
12 meanwhile it's lost, his own real cheese.

As this example proves and says,
the greedy need to mend their ways:
craving to have more than their right
16 they set themselves up for defeat.
They often lose their good; worse luck,
gain not a thing from other folk.

Fable 9

The City Mouse and the Country Mouse

There was a mouse, a city sort,
who, for diversion and for sport
to a town nearby wished to go.
4 Her way was through a forest, though.
In the woods dark came on apace.
She found a small hut in that place,
that a wood mouse had fashioned for
8 the gathered food she wished to store.
The city mouse then asked of her,
did she have any food right there?
The country mouse said, "Certainly!
12 Come over here and you will see.
And if you've brought some friends with you,
Plenty of dinner for them, too!"
When town mouse had been there a bit,
16 to her companion she spoke out,
So shabby was her place, so poor!
She'd leave! She would no more endure!
But if wood mouse would come to town,
20 delightful chambers she'd be shown,
great pantries, cellars, fine and full,

---

2. The dog carries a piece of meat in the Latin versions of the story. See p. 307 of this
volume for Phaedrus's version.

good drinks, and food delectable.
The country mouse believed it all
24 and came. What splendid rooms she saw!
Those lovely chambers, sure enough,
those pantries, cellars, full of stuff,
wheat and honey she was given—
28 she thought she'd died and gone to heaven.
        But now the butlers—Ha! Surprise!—
came to the cellar for supplies.
Soon as they opened up the door
32 she found a hole and fled in there.
Bewildered, the poor country mouse
hardly knew who and what she was.
But when the butlers left the scene
36 the mice returned to feast again.
The wood mouse, though, was full of fear,
dejected, from her deathly scare.
Now her companion looked at her
40 and sweetly commented, "My dear,
such a long face! What's wrong?" she said.
The other cried, "I'm half destroyed
by fear, I was so terrified!
44 Why did I let thee be my guide?
Of good things much I heard from thee,
of bad things not a word to me!
Here thou hast human beings to fear,
48 cats, birds too—evils similar!
and traps that humans set for thee.
I love my woods much more! For me
better peace and security
52 than these rooms with anxiety!"

So here's the moral, from a mouse:
we love our own way, each of us,
prefer our peace, from terrors free,
56 than others' wealth, with misery.

Fable 11A[3]

The Lion, Hunting

At one time law and custom said
the lion should be king and head

---

3. This is the first of two ancient versions of the same tale. See note 5 on p. 184.

of all the beasts on earth, and all
4 that thrived there, every animal.
The ox he made his seneschal;
loyal he thought him, brave withal.
The wolf, too, was the king's grantee,
8 his steward. In the woods these three
found a stag and pursued it, then
after they took it, stripped the skin.
The wolf then asked the ox, what share
12 should each of them have in the deer?
"Our King," the ox said, "must decide.
Honor is his; he must divide
the prize." The lion spoke; he swore
16 he should have all the prize, for sure.
One part he was entitled to
because, as king, it was his due.
A second part he claimed, for he
20 was their companion, one of three.
He claimed another portion still,
for it was he who made the kill.
Who tried to claim the fourth would be
24 he said, his mortal enemy.[4]
None touched the stag then—did not dare!
they left it for the lion's share.

Fable 11B

The Lion, Hunting[5]

Another time the lion went
with other confreres to the hunt;
this time they were the goat and sheep.[6]
4 A stag they took, to kill and keep.
Four parts they wished to cut from it;
the lion said: "I claim each bit.
The greater part is due to me,
8 for I am King, the court's grantee.
Second, too; I ran down the deer,

---

4. These are not drawn from Harley 978 (MS A in *Fables*) but another manuscript, Y (York Minster XVI, k. 112). In A and in some other MSS the fourth part of the deer and the lion's claim on it are not mentioned.
5. "*Romulus Nilantii*, Marie's probable source, treats these [two stories] as two fables, as they are classically, the first from Babrius, the second Phaedrus. The majority of manuscripts treat them as a single fable" (Spiegel 268). I follow Spiegel in treating them as two versions of the same story.
6. In Marie's sources—*Rom. Nil.* and Phaedrus—there is also a cow.

and third, for I'm the strongest here.
The rest I've cut in such a way
12   your claims would make a mad melee."
When his companions heard this claim
they ran away and left the game.

    By the same token—doubt me not—
16   if a poor man will cast his lot
with one more powerful than he
he'll never have prosperity.
The rich man's honored in the end—-
20   at the expense of his poor friend.
And if there's profit to be split
the wealthy man wants all of it.

Fable 13

The Crow and the Fox

    It happened once—as well it could—
that by a window with a good
pantry just next to it, inside,
4   a crow flew by; and there he spied
some cheeses lying on display,
spread out upon a wicker tray.
He snatched one up, and flew away.
8   He met a fox while on his way.
Now a great longing had this fox
to share the cheese; he thought some tricks
he'd try, some cunning stratagem,
12   and the crow might be fooled by him.
    "Dear God, Sire," said the fox, "I see
a bird of such gentility!
No fairer fowl has lived on earth.
16   Never have I beheld such worth!
Does the song match the form? If so,
fine gold's naught to this beauteous crow!"
    This praise the crow was bound to hear.
20   On earth he thought he had no peer,
and he resolved to sing, for he
as chanteur, got much flattery.
He sang; his beak was all agape,
24   the cheese, of course, made its escape,
and fell right down upon the ground.

And the fox snapped it with a bound.
Now he'd no care for song, no praise;
28   he had his object, and his cheese.

Example take: the proud must have
the praise and plaudits that they crave;
by lies and tricks and blandishments
32   they're made to service others' wants.
Fools, squanderers, they've not a chance
with cunning frauds and sycophants.

Fable 14

The Sick Lion

Of an old lion is my text,
with age and frailty much vexed.
Long he'd lain ill, poor animal,
4   and now could not get up at all.
All the beasts in a congress met;
to see the lion, came to Court.
Sorrow most felt for him, regret,
8   —there were those not the least upset!
But since the lion was old and ill,
some gift they hoped for in his will,
and most of them were keen to see
12   whether he made recovery.
Then the goat made a nasty pass,[7]
butted him with his horns; the ass
struck with his hoof the lion's chest.
16   The fox, for his part, did his best
and bit the old king on his ears.
"Wondrous!" the lion said, "these jeers!
Well I remember, in my prime,
20   when youth and health and strength were mine,
the other beasts knew me with fear,
and honored me as their seigneur.
When I was joyful, joy was theirs;
24   when in my wrath, how great their fears!
Now, sick and weak, I am reviled
and trampled, and my worth defiled.

---

7. A number of manuscripts here supply *bues*, ox, instead of *bucs*, goat. In *Rom. Nil.* and
Phaedrus, the attackers are the *aper*, boar; *taurus*, bull; and *asinus*, ass.

What is the worst ignominy:
28 those who were once close friends to me,
    whom I gave honor, riches, love—
    that they've no recollection of;
    they're just like those I caused distress!
32 How few friends have the powerless!"

    By this example and this case
    note how the lion fell from grace:
    he who from power's forced to fall
36 loses force, knowledge, wisdom, all—
    contempt from many he will have;
    many who once professed their love.[8]

Fable 21

The Wolf and the Sow

    Along a road a wolf once fared.
    A pregnant sow, as it occurred,
    he met, a fellow traveler.
4   Speedily, he accosted her.
    He said that he would let her be
    if she gave birth immediately,
    for he would have those piglets, now!
8   Sagaciously then spoke the sow:
        "Sire, how can I make such haste!
    So close to me I see you placed,
    I cannot possibly deliver!
12 Shame at your nearness makes me shiver!
    You don't see the significance?
    Such deep disgrace all females sense
    when male hands touch them, when they dare!
16 Sire, stay away from this affair!"
        The wolf went off then, to conceal
    himself; he saw he'd missed his meal.
    The sow continued on, set free
20 by her own ingenuity.

8. The lion's plight here seems pitiable, but in Fable 36, "The Sick Lion and the Fox," the lion, pretending to be sick, lures all the other hunting animals to his den and eats them; only the fox is clever enough to see what is afoot. In Fable 71, "The Sick Lion, the Deer, and the Fox," the deer is suspicious but finally capitulates, comes to see the lion, and is killed. The lion claims to need to eat the deer's heart for his illness, but the fox steals it and outwits everyone in the subsequent investigation. The fox as supreme trickster, of course, figures often in medieval European tales, such as the Reynard the Fox series.

Women all, here's one you should heed
and keep in mind for time of need:
Don't scorn, one time, to tell a lie;
24   Better your children live than die![9]

Fable 25

The Widow[1]

My text here offers up a word
about a man dead and interred.
On his tomb night and day his wife
4   lamented, wept, displayed her grief.
Now, nearby, there had been a thief
hanged; his misdeeds had cost his life.
A chevalier, the thief's own kin
8   had cut him down and buried him.
Now through the region came the cry—
whoever stole the thief must die!
Judgment same as the thief's was just,
12   if apprehended, hang he must.
No help or counsel found this knight,
or a solution for his plight,
for many people knew, too well,
16   he was kin to the criminal.

He quickly to the graveyard went,
where the good widow made lament
and wept above her husband's grave.
20   The knight spoke, devious and suave:
"Comfort yourself! Take heart, be brave!
I would rejoice to have your love."
She looked at him; made careful study;
24   then joyously agreed, this lady,
to grant his wish. The chevalier
explained his fearful plight to her,

---

9. In the Latin story, the wolf offers his services as a midwife. Spiegel sees a problem with lines 23–24, as neither the wolf nor the sow has said anything untrue. She further comments: "The point of Marie's tale seems to be that men should not be present at childbirth, a sentiment supported in a roughly contemporary guide for women, which says that a woman should consult another woman to examine her. 'A man ought to avoid the secrets of women and fly from their intimate association . . .'" (269). Spiegel cites Beryl Rowland, editor and translator, *The Medieval Woman's Guide to Health* (Kent, Ohio: Kent State University Press, 1981), 9–10.
1. Marie's famous source is "The Widow of Ephesus" in the *Satyricon* XI of Petronius. The story is portrayed in the film *Satyricon* by Federico Fellini. (See p. 308–09 and 313–16 of this Norton Critical Edition.)

his sure disaster and his grief
28 because he'd taken down the thief.
If she'd no counsel to bestow,
out of the country he must go.
But then the worthy woman said:
32   "Let us dig up my lord, who's dead;
where the thief hung, hang him instead.
Who'll ever note a change was made?
The dead must help us; through their giving
36 we still take comfort from the living."

Notice the import of this tale:
between the quick and dead, how frail
a trust exists; how devious
40 the world, how false and frivolous!

Fable 42

The Rich Man Who Was Bled

A doctor once—so it is said—
had a rich patient, whom he bled,
a serious case. The specimen,
4   the drawn blood, was entrusted then
to the man's daughter, so she would
guard and protect the precious blood,
for it would, once examined, be
8   clue to her father's malady.
She took the sample to her room
and put it on a bench; but harm
came to the specimen after all.
12 Oh, dreadful luck! It chanced to spill.
She lacked the courage to confess,
had no solution to this mess,
except that her own blood be shed
16 in secret, cooled, and used instead.
Soon as the doctor saw the blood,
immediately he understood
he had a pregnant donor here!
20 Now the rich man was wild with fear—
was he with child? Thus terrified,
he called his daughter to his side.
Partly for love, partly distress,
24 the daughter managed to confess

she'd spilled her father's blood and then
donated her own specimen.

With frauds and tricksters it's the same:
28   deceivers, thieves; they try some game;
many who do some wickedness
engulf themselves in more distress.
However shrewd their play, and skilled,
32   they meet their match, and end up killed.[2]

Fable 43

The Rustic and the Beetle

A peasant once was lying down,
sleeping and snoozing in the sun.
Face down and naked he was curled,
4   his butt-hole open to the world.
A beetle crawled inside his butt,
waking him as it climbed his gut.
Sick, wretched, he sought a physician,
8   spoke to him of his condition.
The doctor said, "You're pregnant, man!"
Now he was worse off than he'd been,
for he believed it to be true.
12   Now fools who heard believed it too;
it was a portent, they all said,
and they were full of fear and dread.
His sins, bad faith, would curse them all;
16   great evil on them must befall.
Foolish folk are so credulous,
they follow the ridiculous,
put faith and hope in nonsense, thus.
20   Their watch was most assiduous—
by what means would the child be born?
From human window bug crawled down;
where it came in, came out again,
24   Thus hoodwinked were they, everyone.

---

2. Spiegel is right, I believe, when she comments that "Marie's moral seems unnecessarily
harsh"; it almost seems to me to have been attached to the wrong fable or a wrong
version.

By this example, let me say,
the ignorant behave this way;
believing that which cannot be,
28   they're fooled by silly vanity.

Fable 44

The Woman Who Tricked Her Husband[3]

A peasant once stood just inside
his door; he waited there and spied
a man upon his bed, who lay
4   joyously with his wife, in play.
"What have I seen," he said, "Alas!"
His wife at once responded thus:
"Dear heart, whatever's wrong with you?"
8   "Another man! I saw, I knew—
I saw him take you, on our bed!"
Furious, the peasant's wife then said,
"Oh, not again! When will I learn!
12   I knew this madness would return!
Illusions, lies! You think them true!"
"Wife, I know what I saw of you."
"You're crazy if you take," said she,
16   "for truth this thing you've claimed to see."
She led him by the hands, at that,
where, full of water, sat a vat;
she made him look inside of it.
20   Then she began to ask him: what
he saw in there; he said to her,
just his own self, an image there.

---

3. Cf. Chaucer's "The Merchant's Tale," from *The Canterbury Tales,* in which an old man recovers his eyesight (suddenly, by means of a supernatural agency) just in time to see his young wife and her young lover *in flagrante delicto* in a tree. The wife insists that her husband has not seen what he has seen but first misinterpreted a magic protocol she was trying to cure his eyesight; finally she insists that he in the first moments of recovering vision misinterpreted what he saw, as people do when they are waking up and still not fully conscious. The old husband gives in. (See p. 309 of this Norton Critical Edition.)

    Versions of this story have been generated for centuries, and many are very amusing. See especially Louise O. Vasvari, "Cunningly Lingual Wives in European Ballad Tradition," *Tradiciones Culturas y Populares,* Mexico, Distrito Federal I, July–August 2008, Numero 15, 69–81; also Child Ballad #274 (in Volume V of *English and Scottish Popular Ballads*). In the Scots-Irish tradition the husband comes home drunk and sees various signs that another man is in his home and his bed, of which the wife gives ridiculous explanations. In addition to Child Ballad #274, "Our Goodman," (known in other sources as "Seven Drunken Nights," "Four Nights Drunk" and ten other titles) there are numerous versions collected in the Appalachians in the 1930s; The Weavers adapted them to create their popular and delightful song known as "You Old Fool, You Blind Fool."

Then she said, "Surely, dear, you're not
24 with all your clothes, inside that vat;
you see an empty likeness that
you must not trust—dismiss the thought!
Your eyes lie; they misrepresent!"
28   The husband said: "Oh, I repent!
Surely a man, to prosper, must
give what his wife says all his trust,
rather than what his false eyes see—
32 sight makes the fool, so easily!"

We, by this moral tale, can see
how plain sense and sagacity
are of great worth in people's lives;
36 more than goods, more than kin—or wives!

Fable 45

A Second Time, a Woman Tricks Her Husband

Of one more peasant I will say,
his wife he noticed on her way
into the forest with her lover.
4 He pursued both; the man took cover,
and fled into the foliage.
The husband came back in a rage,
scolding the woman furiously.
8 His wife, however, asked him why
the anger, why was she to blame?
The husband answered to his dame,
he'd seen her lecher! Seen the shame,
12 seen the dishonor, done to him,
when those two sneaked into the trees.
"Sire," said the woman, "if you please,
for God's love, tell me truthfully,
16 do you think that you saw with me
a man? Tell me! Keep nothing hid!"
"I saw him go into the wood!"
"Alas, I'm dead!" she said, "I'll die
20 tomorrow, possibly today.
My grandmother died this same way,
my mother—I saw that, I say!
A bit before their deaths, each one
24 (this I am saying is well known!)

were led away by a young man
where, otherwise, they'd not have gone.
I know so well my end is near!
28　Summon my cousins; bring them here;
our goods we must divide and share—
Stay in this world I do not dare!
My worldly goods I'll take with me
32　and go into a nunnery."
　　Hearing, the husband cried, "Mercy!
Let it all be, my sweet *amie*!
Please do not go away from me!
36　I lied! No lecher did I see!"
　　Said she, "I can't delay, don't dare,
for of my soul I must take care,
now, most especially, you see,
40　for you have shamed me publicly.
Shamed and condemned I'd always be,
thought to have wronged you vilely,
unless an oath you swear to me
44　—one all my relatives can see—
you never saw me with a man.
Swear on your faith; not once again
will you lambaste or scold me, ever,
48　or raise this matter of a lover."
　　"Willingly, dame," he answered, "never."
And to a church they went together,
and there, to all she asked, he swore,
52　not only that, but plenty more.

　　Thus men fault women; say they see
how women use chicanery.
Ingenious, devious, crafty, evil—
56　They've more art than the very devil!

Fable 53

The Hermit

　　This tale is of a hermit, one
whose peasant servant lived with him.
When he spoke of the Deity,
4　the peasant asked repeatedly
why Adam of the apple ate,
causing man's downfall and his fate,

and why, once he'd consumed the fruit,
8   there was no pardon, no commute
of sentence. Now, the anchorite,
distressed, resolved to set things right,
calm down the peasant, end the query
12   of which the hermit had grown weary.
He asked that a big bowl be brought,
upside down on the table set,
and underneath he placed a mouse.
16   Then he forbade, for any cause,
the peasant to come anywhere
near the bowl, or look under there.
Meanwhile, he would to church repair
20   and to God offer up a prayer.
No sooner was he out of sight
before the peasant thought he might
see what great marvel lay below
24   the upturned bowl he guarded so.
There was no way he could refrain
from looking, or himself restrain
from spying what the bowl might house.
28   He raised the bowl; he saw the mouse,
which ran off and escaped him thus.
    His master came home, furious,
in a great rage, a tearing wrath,
32   demanded why he'd looked beneath
the bowl, why he had disobeyed
commands. He had his trust betrayed!
    The peasant answered after this:
36   "Sire, I could simply not resist.
Either my heart would burst from me,
or I would peek beneath and see."
    "What has become then of the mouse?
40   If you had caught it where it was,
I'd have excused your foolishness."
    "It moved too fast, sire, I confess."
    "Well, then, friend, let your queries go;
44   don't wish to blame poor Adam so,
though he did eat the fruit and did
what Our Lord specially forbade.
The Devil gave him counsel there,
48   and through his wife set him a snare,
promised him honor such that he
God our Creator's peer would be!"

And so we shouldn't inculpate
52 the deeds of others, small or great,
accuse our neighbors or our kin;
let each disparage his own sin!
He who would others criticize,
56 better he should himself chastise.

Fable 57

The Peasant and the Dwarf-Man[4]

A peasant caught a dwarf-man once;
long had he waited for the chance.
The dwarf-man gave him wishes three
4 for dealing with him secretly.
Gleeful, the man was, jubilant.
When homeward to his wife he went
he gave her, of the wishes, two;
8 he kept one—not with much ado.
Some time passed, quite an interval;
the wishes were not used at all.
There came a day, though, after that,
12 when at a feast the couple sat
eating sheep's bones and spine parts, which
were full of marrow, thick and rich.
How the wife craved this lovely treat!
16 Willingly she'd have it to eat,
but couldn't reach it. For her fill,
she wished her husband had a bill,
long, like a woodcock's; then the peasant
20 could reach the marrow; oh, how pleasant!
She made her wish; the poor man thus
with horror saw his change of face
and wished he were away, long gone,

---

4. Cf. the ribald medieval French fabliau "The Four Wishes of St. Martin" (anonymous) in which the saint bestows the four wishes on a devoted follower, who then quarrels with his wife. Each in an access of sheer spite wishes the other's body to be made up of nothing but genitals (male for the husband, female for the wife). The remaining two wishes are used to restore the couple's normal anatomies.

    Spiegel comments on Marie's tale: "The granting of three wishes is a common folk motif (see Stith Thompson J2071)" [i.e., Thompson's *Motif-Index of Folk Literature* (2nd ed., Bloomington: University of Indiana Press, 1955]. Spiegel further remarks that "the waste of the three by a quarreling married couple is a usual theme . . . Marie's tale is unusual (but perhaps not incomplete) in presenting only two wishes, although the goblin [or dwarf-man] gives them three" (273).

24 and had his own face back again!
Thus did two wishes go to waste;
all their good squandered and effaced.

Often things do turn out this way;
28 thus many folk are led astray.
Too credulous, they have believed
some foolishness, and been deceived.
A fool will fall for some device
32 and ask some trickster for advice
on how things are—but it's a loss;
no knowledge there, no worth; just dross.

Fable 95

The Peasant and His Contentious Wife

A peasant wed a wife, and she
was quarrelsome and contrary.
The two of them walked out one day
4 for pleasure, where a meadow lay.
The man said he had never known
—never had he laid eyes upon—
a meadow scythed so evenly.
8 And she replied immediately:
"Oh, shears were used for mowing that!"
"No, it's been scythed!" was his retort.
"No, sheared!" said his insistent spouse.
12 The peasant now was furious.
"You're plainly crazy!" said the man.
"They scythed this grass to cut it down!
You're stupid! and you're insolent.
16 You talk right over me; you want
to cut me off entirely!
Crazy fool, will you silence me?"
He threw her to the ground, at that,
20 grabbed her, and cut her tongue right out,
then asked her what advice she had,
and whether now she understood—
had the field with a scythe been cleared,
24 or did she think it had been sheared?
Now the old dame, who couldn't say,
signaled with fingers to display

her thought; with shears it had been mown!
28 Not with a scythe had it been done!

What this example serves to state
human beings often demonstrate.
When a fool speaks in ignorance
32 and someone wiser then talks sense,
the fool rejects it, and gets mad,
though he may know his case is bad.
He lies; he cuts in; he won't stop,
36 and there's no way to shut him up.

Fable 96

The Hare and the Stag

A hare once saw a stag, who stood
as the hare gazed upon his head.
The antlers were so beautiful!
4 He, hare, was vilest beast of all,
he thought, a hornless animal,
created, oh! so low and small.
To Goddess Nature went the hare,[5]
8 and there made his complaint to her:
why, at the time he had been formed,
was he not, like the stag, adorned
with horns like those he'd noticed? Why?
12 The Goddess made him a reply:
"Stop it, wrong-headed animal!
Antlers! You could not cope at all!"
"I could, and do it well!" he said.
16 Then there were antlers on his head!
He could not hold these horns up, though,
and how to move he did not know;
more weight the horns had than the hare,
20 a little animal, could bear.

By this example one can see
the covetous and miserly
will always wish to instigate

---

5. A Latin analogue, the *Romulus Robertii*, slightly later than Marie (see Spiegel 263, Hervieux II, 549–62; Spiegel 277), has Jupiter for the deity consulted here. Nature is Marie's goddess.

24   pomp and prestige for their estate.
      Presumptuous, immoderate,
      they harm themselves, and learn too late.

Fable 100

The Knight and the Old Man

I'll tell now of a chevalier—
—there's an instructive story here—
who met an old man by the way.
4   Together they kept company.
The knight thought he seemed wise, this man;
to many places had he been;
the knight hoped he'd advice to give.
8   Where, in what country, should he live,
since he himself was not so wise?
And the old man had this advice,
that in some country he should dwell
12   where everyone would love him well.
      "If I can't find it," said the knight,
tell me, what region would be right
for me to seek my residence?"
16   The old one said, with great good sense:
      "Then go and stay—take heed from me—
where all the folk have fear of thee."
      "And what then," said the chevalier,
20   if I can't find that land of fear?"
      "Go where you know no one; so far
that not a soul knows who you are."

This story teaches us a rule:
24   when one converses with a fool
who asks too much and won't desist;
the fool finds out more than he wished!

Fable 101

The Bishop Cat

There sat a cat upon a stove,
waiting and spying from above.
He saw a vole and mouse; to each

4   he spoke in fair and honeyed speech.
He was their bishop, so he said:
through bad advice they'd been misled,
no confirmation[6] had they had!
8   But the mouse made reply; he said:
    "I'd rather die! It would be worse
to be beneath those claws of yours!"
Mouse and vole fled; the cat, intent,
12   came chasing after on the hunt.
The rodents reached the wall; inside
they thought it preferable to hide
crouched in the wall, move not at all,
16   than heed the bishop and his call
—his confirmation, terrible!—
They knew that cat was criminal!

So here we can a moral fit:
20   to someone's power one can't submit
if their intent's an evil one;
Shun them, and then no harm is done!

Fable 102

The Old Woman and the Hen

A woman, one time heretofore,
seated herself just by her door
and watched her hen; she saw her scratch
4   and seek her food there in a patch,
laboring greatly every day.
The woman spoke up lovingly:
    "Pretty one, stop! Don't work so much!
8   I do not wish to see you scratch!
I'll give you all the grain you want,
full measure! You won't have to hunt!
    The hen, though, made her this reply:
12   "Madame, what's this you say to me!
Do you think I prefer your wheat
to things I've always had to eat?
No, no!" the hen said, "not at all!
16   Give me a bushel always full;

6. All but two manuscripts have not *cunfermeisun* (confirmation) but *beneicun* (benedic-tion) (Spiegel's note, 278). The last line of all but three manuscripts has *en altre tere*, "to another land."

you may be sure I will not wait,
omit a chance, or hesitate
to seek and scratch here every day—
20　　such is my nature, such my way."

Here is a case to keep in mind:
many discover how to find
wealth, and enjoy prosperity;
24　　but change they cannot; all they see
is their own nature, their own ways.
They crave those in their hearts, always.[7]

Epilogue

At the conclusion of this text
I've set in French, it's right that next
I name myself, for memory.[8]
4　　I am from France; I'm called Marie.
It's possible the work I've done
some clerics might claim for their own—
I wish no one to make that claim!
8　　A fool lets others steal his fame.
For love of William, noble count
—no realm knows man more valiant—
this writing task I undertook,
12　　in French, from English, made this book.
Aesop men call this book, for he
translated it originally
from Greek into the Latin tongue.
16　　King Alfred loved this work; he then
translated it in English rhyme.
I in French verse have done the same,
rightly, or such was my intent.
20　　Now I pray God omnipotent
that I may to this work attend
and thus to Him my soul commend.

---

7. Spiegel translates *coveitent* in the last line as "lust"; she cites collections of Latin fables in which Venus, questioning Juno's chastity, compares the hen's scratching to the natural and never satisfied lust of women (Spiegel 278). Cf. the Latin fable of "Juno, Venus, and the Hen" on page 308 of this Norton Critical Edition, excerpted from *Babrius and Phaedrus*, trans. Ben Edwin Perry, Loeb Classical Library No. 436 (London: Heinemann, and Cambridge, MA: Harvard University Press, 1945), 387. There is a good argument for her choice—this particular tradition—but I think the word "lust" puts too much emphasis on sexual desire in the context of this story, hence my choice "crave."
8. I.e. for the sake of the record, and for posterity.

Espurgatoire de Seint Patriz[†]
(Saint Patrick's Purgatory)
SELECTED TRANSLATIONS

Prologue

In the name of God—may He
send us His grace, and with us be—
I wish to write down in *Romanz*,[1]
4 for memory and reference,
what the book[2] tells us; tell the story,
the sufferings of Purgatory.
Saint Patrick God desired to show
8 the entrance, where the soul must go.

Dedication

Some time ago, a worthy man
asked of me what I now take on,
a work I do with reverence,
12 to honor him, all diligence.
If he is pleased, and in accord,
I shall recount all I have heard,
may I stand always in his grace!

[†] The edition of Marie's original I have used as my copy text is the French text edited by
Karl Warnke: *Das Buch vom Espurgatoire S. Patrice der Marie de France und seine Quelle*
(Halle: Max Niemeyer, 1938). I have also consulted Michael J. Curley's *Saint Patrick's
Purgatory: A Poem by Marie de France* (Center for Medieval and Renaissance Studies,
State University of New York at Binghamton, 1993), whose text is based on Warnke and
whose notes and commentary are astute and useful.

1. I.e., into French.
2. I.e., the Latin treatise by H. of Saltrey, an English Cistercian monk. It was a work of
enormous popularity: Curley calls it an "instant best seller" (1), and Jacques Le Goff
has credited it with initiating "the vision of genuine Purgatory" (Le Goff, *The Birth of
Purgatory*, trans. Arthur Goldhammer, [Chicago: University of Chicago Press, 1984],
108, 193–201). Marie's version made the story available to a French-speaking public
and also transformed it into a chivalric tale, a hugely popular form at that time. (See
Curley 1–2.)

16 Dear father, listen now to this.
However much I truly might
wish to work a great benefit
for many folk, so that they could
20 amend their ways, more serve our God
and fear Him, I would not have thought,
ever, to make this task my lot,
my study, but for your request;
24 sweet and dear to my heart, the task.
Little I've heard of this concern,
or seen; yet from all that I learn,
my love of God has grown much greater,
28 too, my wish to serve my Creator.
And thus I wish to open here
this text, and make its matter clear.

Preface

In his sermons, Saint Gregory
32 shows examples for us to see:[3]
spirits, that in our bodies live;
others, outside, around us thrive,
vicious things, that can terrify,
36 loathsome, that do great injury—
thus to put fear into the hearts
of fools and sinners, he imparts
warnings of griefs their sins will bring,
40 and of their souls' sure suffering,
and to arouse compunction,
more devotion, in anyone
wishing to please God, serving Him,
44 deserving, too, His blessed realm.
With great care, thus, I show this book,
to benefit the simple folk,
wishing this task to undertake
48 with pains and effort for God's sake.
My lord, know that when souls depart
and from the body they set out,
angels are there, beneficent,
52 also spirits malevolent.
And the good angels—this, in sum—

3. See *The Dialogues of Saint Gregory, Surnamed the Great,* trans. Edmund G. Gardner (Boston: Philip Lee Warner, 1911), Book 4.

receive the soul of the good man,
place it in joyousness and rest.
56 The devils move to the arrest:
the wicked souls seize and torment,
lead to peril and punishment.
There the reward these souls will earn
60 is fitting for the toil they've done.
Plainly we're told, and openly
that many souls, most certainly
know what's to come to them, before
64 they leave the body, what's in store.
Some learn by revelation; some
learn through a vision what's to come;
some know directly, insofar
68 as they're permitted—but no more.
And truly there are souls who see
envisionings before they die;
enraptured, they're transported hence,
72 but back to body come, and sense,
and there reveal what they have seen
of torment and salvation:
that which awaits the good, for sure;
76 that which the wicked folk must fear.
And in the spirit, they can see
what appears flesh—corporally.
Rivers appear to them, raised bridges,
80 fire, fields, woods, they see, and houses,
men, whose diversity is great,
some black in color, and some white;
and many other things they see—
84 some seem in sorrow, some in joy.
And certain folk are by them seen
by hands, by feet, dragged to their pain;
where they are hanged and flogged, and then
88 into vile, filthy places thrown.
Other pains they experience:
these not at all at variance
with our tale, which we wish made known,
92 which we already have begun . . .

*   *   *

But it must happen, nonetheless,
112 we shall suffer, more or less,
doing our works, in Purgatory;
even those who await true glory

must come to torment, suffer it;
116 know pain and travail as their fate.
Those who are just and righteous here,
least desire sin, thus to be sure
to have eternal life; they, too,
120 —no doubt of it—they must pass through,
and of their sins be purged at last;
then, saved, depart, and be at rest.
Here we shall show you pains; all full
124 of agony most terrible.
They are prepared in such a way
they seem experienced bodily.
Such is God's plan and foresight that
128 the greater torments, without doubt,
are deep down; those more arduous.
The lesser, less laborious,
less grievous, are for those who most
132 mercy await; who won't be lost.
But there is also Hell, beneath,
dark and deep, under the earth,
a prison, gloomy, tenebrous,
136 to sinners dread and perilous.
But on earth there is Paradise,
toward the East, in the very place
God set it, where the souls are drawn
142 when they have been released from pain;
in our text it is written thus:
there they live in delight and bliss.

[*Marie refers then to beliefs of St. Augustine and St. Gregory regarding
the physical penances of souls and spirits and mentions that others write
on the corporeal suffering of souls.*]

God Reveals Purgatory to Saint Patrick

My lord, listen to the account.
Hear of Patrick; hear of the saint;
a most religious, noble man.
192 So that God's word he might make known,
He went to Ireland; he set out
to preach, his purpose all devout.
He was the second man to fare
196 to see God's law established there.
God made him signs and powers, because
of Patrick's worth; made miracles.

Devoutly Patrick strove to give
200 understanding to such as live
by fools' beliefs, which he could rout;
from error he could cast folk out.
Hearts fickle, brutish, bestial,
204 he wished to make acceptable
to God; and often terrible
accounts he gave, of pains of Hell,
of suffering of those who have
208 no faith, do not in Christ believe.
Often, though, he would gladden them,
speaking of joys that were to come,
joys wonderful, and surely had
212 by those who wish to serve their God.
He made them understand; know; see;
so that they could believers be.

[*An old man comes to Patrick to receive communion and confession but
is unaware that in killing five people he has sinned. Patrick instructs him
and imposes a penance on him. Saint Patrick receives a visitation from
Jesus Christ, who gives him a full text of the Gospels and a staff to carry
with him when he preaches to the people*].

After that visitation God
led away Patrick, and he showed
the saint a waste place, desolate
304 and uninhabited. A pit
lay there, completely round, and steep,
enormous, and profoundly deep,
and, you must know, dark and obscure,
308 fearful, dreadful beyond measure.
The entrance, God said, could be found
to Purgatory, in that ground,
that pit. He with faith firm and sure,
312 who lived in hope of our *Seigneur,*
confessed his sins, and afterward
received Communion; this one could
enter the pit and sojourn there;
316 and if then he could persevere,
and a full day and night could stay,
returning up by the same way,
his sins would all be cleansed away,
320 his misdeeds purged entirely,
all his life's errors. He'd be free.
And without fail he now could see

the dreadful suffering, the keen
324   torment of sinners, their deep pain.
The elect's joy he'd see; he could;
if he were perfect before God.

When God had spoken in this wise
328   he vanished before Patrick's eyes.
Patrick returned then strengthened thus:
replenished, furnished, by God's grace.
In his *Seigneur*, who had that day
332   appeared to him, he felt much joy;
truly, joy of the pit he felt.
The people he could tell of it,
could show it, saving many thus
336   from error and from dreadful loss.
He built an abbey in that place,
And people of great holiness
put there, and canons regular.
340   Their order's rules he taught them there.
And where he had the graveyard placed
truly, the pit lies, toward the East . . .

[*Many in Saint Patrick's time receive permission to go to Purgatory to do
penance; they suffer greatly but rejoice afterward. They recount their expe-
riences to Patrick, who keeps a record of them.*]

Since those who go there, enter in
that place, are purged of all their sin,
as Purgatory it shall be
372   forever held in memory.
And since Saint Patrick first was shown
by God, the entrance, it is known
always, thanks to this blessed story,
376   as Saint Patrick's Purgatory.
The site the church was founded on
by the name Rigles is well known.[4]

[*A story is told of an old Irish prior who lives in a cell near Saint Patrick's
church. He has one tooth and lives on cold water, salt, and bread, and
suffers greatly, longing to go to a better place. Angels appear and bless him,
shortly before his death.*]

---

4. "'Reglis' is the form which appears in most manuscripts of Henry of Saltrey. The word
derives from the Irish *réiclés* (var. *reglés*, *rigles*) and originally signified an oratory or
a small church, a monastic cell or anchorite's hut. Later it came to apply to a church
associated with a monastery or to the abbey itself (*Dictionary of the Irish Language*
[Dublin: Royal Irish Academy, 1983], 503: *reiclés*). The word may derive from the Latin
reclusum, or possibly *ro-eccles* (< *ecclesia*), a large church. Marie appears to take it as a
place-name." Curley's note, loc. cit., p. 65.

Preparatory Ceremonies for Entering Purgatory

My lord, it's set down in the book:
in Patrick's time were many folk
then, and in later times as well,
424 just as we have ourselves heard tell,
who went to Purgatory, then
soon came back up to earth again;
some were retained, for dreadful cost—
428 they died and were forever lost.
Those who returned told what had been;
the canons took down what they'd seen,
to tell the edifying story—
432 no doubts then about Purgatory!
It has been told us, furthermore,
custom and use was, heretofore,
that those who wished this trial to make
436 and Purgatory's chance to take,
must first to the lord bishop go,
and their confession make and show.
After confession had been heard,
440 this was the sermon and the word:
"My lord, by God, seek not this quest!
What you will find there is no jest!
Many have been retained there; never
444 seen again; they were lost for ever."
But when the bishop could be sure
their purpose still was firm and pure,
he sent them to the prior; he wrote
448 letters requesting that these folk
be guarded, cared for, and be put
as they desired, in the dark pit.
When they came to the prior, he
452 received these folk all properly,
kindly exhorted them; he meant
they should abandon their intent,
and in this earthly life, take on
456 penitence, and here see it done.
If he could not dissuade or warn
these folk, their purpose overturn,
he placed them in the church, and there
460 kept them for fifteen days, in prayer,
fasting and vigils, penitences,
mortifying flesh and senses.

Local clergy, then, were sent for.
464 Their friends, too, were invited there;
Mass, in the morning, sung and said;
up to the altar all were led
who chose the pit. Communion, then;
468 benediction; the Cross; the sign;
holy water on them was thrown
by clerics and their friends, who'd come
with song and with procession, for
472 such was the custom heretofore.
Those choosing they led to the door;
all saw as it was opened there.
And in a homily the prior
476 spoke of the suffering most dire
that they would there be sure to find,
never escape, or leave behind,
if their faith was not absolute,
480 their hope in God thus resolute.
In Patrick's time, the prior said,
many had failed, and there had died.
To those who held their purpose still,
484 and firmly exercised their will,
and would not leave, he spoke no more;
the prior opened up the door.
They crossed themselves; they entered in
488 before the people watching them;
the prior closed the door again.
To God's loved church, the clerics then
followed the prior, and in prayer
492 sought for the entrants God's great care.
Next morning, they all went to learn
who had been strong and could return,
what stalwart made it back, and he
496 received was, welcomed joyously.
There in the church full fifteen days,
he served the Lord in sundry ways,
and his adventure he made known;
500 in writing it was taken down.
And if someone did not return
it was known he was lost; gone; done.

The Story of the Irish Knight Owen

During the time of Stephen's reign,[5]

504   as in our text it's written down,
in Ireland lived a worthy man,
Owen, his name; a knight, of whom
we wish to speak, and tell aright,
508   truly, the history of this knight.
The local bishop he sought out
at Purgatory's site; he thought
to make confession to this man
512   and pardon for his sins obtain.
Often with evil works he had
cruelly striven against God.
All that he spoke the bishop heard,
516   how he confessed, how chose his word,
much he condemned and blamed the man
for the dark works that he had done.
Living so, in these sins, he had
520   much angered his Creator, God;
for his trespasses Owen knight
felt dismay, sorrow, and regret.
Some worthy penitence he thought
524   to make; God's help, His will, he sought.
The bishop wished to designate
a penitence appropriate
to Owen's sins, to what he'd heard,
528   lighten his burden; to this word
the chevalier said briefly: "Sire,
Lord Bishop, I have no desire
to thus so lightly expiate
532   my errors, as you designate.
To my Creator, my *Seigneur*,
I owe, for my great sins, much more;
let me choose, for my rank offense,
536   to do the heaviest penitence.
To Purgatory I shall go,
Saint Patrick's Pit shall enter; so
I shall be purged, I shall be free,
540   of sins, of my iniquity."
The Bishop warned him much, at that;
he must abandon such a thought!

---

5. Stephen of Blois was king of England from 1135 to 1154.

"Where devils keep their habitat
544 men must not go; it is not fit!
Many who went there, it's well known,
never, ever, came back again."
No fear of torment or of pain
548 could move the courage of the man.
The Bishop saw his will and heart
and thought it best that he exhort
Owen to seek a convent where
552 good monks, or canons, lived, and there
follow his purpose, far more sure
he could succeed and live secure.
Owen refused; his mind was set.
556 No habit would he wear, save that
he now wore, till he'd gone, he'd been,
and Purgatory he had seen.
The Bishop saw how resolute
560 Owen was, firm and absolute,
and to the prior then he wrote,
giving instructions in his note:
the prior must receive this knight,
564 and follow proper form and right,
placing the man in Purgatory,
with all due rite, and customary.
The knight went to the prior, and he
568 received the man most lovingly.
Much he spoke; much in sermon sought
to persuade Owen from his thought.
This burden human could not bear,
572 to enter such perdition there.
So fervent, though, the knight's desire,
no success had the kindly prior.
So to the church he brought the knight,
576 as was the custom and the rite,
and fifteen days Sir Owen passed
there to keep vigil, pray, and fast.
When fifteen days had passed and gone,
580 local clergy were asked to come.
That morning Mass was sung and said,
which Owen at his leisure heard,
then received, with this blessed Word,
584 devout, the body of Our Lord.
Holy water on him was thrown;
after that he was led along
with litany, orison, prayer,

588   and beautiful procession, where
he was to enter in the pit;
with great speed he came up to it.
The prior opened up the door
592   and speaking to the chevalier
showed to him, before the crowd,
the entrance. Then he spoke this word:
"Friend, if you could take my advice
596   you would not enter in this place!
Your life you can amend right here,
honor and serve God without fear.
Many who entered here are lost,
600   no one knows to what fate, what cost;
their belief was not firm, not pure,
their faith and hope not strong, not sure;
the torments they could not endure;
604   there they have gone forevermore.
In seeing such appalling pain
they forgot God; died; there remain.
If you still wish to enter here
608   in spite of all I've made you hear,
more I shall make you hear! of all
that you shall find, that will befall."
     The chevalier heard all, and said
612   "I shall enter. I trust in God,
that for my sins I can atone,
thus pleasing God for what I've done."
     The prior said, "Sire, listen, do!
616   Hear what I must make plain to you!
In God's name—you've sworn faith in it—
you will now go into the pit.
Through earth's deep caves you'll find your way
620   to a great meadow, where you'll see
a great hall, beautifully built
and fashioned. You will enter it.
Much he knew workmanship and fine
624   craft, he who made that hall's design.
There you shall be; you shall receive
good, kindly messengers. They'll have
in God's name, goodly speech with you,
628   comfort you, say what you must do,
instructing you sufficiently
in all you are required to be.
They will depart then, afterward,
632   leave you, commending you to God.

After that, quickly, straightaway,
the evil messengers you'll see.
Those who've come back from Purgatory
636   recounted to us this same story,
and there are texts which we have read
telling these things which we have said."
The knight assumed a pleasant mien,
640   and speaking before everyone,
said he had no such fear or doubt
as others, thus exiled, had felt.
Rather much more he felt the force,
644   the fear, of sin, felt his remorse;
he'd hear no tale, no argument,
never abandon his intent.
His sins he felt, and his great wrong;
648   These crushed his heart and weighed him down,
and thus of pain no fear he had,
of torment pleasing to his God.
He who was so well armed before,
652   and well his iron weapons bore,
and fought with such great bravery
in combat, to gain victory,
now in such fashion bore such arms
656   he had no fear of devils' harms,
with faith and hope so fortified
belief and justice on his side.
He with these virtues, without fail,
660   against the Devil would prevail.
He said to all: "Pray, pray for me!"
before him raised the Cross; boldly,
a pleasant look upon his face,
664   into the pit stepped; took his place.
The prior closed the door. All went
from the pit; in procession blent,
moved toward their convent. Orisons
668   they offered, for God's benisons,
that pity, mercy, Him might move
for the knight I have spoken of.

Owen Enters Purgatory

Through the pit went the chevalier;
672   as he went he did not feel fear.
He sought, he strove, there is no doubt,

new knightly tasks; harsh, difficult.
A wonder he was safe, for sure!
676 Darker his way grew, more obscure,
until was lost all human sight.
Then came to him another light,
Tiny; however, strong enough
680 that by it he could find his path.
He wandered through the earth, dim-lit
until he found the field he sought.
A great house, lovely, he saw there,
684 which he'd heard spoken of before.
The light he saw was in that place
like winter dusk, a darkling space.
This palace had, encircling all,
688 surrounding it, one entire wall;
of pillars, arches, it was built,
wandiches;[6] here and there a vault.
A cloister it resembled, where
692 religious folk might dwell in prayer.
Wonderstruck, Owen chevalier
saw this work; could but stand and stare.
When all the palace he had seen,
696 all round the outside he had been,
quickly, in haste, he entered in.
And even more he marveled then,
at all that there appeared to him,
700 and, praising Jesus, he sat down.
Up and down, stunned, he turned his eyes;
he could but wonder, be amazed;
he could not think or understand
704 such work was done by human hand.

[*Owen has barely arrived when fifteen people approach him, led by a prior,
who praises his divinely inspired courage and warns him that he will be
assailed by devils. If he believes their deceitful ploys or is overwhelmed by
fear of them, he will be lost forever. But if he resists them he will be
cleansed of his sins and set free. Owen again remains steadfast, prepared
for the worst.*[7]

6. A *hapax legemonon* (one-time occurrence) whose meaning is unknown. Curley suggests
several possibilities (81), including scribal error; he notes that "'wandyd' or 'wanded'
meant 'made of wicker work' or 'wattled' (of a building). Cf. 'wand,' 'a young shoot of a wil-
low cut to be used in basket-making, wattled buildings, or the like,' and the example pro-
vided in the OED (c. 1450): 'A litill chapel of wandes pei made.'"

7. Lines 787–816, summarized in this text: much of this material, describing the Christian
hero arming himself with Justice, Faith, and Hope, carrying the sword of the Holy Spirit,
comes no doubt from Saint Paul, *Epistle to the Ephesians*, 6:11–17, cited in Curley 87. Here
Owen learns to call on Jesus's name, which will protect him throughout his adventure.

*The devils arrive. They are hideous in appearance and make a terrible
noise.*[8] *They behave as Owen was told they would, trying to frighten and
tempt him. He refuses to speak to them.*

*Owen then begins to experience the torments. In the First Torment,
the devils throw him in a fire and push him down with an iron hook.
Owen calls upon Jesus; the Holy Name protects him.*[9] *In the Second Tor-
ment, the devils take him to a dark obscure land where a wind pierces
him. The devils drag him on, eventually coming to a field full of the
sound of lamentation and of people naked on the ground with nails
through their hands and feet. They do the same to Sir Owen, but he calls
upon God and Christ, and his torment is dispelled.*[1] *In the Third Tor-
ment, in another field people lie on their backs with nails driven through
them and fiery dragons striking and devouring them. As always, he calls
upon Jesus. In the Fourth Torment, in a third field Owen finds people
fastened to the ground with burning nails from head to foot and assailed
by cold winds. The devils tie up Owen and try to include him in this
torture, but he calls upon Christ once more and is delivered.*]

The Fifth Torment

> Between them devils dragged him on;
> to the fourth field they dragged the man.
> Every possible form of pain
> ₁₀₇₂ the knight saw there, before him plain.[2]
> By their feet were many hung;
> in burning chains their bodies swung;

8. Lines 821ff. (summarized in this text). Cf., quoted in Curley 89: "*The Vision of Adamnán*
   in *An Irish Precursor of Dante*, trans. Charles Boswell (London: David Nutt, 1908), 35:
   'In the main doorway of the [heavenly] city they are confronted by a veil of fire and a
   veil of ice, smiting perpetually one against the other. The noise and din of these veils,
   as they clash together, are heard throughout the world, and the seed of Adam, should
   they hear that din, would be seized thereat with trembling and intolerable dismay. Faint
   and dazed are the wicked at that din; howbeit, on the side of the Heavenly Host, naught
   is heard of that rude discord, save a very little only, and that sweeter than any music.'"
9. Line 892ff: Curley in his note 12 (93) cites *The Apocalypse of Peter* in *The Apocryphal New
   Testament*, trans. Montague Rhodes James (Oxford: The Clarendon Press, 1924), 510,
   36; also *The Vision of Adamnán*, in *An Irish Precursor of Dante*, trans. Charles Boswell
   (op. cit); and *The Vision of Tnugdal*, trans. Jean-Michel Picard and Yolanne de Pontfarcy
   (Dublin: Four Courts Press, 1989), 117. In this last work, Curley sums up for us: "homi-
   cides, parricides and fratricides [are thrown into] a deep pit of burning charcoal"; he
   then cites the text: ". . . A multitude of wretched souls was falling onto this red-hot metal
   plate, and there they burnt until completely melted like cream which is reduced in a
   skillet. Then . . . they were sieved through this metal plate as wax is sieved through a
   cloth, and their torment was again renewed, this time in the charcoals glowing with fire."
1. Tortures similar to those in the Second Torment are described in the *Apocalypse of Paul*
   in *The Apocryphal New Testament* (op. cit), 544; *The Vision of Drychthelm* (in Bede, *The
   History of the English Church and People*, trans. Leo Sherley-Price, rev. R. E. Latham
   [Harmondsworth: Penguin Books, 1968], 290); and *The Vision of Tnugdal*, 118: "On the
   one side of this path was a stinking, sulphureous and tenebrous fire, but on the other
   side was icy snow and a horrific wind with hail."
2. The tradition of the visitor to the world of the dead finding numerous people whom he
   lists and describes is at least as old as *The Odyssey* and *The Aeneid*. In *The Aeneid* (Book 6,

many of them were hanging there
1076   by hands, arms, in that wretched snare;
others in that space had a share
who were suspended by their hair.
Heads hanging downward, too, were some
1080   pendant in an infernal flame;
and by their legs they swung, these folk,
in the sulfurous fire and smoke;
and some most cruelly were stuck
1084   upon a burning, flaming hook
by eyes or ears, or by the nose—
(how marvelous a thing that was!)
by neck, by chin, and by the mouth
1088   and by the breasts; we find, in truth,
and by the genitals, still more;
hooked by the cheeks, a number were.
Those hanging there the knight could see
1092   in fire that burned eternally;
and some in furnaces were burned,
their bodies into sulfur turned
and charred and blackened; others still
1096   he saw were roasted on a grill;
others impaled on spits[3] to toast
with sulfur and with pitch were roast.
Some devils, at rotisserie,
1100   poured on them a variety
of metals; other devils took
maces of iron, and beat the folk.
Of torment, all varieties
1104   displayed themselves to Owen's eyes;
and old companions, from old ties,
many of whom he recognized,
who in the world of flesh he'd known
1108   and who much evil work had done.[4]
No one could speak of, or portray

---

especially lines 426–49) Aeneas comes upon the Fields of Mourning, where all sorts
and conditions of people suffer, not necessarily from guilt or punishment but from sad-
ness at the vicissitudes of life. Similar, often imitative short passages are found in
medieval literature: cf. the Middle English lay, imitating an Anglo-Norman or French *lai,
Sir Orfeo* (lines 385–406), where the hero, a king and minstrel (obviously a borrowing
of the Orpheus myth!), goes in search of his wife who has been stolen by fairies. Parts of
the fairyland seem to be a place of the dead, and the passage describes people who have
died violently or with much suffering. Dante, of course, took the whole idea to a whole
new level or series of levels.

3. *Espeiz:* sword; spear.
4. Recognition scenes in the world of the dead are frequent in older literature and often
accompany lists and descriptions mentioned in the note to line 1072. The most famous,
probably, are the appearance, in Book 11 of *The Odyssey*, of the dead soldier Elpenor

in book, such shrieks of agony
such tears. This field did not contain
1112   just those who struggled in their pain,
but devils, their tormentors, who
tortured them in this field of woe.
Now they seized Owen, and they sought
1116   to torture him. But they could not,
for he called out, in Jesus' name,
and so to him deliverance came;
to name this name is good; for thus
1120   one frees oneself from wickedness.

The Sixth Torment

From there they led him on; he saw
a torment great and horrible,
a burning, flaming, fiery wheel;
1124   sulfuric flames engulfed the reel.
Around the rim, just where the spokes
were joined, were flaming iron hooks
thickly affixed to rim and rung;
1128   on these hooks, thickly, people hung.
Half of the wheel touched on the ground;
the other in the air; it burned.
The wretched people hanging thus
1132   burned in the flames, so sulfurous,
that roared up from the earth; it was
dark as dark gets, or ever is.
The devils made it very plain,
1136   exhibiting to him each pain,
and sparing Owen no detail:
if he refused them, without fail
these were the torments he would feel,
1140   that he would know, up on that wheel.
"Before we hang you, chevalier,
we'll show to you, we'll make it clear,
what they feel, wretched captive folk,

---

and of Odysseus's mother Antikleia, neither of whom Odysseus knows is dead (*Od.*
11.51–83, 84–89, 140–224); the appearance of Aeneas's cast-off lover Dido in the Fields
of Mourning (*Aeneid* 6. 450–76); and the figure Montefeltro, a false counselor shut up
in a flame in Dante's *Inferno*, who tells him that if Dante were to return to the upper
world he would never confide in him what he is about to say (*Inferno* 27.61–66), a pas-
sage used to great effect in the epigraph of T. S. Eliot's poem "The Love Song of
J. Alfred Prufrock." The shock of seeing someone one knows in such a place under-
scores and intensifies the knowledge of mortality and experience of suffering.

1144 who hang up there by hook and spoke."
      Forward the devils came. They turned
      this great wheel as it flamed and burned;
      some of them on one side of it
1148 and others working opposite,
      holding great bolts of iron, all fire.
      Up from the earth they lifted higher
      the wheel, pushing it through the air
1152 to display folk who dangled there.
      Others were working in reverse,
      pushing the wheel down with great force;
      so violently was this done
1156 so swiftly was the great wheel spun,
      that in all honesty no one
      could see the people as they hung,
      the speed and flame were so intense.
1160 Sorrow and misery, immense
      beyond belief, the people there
      bore; torments mortals cannot bear.
      The devils seized the knight; took him
1164 and put him up upon the rim;
      raised him up in the air; but then
      just as the wheel was coming down
      he spoke the name of Jesus Christ;
1168 quickly was saved. That name sufficed.

The Seventh Torment

      But from that place they led him on;
      between them devils led the man
      until from far he saw a house
1172 enormous, smoky, vaporous.
      So great the width, the length, one's eyes
      could not discern the house's size.
      Viciously now they dragged the man;
1176 they were still at some distance when
      the heat became so great, Owen
      could not endure it and go on.
      He stopped. They dragged him forcibly.
1180 "Sir Knight, you cringe! You dawdle! Why?
      That is a bathhouse. You will go
      into it, whether you will or no.
      You will be bathed along with those
1184 who so deserved it, and so chose."

Now they could hear from those inside
how wretchedly they wept and cried.
He was dragged in the house. He saw
1188   many torments, all horrible.
Encircling the interior
were pits, all dug into the floor,
wide, they were, ghastly and profound,
1192   and to the bottom, carved out round,
placed near each other; thus was seen
no sign of passages between.
Each pit of which we speak, each hole,
1196   we have discovered, was brim full
of seething liquids, every kind,
of burning metals, all those mined.
Of people a great multitude
1200   he saw around him, and he could
see in age great diversity,
young and old tortured horribly.
All were plunged in this metal that
1204   was smoking, flaming, seething hot,
some to their breasts stood, in a pit,
some to their navels, stewed in it,
some to the thighs, some to the knees,
1208   all in most grievous agonies.
Some stood in metal and in heat
up to their legs or to their feet,
some stood with one hand held in it,
1212   or both, in torment éxquisite.
As with one voice they all cried out
Grieving, lamenting their hard fate.
Viciously now the devils said
1216   that these same torments Owen would
be put to, and would suffer too,
if all their will he would not do.
They went to plunge him in the bath.
1220   The knight remembered then his faith,
and Jesus' name; he called on it,
saved himself from the pain, the pit.

The Eighth Torment

They led him from that seething deep
1224   up to a mountain, great and steep.
People he saw of every age

gathered together in that place.
Crouched on their toes, bowed down, they were,
1228 all in great pain, and all stripped bare.
So many squatted on that slope
that, if on Earth were no more folk,
there were enough there, Owen thought,
1232 to cover Earth, if they spread out.
They were like folk awaiting death,
all of them turned and facing north,[5]
and Owen marveled, looking on,
1236 at all these folk, abject, crouched down,
since, so bent down, they seemed to be
imploring mercy, piteously.
One of the devils asked him why
1240 he marveled at them, crouched this way,
waiting in fear, and forced to feel
such suffering and such ordeal:
    "Just such a labor you shall earn,
1244 should you refuse to serve our turn."
    From Owen not one word they got.
Up the slope now the devils thought
to force him; but then from the north
1248 a tempest, violent, roared forth,
lifting them all up horribly,
throwing them down again, to be
dunked in a cold and reeking river,
1252 weeping, lamenting, on the other
side of the mountain. All their cries
Owen shared, with their agonies.
In the deep cold they felt deep pain;
1256 they struggled to rise up again.
The devils with iron hooks thrust down;
in congealed stink swam everyone.
The chevalier remembered; thought
1260 to call on Jesus Christ; cried out;
at once delivered as he cried
stood on the river's other side.

5. Curley (note 30, 115) cites Isaiah 14:13–14 and the Song of Songs 4:16 in connection
   with this passage, lines 1234ff.

The Ninth Torment

But soon again the devils came
1264   and dragged him south. He saw a flame
dark, sulfurous, its reek intense
beyond all measure and all sense.
Folk of all ages he saw there
1268   tossed by the flames up in the air,
their bodies bright with snap and spark
as they were swept up from the dark.
Up they were swept, then fell again
1272   into the fire from which they came,
the incandescent place of fear,
sorrow and terrible dolor.
The devils, as they dragged him near,
1276   now remarked to the chevalier:
    "See you this flaming hole, just there?
That, knight, is flaming hell; the door.
There are our mansions; there shall be
1280   our homeland, for eternity.
And since you have served us so well,
you shall be with us there in hell,
for all of those who serve us shall
1284   join us, and there forever dwell.
Place yourself in this pit, this hole,
and you shall die, body and soul;
if to serve you do not intend,
1288   there, perforce, you shall surely end.
If to return you do prefer,
back we shall lead you, chevalier,
safe and sound, without injury,
1292   to enjoy your longevity."
    Such was his faith in Jesus Christ
he scorned their counsel and advice.
The devils leaped inside the pit
1296   dragging him with them into it.
So sudden was the torment that
almost, the chevalier forgot
to name the Name of his Seigneur;
1300   then sweetly did so, to his cure.
He called on Christ; after his cry
the firestorm flung the knight on high,
with all the others, in the air.
1304   How perilous a leap was there!

Down in the pit's edge he was flung;
just for an instant there he hung
amazed that he had landed there.
1308 But devils came at him once more,
and these he did not recognize;
they were not those who met his eyes
before. They said,
"Ah, chevalier,
1312 now solitary, are you, here?
Our colleagues lied to you, of course,
saying the entrance and the course
leading to hell was this same pit.
1316 They lied to you; be sure of that;
such lying is, you know, their wont;
after all, it is their intent
so to betray, so to seduce,
1320 when to be truthful is no use.
This is most surely not the true
entrance to hell they showed to you,
but understand our counsel well:
1324 We, knight, shall show you the true hell."

The Tenth Torment

Dragging and pulling him once more
they brought him to a river shore
reeking, deep, ghastly to the sense.
1328 Cries, he heard, shrieks and noise immense.
The sulfurous flame and smoke, intense,
covered the river, which was dense,
crowded with evil spirits, full
1332 of suffering most horrible.
The leader demon turned and spoke:
"Notice that river? Flame and smoke?
Hell's own pit blows heat through that river—
1336 Hell, where we shall be damned forever.
That river has a bridge. To cross
is, for all, greatly hazardous.
Over this bridge, knight, you must go;[6]

---

6. Curley (note 33, 123) mentions two fascinating and detailed analogous descriptions of
an "otherworld bridge over a noisome river": one is from the *Dialogues of Saint Gregory*,
Book 4 (op. cit), chapter 36, 22–25; the other from *The Vision of Tnugdal* (op. cit), 119,
123–25. There is also a striking similarity of this bridge to bridges in other stories from
very different cultures. For instance, in the California Native American story (Yokut and

1340 meanwhile we cause the wind to blow
that from the mountain bore you down.
Into the river you'll be blown,
just as it seized you to deliver,
1344 plunging you, to that other river.
You'll be delivered, be sure of that,
by our friends, into Hell's own pit.
First the bridge you must try to pass.
1348 Prove yourself! See if you can cross!"
They raised him up; they raised him high,
they set his feet upon the way.
Of perils on that bridge were three;
1352 great they were, full of treachery.
First, it was slimy, slippery;
one lost one's footing constantly,
would, even if the bridge were broad,
1356 if one had no help from the Lord.
And then there was another peril:
this was a bridge extremely narrow;
it seemed to him no mortal could
1360 not fall, but keep grasp firm and good.
The third one so inordinate
was that the bridge had such great height
over the searing, burning river.
1364 It terrified those passing over,
Their courage failed, their strength, their faith;
they fell to Hell's pit and to death.
The demons once again spoke, thus,
1368 so wicked and so treacherous:
"Once more, Sir Knight, we counsel you:
be with us; serve our retinue.
We shall escort you to the door
1372 you entered; you'll be free once more."
The chevalier, though, thought of threat
from which the Lord had thrust him out,
and called on Jesus Christ at once.
1376 Then step by step he could advance.
As he went forward he could sense

Western Mono tribes, in the San Joaquin Valley) "The Man's Wife," in Theodora Kroe-
ber's *The Inland Whale: Nine Stories Retold from California Indian Legends* (Berkeley
and Los Angeles, 1959), there is a strikingly similar bridge. In this moving Orpheus-like
tale a young man's wife dies; unable to accept her death he follows her to the Other-
world. One of the many dangers he must face as a living person is this bridge, "treacher-
ous in its erratic swaying and dipping . . . many fell from it into the river, from which
there was no chance of rescue and where monstrous fish devoured them . . . also demon
birds would fly up, trying to frighten them so they would miss their footing and fall" (145).

with each step he gained confidence,
for the bridge broadened on each side,
1380 so he could see, it was so wide.
Soon the bridge could, being so broad,
carry a cart with a full load.
Soon after, it had grown so large,
1384 two carts could pass, with all their charge,
and travel freely in that place
with room to spare, with ample space.
The devils who had held him swam
1388 beneath, and they stared up at him
as he passed over easily.
Then they cried out, so hideously,
earth and air trembled horribly.
1392 No greater danger could there be;
of their shrieks Owen had more fear
than all his perils heretofore.
Deeper down Owen could espy
1396 more devils; they held hooks on high,
of iron, to catch him, make him fall;
but they could not touch him at all.
Freely he passed, high above Hell,
1400 sans incident or obstacle.

A Homily

The author would have us perceive
example[7] here; take it; believe
the torments of which we have heard
1404 which the book sets out in plain word,
of Purgatory's miseries,
and this world's strife and agonies.
If all these torments here set down
1408 were judged against all others known,
no likeness could be made at all.
Eagle and finch? So great, so small?
The agonies of Hell are such,
1412 the pains, the sufferings are much
as if one could enumerate
sands of the sea. They are that great.
He who can often contemplate

---

7. *Dialogues of Saint Gregory*, Book 4, chapters 55 and 58, pp. 248–52, 255–56, similarly urge us on to pray for our relatives suffering in Purgatory.

1416 these sufferings, gives little weight
to worldly vanities; delight
in them he scorns, and holds them slight.
The cloistered monks cannot conceive
1420 —though in confinement they believe
their life a hard one, full of strain—
they too cannot conceive the pain
in regions we have spoken of
1424 and shown to you who live above.
If they thought of that suffering,
their own lives, above everything,
they'd prize. Oh, so much easier,
1428 when, soul and body joined, both share
in life, no fears assail the soul,
and clothes and food are plentiful,
than when great pain is all one sees,
1432 all things arouse great agonies.
This is why I exhort you all—
think of these pains, so terrible,
think of your friends, who suffer there—
1436 help them! and bring them aid and care.
As was said to the chevalier,
those who, to purge their sins, go there,
will be from suffering set free—
1440 or else damned to eternity.
Those who now suffer, those shall be
delivered from there, certainly,
by masses and by orisons,
1444 by alms and gifts and benisons,
which, for their sake, we give the poor;
release they'll have, excepting for
those who are lost and in Hell's mouth,
1448 know not God's mercy, but true death.
Those tried, tormented, are our fathers,
mothers, sisters, kin—our brothers;
our kind deeds they await, for these
1452 God will know of, and grant release.
If these, among us, we could see,
suffering torments bodily,
ours would be wicked viciousness
1456 if we did not help their distress.
Much greater need do they have there
than when they lived among us here.
As witnesses Saint Gregory
1460 speaking of our mortality

and those who with this life have done
and are to Purgatory gone,
their pains are greatly lessened when
1464 gifts and good works are done for them.
In church, what a great shame it is
when we should hear the services
we think of other things instead
1468 of prayers to God, prayers for the dead.
We say this to chastise—for shame!—
those who leave worship at such time
when service for the dead is sung.
1472 They should remain, and be among
others, and pray devotedly
that God relieve souls' agony,
for those who are set free from sin
1476 are soon relieved, and soonest gone.
If folk remembered as they should
what we have spoken of, they would
bear in mind torment and dolor—
1480 they too should think of it in fear!—
that wretched folk forever know,
and the joys, for the ones who go
to where they their Creator serve,
1484 in perfect faith and perfect love.

Owen Is Led into Earthly Paradise

The knight I've spoken of had passed
over the bridge. After he crossed
he traveled confident and free.
1488 And now a huge wall he could see,
high over earth, looming in air;
what wonders Owen could see there!
One could not speak of, try to tell,
1492 the design or material.
Within the wall, he saw a gate—
from far off he could notice it;
it was of precious metals made
1496 and gloriously was inlaid
with the most marvelous bright stones,
most precious and most costly ones.
Wonderstruck, Owen the good knight
1500 gazed at the lovely glowing gate,
for it gave off a splendid light

from the rich stones, so rare and bright.
He hastened toward it; as he came
1504   the portal opened up to him.
Half a league from it—more, a bit,
he was; then he approached the gate.
A fragrance he sensed came from it,
1508   wondrously sweet and delicate.
If all the things upon the earth,
here at one time, here now, or both,
possessed a fragrance, not a one
1512   could equal, by comparison,
the sweetness he experienced.
It filled his body; and he sensed
his strength returning, to the full.
1516   His torments, fierce and terrible,
seemed, through this fragrance, truly done;
all of his pain was lost and gone.
Still he approached, and gazing in,
1520   a land, resplendent, saw within,
with greater incandescence than
comes to us from the summer sun.
Longing he felt to enter, then,
1524   and to receive there benison
for the great labor he had done.
That such a gate should welcome him!
No deceit was meant, certainly
1528   by One who caused the knight to see
what he desired so; by His grace
Owen could come into this place . . .

[Owen sees people carrying palm branches, banners, candelabras, and a procession of religious folk of all orders, and also lay people. Two archbishops come to Owen and congratulate him. The land is so bright he can't fully see it, but it is like a field full of trees, flowers, fragrant grasses, and fruit. He sees a great multitude of people, secular but devout, who differ in the light that they give off, as stars do: gold, green, purple, hyacinth, blue, and white like a flower ("u bloie u blanche cum flur," line 1620). Owen can discern from their clothing what occupation ("mestier") they followed in life. All are singing with joy at having been freed from Purgatory.]

. . . Each of them in that place rejoiced
1640   at their great happiness vouchsafed;
from suffering and Purgatory
they had been freed and led to glory.
So full, this country, of God's grace,

1644 so fortified, this blessed place,
the soul might, by this grace alone,
be nourished and sustained and strong.
Many houses the knight could see
1648 and there within, much company,
and every house was shining, full
of the great light celestial.
All those who saw the chevalier
1652 praised and blessed the Creator, for
this knight, this brother, who had come,
escaping death, to be with them.
He saw how jubilant they were,
1656 all of them, at his being there,
melody reached him, song, so sweet,
from God's saints who were chanting it.
No heat's or cold's extremity
1660 was there, or hurt or injury,
but all was pleasing to the soul,
peaceful, acceptable withal.
In this repose, this happiness,
1664 he saw great joys, so plenteous,
such that none in the earthly state
could know, or could enumerate.
God grant us worthiness, that we
1668 strive for such possibility!

[*Following these expressions of joy, the archbishops deliver a homily to Owen. They tell him that he has now seen all he desired to see. Owen has seen the torments of the sinners and the joy of the good people; now for the significance. This is the land from which Adam was exiled. Since Adam's fall we are born into "misery and wretchedness" (Curley, line 1711), but through faith in Christ we can come into this land. Those who are released from their pain come to us and are received with joy and a beautiful procession. Those who are in the pain of Purgatory do not know how long they will suffer, but our prayers—and masses, donations, gifts—can relieve or at least alleviate their pain. Similarly with us here in the Earthly Paradise: we remain here for the period we have deserved before we are called to the greater glory of heaven.*]

Owen Visits the Gates of the Celestial Paradise

Now the archbishops led the knight
1796 up a steep mountain, a great height.
There they directed him to cast

upward his eyes; after he must
tell them: what color met his eyes
1800   there in the radiance of the skies?
And he replied at once to them
it was like gold that was aflame.
So dazzling its brilliancy
1804   all seemed on fire that he could see.
      "Dear friend: this gate before your eyes
is to celestial Paradise.
When someone leaves us, goes on high,
1808   this is the gate he enters by;
for those who rise up, you must know,
this is the portal where they go.
And here Our Father, here Our Lord
1812   bestows on us celestial food.[8]
Once every day He feeds us thus,
with His sweet grace, so bounteous.
You too shall now partake with us
1816   this food He gives, so plenteous."
      Just barely had he spoken this
when fire of Sanctus Spiritus
seemed to descend from heaven, and all
1820   the country round it seemed to fill
with light, effulgent, like sun's rays.
Easily such light greets the eyes!
Circling, the Spirit wafted round
1824   heads; then its way inward found,
and, do not doubt at all, the knight
shared this celestial food, this light.
Joy beyond everything, delight
1828   he felt at heart, so perfect that
he knew not, so suffused, so full,
if he were dead, or living still.
      Soon past and gone, this hour, alas,
1832   when blessed souls received such grace.
With such good food the souls are fed
when into Heaven they are led.
The chevalier now longed to stay
1836   forever, had he had his way;
after a happiness so great
a mortal sadness was his fate.
      And the archbishops presently

---

8. Curley points out in his note 35 (145): "Reference to the concept of divine light as 'viande celestiël' (Latin 'cibum celeste') is also found in Langland's *Piers Plowman*, BV, 500."

1840 spoke to him, saying what must be.
　　　"Return you must, knight, certainly.
　　You have seen what you longed to see:
　　In Paradise, the greatest joys;
1844 the wretched folks' worst agonies.
　　You must return now, chevalier,
　　along the path that brought you here;
　　live in the world; live in good faith;
1848 and be assured that at your death
　　you shall most certainly return,
　　share in the joys that you have seen.
　　If into wicked ways you fall
1852 —God grant you not do so at all!—
　　to all the torments that you know
　　to again purge yourself, you go.
　　Haste you! And now depart! You know
1856 the devils that have tried you so
　　cannot approach you, and their threat
　　of torment has no power in it."
　　　But the knight Owen wept and sighed.
1860 To the archbishops' speech he cried
　　Oh, no! He did not want to leave,
　　never to come again! To live
　　on earth, with all its grievous sins
1864 which so encumber human beings.
　　　"I only know I wish to be
　　here, as I am! God pity me!"
　　　The two archbishops told him, still:
1868 　"Brother, you shall not have your will."

Owen's Return Journey

　　　Out of the gate the knight was led;
　　commended to the Christ Our Lord.
　　They closed the gate; and Owen then
1872 passed all the places where he'd been;
　　the devils saw him as he came
　　and fled; they all were full of shame.
　　Of torments, hurts, no fear had he,
1876 immune to all their injury.
　　　The wondrous palace where he'd seen
　　the devils first, he saw again,
　　and went inside. He sat down there
1880 and marveled—could not marvel more—

at the design of the great house.
And the men came, soon after this,
who had been first to speak to him;
1884   they greeted him now, in God's name.
The men praised God's omnipotence,
His everlasting permanence
which strengthened Owen against evil,
1888   caused him to overthrow the devil
and from his sins set Owen free,
purged him and brought him liberty.
        "Dear fair brother, make haste! Due speed!
1892   For that there is most urgent need,
be not surprised or taken here!
In your land day breaks, chevalier.
The prior comes to meet you; he,
1896   jubilant at your victory,
rejoicing, will receive you then,
into the church will lead you; soon
after that they will close the door
1900   by which you entered to come here."
        Owen received their benison,
then left the house; continued on.
        Then at the door he saw broad day.
1904   He saw the prior make his way
toward him rejoicing at the sight,
jubilant to receive the knight.
        Into the church he led him, where,
1908   for fifteen days he sojourned there,
in vigil, orison, and fast,
and mortified his flesh. That past,
Owen recounted all he'd seen,
1912   all he had done; he wrote it down.
        To honor his Creator, he
took up the Cross most lovingly;
he wished to seek Him in that land
1916   where the Jews had Our Lord condemned.
Thus he went to Jerusalem
to seek Him; then returned again
to serve his king, his sovereign,
1920   who happily retained the man.
All in good order Owen then
told his king what his life had been:
he asked his king for his advice,
1924   what sort of life he should embrace.
Should he become a monk? If so,

then to what order should he go?
But the king said, a chevalier
1928 he should remain, in service here
on earth; he should retain his post;
this was how he could serve God best.
And so throughout his life he did;
1932 in that way chose to serve his God.

Gilbert's Visit to Ireland

Just at the time of this event
a monk of Citeaux came there, sent
by his abbot to Ireland
1936 to obtain from the king some land
promised the abbot formerly;
and thus the monk was sent to see
about this land, determine where
1940 it lay, to build an abbey there.
This abbot had the name Gervaise;
a most religious man, he was,
abbot of Citeaux, and he sent
1944 to Ireland's king, with this intent,
Gilbert, a brother monk. (He was
abbot when death had claimed Gervaise.)
Gilbert was sent with inquiry—
1948 where was the abbey's site to be?
The king had Gilbert shown the place
he wished to build this edifice.
But then the monk expressed a fear—
1952 how could he work or function there?
He did not know or understand
the language spoken in that land!
But the king said, "Oh, have no fear!
1956 I'll give you an interpreter,
a good man; no man's worthier."
And then he called the chevalier
Owen, said he should go along
1960 with Gilbert, teach to him the tongue.
And Owen told the king that he
would do this service willingly,
at the king's pleasure. Candidly,
1964 great desire for this task had he.
"This is a whole truth I will share.
I lived another life, and there

I saw—I keep in memory—
1968   great glory; greater sanctity
within their order, had these men
than any folk I knew of, then."
    Owen remained with Gilbert there;
1972   he served him well, this chevalier,
but never changing his estate
to monk, lay brother; for his fate
was as a knight to die, to live;
1976   no other habit he'd receive.
The abbey they established, both;
placing there people of good faith;
Gilbert became the cellarer[9]
1980   and Owen his interpreter.
Owen a loyal servant was,
aiding in every need and cause.
Two and a half years was his stay,
1984   and then Sir Owen went his way.
Gilbert said Owen, staying there
lived a life holy, truly pure,
becoming to a chevalier;
1988   his leaving a great loss, for sure.
It must be said, though, after this,
the monks abandoned, quit this house,
and sought another one; in truth,
1992   they went to England and to Louth.[1]
    Owen remained in Ireland; there
he lived a life devout and pure.
Then he died, yielding up his soul
1996   to God, whom he had served so well.
    This Gilbert often said and spoke
of Owen's life to many folk
to edify them, for he thought
2000   that they would greatly benefit.
But one man doubted all the story
that Owen went to Purgatory.
Gilbert responded to that thought;
2004   those folk were not at all devout
who said that sight was spiritual,
and not at all corporeal,
when people entered in that house

---

9. The provisioner of food and drink in an abbey.
1. On the east coast of England, north of The Wash and south of the mouth of the Humber River.

2008   where God's purgation ordered was,
       the frightful torment and the pain
       that one was sure to find within.
       The chevalier rejected all;
2012   what he knew was corporeal!
       It was in flesh, it was in bone
       that he had all these torments known.
           "If suffering corporeal
2016   you won't accept, or Owen's tale,
       believe me; with my eyes, I knew
       something I shall recount to you.
           "I was in a religious house,
2020   and we had living there with us
       a monk, devout, who greatly strove
       to serve God well, and with much love.
       One time, though, in his cell at night,
2024   about to sleep, he had a sight
       —as he lay in his convent there—
       of devils who were drawing near.
       They came, they seized him bodily,
2028   and the poor monk they stole away.
       None of his brothers knew of it.
       The devils longed his goods to get!
       Three days, three nights, they held him; none,
2032   no brothers, knew that he was gone.
       Back to his bed then he was borne;
       they threw him down in furious scorn,
       whipped him and beat him; in their wrath
2036   they wounded him almost to death.
       His injuries were so profound,
       so wide, his body seemed all wound.
       Freely he came to me, to show
2040   his wounds, and tell this tale of woe.
       And, take note: never could he cure
       these wounds, of that you can be sure.
       Great they were, always horrible,
2044   fresh and raw, and as if like new.
       One wound, most ghastly and profound,
       dreadfully wide, was also round.
       His longest finger was too short
2048   to probe the bottom of this hurt.
       Whenever he saw younger folk
       act foolish, silly, mock and joke,
       he'd chide them candidly, and state
2052   if they could know what lay in wait,

griefs forced on them, and torments done—
they'd not make fun of anyone!
    In fifteen years he passed away—
2056 never forgotten, though, by me!"
    Gilbert told all this story, thus:
our author told, who then told us,[2]
just as Sir Owen told the tale,
2060 the monk I spoke of, he as well.
All of it I have here set down,
and in my text the story shown.
    Two abbots I consulted then,
2064 good ordained clergy, Irishmen.
I queried them: could these things be
the truth, in all sincerity?
    One of them said that all was true
2068 of Purgatory; and he knew
some who assayed that realm of pain;
but they did not return again.

Bishop Florentien's Story

    The very year I met these folk
2072 I also with a bishop spoke.
Nephew of Patrick Number Three,[3]
companion of Saint Malachy,[4]
he was, and named Florentien.
2076 Quite a sermon he said me then,
that Purgatory could be found
in his own diocese, his ground.
    Most eagerly I sought his word,
2080 if it was true, what I had heard;
and he said to me, certainly
true it was, and explained to me:
indeed, when many entered in,

---

2. I.e., H. of Saltrey.
3. Mentioned only in H. of Saltrey's *Tractatus* and then in Marie's poem, as *"tierz seint
   Patriz."* The idea that there were two Saint Patricks comes from a confusion between
   Saint Palladius, a Roman deacon who was the first bishop sent to Ireland and who seems
   to have been unsuccessful and stayed only a short time, and Saint Patrick, who is thought
   to have served Ireland in the second half of the fifth century and who affected the Irish
   people far more deeply. Curley mentions some church officials who could possibly be
   identified as the third Saint Patrick (10), but there is no good evidence that any of them
   were the person so named by H. or Marie.
4. A Cistercian who worked for the reform of Ireland in the early twelfth century. He died
   November 2, 1148, and was canonized in 1190. He may have been popularly thought
   of as a saint before canonization.

2084 they did not gain this world again,
     but there were those who did return,
     who had the torments seen and known.
     Forever after they were frail,
2088 their once good color blanched and pale,
     for all the suffering they had known,
     anguish that weighed on flesh and bone.
     If they led good lives, and devout,
2092 they would be saved, there was no doubt,
     and of their sins they would be free,
     pure, purged of them entirely.
          "Nearby there lives a saintly man,
2096 we believe a most worthy one,
     a hermit, virtuous, devout.
     Each night it happens, without doubt,
     he hears the devils gathering,
2100 around his precinct nattering.
     After sunset, in open air,
     he used to see them gather there,
     coming to hold their parliament;
2104 before the break of day, they went.
     But while assembled there, each one
     would tell their master what he'd done.
     The hermit could the devils see;
2108 he heard their stories frequently.
     They came to tempt him in his cell,
     but entrance found impossible.
     As naked women, in that form,
2112 they came and showed themselves to him,
     to trick him, trap him; this was how
     they thought they'd make him break his vow.
     From them he often learned the state
2116 of many folk, and of their fate."

Bishop Florentien's Chaplain's First Story

          He finished then, Lord Florentien.
     One of his chaplains rose up then.
          "Sire, let me tell a story, too,
2120 if I may have good leave from you,
     about this holy man, as well.
     What I have seen and heard, I'll tell."
          "Tell us! And we will lend an ear."
2124   The chaplain said, "Now, fair sire, hear.

The cell where lives this holy man
is, from the Mount of Saint Brendan[5]
one hundred long leagues; many a year
2128　another man has sojourned there,
choosing that way of life, that site,
and thought to be an eremite.[6]
To the first hermit—our first one—
2132　I went; he said—this is the sum—
nothing there was he wanted more
than to speak to this man, for sure.
His frequent wish, his keen intent:
2136　talk to him to his heart's content.
I asked the hermit, then, fair sire,
why he had such a keen desire.
　　"Because I have so often heard
2140　the devils talk of him. Their word
holds his life up to ridicule.
No hermit is this man, at all!
When the devils come here, at night,
2144　it is their joy and their delight
to tell of him and other folk,
often, whom they make do their work.
Truly I heard, the other night,
2148　one tale that, briefly, I'll recite.
The other night the devils went
to meet up in their parliament,
and to their *seigneur* to recount
2152　each one, the day's accomplishment.
They all approached him, one by one.
The master asked one what he'd done:
his question to this devil: had
2156　he brought the company some food?
　　"'Indeed, both bread and flour,' said he,
'butter and cheese I have with me.'
　　"'And where did you acquire this food?'
2160　　"'Oh, let me tell you; I'll be glad!
Two clerics met a peasant; said,
could he donate to them some bread,
for good works and for charity?
2164　The peasant told them no, though he
was well supplied; most plentiful

---

5. "Brandan Mountain is located on the Dingle Peninsula (Co. Kerry) in southwestern Ireland" (Curley's note, 163).
6. I.e., a hermit.

his bread and meat; his house was full.
He swore by charity he could
2168 not help, because he had no food.
Since he committed perjury
I took it all; with it made free;
He lost it. What I'd power to do,
2172 I did, and brought the food to you.'"
      "At that the devils went away,
they left the food just where it lay,
abandoning the stolen food
2176 that had been all the peasant's good.
      "I came that morning, found it there.
I tossed it in a ditch, for fear
that someone else, in passing, would
2180 find it, and eat this evil food."

Bishop Florentien's Chaplain's Second Story: Of a Priest's Temptation

      "Another tale I know, and it
should change you, to your benefit.
Beware the Devil! For he is
2184 most subtle and ingenious.
      "There was a holy man, a priest;
to serve his God he never ceased.
Mornings, to serve, this good priest rose;
2188 before he entered church, he chose
the graveyard for his services;
he sang full fifteen psalms, for those
good folk who lay at rest, in death,
2192 their souls; the souls of all on earth.
Chaste was his life; his teaching was
good, full of wisdom; virtuous,
for all those people, all those folk
2196 who sought his counsel; all his flock.
      "Devils bemoaned, with rage and grief,
that he led such a blameless life,
nothing could make him turn away
2200 from service to the Deity.
The master Devil, with contempt
fumed at his men, who could not tempt
this priest, or turn him from his way.
2204   "One devil told him: 'Many a day

I have been haunting this fine man.
Now, for the first time, I've a plan
that within fifteen years will work.
2208 Bewitched, betrayed, he'll be; my trick
will get this man; but not until
time is ripe shall we have our will.
By a woman I shall supply,
2212 he'll be seduced then easily.'
      "The master said, 'Much you'll have done
if you accomplish in this term
this task, to tempt him into sin.
2216 A fat reward from me you'll win!'
      "The next day, just as came the dawn,
the priest arose, and he had gone
into the cemetery, where
2220 a cast-off infant he saw there,
thrown down, it was, just by the Cross.
A girl. He picked her up. A nurse
was found for her; but still he thought her
2224 tiny girl, as like a daughter.
Reading and writing both he taught her,
and in God's service hoped to put her.
      "Then she became fifteen. By then
2228 she was a beauty, and well grown.
Often he gazed on her, with thought
the devil prompted, to exhort
and urge him, with his dreadful art;
2232 he coveted her in his heart.
Her beauty stunned him; more and more
taken he was with lust for her.
And then he asked her; and she said
2236 whatever pleased him, grant she would.
      "The very next night, just before
he planned to do his will with her,
the devils met in parliament,
2240 each to tell his accomplishment.
The devil stalking round the priest,
before them all could not resist
saying: what fifteen years before
2244 he'd promised, now was to occur.
Tomorrow would the priest be won,
while lost; by woman all undone.
She whom he'd sheltered as his daughter,
2248 carnally, in his bed, he'd get her,

well before noon! Each of them, hear!
"At this the devils made huge cheer:
"'Both we'll have taken, he and she!
2252   A double triumph this will be!'
"'Do you need help?' the master said.
"'No, sire: there's nothing that I need.'
The master grateful was, and pleased.
2256   "Hear now the deed done by the priest!
That morning to the girl he said,
"'Now, fair one, go up to my bed;
lie down in it, be sure you do;
2260   my pleasure I shall take with you.'
"The young girl went immediately
to do his will. He came to see
her lying there; he studied her;
2264   fiercely he thought on this affair.
The work he was about to do
the devil urged him to. He knew
all would be lost that he had done,
2268   all that he stood for, priest and man.
"He felt the Spirit work in him.
He rushed outside; left her within;
he took a knife—he was not false!—
2272   and he hacked off his genitals,
threw them far from him, instantly;
then to the devil up spoke he:
"'Hear, vicious spirit! Enemy!
2276   Pleasure you'll never have from me
or my damnation! Now you see,
lost, your cursed opportunity!'
"Night came. Soon after this event
2280   the devils met in parliament.
And now the master called upon
the man who'd promised everyone
that, before noon, he'd catch this priest
2284   with lust, the madness of a beast.
"'So,' said the chief, 'How did it go?'
"'Badly! This is a tale of woe!
All of my labor's come to naught!'
2288   "He told them all, he had not caught
the priest, who had escaped his snare.
"Oh, what disfavor had he there!
The master bade his servants: 'Go!
2292   Beat him for me! Whip, flail him so

you see he suffers horribly!'
Parliament done, they went their way.
   "The girl was in a convent placed
2296   to do God's service, by the priest."

Epilogue

   I, Marie, have put this book,
of Purgatory, for lay folk,
into French; may it useful be,
2300   understood, held in memory.
Now we pray God that through His grace
from our sins He deliver us.
Amen.

BACKGROUNDS
AND CONTEXTS

The Supernatural

MAN-WOLF, WEREWOLF: LEGENDS AND TRADITIONS

OVID

Ovid (Publius Ovidius Naso, 43 B.C.E–18 C.E.) was a Roman poet most famous for his mythological work *Metamorphoses*, but also known for the mythological *Fasti*, the love poetry of the *Amores* (Loves), the *Ars Amatoria* (Art of Love), and the tongue-in-cheek *Remedia Amores* (Cures for Love), as well as the *Heroides*, imaginary letters written by the wives of classical heroes to their husbands (e.g., Penelope to Odysseus). In 8 C.E. Ovid, who had somehow deeply offended the very upright Emperor Augustus, was exiled to Tomis, a small town on the Black Sea, where he lived, honored by its inhabitants but miserable and homesick, until his death; there he wrote eight poems of exile, the *Tristia*.

From The Metamorphoses[†]

Lycaon's Feast

> Now when great Jove, the son of Saturn, saw
> all this from his high citadel, he groaned,
> recalling an event then still too recent
> to be widely known: Lycaon's filthy banquet!
> And stirred by anger worthy of himself,
> he called a council of the gods to session:
> none of those summoned was the least bit late.
>   When the nighttime sky is clear, there can be seen
> 230 a highway visible in heaven, named
> the Milky Way, distinguished for its whiteness.
> Gods take this path to the royal apartments
> of Jove the Thunderer; on either side
> are palaces with folding doors flung wide,
> and filled with guests of their distinguished owners;

[†] From *Ovid's Metamorphoses*, translated by Charles Martin (New York: Norton, 2004), pp. 21–25. © 2004 by Charles Martin. Used by permission of W. W. Norton & Company, Inc.

plebeian gods reside in other sections,
but here in this exclusive neighborhood,
the most renowned of heaven's occupants
have *their* own household deities enshrined;
240 and if I were permitted to speak freely,
I would not hesitate to call this enclave
the Palatine of heaven's ruling class.
     So when, within their marble council chamber,
all of the gods assembled took their seats,
and Jove, above the others, leaned upon
his staff of ivory and shook three times
and four his awe-inspiring thick head
of hair, which makes the very cosmos tremble,
these words escaped from his indignant lips:
250 "I've never been more anxious for my realm,
not even when the serpent-footed Giants
were each preparing to take heaven captive
in the fierce embrace of his one hundred arms!
—That enemy was savage, to be sure,
but all the trouble came from just one source;
yet now, wherever Nereus is heard
resounding as he flows around the world,
the human race must perish; this I swear
by the rivers flowing underneath the earth
260 through Stygian groves; we have tried everything
to find a cure, but now the surgeon's blade
must cut away what is untreatable,
lest the infection spread to healthy parts.
     "I have my demigods to think about,
rustic divinities, the nymphs, the fauns,
the Satyrs, and the spirits of the forest
that dwell on mountainsides; although, as yet,
we haven't honored them with residence
in heaven, we must guarantee their safety
270 upon the earth which we have given them.
     "But can we? O my gods, can you believe
they will be safe, when I, who lord it over
lesser immortals *and* the thunderbolt,
have had snares set against me by a mortal
noted for beastliness? I mean—Lycaon!"
     All hell broke loose in heaven—what an uproar,
with everyone excitedly demanding
a punishment to fit such infamy!
It was as when that band of traitors raged
280 to annihilate the name of Rome by shedding

the blood of Caesar's heir; stunned by the frightful
prospect of utter ruin, the human race
throughout the world, as one, began to shudder;
nor was the piety of your own subjects,
Augustus, any less agreeable
to you than that of Jove's had been to him.
By voice and gesture, he suppressed the riot.
All held their peace.

                When the clamor had subsided,
curbed by the weight of his authority,

290 great Jove once more broke silence with these words:
"He has been dealt with—have no fears of that!
But I will now inform you of his crimes
and of their punishment.

                  "The age's infamy
had reached our ears; hoping to disprove it,
I glided down from the summit of Olympus,
concealing my godhood in a human form,
and walked upon the earth. Long would it take
to enumerate the evils that I found
in such abundance, everywhere I went:

300 the truth was even worse than I had heard.
    "I crossed Maenala, where the wild beasts roam,
Cyllene, and the pine groves of Lycaeus;
then on to the inhospitable abode
and seat of the tyrant of Arcadia,
approaching it as evening turned night.
    "By signs I let them know a god had come,
and common folk began to offer prayers;
at first Lycaon mocked their piety,
and then he said, 'I will make trial of him,

310 and prove beyond a shadow of a doubt
whether this fellow is a god or man.'
    "He planned to take me, overcome with sleep,
and murder me as I lay unawares;
that was his way of getting at the truth.
Nor was he satisfied with this: he took
a hostage sent by the Molossians,
and after severing his windpipe, cut
his body into pieces and then put
the throbbing parts up to be boiled or broiled.

320   "As soon as he had set this on the table,
I loosed my vengeful bolts until that house
collapsed on its deserving household gods!
    "Frightened, he runs off to the silent fields

and howls aloud, attempting speech in vain;
foam gathers at the corners of his mouth;
he turns his lust for slaughter on the flocks,
and mangles them, rejoicing still in blood.
    "His garments now become a shaggy pelt;
his arms turn into legs, and he, to wolf
330 while still retaining traces of the man:
greyness the same, the same cruel visage,
the same cold eyes and bestial appearance.
    "One house has fallen: many more deserve to;
over the broad earth, bestiality
prevails and stirs the Furies up to vengeance."

The Great Flood

Some of the gods give voice to their approval
of Jove's words and aggravate his grumbling,
while others play their roles with mute assent.
    Nevertheless, all of them were saddened
340 by the proposed destruction of the human race
and wondered what the future form of earth
could possibly be like, without men on it:
why, who would bring the incense to their altars?
    Was it his purpose to surrender earth
for wild beasts to plunder? As they debated,
the king of gods bade them not to worry,
for he would tend to everything himself,
and promised to provide them with a race
which, quite unlike the one he would destroy,
350 would be miraculous in its origin.
    Now he was just about to sprinkle earth
with thunderbolts, yet held back out of fear
that such a conflagration could ignite
the sacred heavens and set the skies ablaze;
and he recalled a time the Fates predicted,
when land and seas and heaven's palaces,
the universe so artfully devised,
should come to total ruin in a fire.
    He puts away those bolts the Cyclops forged;
360 another punishment now pleases him:
to sink the mortal race beneath the waves
and send down sheets of rain from up above.

*   *   *

PETRONIUS ARBITER

[Niceros's Story]†

* * *

Trimalchio now turned to his old friend Niceros. "You used to be better company, my friend," he said, "but now you're solemn and glum, and I don't know why. But if you'd like to make your host happy, why not tell us the story of your famous adventure?"

Niceros was delighted to have been singled out. "So help me," he said, "but may I never earn a thing, if I'm not ready to burst at your kind words. Well, here goes. Happiness here we come! Though I confess I'm a bit nervous our learned professors are going to laugh me down. Still, so what? I'll tell you my story and let them snicker. Better to tell a joke than be one, I say."

With these "winged words" our storyteller began. "When I was still a slave, we used to live in a narrow little street about where Gavilla's house stands now. There the gods decreed that I should fall in love with the wife of the tavernkeeper Terentius. You remember Melissa, don't you? Came from Tarentum and a buxom little package, if ever I saw one. But, you know, I loved her more for her moral character than her body. Whatever I wanted, she gladly supplied, and we always went halves. I gave her everything I had, and she'd stow it all safely away. What's more, she never cheated.

"Well, one day, down at the villa, her husband died. Needless to say, I moved heaven and earth to get to her, for a friend in need is a friend indeed. By a stroke of real luck my master had gone off to Capua to do some odds and ends of business. So I grabbed my chance and persuaded one of our guests to go with me as far as the fifth milestone. He was a soldier and strong as the devil. Well, we stumbled off at cockcrow with the moon shining down as though it were high noon. But where the road leads down between the graves, my man went off among the tombstones to do his business, while I sat by the road mumbling a song to keep my courage up and counting the graves. After a while I started looking around for him and suddenly I caught sight of him standing stark naked with all his clothes piled up on the side of the road. Well, you can imagine: I stood frozen, stiff as a corpse, my heart in my mouth. The next thing I knew he was pissing around his clothes and then, presto! he changed

† From *The Satyricon of Petronius* (dated to first century c.e.), translated by William Arrowsmith (Ann Arbor: University of Michigan Press, 1959), pp. 59–61. Translation copyright © 1959, renewed © 1987 by William Arrowsmith. Used by permission of Dutton Signet, a division of Penguin Group, and by the Estate of William Arrowsmith.

into a wolf. Don't think I'm making this up. I wouldn't kid you for anything. But like I was saying, he turned into a wolf, then started to howl and loped off for the woods. At first I couldn't remember where I was. Then I went to get his clothes and discovered they'd been changed into stones. By now, let me tell you, I was *scared*. But I pulled out my sword and slashed away at the shadows all the way to my girlfriend's house. I arrived as white as a ghost, almost at the last gasp, with the sweat pouring down my crotch and my eyes bugging out like a corpse. I don't know how I ever recovered. Melissa, of course, was surprised to see me at such an hour and said, 'If you'd only come a little earlier, you could have lent us a hand. A wolf got into the grounds and attacked the sheep. The place looked like a butchershop, blood all over. He got away in the end, but we had the last laugh. One of the slaves nicked him in the throat with a spear.'

"That finished me. I couldn't sleep a wink the rest of the night and as soon as it was light, I went tearing back home like a landlord chasing the tenants. When I reached the spot where my friend's clothing had been turned into stones, there was nothing to be seen but blood. But when I got home, I found the soldier stretched out in bed like a poleaxed bull and the doctor inspecting his neck. By now, of course, I knew he was a werewolf and you couldn't have made me eat a meal with him to save my own life. You're welcome to think what you like of my story, but may the gods strike me dead if I'm feeding you a lie."

Far from doubting him, we were all dumb with astonishment. "I, for one," said Trimalchio, "wouldn't dream of doubting you. In fact, if you'll believe me, I had goosebumps all over. I know old Niceros and he's no liar. Nope, he's truth itself and never exaggerates. * * *

GIRALDUS CAMBRENSIS

Of the Prodigies of Our Times, and First of a Wolf Which Conversed With a Priest†

I now proceed to relate some wonderful occurrences which have happened within our time. About three years before the arrival of Earl John in Ireland, it chanced that a priest, who was journeying from Ulster towards Meath, was benighted in a certain wood on the borders of Meath. While, in company with only a young lad, he was watching by a fire which he had kindled under the branches of a

†   From *Topographica Hibernica*, trans. Thomas Forester, 1913, in *A Lycanthropy Reader: Werewolves in Western Culture*, ed. Charlotte F. Otten.

spreading tree, lo! a wolf came up to them, and immediately addressed them to this effect: "Rest secure, and be not afraid, for there is no reason you should fear, where no fear is!" The travellers being struck with astonishment and alarm, the wolf added some orthodox words referring to God. The priest then implored him, and adjured him by Almighty God and faith in the Trinity, not to hurt them, but to inform them what creature it was that in the shape of a beast uttered human words. The wolf, after giving catholic replies to all questions, added at last: "There are two of us, a man and a woman, natives of Ossory, who, through the curse of one Natalis, saint and abbot, are compelled every seven years to put off the human form, and depart from the dwellings of men. Quitting entirely the human form, we assume that of wolves. At the end of the seven years, if they chance to survive, two others being substituted in their places, they return to their country and their former shape. And now, she who is my partner in this visitation lies dangerously sick not far from hence, and, as she is at the point of death, I beseech you, inspired by divine charity, to give her the consolations of your priestly office."

At this word the priest followed the wolf trembling, as he led the way to a tree at no great distance, in the hollow of which he beheld a she-wolf, who under that shape was pouring forth human sighs and groans. On seeing the priest, having saluted him with human courtesy, she gave thanks to God, who in this extremity had vouch-safed to visit her with such consolation. She then received from the priest all the rites of the church duly performed, as far as the last communion. This also she importunately demanded, earnestly supplicating him to complete his good offices by giving her the viat-icum. The priest stoutly asserting that he was not provided with it, the he-wolf, who had withdrawn to a short distance, came back and pointed out a small missal-book, containing some consecrated wafers, which the priest carried on his journey, suspended from his neck, under his garment, after the fashion of the country. He then intreated him not to deny them the gift of God, and the aid destined for them by Divine Providence, and, to remove all doubt, using his claw for a hand, he tore off the skin of the she-wolf, from the head down to the navel, folding it back. Thus she immediately presented the form of an old woman. The priest, seeing this, and compelled by his fear more than his reason, gave the communion, the recipient having earnestly implored it, and devoutly partaking of it. Immediately afterwards, the he-wolf rolled back the skin, and fitted it to its original form.

These rites having been duly, rather than rightly, performed, the he-wolf gave them his company during the whole night at their little fire, behaving more like a man than a beast. When morning came, he led them out of the wood, and, leaving the priest to pursue his jour-ney, pointed out to him the direct road for a long distance. At his departure, he also gave him many thanks for the benefit he had conferred, promising him still greater returns of gratitude, if the Lord should call him back from his present exile, two parts of which he had already completed. At the close of their conversation, the priest inquired of the wolf whether the hostile race which had now landed in the island would continue there for the time to come, and be long established in it. To which the wolf replied:—"For the sins of our nation, and their enormous vices, the anger of the Lord, falling on an evil generation, hath given them into the hands of their enemies. Therefore, as long as this foreign race shall keep the commandments of the Lord, and walk in his ways, it will be secure and invincible, but if, as the downward path to illicit pleasures is easy, and nature is prone to follow vicious examples, this people shall chance, from living among us, to adopt our depraved habits, doubtless they will provoke the divine vengeance on themselves also."

The like judgment is recorded in Leviticus:—"All these abominations have the inhabitants of the land done, which were before you, the land is defiled. Beware, therefore, that the land spue not you out also, when ye defile it, as it spued out the nation which was before you." All this was afterwards brought to pass, first by the Chaldeans, and then by the Romans. Likewise it is written in Ecclesiasticus:—"The kingdom is made over from one nation to another, by reason or their unjust and injurious deeds, their proud words, and divers deceits."

It chanced, about two years afterwards, that I was passing through Meath, at the time when the bishop of that land had convoked a synod, having also invited the assistance of the neighbouring bishops and abbots, in order to have their joint counsels on what was to be done in the affair which had come to his knowledge by the priest's confession. The bishop, hearing that I was passing through those parts, sent me a message by two of his clerks, requesting me, if possible, to be personally present when a matter of so much importance was under consideration, but if I could not attend, he begged me at least to signify my opinion in writing. The clerks detailed to me all the circumstances, which indeed I had heard before from other persons, and, as I was prevented by urgent business from being present at the synod, I made up for my absence by giving them the benefit of my advice in a letter. The bishop and synod, yielding to it, ordered the priest to appear before the pope with letters from them, setting forth what had occurred, with the priest's confession, to which instrument the bishops and abbots who were present at the synod affixed their seals.

It cannot be disputed, but must be believed with the most assured faith, that the divine nature assumed human nature for the salvation of the world; while in the present case, by no less a miracle, we find that at God's bidding, to exhibit his power and righteous judgment, human nature assumed that of a wolf. But is such an animal to be called a brute or a man? A rational animal appears to be far above the level of a brute; but who will venture to assign a quadruped, which inclines to the earth, and is not a laughing animal, to the species of man? Again, if any one should slay this animal, would he be called a homicide? We reply, that divine miracles are not to be made the subjects of disputation by human reason, but to be admired. However, Augustine, in the 16th book of his Civit. Dei, chapter 8, in speaking of some monsters of the human race, born in the East, some of which had the heads of dogs, others had no heads at all, their eyes being placed in their breasts, and others had various deformities, raises the question whether these were really men, descended from the first parents of mankind. At last, he concludes, "We must think the same of them as we do of those monstrous births in the human species of which we often hear, and true reason declares that whatever answers to the definition of man, as a rational and mortal animal, whatever be its form, is to be considered a man." The same author, in the 18th book of the Civit. Dei, chapter 18, refers to the Arcadians, who, chosen by lot, swam across a lake and were there changed into wolves, living with wild beasts of the same species in the deserts of that country. If, however, they did not devour human flesh, after nine years they swam back across the lake, and reassumed the human form. Having thus further treated of various transformations of man into the shape of wolves, he at length adds, "I myself, at the time I was in Italy, heard it said of some district in those parts, that there the stable-women, who had learnt magical arts, were wont to give something to travellers in their cheese which transformed them into beasts of burthen, so that they carried all sorts of burdens, and after they had performed their tasks resumed their own forms. Meanwhile, their minds did not become bestial, but remained human and rational." So in the Book which Apuleius wrote, with the title of the Golden Ass, he tells us that it happened to himself, on taking some potion, to be changed into an ass, retaining his human mind.

In our time, also, we have seen persons who, by magical arts, turned any substance about them into fat pigs, as they appeared (but they were always red), and sold them in the markets. However, they disappeared as soon as they crossed any water, returning to their real nature; and with whatever care they were kept, their assumed form did not last beyond three days. It has also been a frequent complaint, from old times as well as in the present, that certain hags in Wales, as well as in Ireland and Scotland, changed themselves into the shape of hares, that, sucking teats under this counterfeit form, they might stealthily rob other people's milk. We agree, then, with Augustine, that neither demons nor wicked men can either create or really change their natures; but those whom God has created can, to outward appearance, by his permission, become transformed, so that they appear to be what they are not; the senses of men being deceived and laid asleep by a strange illusion, so that things are not seen as they actually exist, but are strangely drawn by the power of some phantom or magical incantation to rest their eyes on unreal and fictitious forms.

It is, however, believed as an undoubted truth, that the Almighty God, who is the Creator of natures, can, when he pleases, change one into another, either for vindicating his judgments, or exhibiting his divine power; as in the case of Lot's wife, who, looking back contrary to her lord's command, was turned into a pillar of salt; and as the water was changed into wine; or that, the nature within remaining the same, he can transform the exterior only, as is plain from the examples before given.

Of that apparent change of the bread into the body of Christ (which I ought not to call apparent only, but with more truth transubstantial, because, while the outward appearance remains the same, the substance only is changed), I have thought it safest not to treat, its comprehension being far beyond the powers of the human intellect.

CHARLOTTE F. OTTEN

From A Lycanthropy Reader†

* * *

In English usage the word *werewolf* antedates the word *lycanthrope* by about five centuries. According to Ernest Weekley in *More Words Ancient and Modern*, the word *wer* [*were*] "is found in all the Teutonic languages and is cognate with Lat. *vir*, Gaelic *fear*, Welsh *gwr*, Sanskrit *vira*.,"[1] The first recorded use of the word *werewolf* appears in the Ecclesiastical Ordinances of King Cnut (1017–1035):

> Thonne moton tha hyrdas beon swydhe wacore and geornlice clypigende, the widh thonne theodsceadhan folce sceolan scyldan, thaet syndon biscopas and maessepreostas, the godcunde heorda bewarian and bewarian sceolan, mid wislican laran, thaet se wodfreca werewulf to swidhe ne slyte ne to fela ne abite of godcundse heorde. [Therefore must the shepherds be very

---

† From *A Lycanthropy Reader: Werewolves in Western Culture*, Charlotte F. Otten, ed. (Syracuse: Syracuse University Press, 1986), pp. 5–9. Copyright © 1986 by Syracuse University Press. Reprinted by permission of the publisher.
1. Ernest Weekley, *More Words Ancient and Modern* (London, 1927), 181–84.

watchful and diligently crying out, who have to shield the people against the spoiler, such are bishops and mass-priests, who are to preserve and defend their spiritual flocks with wise instructions, that the madly audacious were-wolf do not too widely devastate, nor bite too many of the spiritual flock.][2]

Obviously symbolic, this Old English werewolf in ecclesiastical jurisprudence is rooted in the Scriptures. The image of the wolf attacking the flock appears in Christ's Sermon on the Mount: "Beware of false prophets, which come to you in sheep's clothing, but inwardly they are ravening wolves" (Matt. 7:15, AV); and in Paul's address to the Ephesians: "For I know this, that after my departing shall grievous wolves enter in among you, not sparing the flock" (Acts 20:21 AV). The shift in the image of wolf to werewolf may well indicate the perception of a closer alliance with Satan than the word *wolf* (although ravening and grievous) connotes. The image cluster in the Ecclesiastical Ordinances has roughly the following equivalences:

sheep/flock = Christian parishioners who are vulnerable to spiritual attack by Satanic forces.

shepherds = bishops and priests who are instructed to protect their "flock" from diabolic attack.

werewolf = Satan and his cohorts who wish to destroy the faith of the "sheep" and to damn them to perdition.

In these Laws of the Church there is no hint that the word *werewolf* could refer to a human being whose mental state of aberration is associated with lycanthropic delusion, a psychological condition recognized for centuries in medicine. Nor is this a reference to St. Augustine's well-known pronouncements on physical metamorphosis:

It is very generally believed that by certain witches' spells and the power of the Devil men may be changed into wolves . . . but they do not lose their human reason and understanding, nor are their minds made the intelligence of a mere beast. Now this must be understood in this way: namely, that the Devil creates no new nature, but that he is able to make something appear to be which in reality is not. For by no spell nor evil power can the mind, nay, not even the body corporeally, be changed into the material limbs and features of any animal . . . but a man is fantastically and by illusion metamorphosed into an animal, albeit he to himself seems to be a quadruped.[3]

What is remarkable in this Anglo-Saxon legal use of the word *werewolf* is the substitution of *werewolf* for the Scriptural *wolf*. Satan is seen as

---

2. *Ancient Laws and Institutes of England*, edited by B. Thorpe (London, 1840), 160–61.
3. St. Augustine, *De Spiritu et Anima*, cap. 26; *De Civitate Dei*, lib. 18, cap. 17.

enlisting humans as allies and servants, adding them to his demonic hosts. This is a covert acknowledgment of Satan's capacity to change humans into werewolves, that is, the instigation to werewolfism is Satan's, but the human will collaborates in the spiritual metamorphosis. Bishops and priests are warned about the subtle, undetectable transformations threatening the spiritual life, of the flock.

The spiritual symbolic use continues in Middle English. *Pierce the Ploughmans Crede* (c. 1394) paraphrases Matt. 7:15 and uses *werwolves* in place of *wolves:*

> *In vestimentis ouium* but onlie with-inne
> Thei ben wilde wer-wolues that wiln the folk robben. (458–9)[4]

Satan is the specific source of evil: werewolves are his captive agents.

Simultaneous with this use in ecclesiastical and spiritual contexts is the emergence of the werewolf in narrative contexts. Reminiscent of the physical transformation in ancient myth (Homer, Virgil, Ovid, Petronius), these narratives return to physical metamorphosis; the werewolf in the Middle English narratives, however, is not the generalized moral evil of ancient mythology but the helpless victim of domestic crime, usually adultery. The scheming wife (and her lover) are the agents of the transformation. The Celtic tale of *Arthur and Gorlagon* (Latin version, late fourteenth century) is a story of physical transformation through female betrayal. The etymology of *Gorlagon* reveals the werewolf, according to Alfred Nutt: "*Gorlagon* is by metathesis for *Gorgalon*, an expanded form of *Gorgol* = Old Welsh *Guruol* or *Guorguol*, the first syllable of which is cognate to Latin *vir*, Anglo-Saxon *wer*.) * * *

Sir Thomas Malory's *Le Morte Darthur* (1470) has a similar betrayal: a good knight was "bitrayed with his wyf for she made hym seuen yere a werwolf."[5]

In the French *Roman de Guillaume de Palerne*, translated into Middle English about 1350, the werewolf is a Spanish prince who has been transformed by his cruel stepmother. The word *werwolf* occurs frequently throughout the poem, whose subtitle is *William and the Werwolf:*

> For i wol of the werwolf a wile nov speke.
> Whanne this werwolf was come to his wolnk denne. (79–80)[6]

In the narratives of the Middle Ages the werewolf shifted its shapes away from the ancient myths of Greece and Rome, the spiritual uses

---

4. *Pierce the Ploughbmans Crede*, edited by W. W. Skeat, Early English Text Society (London, 1867), 17.
5. Sir Thomas Malory, *Le Morte Darthur*, edited by H. Oskar Sommer, Vol. I (London, 1889), 793.
6. *William of Palerne*, edited by W. W. Skeat, Early English Text Society, (London, 1867), 9.

of the ecclesiastical courts, and the paraphrases of the Scriptures. The ancient myths told of moral changes in humans that converted them into animals, Odysseus's men, for example, were changed by Circe into beasts. Ovid's *Metamorphoses* records the story of Lycaon, the savage king of Arcadia, who, when visited by the god Jupiter in disguise, served him a dinner of human flesh. Outraged by this display of cannibalism, Jupiter transformed Lycaon into what corresponded to his moral appetites: into an irrational, bestial human-wolf. These myths are a realistic (though symbolic) assessment of the moral dimensions of human life * * *. The werewolves of the ecclesiastical courts and the Scriptures were manifestations of the Devil's power in human lives. But the werewolves of medieval narratives were victims of domestic plotting. It is a puzzling change, although the anti-feminist bias of the period may be a factor in the shift. The effect on the reader also undergoes a radical change. While the ancient myths are powerful warnings to humans to abstain from indulging bestial appetites and from obeying irrational promptings, and the ecclesiastical and Scriptural werewolves are to be feared because of the wily stratagems of the Devil who goes about "seeking whom he may devour" (I Peter 5:8 AV), the werewolf in the medieval narratives evokes pity and sympathy for the werewolf, who, banished by fellow humans, was barbarized by his shape and excluded from human fellowship and love.[7]

THE FAIRY LOVER

THOMAS CHESTRE

From Sir Launfal[†]

* * *

A gerfawcon[1] sche bar on her hond,
A softe pas[2] her palfray fond,

---

7. For a curious etymology, see Montague Summers, *The Werewolf* (New York: University Books, 1966), 12, who quotes from *The Booke of huntynge or Master of game* (c. 1400), chap vii: "Of ye Wolf and of his nature ther ben some that eten chyldren & men and eteth noon other flesh from that tyme that thei be a charmed with mannys flesh, ffor rather thei wolde be deed. And thei be cleped Werewolfes for men shulde be war of him," Bodley MS. 546, 35ᵛ.

† From *The Breton Lays in Middle English*, ed. Thomas C. Rumble (Detroit: Wayne State University Press, 1965), pp. 40–43. Copyright © 1965 Wayne State University Press. Reprinted with the permission of the publisher and Clayton T. Rumble and Bruce B. Rumble, sons of Thomas C. Rumble. Dated to late fourteenth century.

1. Hunting falcon.
2. An easy pace.

That men her schuld beholde;
Thorugh Karlyon rood that lady;
Twey whyte grehoundys ronne hyr by;
966   Har colers were of golde.

And whan Launfal sawe that lady,
To alle the folk he gon crye an hy,
Bothe to yonge and olde:
"Here," he seyde, "comyth my lemman swete!
Sche myghte me of my balys bete,[3]
972   Yef that lady wolde!"

Forth sche wente ynto the halle,
Ther was the quene and the ladyes alle,
And also Kyng Artour;
Her maydenes come ayens her ryght,
To take her styrop whan sche lyght,
978   Of the lady, Dame Tryamour.

Sche dede of her mantyll on the flet[4]
That men schuld her beholde the bet,[5]
Wythoute a more sojour;[6]
Kyng Artour gan her fayre grete,
And sche hym agayn wyth wordes swete,
984   That were of greet valour.

Up stod the quene and ladyes stoute,[7]
Her for to beholde all aboute,
How evene sche stod upryght;[8]
Than wer they wyth her al so donne
As ys the mone ayen the sonne,
990   A-day whan hyt ys lyght.[9]

Than seyde sche to Artour the kyng:
"Syr, hydyr I com for swych a thyng,
To skere[1] Launfal the knyght—
That he never, yn no folye,

---

3. *I.e.* she might set right my troubles.
4. Floor.
5. Better.
6. Delay.
7. Tall, graceful.
8. How stately was her bearing.
9. Compared with her, they were as pale as the moon against the sun in daylight.
1. To prove the innocence of.

Besofte the quene of no drurye,[2]

996 By dayes ne be nyght.

Therfor, Syr Kyng, good kepe thou nyme:[3]
He bad naght her, but sche bad hym
Here lemman for to be;
And he answerede her and seyde
That hys lemmannes lothlokest mayde

1002 Was fayryr than was sche."

Kyng Artour seyde, wythouten othe,
"Ech man may yse that ys sothe,
Bryghtere that ye be!"[4]
Wyth that, Dame Tryamour to the quene geth,
And blew on her swych a breth

1008 That never eft[5] myght sche se.

The lady lep an hyr palfray,
And bad hem alle have good day;
Sche nolde no lengere abyde.
Wyth that com Gyfre all so prest,[6]
Wyth Launfalys stede out of the forest,

1014 And stode Launfal besyde.

The knyght to horse began to sprynge,
Anoon, wythout any lettynge,
Wyth hys lemman away to ryde.
The lady tok her maydenys achon,[7]
And wente the way that sche hadde er gon,

1020 Wyth solas and wyth pryde.

The lady rod thorugh[8] Cardeuyle,
Fer ynto a jolyf ile,
Olyroun that hyghte;[9]
Every yer,[1] upon a certayne day,

---

2. Adultery.
3. Ms. *myne*; I have emended to derive the word from O.E. *nimman*, "to take"; thus "take good keep," an idiom still heard (Rumble's note).
4. Everyone can see that it is the truth: you are the fairer.
5. Again, after.
6. Quickly.
7. Each one.
8. Ms. *dor3*.
9. Was named.
1. Ms. *er*.

Me may here[2] Launfales stede nay,
1026   And hym se wyth syght.

Ho[3] that wyll ther axsy justus,[4]
To kepe hys armes fro the rustus,
In turnement other fyght,
Dar[5] he never forther gon:
Ther he may fynde justes anoon
1032   Wyth Syr Launfal the knyght.

Thus Launfal, wythouten fable,
That noble knyght of the Rounde Table,
Was take ynto fayrye;[6]
Sethe[7] saw hym yn thys lond no man,
Ne no more of hym telle Y, ne can,
1038   For sothe, wythoute lye.

Thomas Chestre made thys tale
Of the noble knyght, Syr Launfale,
Good of chyvalrye;
Jhesus, that ys Hevene-Kyng,
Yeve us alle Hys blessyng,
And Hys Modyr Marye!

                                         Amen
                              Explicit Launfal

ANONYMOUS

This ballad, drawn from a Middle English romance thought to be
dated about 1400 (from which the ballad tale differs in some respects)
and from legends about the thirteenth-century Scots laird Thomas of
Ercildoune, was first published by Walter Scott (1803), who wrote a lon-
ger version himself, and later by Robert Jamieson (1806); their source
was an informant named Mrs. Brown of Falkland (1747–1810). See
Bertrand S. Bronson, "Mrs. Brown and the Ballad," *California Folklore
Quarterly* 4. 2 (1945): 129–40. Child made good use of Scott's and Jamie-
son's work and of their informants' material. Susan Stewart suggests that
Keats's poem "La Belle Dame Sans Merci" is based on the Thomas
legend, which seems very likely; see her *Poetry and the Fate of the
Senses* (Chicago: University of Chicago Press, 2002), p. 26.

2. One may hear.
3. Whoever.
4. Ask to loust.
5. Need.
6. The land of faery.
7. Afterward; ms. *seppe*.

Thomas Rymer[†]

Child Ballad #37

37A.1 True Thomas lay oer yond grassy bank,
And he beheld a ladie gay,
A ladie that was brisk and bold,
Come riding oer the fernie brae.

37A.2 Her skirt was of the grass-green silk,
Her mantel of the velvet fine,
At ilka tett of her horse's mane
Hung fifty silver bells and nine.

37A.3 True Thomas he took off his hat,
And bowed him low down till his knee:
'All hail, thou mighty Queen of Heaven!
For your peer on earth I never did see.'

37A.4 'O no, O no, True Thomas,' she says,
'That name does not belong to me;
I am but the queen of fair Elfland,
And I'm come here for to visit thee.

• • • • •

37A.5 'But ye maun go wi me now, Thomas,
True Thomas, ye maun go wi me,
For ye maun serve me seven years,
Thro weel or wae as may chance to be.'

37A.6 She turned about her milk-white steed,
And took True Thomas up behind,
And aye wheneer her bridle rang,
The steed flew swifter than the wind.

37A.7 For forty days and forty nights
He wade thro red blude to the knee,
And he saw neither sun nor moon,
But heard the roaring of the sea.

37A.8 O they rade on, and further on,
Until they came to a garden green:
'Light down, light down, ye ladie free,
Some of that fruit let me pull to thee.'

37A.9 'O no, O no, True Thomas,' she says,
'That fruit maun not be touched by thee,
For a' the plagues that are in hell
Light on the fruit of this countrie.

---

† From *The English and Scottish Popular Ballads*, ed. Francis James Child (Boston: Houghton Mifflin, 1884–98), Vol. I (1884), pp. 317–29.

37A.10 'But I have a loaf here in my lap,
        Likewise a bottle of claret wine,
        And now ere we go farther on,
        We'll rest a while, and ye may dine.'

37A.11 When he had eaten and drunk his fill,
        'Lay down your head upon my knee,'
        The lady sayd, ''re we climb yon hill,
        And I will show you fairlies three.

37A.12 'O see not ye yon narrow road,
        So thick beset wi thorns and briers?
        That is the path of righteousness,
        Tho after it but few enquires.

37A.13 'And see not ye that braid braid road,
        That lies across yon lillie leven?
        That is the path of wickedness,
        Tho some call it the road to heaven.

37A.14 'And see not ye that bonny road,
        Which winds about the fernie brae?
        That is the road to fair Elfland,
        Whe[re] you and I this night maun gae.

37A.15 'But Thomas, ye maun hold your tongue,
        Whatever you may hear or see,
        For gin ae word you should chance to speak,
        You will neer get back to your ain countrie.'

37A.16 He has gotten a coat of the even cloth,
        And a pair of shoes of velvet green,
        And till seven years were past and gone
        True Thomas on earth was never seen.

GEOFFREY CHAUCER[†]

The Tale of Sir Thopas is a burlesque of popular romances. These were stripped-down, cliché-ridden versions of French chivalric romances, composed and recited by minstrels for unsophisticated English audiences with little or no French and no taste for the stylistic refinements and psychological subtleties that appealed to more courtly audiences in both France and England. The emphasis was on plenty of action— love and adventure; the slaying of giants, dragons, and wicked knights; the rescue of fair maidens. Chaucer doubtless enjoyed such medieval horse operas for their very absurdities, and his satire shows a connoisseur's

† From *The Norton Anthology of English Literature,* Fifth Edition, Vol. 1, ed. M. H. Abrams et al. (New York: Norton, 1986), p. 201, note 1. Copyright © 1986, 1979, 1974, 1968, 1962 by W. W. Norton & Company, Inc. Used by permission of W. W. Norton & Company, Inc.

eye for hackneyed and inane detail. His hero Sir Thopas, in ancestry, personal appearance, costume, sports, love-longing, horsemanship, oaths, and encounter with a three-headed giant, lampoons such popular derring-do heroes as Bevis of Hampton and Guy of Warwick. Sir Thopas's birthplace in Flanders would mark him to the English as ultra-bourgeois; his exaggeratedly white complexion and rosy lips link him to the heroines of the romances.

Chaucer burlesques not only the plot but also the style of such performances. Oral delivery demanded first of all a dogtrot rhythm, and, secondly, a handy store of formulas to fit all occasions, especially those occasions when the poet was stuck for a rhyme. Chaucer's imitation is an exercise in brilliant monotony and witty banality.

But within the frame story of the *Canterbury Tales*, Chaucer's parody turns into a truly Olympian jest about the nature of art and artists. The Introduction to the tale brings onstage again the narrator who described his fellow pilgrims with such wide-eyed enthusiasm in the General Prologue and apologized for the fact that a strict adherence to truth obliged him to relate every word spoken on the pilgrimage, no matter how vulgar and offensive. Here the Host draws a portrait of this pilgrim, inviting him to tell a tale, and the pilgrim apologizes once again—the only story he knows is a rhyme he learned long ago. Thus on the literal level of the frame story the creator of the entire pilgrimage knows only one tale, and that one so wretched that he is not allowed to finish it. The supreme irony of the Tale of Sir Thopas may be the author's humble acknowledgment, within the frame of his fiction, that he, too, is a member of the tribe of versifiers who strove according to their greatly varying talents to provide the best rhymes and entertainment that they could.

The Tale of Sir Thopas (ca. 1390)[†]

Whan seyd was al this miracle,° every man	*i.e., the Prioress's tale of a miracle*
As sobre was° that wonder was to se,	*Was so grave, serious*
Til that our Hoste japen tho bigan,°	*began then to jest, joke*
And than at erst° he loked upon me	*for the first time*
And seyde thus: "What man artow?"° quod he.	*art thou*
"Thou lokest as° thou woldest finde an hare,	*as if*
For ever upon the ground I see thee stare.	
Approche neer° and loke up merily.	*nearer*
Now war yow,° sirs, and lat this man have place.	*pay attention*

695 is the line number marked at "And seyde thus."

† From *The Canterbury Tales: A Norton Critical Edition*, Second Edition. ed. V. A. Kolve and Glending Olson (New York: Norton, 2005), pp. 255–61. Copyright © 2005, 1989 by W. W. Norton & Company, Inc. Used by permission of W. W. Norton & Company, Inc.

700 He in the waast° is shape as wel as I.	*waist*
This were a popet° in an arm t'enbrace°	*little doll / to embrace*
For any womman, smal and fair of face.	
He semeth elvish by his contenaunce,[1]	
For unto no wight° dooth he daliaunce.°	*person / is he sociable*
705 Sey now somwhat, sin° other folk han sayd.°	*since / have spoken*
Tel us a tale of mirthe, and that anoon."	
"Hoste," quod I, "ne beth nat yvel apayd,°	*do not be displeased*
For other tale certes° can° I noon,	*certainly / know*
But of° a ryme I lerned longe agoon."	*Except*
710 "Ye, that is good," quod he. "Now shul we here	
Som deyntee° thing, me thinketh by his	*pleasant / look,*
chere."°	*expression*

The Tale

[THE FIRST FIT][2]

Listeth,° lordes, in good entent,°	*Listen / with good will*
And I wol telle verrayment°	*truly*
Of mirthe and of solas:	
715 Al of a knyght was fair and gent°	*noble, elegant*
In bataille and in tourneyment;	*topaz (a yellow*
His name was sir Thopas.°	*semiprecious stone)*
Y-born he was in fer° contree,	*far, distant*
In Flaundres° al biyonde the see,	*Flanders (Belgium)*
720 At Popering,° in the place.	*a Flemish market town*
His fader was a man ful free,°	*noble, generous*
And lord he was of that contree,	
As it was Goddes grace.	
Sir Thopas wex a doghty	*grew into a bold young*
swayn.°	*man, squire*
725 Whyt was his face as payndemayn,°	*fine white bread*
His lippes rede as rose.	
His rode° is lyk scarlet in grayn,°	*complexion / scarlet dye*
And I yow telle in good certayn,°	*in certainty*
He hadde a semely° nose.	*seemly, handsome*

1. He seems elfish, from the look of him. "Elvish" is often glossed as "distracted, abstracted" but literally means someone mysterious, from another world of being; cf. the realm of "Fairye" (l. 802).
2. We follow John Burrow's argument that the Tale of Sir Thopas is divided into three parts or "fits" (see l. 888), the second fit half as long as the first, the third half as long as the second.

730 His heer, his berd was lyk saffroun,°	saffron (deep yellow)
That to his girdel° raughte° adoun;	belt / reached
His shoon° of Cordewane.°	shoes / cordovan (Spanish) leather
Of Brugges° were his hosen	Bruges (in Flanders)
broun,°	brown tights
His robe was of ciclatoun,°	costly embroidered silk
735 That coste many a jane.°	a silver coin of Genoa

He coude° hunte at wilde deer,°	knew how to / animals
And ryde an hauking for riveer°	go hawking for waterfowl
With grey goshauk° on honde.	a kind of hawk
Therto° he was a good archeer;	In addition
740 Of wrastling was ther noon his peer,°	equal
Ther° any ram shal stonde.°	Where / be put up as a prize

Ful many a mayde, bright in bour,°	bedchamber
They moorne° for him paramour,°	yearn / with love-longing
Whan hem were bet° to slepe.	it would be better for them
745 But he was chast° and no lechour,°	chaste / lecher
And sweet as is the bremble-flour°	bramble flower (dog rose)
That bereth the rede hepe.°	rose hip

And so bifel° upon a day,	it happened
For sothe,° as I yow telle may,	In truth
750 Sir Thopas wolde out ryde.°	decided to ride out
He worth upon° his stede° gray,	gets up on / steed
And in his honde a launcegay,°	a light lance
A long swerd by his syde.	

He priketh° thurgh a fair forest,	pricks, spurs his horse
755 Therinne is many a wilde best,	
Ye, bothe bukke° and hare;	buck, male deer
And as he priketh north and est,	
I telle it yow, him° hadde almost°	(to) him / almost
Bitid° a sory care.°	Happened / sad misfortune

760 Ther springen herbes grete and smale,	
The lycorys° and cetewale,°	licorice / zedoary (like ginger)
And many a clowe-gilofre;°	clove
And notemuge° to putte in ale,	nutmeg
Whether it be moyste° or stale,°	fresh / stale, old
765 Or for to leye in cofre.°³	put in a chest

3. None of the spice-bearing plants named in this stanza would be found growing in Flanders. Like many other details in the story, they are part of the exotic landscape of romance that Chaucer playfully invokes throughout.

The briddes singe, it is no nay,°   *it cannot be denied*
The sparhauk° and the papeiay,°   *sparrow hawk / parrot*
    That joye it was to here.°   *hear (them)*
The thrustelcok° made eek his   *male thrush*
        lay,°   *also sang (composed) his song*
770 The wodedowve° upon the spray°   *wood pigeon / branch*
    She sang ful loude and clere.

Sir Thopas fil° in love-longinge   *fell*
Al whan he herde the thrustel° singe,   *thrush*
    And priked° as he were wood.°   *rode / mad*
775 His faire stede° in° his prikinge   *steed / because of*
So swatte° that men mighte him wringe;   *sweated*
    His sydes were al blood.°   *covered with blood*

Sir Thopas eek so wery was
For prikinge on the softe gras
780   (So fiers° was his corage°)   *fierce, ferocious / heart, spirit*
That doun he leyde him in that plas°   *place*
To make° his stede som solas,°   *give / respite, comfort*
    And yaf° him good forage.°   *gave / feeding*

"O seinte Marie, *benedicite!*°   *bless me*
785 What eyleth this love at me°   *does love have against me*
    To binde me so sore?
Me dremed al this night, pardee,°   *by God*
An elf-queen° shal my lemman° be,   *fairy queen / lover, sweetheart*
    And slepe under my gore.°   *robe, cloak*

790 An elf-queen wol I love, ywis,°   *indeed*
For in this world no womman is
    Worthy to be my make°   *mate, match*
            In toune.°   *in (any) town*
Alle othere wommen I forsake,
795 And to an elf-queen I me take
    By dale° and eek by doune."°   *valley / hill*

Into his sadel he clamb anoon°   *quickly climbed*
And priketh over style° and stoon   *stile*
    An elf-queen for t'espye,°   *to discover*
800 Til he so longe had riden and goon
That he fond, in a privee woon,°   *secret place*
    The contree of Fairye
                So wilde.
For in that contree was ther noon

805	That to° him dorste° ryde or goon—	*against / dared*
	Neither wyf ne childe—	
	Til that ther cam a greet geaunt;°	*giant*
	His name was sir Olifaunt,°	*Sir Elephant*
	A perilous man of dede.°	*in (his) actions*
810	He seyde, "Child,° by	*Noble youth*
	Termagaunt,°	*(supposedly a Saracen god)*
	But if° thou prike° out of myn haunt,°	*Unless / ride / territory*
	Anon I slee° thy stede	*will slay*
	With mace.°	*a spiked warclub*
	Heer is the queen of Fayerye,°	*the magical otherworld*
815	With harpe and pype and simphonye°	*a stringed instrument*
	Dwelling in this place."	
	The child seyde, "Also mote I thee,°	*So may I thrive (I swear)*
	Tomorwe wol I mete thee	
	Whan I have myn armoure;	
820	And yet I hope, *par ma fay,*°	*by my faith*
	That thou shalt with this launcegay°	*light lance*
	Abyen it ful soure.°	*Pay for it very sourly, bitterly*
	Thy mawe°	*stomach, belly*
	Shal I percen,° if I may,	*pierce*
825	Er it be fully pryme° of day,	*9 A.M.*
	For heer thou shalt be slawe."°	*slain*
	Sir Thopas drow° abak ful faste;	*drew*
	This geaunt at him stones caste	
	Out of a fel staf-slinge.°	*terrifying sling-shot*
	But faire° escapeth child Thopas,	*fairly, safely*
830	And al it was thurgh Goddes gras°	*grace*
	And thurgh his fair beringe.°	*behavior, conduct*

[THE SECOND FIT]

	Yet listeth,° lordes, to my tale	*listen*
	Merier than the nightingale,	
	For now I wol yow roune°	*tell (whisper)*
835	How sir Thopas, with sydes smale,°	*slender waist*
	Priking over hil and dale,	
	Is come agayn to toune.	
	His merie men° comanded he	*companions in arms*
840	To make him bothe game and glee,°	*entertainment and music*
	For nedes moste he fight	

With a geaunt with hevedes° three,   *heads*
For paramour° and jolitee°   *love / pleasure*
     Of oon° that shoon ful brighte.   *i.e., the elf queen*

845 "Do come,"° he seyde, "my minstrales,   *Summon*
And gestours° for to tellen tales—   *storytellers*
     Anon in myn arminge—
Of romances that been royales,
Of popes and of cardinales,
850 And eek° of love-lykinge."°   *also / love delights*

They fette° him first the swete wyn,   *fetched*
And mede° eek in a maselyn,°   *mead / mazer (wooden bowl)*
     And royal spicerye°   *mixtures of spices*
Of gingebreed° that was ful fyn,   *preserved ginger*
855 And lycorys,° and eek comyn,°   *licorice / cumin*
     With sugre that is trye.°   *choice, excellent*

He dide° next° his whyte lere°   *put on / next to / flesh*
Of clooth of lake° fyn and clere°   *fine linen / bright*
     A breech° and eek a sherte;   *pair of trousers*
860 And next his sherte an aketoun,°   *padded jacket*
And over that an habergeoun°   *coat of mail*
     For° percinge of his herte;   *To prevent*

And over that a fyn hauberk°   *armor for chest and back*
Was al y-wroght of° Jewes werk,   *made, crafted by*
     Ful strong it was of plate;°   *plate armor*
865 And over that his cote-armour°   *heraldic surcoat*
As whyt as is a lily-flour,
     In which he wol debate.°   *fight*

His sheeld was al of gold so reed,°   *red*
870 And therin was a bores° heed,   *boar's*
     A charbocle° bisyde;   *carbuncle (a red gemstone)*
And there he swoor on ale and breed
How that the geaunt shal be deed,
     Bityde what bityde.°   *Come what may*

875 His jambeux° were of quirboilly,°   *leg armor / hardened leather*
His swerdes shethe of yvory,
     His helm° of laton° bright.   *helmet / latten, brass*
His sadel was of rewel-boon,°   *whalebone, ivory*
His brydel as the sonne shoon,°   *shone*
880 Or as the mone light.

His spere was of fyn ciprees,°   *cypress*
That bodeth werre° and nothing   *forebodes war*
 pees,°   *in no way peace*
  The heed ful sharpe y-grounde.
His stede was al dappel gray,
885 It gooth an ambel° in the way   *goes at a slow walk*
 Ful softely and rounde°   *easily*
  In londe.
Lo, lordes myne, heer is a fit!°   *canto or section of a poem*
If ye wol any more of it,
890 To telle it wol I fonde.°   *strive, try*

[THE THIRD FIT]

Now hold your mouth, *par charitee*,°   *for charity's sake*
Bothe knight and lady free,°   *noble, generous*
 And herkneth to my spelle.°   *listen to my story*
Of bataille and of chivalry,
895 And of ladyes love-drury°   *love service, courtship*
 Anon I wol yow telle.

Men speke of romances of prys,°   *worthy, excellent*
Of Horn child and of Ypotys,
 Of Bevis and sir Gy,
900 Of sir Libeux and Pleyn-damour.
But sir Thopas—he bereth the flour°   *bears the prize*
 Of royal chivalry.[4]

His gode stede al he bistrood,°   *bestrode*
And forth upon his wey he glood°   *glided, traveled*
905 As sparkle° out of the bronde.°   *sparks / burning brand, torch*
Upon his crest° he bar a   *the top of his helmet*
 tour,°   *bore a tower ornament*
And therin stiked° a lily-flour—   *stuck, was fixed*
 God shilde his cors fro shonde!°   *keep his body from harm*

And for° he was a knight auntrous,°   *because / adventurous*
910 He nolde° slepen in non hous,   *would not*
 But liggen° in his hode.°   *lie / hood (i.e., outdoors)*

---

4. Chaucer claims that his hero surpasses those of the popular romances that he parodies in this tale: King Horn (also known as Child Horn), Ypotis (a pious child, Epictetus, who instructs the emperor Hadrian in the Christian faith), Bevis of Hampton and Guy of Warwick, who furnished Chaucer much to satirize here, along with Lybeaux Desconus ("sir Lybeux"), whose disguise-name means "The Fair Unknown," and the almost wholly unknown "Pleyn-damour," whose name means "full of love."

His brighte helm° was his wonger,°   *helmet / pillow*
And by him baiteth° his dextrer°   *feeds, grazes / warhorse*
    Of herbes° fyne and gode.   *On grasses*

915 Himself drank water of the wel,°   *spring*
As did the knight sir Percivel,°   *Percival (a chaste romance hero)*
    So worly under wede,°   *worthy in his armor, clothing*
Til on a day—[5]

"No more of this, for Goddes dignitee,"
920 Quod oure Hoste, "for thou makest me
So wery of thy verray lewednesse°   *sheer incompetence*
That, also wisly° God my soule blesse,°   *as surely as / may bless*
Myn eres° aken of° thy drasty° speche.   *ears / ache from foul, vile*
Now swiche a rym° the devel I   *rhyme, tale in verse /*
    biteche!°   *consign to*
925 This may wel be rym dogerel,"° quod he.   *doggerel verse*
    "Why so?" quod I. "Why wiltow lette° me   *wilt thou prevent*
More of my tale than another man,
Sin° that it is the beste rym I can?"°   *Since / know*
    "By God," quod he, "for pleynly at a word,
930 Thy drasty ryming is nat worth a tord.°   *turd*
Thou doost nought elles but despendest° tyme.   *waste*
Sir, at o word,° thou shalt no lenger ryme.   *in short*
Lat see wher thou canst tellen aught in geste[6]
Or telle in prose somwhat° at the leste,   *something*
935 In which ther be som mirthe or som doctryne."°   *useful teaching*

---

5. After this line the Hengwrt MS has the following rubric: "Here the hoost stynteth [stops] Chaucer of his tale of Thopas and biddeth hym telle another tale."
6. "Let (us) see whether thou canst tell something in alliterative verse."

Love and Romance

CHRISTOPHER MARLOWE

Christopher Marlowe (1564–1593) was an English poet and dramatist. His most famous works, tragedies, are *Tamburlaine*, *Dr. Faustus*, *The Jew of Malta*, and *Edward II*. He is also celebrated for his long poem *Hero and Leander* and for the lyric "Come Live with Me and Be My Love."

Ovid's Elegia 5: *Corinnae concubitus*[†]

In summers heate and midtime of the day
To rest my limbes upon a bed I lay,
One window shut, the other open stood,
Which gave such light as twinkles in a wood,
Like twilight glimpse at setting of the Sunne,
Or night being past, and yet not day begunne.
Such light to shamefast maidens must be showne,
Where they may sport, and seeme to be unknowne.
Then came Corinna in a long loose gowne,
Her white neck hid with tresses hanging downe,
Resembling fayre Semiramis[1] going to bed,
Or Layis of a thousand lovers sped.
I snatcht her gowne: being thin, the harme was small,
Yet strived she to be covered therewithall.
And striving thus as one that would be cast,
Betrayde her selfe, and yeelded at the last.
Starke naked as she stood before mine eye,
Not one wen[2] in her body could I spie.

[†] From Ovid's *Amores*. The subtitle of this elegy translates to "lying with Corinna." For Ovid, see note on page 243 of this Norton Critical Edition.

1. A mythical Assyrian queen, believed to have founded Babylon; she was the wife of Ninus, founder of Nineveh, and succeeded him as ruler. She also conquered Egypt and other cities. She was famous for her beauty and wisdom.

2. Per *Webster's Unabridged Dictionary*, Second Edition: "Any excrescence or imperfection: a blemish." That definition is now obsolete.

What armes and shoulders did I touch and see,
How apt her breasts were to be prest by me.
How smooth a belly under her wast saw I,
How large a legge, and what a lustie thigh?
To leave the rest, all liked me passing well,
I clinged her naked body, downe she fell,
Judge you the rest, being tirde she bad me kisse;
Jove send me more such afternoones as this.

JOHN DRYDEN

This translation is by John Dryden (1631–1700) and, because Dryden
did not finish his project, by William Congreve (1670–1729).

Dryden, the first official poet laureate of England and a prolific writer
in many fields, is known for his plays, *The Conquest of Granada,
Marriage-a-la-Mode, All for Love, Don Sebastian,* and *Amphitrion,* all of
different genres, and for many poems, among them *Absalom and Achi-
tophel* (in collaboration with Nahum Tate), *Annus Mirabilis, The Hind
and the Panther, Alexander's Feast,* and the satiric *McFlecknoe.* He was
a brilliant and prolific translator of Homer, Lucretius, Ovid, Boccaccio,
Chaucer and Virgil; by some he is regarded as the greatest translator of
Virgil's *Aeneid.*

Congreve, a disciple of Dryden's, is best known for his Restoration
dramas *The Old Bachelour, The Double Dealer, Love for Love, The Way
of the World*—his masterpiece—and for a tragedy, *The Mourning Bride.*

From Ovid's The Art of Love: Book I[†]

*   *   *

You, who in Cupid's roll inscribe your name,
First seek an object worthy of your flame;
Then strive, with art, your lady's mind to gain;
And last, provide your love may long remain.
On these three precepts all my work shall move:
These are the rules and principles of love.
Before your youth with marriage is oppress't,
Make choice of one who suits your humour best
And such a damsel drops not from the sky;
She must be sought for with a curious eye.
The wary angler, in the winding brook,
Knows what the fish, and where to bait his hook.
The fowler and the huntsman know by name

† From *Ovid's Art of Love (in Three Books), the Remedy of Love, the Art of Beauty, the
Court of Love, the History of Love,* and *Amours* (New York: Calvin Blanchard, 1855).

The certain haunts and harbour of their game.
So must the lover beat the likeliest grounds;
Th' assemblies where his quarries most abound:
Nor shall my novice wander far astray;
These rules shall put him in the ready way.
Thou shalt not fail around the continent,
As far as Perseus or as Paris went:
For Rome alone affords thee such a store,
As all the world can hardly shew thee more.
The face of heav'n with fewer stars is crown'd,
Than beauties in the Roman sphere are found.
Whether thy love is bent on blooming youth,
On dawning sweetness, in unartful truth;
Or courts the juicy joys of riper growth;
Here may'st thou find thy full desires in both:
Or if autumnal beauties please thy sight
(An age that knows to give and take delight;)
Millions of matrons, of the graver sort,
In common prudence, will not balk the sport.
In summer's heats thou need'st but only go
To Pompey's cool and shady portico;[1]

* * *

And if the hall[2] itself be not belied,
E'en there the cause of love is often tried;
Near it at least, or in the palace yard,
From whence the noisy combatants are heard.
The crafty counsellors, in formal gown,
There gain another's cause, but lose their own.
Their eloquence is nonpluss'd in the suit;
And lawyers, who had words at will, are mute.
Venus from her adjoining temple smiles
To see them caught in their litigious wiles;
Grave senators lead home the youthful dame,
Returning clients when they patrons came.
But above all, the Playhouse is the place;
There's choice of quarry in that narrow chace:
There take thy stand, and sharply looking out,
Soon may'st thou find a mistress in the rout,

1. Pompey (106–48 B.C.E.), sometimes known as The Great, a Roman general and a rival of Julius Caesar. The grand garden portico of Pompey the Great, built in the Campus Martius of Rome, was one of the most popular promenades frequented by ancient Romans; it was built between 62 and 52 B.C.E.
2. I.e., the Forum, where a number of activities took place, from the market to civic meetings and public affairs. Here—see following lines—it means the law-courts.

For length of time or for a single bout.
The Theatres are berries for the fair;
Like ants or molehills thither they repair;
Like bees to hives so numerously they throng,
It may be said they to that place belong:
Thither they swarm who have the public voice;
There choose, if plenty not distracts thy choice.
To see, and to be seen, in heaps they run;
Some to undo, and some to be undone.

NAHUM TATE

Nahum Tate (1652–1715), Irish, born in Dublin, settled in London and was made third poet laureate of England in 1692; he is best known as a collaborator and adaptor of other authors' plays, chiefly those from the Renaissance period: Shakespeare, Webster, Chapman and Marston, and Fletcher. His version of *King Lear,* which omits the Fool and ends happily with Cordelia marrying Edgar (it resembles the ancient version, centuries before Shakespeare), drew audiences up to the nineteenth century.

From Ovid's *Remedia amoris* (The Remedy of Love)[†]

*   *   *

To me, ye injured youths, for help repair,
Who hopeless languish for some cruel fair;
I'll now unteach the art I taught before,
The hand that wounded shall your health restore.
One soil can herbs and pois'nous weeds disclose:
The nettle oft is neighbour to the rose.

*   *   *

By reading me, you first receiv'd your bane;
Now, for an antidote, read me again:
From scornful beauty's chains I'll set you free,
Consent but you to your own liberty.
Phoebus, thou god of physic and of verse,
Assist the healing numbers I rehearse;
Direct at once my med'cines and my song,
For to thy care both provinces belong.

*   *   *

---

† From *Ovid's Art of Love (in Three Books), the Remedy of Love, the Art of Beauty, the Court of Love, the History of Love, and Amours* (New York: Calvin Blanchard, 1855).

[Ovid then recommends strongly against leisure: Venus loves it, Cupid loves sloth. Defend your friends in the law courts; take up soldiering; country life and farming are hard manly work and rewarding; take up travel, and don't find excuses, such as weather or business affairs, that can wait to delay it; *distance yourself* from the scene of your romantic debacle! Then, reflect on your ex-lover's faults.]

> Think, till the thought your indignation move,
> What damage you've receiv'd by her you love:
> How she has drain'd your purse; nor yet content,
> Till your estate's in costly presents spent,
> And you have mortgaged your last tenement.
> How she did swear, and how she was forsworn;
> Not only false, but treated you with scorn:
> And, since her avarice has made you poor,
> Forc'd you to take your lodgings at her door:
> Reserv'd to you, but others she'll caress:
> The foreman of a shop shall have access.
> Let these reflections on your reason win;
> From seeds of anger hatred will begin;
> Your rhet'ric on these topics should be spent.
> Oh, that your wrongs could make you eloquent!
> But grieve, and grief will teach you to enlarge,
> And, like an orator, draw up the charge.

✻   ✻   ✻

> E'en truth and your own judgment you must strain,
> Those blemishes you cannot find, to feign:
> Call her blackmoor, if she's but lovely brown;
> Monster, if plump; if slender, skeleton.
> Censure her free discourse as confidence;
> Her silence, want of breeding and good sense.
> Discover her blind side, and put her still
> Upon the task which she performs but ill;
> To dance, if she has neither shape nor air;
> Court her to sing, if she wants voice and ear;
> If talking misbecomes her, make her talk;
> If walking, then in malice make her walk.
> Commend her skill when on the lute she plays,
> Till vanity her want of skill betrays.
> Take care, if her large breasts offend your eyes,
> No dress does that deformity disguise.
> Ply her with merry tales of what you will,
> To keep her laughing, if her teeth be ill.
> Or if blear-eyed, some tragic story find,

Till she has read and wept herself quite blind.
But one effectual method you may take,
Enter her chamber ere she's well awake:
Her beauty's art, gems, gold, and rich attire,
Make up the pageant you so much admire:
In all that specious figure which you see,
The least, least part of her own self is she;
In vain for her you love, amidst such cost,
You search; the mistress in the dress is lost.
Take her disrob'd, her real self surprise,
I'll trust you then for cure, to your own eyes.
(Yet have I known this very rule to fail,
And beauty most, when stript of art prevail.)
Steal to her closet, her close tiring place,
While she makes up her artificial face.
All colours of the rainbow you'll discern,
Washes and paints, and what you're sick to learn,
I now should treat of what may pall desire,
And quench in love's own element the fire;
For all advantages you ought to make,
And arms from love's own magazine to take:
But modesty forbids at full extent
To prosecute this luscious argument,
Which, to prevent your blushes, I shall leave
For your own fancy better to conceive,
For some of late censoriously accuse
My am'rous liberty and wanton muse.

                         *   *   *

Now to perform a true physician's part,
And show I'm perfect master of my art;
I will prescribe what diet you should use,
What food you ought to take, and what refuse.
Mushrooms of ev'ry sort provoke desire,
Salacious rockets set your veins on fire;
The plant I recommend is wholesome rue,
It clears the sight and does the blood subdue:
But, in a word, of all the herbs that grow,
Take only such as keep the body low.
If my opinion you would have of wine,
It quenches love, and does to love incline.
A little breath of wind but fans the fire,
Whose flame will in a greater blast expire.
In wine you must no moderation keep;
You must not drink at all; or drink so deep,

So large a dose, as puts your cares to sleep.
Now to our port we are arriv'd; bring down
The jolly wreath, our weary barque to crown.
Your grief redrest, and now a happy throng,
Ye nymphs and youths applaud my healing song.

ANDREAS CAPELLANUS

From De arte honeste amandi
(The Art of Courtly Love)[†]

Introduction to the Treatise on Love

We must first consider what love is, whence it gets its name, what the effect of love is, between what persons love may exist, how it may be acquired, retained, increased, decreased, and ended, what are the signs that one's love is returned, and what one of the lovers ought to do if the other is unfaithful.

CHAPTER I. WHAT LOVE IS

Love is a certain inborn suffering derived from the sight of and excessive meditation upon the beauty of the opposite sex, which causes each one to wish above all things the embraces of the other and by common desire to carry out all of love's precepts in the other's embrace.

That love is suffering is easy to see, for before the love becomes equally balanced on both sides there is no torment greater, since the lover is always in fear that his love may not gain its desire and that he is wasting his efforts. He fears, too, that rumors of it may get abroad, and he fears everything that might harm it in any way, for before things are perfected a slight disturbance often spoils them. If he is a poor man, he also fears that the woman may scorn his poverty; if he is ugly, he fears that she may despise his lack of beauty or may give her love to a more handsome man; if he is rich, he fears that his parsimony in the past may stand in his way. To tell the truth, no one can number the fears of one single lover. This kind of love, then, is a suffering which is felt by only one of the persons and may be called "single love." But even after both are in love the fears that arise are just as great, for each of the lovers fears that what he has acquired with so much effort may be lost through the effort of someone else, which is certainly much worse for a man than if, having

† From Andreas Capellanus, *The Art of Courtly Love*, ca. 1190, translated by Jay Parry, edited and abridged by Frederick W. Locke (New York: Frederic Ungar, 1957), pp. 2–3, 15–19.

no hope, he sees that his efforts are accomplishing nothing, for it is worse to lose the things you are seeking than to be deprived of a gain you merely hope for. The lover fears, too, that he may offend his loved one in some way; indeed he fears so many things that it would be difficult to tell them.

That this suffering is inborn I shall show you clearly, because if you will look at the truth and distinguish carefully you will see that it does not arise out of any action; only from the reflection of the mind upon what it sees does this suffering come. For when a man sees some woman fit for love and shaped according to his taste, he begins at once to lust after her in his heart; then the more he thinks about her the more he burns with love, until he comes to a fuller meditation. Presently he begins to think about the fashioning of the woman and to differentiate her limbs, to think about what she does, and to pry into the secrets of her body, and he desires to put each part of it to the fullest use. Then after he has come to this complete meditation, love cannot hold the reins, but he proceeds at once to action; straightway he strives to get a helper to find an intermediary. He begins to plan how he may find favor with her, and he begins to seek a place and a time opportune for talking; he looks upon a brief hour as a very long year, because he cannot do anything fast enough to suit his eager mind. It is well known that many things happen to him in this manner. This inborn suffering comes, therefore, from seeing and meditating. Not every kind of meditation can be the cause of love, an excessive one is required; for a restrained thought does not, as a rule, return to the mind, and so love cannot arise from it.

* * *

SEVENTH DIALOGUE. A MAN OF THE HIGHER NOBILITY SPEAKS WITH A WOMAN OF THE SIMPLE NOBILITY.

When a man of the higher nobility addresses a woman of the simple nobility, let him use the same speeches that a nobleman and a man of the higher nobility use with a woman of the middle class, except that part dealing with the commendation of birth, and he must not boast very much of the fact that he is noble. In addition he might begin with this formula:

"I ought to give God greater thanks than any other living man in the whole world because it is now granted me to see with my eyes what my soul has desired above all else to see, and I believe that God has granted it to me because of my great longing and because He has seen fit to hear the prayers of my importunate supplication. For not an hour of the day or night could pass that I did not earnestly pray God to grant me the boon of seeing you near me in the flesh. It is no wonder that I was driven by so great an impulse to see you and was tormented by so great a desire, since the whole world extols your virtue and your wisdom, and in the farthest parts of the world courts are fed upon the tale of your goodness just as though it were a sort of tangible food. And now I know in very truth that a human tongue is not able to tell the tale of your beauty and your prudence or a human mind to imagine it. And so the mighty desire, which I already had, of seeing you and serving you has greatly increased and will increase still more."

THE WOMAN SAYS: "We are separated by too wide and too rough an expanse of country to be able to offer each other love's solaces or to find proper opportunities for meeting. Lovers who live near together can cure each other of the torments that come from love, can help each other in their common sufferings, and can nourish their love by mutual exchanges and efforts; those, however, who are far apart cannot perceive each other's pains, but each one has to relieve his own trouble and cure his own torments. So it seems that our love should go no further, because Love's rule teaches us that the daily sight of each other makes lovers love more ardently, while I can see on the other hand that by reason of distance love decreases and fails, and therefore everybody should try to find a lover who lives near by."

THE MAN SAYS: "You are troubling yourself to say what seems to be against all reason, for all men know that if one gets easily what he desires he holds it cheap and what formerly he longed for with his whole heart he now considers worthless. On the other hand, whenever the possession of some good thing is postponed by the difficulty of getting it, we desire it more eagerly and put forth a greater effort to keep it. Therefore if one has difficulty in obtaining the embraces of one's lover and obtains them rarely, the lovers are bound to each other in more ardent chains of love and their souls are linked together in heavier and closer bonds of affection. For constancy is made perfect amid the waves that buffet it, and perseverance is clearly seen in adversities. Rest seems sweeter to a man who is wearied by many labors than to one who lives in continual idleness, and a new-found shade seems to offer more to one who is burdened by the heat than to one who has been constantly in air of a moderate temperature. It is not one of Love's rules, as you said it was, that when lovers seldom meet the strength of their love is weakened, since we find it false and misleading. Therefore you cannot properly refuse me your love with the excuse of the long and difficult distance between us, but you should gratify me rather than someone who lives near by; besides, it is easier to conceal a love affair when the lovers do not meet than when they converse frequently with each other."

THE WOMAN SAYS: "So far as hiding one's love goes, I do not think there is any choice between a distant lover and one who is present.

If the lover proves to be wise and clever it doesn't matter whether he is far from his beloved or near her, he will so govern his actions and his will that no one can guess the secrets of their love; on the other hand a foolish lover, whether far or near, can never conceal the secrets of his love. Your argument must therefore fall before this most obvious one on the other side. Besides there is another fact, by no means trivial, which keeps me from loving you. I have a husband who is greatly distinguished by his nobility, his good breeding, and his good character, and it would be wicked for me to violate his bed or submit to the embraces of any other man, since I know that he loves me with his whole heart and I am bound to him with all the devotion of mine. The laws themselves bid me refrain from loving another man when I am blessed with such a reward for my love."

THE MAN SAYS: "I admit it is true that your husband is a very worthy man and that he is more blest than any man in the world because he has been worthy to have the joy of embracing Your Highness. But I am greatly surprised that you wish to misapply the term 'love' to that marital affection which husband and wife are expected to feel for each other after marriage, since everybody knows that love can have no place between husband and wife. They may be bound to each other by a great and immoderate affection, but their feeling cannot take the place of love, because it cannot fit under the true definition of love. For what is love but an inordinate desire to receive passionately a furtive and hidden embrace? But what embrace between husband and wife can be furtive, I ask you, since they may be said to belong to each other and may satisfy each other's desires without fear that anybody will object.

"But there is another reason why husband and wife cannot love each other and that is that the very substance of love, without which true love cannot exist—I mean jealousy—is in such a case very much frowned upon and they should avoid it like the pestilence; but lovers should always welcome it as the mother and the nurse of love. From this you may see clearly that love cannot possibly flourish between you and your husband. Therefore, since every woman of character ought to love, prudently, you can without doing yourself any harm accept the prayers of a suppliant and endow your suitor with your love."

THE WOMAN SAYS: "You are trying to take under your protection what all men from early times down have agreed to consider very reprehensible and to reject as hateful. For who can rightly commend envious jealousy or speak in favor of it, since jealousy is nothing but a shameful and evil suspicion of a woman? God forbid, therefore, that any worthy man should feel jealous about anyone, since this proves hostile to every prudent person and throughout the world is hated by everybody good. You are trying also, under cover of defining love, to condemn love between husband and wife, saying that their embraces cannot be furtive, since without fear that anyone may object they can fulfill each other's desires. But if you understood the definition correctly it could not interfere with love between husband and wife, for the expression 'hidden embraces' is simply an explanation in different words of the preceding one, and there seems to be no impossibility in husband and wife giving each other hidden embraces, even though they can do so without the least fear that anybody may raise an objection. Everyone should choose that love which may be fostered by security for continual embraces and, what is more, can be practiced every day without any sin. I ought therefore to choose a man to enjoy my embraces who can be to me both husband and lover, because, no matter what the definition of love may say, love seems to be nothing but a great desire to enjoy carnal pleasure with someone, and nothing prevents this feeling existing between husband and wife."

THE MAN SAYS: "If the theory of love were perfectly clear to you and Love's dart had ever touched you, your own feelings would have shown you that love cannot exist without jealousy, because, as I have already told you in more detail, jealousy between lovers is commended by every man who is experienced in love, while between husband and wife it is condemned throughout the world; the reason for this will be perfectly clear from a description of jealousy. Now jealousy is a true emotion whereby we greatly fear that the substance of our love may be weakened by some defect in serving the desires of our beloved, and it is an anxiety lest our love may not be returned.

"We find many, however, who are deceived in this matter and say falsely that a shameful suspicion is jealousy, just as many often make the mistake of saying that an alloy of silver and lead is the finest silver. Wherefore not a few being ignorant of the origin and description of jealousy, are often deceived and led into the gravest error. For even between persons who are not married this false jealousy may find a place and then they are no longer called 'lovers' but 'gentleman friend' and 'lady friend.' As for what you tried to prove by your answer—that the love which can be practiced without sin is far preferable—that, apparently, cannot stand. For whatever solaces married people extend to each other beyond what are inspired by the desire for offspring or the payment of the marriage debt, cannot be free from sin, and the punishment is always greater when the use of a holy thing is perverted by misuse than if we practice the ordinary abuses. It is a more serious offense in a wife than in another woman, for the too ardent lover, as we are taught by the apostolic law, is considered an adulterer with his own wife."

References and Similar Themes

ANONYMOUS

Of this anonymous twelfth-century poem, Eric Gerald Stanley writes (22): "*The Owl and the Nightingale* is written in a style of civilized, literary colloquialism. There is an element of direct and honest obscenity . . . but of vulgarity there is not a trace. The tone is light, but much of the matter is serious. Though the poem is not a formal allegory, the Owl stands for the solemn way of life, and the Nightingale for the joyous way of life. The case to be put . . . is which is the better of the two birds; and this implies the question, which of the two is the better way of life. The poet maintains the balance between them; . . . in the end he does not reveal either his own or [the judge's] judgment. . . . The argument is far from neat; it ranges over many aspects of many subjects [central to the interests of people of that age]. . . . Song is the first subject of their debate. . . . The form which the debate takes is influenced by the rhetoric of pleading in a court of law (33). . . . Tricks, wrinkles, *cautelae* were not merely a feature of literary debates, but they were part and parcel of contemporary legal cases" (27). Stanley further points out: "References to the song of the birds are, of course, to be found everywhere in ancient and medieval literature. The cry of the owl is a sinister omen, but the nightingale's song brings joy" (33).

No other long, elaborate debate poems survive in Middle English, but the form is very old, beginning with the fable and with classical Greek pastoral poetry and continuing into Latin, Old English, Old French, and other European languages and treating of such subjects as Winter and Summer (Latin) and the Body and the Soul (Old English) as well as the disputations found in Marie's *Fables* and her Latin sources.

The poet refers not only to Marie's *lai* "Laüstic" but also to fables told by Marie and others, e.g., "The Hawk and the Owl" (79).

From The Owl and the Nightingale[†]

* * *

Hearing these words, the furious Owl,
eyes huge and bright, rushed to the quarrel.

[†] Translated by Dorothy Gilbert for this Norton Critical Edition.

1045 "You say you know these human bowers,[1]
spread round with leaves and lovely flowers,
where, in one bed, two lovers lie
protected,[2] clasping tenderly.
Oh, once you sang—I know well where—
1050 beside a bower, and sought to lure
the lady to a wicked love;
low down you sang, and high above,
tempted her to debauchery
and shamefulness with her body.
1055 Soon her lord husband was aware;
He got much gear, got lime and snare,
traps, and it wasn't long until
you flew to door or window sill
and were caught quickly in a snare;
1060 all tangled in your shins, you were.
Judgment and sentence followed, both:
wild horses, dragging you to death.[3]
Try then, again, to lead astray
virgin or wife, to lechery,
1065 you'll find that your seductive song
has got you dangling before long!"
       The Nightingale took in this word:
if she had been a man, this bird
with sword and spear would have attacked.
1070 But being a little bird, in fact,
she fought with her sagacious tongue.
"Who talks well, fights well," says the song.
And with her tongue, a plan she made:
"Who talks well, fights well," Alfred said.[4]
1075   "What! You say this, to bring me shame?
That lord had sorrow, he had blame.
He was so jealous of his wife

1. The word *bures* has a number of meanings (and spellings): it can mean a dwelling, an inner chamber, a mansion, a cottage, a shelter, or a town. Given the context and the associations of *fin' amor*, the meaning here must surely be still another, found in such literature: a lady's chamber, or a suite for ladies, often with a charming garden.
2. I.e., by the Nightingale, who watches over these lovers as well as, traditionally, over houses. Stanley believes that the Middle English word "bihedde" may be a deliberate scribal substitution for "behedde," "concealed," in a southeastern dialect, a meaning that fits here: "concealed [or 'secure'], embracing tenderly."
3. Dragging and quartering by wild horses as a method of execution occurs in other English poems of the period.
4. This proverb apparently occurs only here. Stanley suggests (131) that in the *Proverbs of Alfred* (458–60) there is a similar idea: "A wise man can enclose much in few words; and a fool's bolt is soon shot." Alfred, sometimes called "the Great," reigned over Wessex and other Saxon territories from 871 to 899 and was revered as a lawmaker and an educator.

that he might not, for his dear life
bear it, if to a man she'd speak;
1080 if she did that, his heart would break.
And so he locked her in a bower:[5]
a hard and bitter fate for her.
I felt such pity for her plight
I was heartsick; for her delight
1085 I sought to please her with my song
well as I might, both soon and long.
The knight was in a rage with me,
pure malice, rage and jealousy,
but all the shame he wished on me
1090 was his, and did him injury.
King Henry[6] found out, by and by—
Jesus preserve his soul on high!—
he banished this malicious knight
who'd brought such viciousness and spite
1095 into so good a monarch's realm.
A little bird, who did no harm,
He robbed of life and limb, because[7]
of pure vindictive odiousness.
Honor and profit, happily,
1100 came to my kinsfolk and to me;
he paid to me a hundred pound,[8]
and now my relatives sit, sound
safe, ever after, full of bliss,
healthy, happy, vigorous.
1105 So well did vengeance come to me,
I dare speak much more easily;
it happened that I got redress,
so I have constant happiness.
Now where I sing is up to me,

---

5. Cf. Marie's *lai* "Guigemar" (p. 5–26 of this volume) and also "Laüstic" (p. 120–24) and "Yönec" (p. 90–119).
6. This is obviously a reference to a dead king and is significant for dating the poem. One of four kings could be meant: Henry I, Henry II, Henry III, or "The Young King," Henry II's eldest son, who died before he could accede to the throne. I follow Stanley in believing that it is Henry II who is meant. He was regarded as a strong king (his subjects were grateful after the devastating civil wars earlier in the twelfth century), and he was, as Stanley says (132), "a generous patron of literature." He died in 1189.
7. Here and later, when the Nightingale delivers her diatribe against the Owl, the deaths of the birds, as known from folklore and literature, are referred to even though the disputants are clearly alive. As Cartlidge comments (76): "As the type of her kind, the Nightingale speaks for each and every individual nightingale. That is why she can talk about her execution as a personal experience—even though, manifestly, she is alive and well."
8. This figure probably just means "as large a sum as one would wish" (Stanley, 132). Stone comments (220) that "One hundred pounds would be four times the maximum fine for homicide under the law." See Brian Stone, *The Owl and the Nightingale, Cleanness, St. Erkenwald* (Harmondsworth: Penguin Classics, 1971).

1110 and I fear no one's perfidy.
      But you, ill spirit! Dismal ghost!
      Wretch, will you find a likely roost,
      a hollow trunk where you may hide
      where I won't tweak and pinch your hide?
1115 Boys of the cloister, servant boys,[9]
      villagers, monks, they all rejoice,
      to bring you torment. They bring stones,
      lobbing them at your nasty bones
      to break them up. They heave, let fly,
1120 break you in bits until you die.
      And if you're tumbled from your spot,
      at last you're useful; if you're shot,
      then you are hung upon a stick[1]
      and your foul carcass, by the neck,
1125 dangles, disgusting. There it rests,
      protecting grain from thieving pests.
      Worthless, you are, with life, with blood,
      But as a scarecrow, very good!
      —When the new seeds lie in the ground.

GIOVANNI BOCCACCIO

From The Decameron (ca. 1350)[†]

The Tenth Day, Tenth Tale

Not many days after that, Gualtieri sent for his son the same way he had for his daughter, and having likewise pretended to have him put to death, he sent him to be brought up in Bologna just as he had done with the girl. In response, his wife said nothing more and did not

---

9. The word "children" has been interpreted by J. W. H. Atkins and the translator Brian Stone as meaning "girls"; Stone writes, "For boy and girl, master and groom" (220). I think Stanley provides more etymological evidence for the meaning "monastery boys": he comments, "The line means that when they pursue the Owl, the people all forget their traditional enmities; the monastery boys run with the lads of the castle and village, the village-folk are at one with the monastics" in their hatred of the Owl as vermin (132–33).

1. See Cartlidge, 76–77, who says that "the killing and displaying of owls in this way is a folkloric tradition designed to ward off bad luck or bad weather," citing Armstrong (118), who writes: "The custom of nailing owls to barn doors or walls, which has only recently been abandoned in England, was too widespread to have arisen through literary influence. Ignorant countryfolk thus disposing of owls explained that they were merely getting rid of vermin, but their actions were really determined by ancient, probably prehistoric, precedent." See Edward A. Armstrong, *The Folklore of Birds: An Enquiry into the Origin and Distribution of Some Magico-Religious Traditions* (London, 1958).

† From *The Decameron*, translated by Wayne Rebhorn (New York: Norton, 2013), pp. 844–50. Copyright © 2013 by Wayne Rebhorn. Used by permission of W. W. Norton & Company, Inc.

change the expression on her face any more than she had in her daughter's case, all to Gualtieri's great astonishment, who told himself that no other woman could do what she did. And if it were not for the fact that he saw her treat the children with the utmost tenderness as long as he permitted her to do so, he would have concluded that she acted as she did because she had stopped caring for them. He knew, however, that her behavior was the product of her wisdom.

Since Gualtieri's subjects believed he had arranged to have his two children murdered, they condemned him, blaming it all on his cruelty, whereas they felt nothing but the most profound pity for his wife. But to the women who mourned with her for her children because they had suffered such a death, she never said anything except that if such was the pleasure of the man who had conceived them, then it was her pleasure as well.

Finally, many years after the birth of his daughter, Gualtieri decided the time had come to put his wife's patience to the ultimate test. Accordingly, he spoke with a large company of his vassals and told them that under no circumstances could he put up with Griselda as his wife any longer. He said that he had come to realize just how bad and immature a decision he had made when he chose her, and that he would therefore do everything he could to procure a dispensation from the Pope so that he could leave Griselda and take another wife. A large number of the worthy men took him to task over this plan, but his only reply was that it had to be done that way.

Upon learning of her husband's intentions, the lady grieved bitterly inside, for it seemed to her that what she had to look forward to was returning to her father's house and perhaps tending his sheep as she had done before, while being forced to see the man she loved with all her heart in another woman's embrace. But still, just as she had borne all of Fortune's other afflictions, she was determined to keep her countenance unchanged and endure this one as well.

A little later Gualtieri arranged to have counterfeit letters sent to him from Rome and led his subjects to believe that they contained the Pope's dispensation, which allowed him to leave Griselda and take another wife. Hence, he summoned her to appear, and in the presence of a large number of people, he said to her: "Woman, through the concession granted me by the Pope I am now free to leave you and choose another wife. Since my ancestors have always been great noblemen and rulers in these parts, whereas yours have always been peasants, I no longer want you as my wife. You should return to Giannucole's house with the dowry you brought me, and I will bring home another woman I've found who is a more appropriate match for me."

When she heard these words, the lady managed to hold back her tears only by making an enormous effort that went well beyond the normal capacity of women.

"My lord," she said, "I have always known that my lowly condition and your nobility were in no way suited to one another, just as I have acknowledged that the position I have held with you was a gift from you and from God, nor have I taken what was given to me and treated it as if it were my own rather than as something lent to me. So, if it pleases you to have it back, then it must also please me—and it does—to return it to you. Look, here's the ring with which you married me: take it. As for your ordering me to carry away the dowry I brought here, to do that will not require a paymaster on your part, nor a purse, let alone a packhorse on mine, for I haven't forgotten that I was completely naked when you took me.[1] And if you think it proper to let everybody see this body that bore the children you sired, I will depart naked as well, but I beg you, in return for the virginity I brought here and cannot take away again, that it may please you to let me take away at least one single shift in addition to my dowry."

Although Gualtieri had a greater desire to weep than anything else, he maintained his stony expression and said: "You may take a shift with you."

The people standing about there begged him to give her a dress so that the woman who had been his wife for thirteen years or longer should not suffer the shame of leaving his house wearing only a shift like a pauper. All their pleading was in vain, however, and thus she left the house in her shift, barefoot, and with nothing to cover her head. After having said good-bye to them all, she returned to her father's home, accompanied by the weeping and wailing of everyone who saw her.

Since Giannucole never really believed it possible for his daughter to last very long as Gualtieri's wife, he had been expecting just such a development every day and had kept the clothes that she had taken off the morning Gualtieri married her. He brought them to her, and after she had put them on, she devoted herself to all the menial chores in her father's house just as she had been accustomed to do, bravely enduring the fierce assault of a hostile Fortune.

As soon as he had sent Griselda away, Gualtieri led his vassals to believe that he had chosen as his wife a daughter of one of the counts of Panago.[2] And having ordered great preparations to be made for the wedding, he sent for Griselda to come to him. When she appeared, he said to her:

"I'm going to bring home the lady whom I have recently chosen to marry, and I want her to be given an honorable reception the moment she arrives. Since you know that I don't have any women in my house

---

1. Compare Job's words (1:21): "Naked came I out of my mother's womb, and naked shall I return thither: the Lord gave, and the Lord hath taken away; blessed be the name of the Lord."
2. Panago (or, more correctly, Panico), located near Bologna, was ruled by counts of the Alberti family.

who can prepare the rooms properly and do many of the things that a festive occasion of this sort requires, and since you understand such household matters better than anyone else, I want you to see to it that all the arrangements are taken care of and that you invite as many ladies as you think necessary and receive them as though you were the mistress of the house. Then, when the wedding celebration is over, you can return home."

Gualtieri's words pierced Griselda's heart like so many knives, for she had not been able to put aside the love she bore him in the same way that she had relinquished the good fortune she once had. Nevertheless, she replied: "My lord, I am ready and willing."[3] And so, clad in homespun garments of coarse wool, she entered the house, which only a little while before she had left in a shift. Then she began sweeping and tidying up the rooms, had bed curtains and bench coverings put in place throughout the great halls, got the kitchen ready to go, and turned her hand to everything just as if she were some little household serving wench, never stopping until it was all as neat and trim as the occasion called for. Finally, after having invitations sent to all the women in those parts on Gualtieri's behalf, she stopped and waited for the celebration to begin. When the wedding day arrived, though the clothes she had on were poor, she displayed the spirit and bearing of a lady, receiving, with a happy smile on her face, all the women who came to the feast.

Gualtieri had seen to it that his children were brought up with care in Bologna by his kinswoman, who had married into the house of the counts of Panago. His daughter, who had now reached the age of twelve, was the most beautiful creature ever seen, and his son was six. Gualtieri sent word to his kinswoman's husband, asking him if he would be so kind as to accompany his daughter and her brother to Saluzzo, to arrange a noble, honorable escort for her, and not to reveal to anyone who she was in reality, but simply to tell them that he was bringing her there as Gualtieri's bride.

The nobleman did everything the Marquis requested, and a few days after he set out on his journey with the girl and her brother and their noble retinue, he reached Saluzzo, arriving around the dinner hour, where he found that all the people there, as well as many others from neighboring communities, were waiting for Gualtieri's new bride. She was received by the ladies, and as soon as she entered the hall where the tables were set up, Griselda, dressed just as she was, happily went to meet her, and said: "You are welcome here, my lady."

The ladies had begged Gualtieri, earnestly but in vain, either to have Griselda remain in another room or to lend her one of the

---

3. Another biblical allusion, this time to Luke 1:38: "Behold the handmaiden of the Lord."

dresses that had once been hers, so that she would not appear in front of the guests looking as she did. But she was nevertheless seated at the tables along with all the rest of them, after which dinner was served. As everyone stared at the girl, they said that Gualtieri had done well by the exchange, and Griselda joined in, praising her warmly, and her little brother, too.

It seemed to Gualtieri that he had now seen as much as he could have ever desired of his wife's patience, for he had observed that no event, however outrageous, had produced any sort of change in her at all. Moreover, he felt sure that her reaction was not the result of obtuseness, since he knew just how wise she was. He therefore decided that it was time to deliver her from the bitter sorrow he guessed she was keeping hidden beneath her impassive exterior, and having summoned her, he smiled and asked her in the presence of all the assembled people: "What do you think of our bride?"

"My lord," replied Griselda, "she seems very fine to me, and if, as I believe, her wisdom matches her beauty, I have no doubt whatsoever that living with her will make you the happiest gentleman in the world. However, I beg you with all my heart not to inflict on her the same wounds you once gave the other spouse you used to have, because I find it hard to believe she'll be able to endure them, considering how much younger she is and also how refined an upbringing she has had, whereas the other one experienced continual hardships from the time she was a little girl."

Seeing that she firmly believed the girl was going to be his wife, and yet had nothing but good things to say, Gualtieri had her sit down beside him.

"Griselda," he said, "the time has finally come both for you to taste the fruit of your long patience, and for those who have thought me cruel, unjust, and brutish to realize that what I've done I've done with a deliberate end in view. For I wanted to teach you how to be a wife, to teach them how to manage one, and at the same time to beget for myself perpetual peace and quiet for the rest of my life with you. When I was at the point of taking a wife, I really feared I'd have no peace, and that's why I decided to choose one by means of a test and have, as you know, inflicted so much pain and suffering on you.

"And since I've never seen you deviate from my wishes in either word or deed, and since it seems to me that you will provide me with all the happiness I've desired, I intend to restore to you in an instant that which I took from you over such a long time, and with the sweetest of cures to heal the wounds I gave you. Receive this girl, then, with a glad heart, the one you believed to be my wife, along with her brother, for they are, in fact, our children, yours as well as mine, the very ones whom you and many others believed for a long time I had cruelly ordered to be put to death. And I am your husband, who loves you more than anything else, since I believe I may boast that there is no one else who could be as content with his wife as I am with you."[4]

When he finished speaking, he embraced her and kissed her, and while she wept for joy, they both got up and went over to where their daughter sat, listening in amazement to what they were saying. Both of them embraced her and her brother tenderly, thus dispelling any confusion that they, like many others present, were feeling. The ladies were overjoyed, and getting up from the tables, they went with Griselda into a chamber where, with a more auspicious view of her future, they divested her of her old clothes and dressed her in one of her own stately gowns. Then, like the lady of the castle, which she always appeared to be even when clad in rags, they led her back into the hall, where her rejoicing with her children was simply wonderful. Indeed, everyone was so happy about what had happened that the feasting and the celebrating were redoubled and continued unabated for many more days. They all declared that Gualtieri was very wise, although they thought that the tests to which he had subjected his wife were harsh and intolerable, but they considered Griselda to be the wisest of them all.

A few days later the Count of Panago returned to Bologna, and Gualtieri, having taken Giannucole away from his drudgery, set him up in a position befitting the man who was his father-in-law, so that he was treated with honor and lived in great comfort during his last remaining years. As for Gualtieri himself, having arranged a noble match for his daughter, he lived a long, contented life with Griselda, always honoring her in every way he could.

What more is there left to say except that divine spirits may rain down from the heavens even into the houses of the poor, just as there are others in royal palaces who might be better suited to tending pigs than ruling men. Who, aside from Griselda, would have suffered, not merely dry eyed, but with a cheerful countenance, the cruel, unheard-of trials to which Gualtieri subjected her? Perhaps it would have served him right if, instead, he had run into the kind of woman who, upon being thrown out of the house in her shift, would have found some guy to give her fur a good shaking and got a nice new dress in the bargain.

---

4. Gualtieri's "I believe I may boast . . ." is a formula used by medieval knights who would boast, often at the dinner table, of some heroic deed they had done or some extraordinary possession they had, challenging those present to match their claim. Cf. Marie's *lai* "Fresne" on page 35.

ANONYMOUS

The narrative similarity of the ballad "Fair Annie" and Marie's *lai* "Le Fresne" (pp. 35–47) has long been noticed. Bertrand H. Bronson notes, "This ballad, running back into the mists through Scandinavian and German analogues, does not appear in the Scottish record until the second half of the eighteenth century. As Child points out, the story—a story is not a ballad, though where there is a story there may be a ballad—is told by Marie de France before the year 1200, in the *Lai de Fraisne* [sic]. From Scotland the ballad appears not to have traveled South, but has been brought West and is found both in New England and in the Southern mountains." Bronson lists seven variants of tunes. See Bertrand Harris Bronson, *The Traditional Tunes of the Child Ballads, with Their Texts, According to the Extant Records of Great Britain and America*, Vol. II (Princeton: Princeton University Press, 1962), 40. Since the 1980s, a number of singers have recorded this ballad, among them Peter Bellamy, Frankie Armstrong, Maggie Boyle, and Martin Simpson.

Fair Annie†

Child Ballad #62A

1   'IT'S narrow, narrow, make your bed,
      And learn to lie your lane;
    For I'm ga'n oer the sea, Fair Annie,
      A braw bride to bring hame.
    Wi her I will get gowd and gear;
      Wi you I neer got nane.

2   'But wha will bake my bridal bread,
      Or brew my bridal ale?
    And wha will welcome my brisk bride,
      That I bring oer the dale?'

3   'It's I will bake your bridal bread,
      And brew your bridal ale,
    And I will welcome your brisk bride,
      That you bring oer the dale.'

4   'But she that welcomes my brisk bride
      Mann gang like maiden fair;
    She maun lace on her robe sae jimp,
      And braid her yellow hair.'

† From *The English and Scottish Popular Ballads*, ed. Francis James Child (Boston: Houghton, Mifflin, 1884–98). Vol. II (1886).

5 'But how can I gang maiden-like,
　　When maiden I am nane?
　Have I not born seven sons to thee,
　　And am with child again?'

6 She's taen her young son in her arms,
　　Another in her hand,
　And she's up to the highest tower,
　　To see him come to land.

7 'Come up, come up, my eldest son,
　　And look oer yon sea-strand,
　And see your father's new-come bride,
　　Before she come to land.'

8 'Come down, come down, my mother dear,
　　Come frae the castle wa!
　I fear, if langer ye stand there,
　　Ye'll let yoursell down fa.'

9 And she gaed down, and farther down,
　　Her love's ship for to see,
　And the topmast and the mainmast
　　Shone like the silver free.

10 And she's gane down, and farther down,
　　The bride's ship to behold,
　And the topmast and the mainmast
　　They shone just like the gold.

11 She's taen her seven sons in her hand,
　　I wot she didna fail;
　She met Lord Thomas and his bride,
　　As they came oer the dale.

12 'You're welcome to your house, Lord Thomas,
　　You're welcome to your land;
　You're welcome with your fair ladye,
　　That you lead by the hand.

13 'You're welcome to your ha's, ladye,
　　Your welcome to your bowers;
　You're welcome to your hame, ladye,
　　For a' that's here is yours.'

14 'I thank thee, Annie; I thank thee, Annie,
 Sae dearly as I thank thee;
You're the likest to my sister Annie,
 That ever I did see.

15 'There came a knight out oer the sea,
 And steald my sister away;
The shame scoup in his company,
 And land whereer he gae!'

16 She hang ae napkin at the door,
 Another in the ha,
And a' to wipe the trickling tears,
 Sae fast as they did fa.

17 And aye she served the lang tables,
 With white bread and with wine,
And aye she drank the wan water,
 To had her colour fine.

18 And aye she served the lang tables,
 With white bread and with brown;
And ay she turned her round about,
 Sae fast the tears fell down.

19 And he's taen down the silk napkin,
 Hung on a silver pin,
And aye he wipes the tear trickling
 A' down her cheek and chin.

20 And aye he turn'd him round about,
 And smiled amang his men;
Says, Like ye best the old ladye.
 Or her that's new come hame?

21 When bells were rung, and mass was sung,
 And a' men bound to bed,
Lord Thomas and his new-come bride
 To their chamber they were gaed.

22 Annie made her bed a little forbye,
 To hear what they might say;
'And ever alas!' Fair Annie cried,
 'That I should see this day!

23 'Gin my seven sons were seven young rats,
     Running on the castle wa,
   And I were a grey cat mysell,
     I soon would worry them a'.

24 'Gin my seven sons were seven young hares,
     Running oer yon lilly lee,
   And I were a grew hound mysell,
     Soon worried they a' should be.'

25 And wae and sad Fair Annie sat,
     And drearie was her sang,
   And ever, as she sobbd and grat,
     'Wae to the man that did the wrang!'

26 'My gown is on,' said the new-come bride,
     'My shoes are on my feet,
   And I will to Fair Annie's chamber,
     And see what gars her greet.

27 'What ails ye, what ails ye, Fair Annie,
     That ye make sie a moan?
   Has your wine barrels cast the girds,
     Or is your white bread gone?

28 'O wha was 't was your father, Annie,
     Or wha was 't was your mother?
   And had ye ony sister, Annie,
     Or had ye ony brother?'

29 'The Earl of Wemyss was my father,
     The Countess of Wemyss my mother;
   And a' the folk about the house
     To me were sister and brother.'

30 'If the Earl of Wemyss was your father,
     I wot sae was he mine;
   And it shall not be for lack o gowd
     That ye your love sall tyne.

31 'For I have seven ships o mine ain,
     A' loaded to the brim,
   And I will gie them a' to thee,
     Wi four to thine eldest son:
   But thanks to a' the powers in heaven
     That I gae maiden hame!'

ANONYMOUS

Lay Le Freine (ca. 1130)[†]

We redeth oft, and findeth ywrite,
And this clerkes wele it wite,[1]
Layes that ben in harping,
Ben yfounde of ferli[2] thing:
Sum bethe of wer and sum of wo,
And sum of joie and mirthe also,
And sum of trecherie and of gile,
Of old aventours that fel while;[3]
And sum of bourdes and ribaudy,[4]
10 And many ther beth of fairy;[5]
Of al thinges[6] that men seth,[7]
Mest o love, forsothe, thai beth,
   In Breteyne, bi hold time,[8]
This layes were wrought, so seith this rime.
When kinges might our[9] yhere
Of ani mervailes that ther were,
Thai token an harp in gle and game,
And maked a lay and gaf it name.
   Now, of this aventours that weren yfalle
20 Y can tel sum, ac[1] nought alle.
Ac herkneth, lordinges, sothe to sain;
Ichil[2] you telle "Lay le Frayn."
   Bifel a cas[3] in Breteyne,
Wherof was made "Lay le Frain";
In Ingliche for to tellen, ywis,
Of an asche[4] forsothe it is
On ensaumple, fair withalle,

† From *The Breton Lays in Middle English*, ed. Thomas C. Rumble (Detroit: Wayne State University Press, 1965), pp. 81–87. Copyright © 1965 Wayne State University Press. Reprinted with the permission of the publisher and Clayton T. Rumble and Bruce B. Rumble, sons of Thomas C. Rumble.
1. Know.
2. Wondrous.
3. Adventures that happened long ago.
4. Coarse jokes and ribaldry.
5. Fairyland.
6. Ms. *þingeþ*.
7. Tell of.
8. In olden times.
9. Anywhere.
1. But.
2. I will.
3. Case, event.
4. Ash-tree.

That sumtime was bifalle.
    In the west-cuntré woned tvay knightes,[5]
30 And loved hem wele in al rightes—
Riche men, in her best liif,
And aither of hem hadde wedded wiif.
That o[6] knight made his levedi[7] milde
That sche was wonder gret with childe;
And when hir time was comen tho,[8]
Sche was deliverd out of wo.
The knight thonked God Almight,
And cleped[9] his messanger an hight:[1]
"Go," he seyd, "to mi neighebour swithe,[2]
40 And say Y gret him fele sithe,[3]
And pray him that he com to me,
And say he schal mi gossibbe[4] be."
    The messanger goth and hath nought forgete,
And fint the knight at his mete;
And fair he gret in the halle
The lord, the levedi, the meyne[5] alle.
And sethen[6] on knes doun him sett,
And the lord ful fair he gret;
"He bad that thou schult to him té,[7]
50 And for love his gossibbe be."
"Is his levedi deliverd with sounde?"[8]
"Ya, sir, ythonked be God the stounde!"[9]
"And whether,[1] a maidenchild other a knave?"[2]
"Tvay sones, sir, God hem save!"
The knight therof was glad and blithe,
And thonked Godes sond[3] swithe,
And graunted his erand in al thing,
And gaf him a palfray for his tiding.
    Than was the levedi of the hous

5. Lived two knights; ms. *knizte.*
6. One.
7. Lady.
8. Then.
9. Called.
1. On high, there.
2. Quickly.
3. Many times.
4. Godparent.
5. Company, household.
6. Then; ms. *sePPen.*
7. Come.
8. Soundly, safely.
9. For the time.
1. Which.
2. Boy.
3. Mercy.

60 A proude dame and an envieous—
Hokerfulliche missegging,[4]
Squeymous[5] and eke scorning.
To ich woman sche hadde envie;
Sche spak this wordes of felonie:
"Ich have wonder, thou messanger,
Who was thi lordis conseiler,
To teche him about to sende
And telle schame, in ich an ende,[6]
That his wiif hath to[7] childer ybore
70 Wele may ich man wite[8] therfore
That tvay men hir han hadde in bour;
That is hir bothe deshonour!"
   The messanger was sore aschamed;
The knight himself was sore agramed,[9]
And rebouked his levedy,
To speke ani woman vilaynie.
And ich woman therof might here,
Curssed hir alle yfere,[1]
And bisought God in heven,
80 For His holy name seven,
That yif hye[2] ever ani child schuld abide,
A wers aventour hir schuld bitide.
   Sone therafter bifel a cas
That hirself with child was.
When God wild, sche was unbounde,
And deliverd al with sounde:
To[3] maidenchilder sche hadde ybore.
When hye it wist, wo hir was therfore;
"Allas," sche seyd, "that this hap come;
90 Ich have ygoven[4] min owen dome![5]
Forboden bite[6] ich woman
To speken ani other harm upon!
Falsliche another Y gan deme:[7]

---

4. Slanderously missaying, lying.
5. Disdainful.
6. All around, everywhere.
7. Two.
8. Know.
9. Angered.
1. Together.
2. She.
3. Two.
4. Given, brought about.
5. Doom, judgment.
6. Be it.
7. Judge.

The selve happe[8] is on me sene.
"Allas," sche seyd, "that Y was born!
Withouten ende Ich am forlorn!
Or Ich mot siggen, sikerly,[9]
That tvay men han yly me by,
Or Ich mot sigge in al mi liif
100 That Y bileighe[1] mi neghbours wiif;
Or Ich mot—that God it schilde![2]—
Help to sle min owhen child.
On of this thre thinges Ich mot nede
Sigge, other don[3] in dede.
Yyf Ich say Ich hadde a bi-leman,[4]
Than Ich leighe[5] meselve opon,
And eke thai wil, that me se,
Held me wers than comoun be;
And yyf Ich knawelethe[6] to ich man
110 That Ich leighe the levedi opon,
Than Ich wold[7] of old and yong
Be hold leighster,[8] and fals of tong.
Yete me is best take mi chaunce,
And sle mi childe and do penaunce,"
    Hir midwiif hye cleped hir to:
"Anon," sche seyd, "this child fordo,[9]
And ever say thou, wher thou go,
That Ich have o child and na mo."
The midwiif answerd thurchout al[1]
120 That hye nil,[2] no hye ne schal.
    [The levedi hadde a maiden fre
Who ther ynurtured hade ybe
And fostered fair ful mony a yere;
Sche saw her kepe this sori chere,
And wepe, and syke,[3] and crye, "Alas!"
And thoghte to helpen her in this cas.
And thus sche spake, this maiden ying,

8. Same thing.
9. Either I must say, surely, . . .
1. Lied about, wronged.
2. Prevent.
3. Do.
4. Second lover, paramour.
5. Lie.
6. Acknowledge.
7. Ms. *worþ* (become).
8. Liar.
9. Slay.
1. To all of this.
2. Will not.
3. Sigh.

"So nolde[4] Y wepen for no kind thing:
But this o child wol I of-bare
130   And in a covent[5] leve it yare.
Ne schalt thou be aschamed at al;
And whoso findeth this childe smal,
By Mary, blissful quene above,][6]
May help it for Godes love!"
       The levedi graunted anon therto,
And wold wele that it were ydo.[7]
Sche toke a riche baudekine[8]
That hir lord brought fram Costentine,
And lapped the litel maiden therin,
140   And toke a ring of gold fin,
And on hir right arm it knitt,
With a lace of silke therin plit.[9]
And whoso hir founde schulde have in mende[1]
That it were comen of riche kende.[2]
       The maide toke the childe hir mide,[3]
And stale oway in an eventide,
And passed over a wild heth;
Thurch feld and thurch wode hye geth
Al the winterlong night.
150   The weder was clere, the mone was light;
So that[4] hye com bi a forest side,
Sche wax al weri and gan abide.
Sone after sche gan herk[5]
Cokkes crowe and houndes berk.
Sche arose and thider wold;[6]
Ner and nere[7] sche gan bihold.
Walles and hous fele[8] hye seighe,
A chirche with stepel fair and heighe;
Than nas ther noither strete no toun,
160   But an hous of religioun,

4. Would not.
5. Convent.
6. The thirteen lines here bracketed are missing from the ms.; the reconstruction is
   Weber's, who followed closely 11. 99–115 of Marie de France's *Lai le Fresne.*
7. Done.
8. Embroidered cloth.
9. Pleated, enfolded; ms. *pilt.*
1. Mind, *i.e.* should recognize.
2. Kind, kin.
3. With.
4. When.
5. Hear.
6. Would go.
7. Nearer and nearer.
8. Many.

An order of nonnes, wele ydight[9]
To servy God bothe day and night.
　The maiden abod no lengore,
Bot yede hir[1] to the chirche dore,
And on knes sche sat adoun,
And seyd, wepeand,[2] her orisoun:[3]
"O Lord," hye[4] seyd, "Jhesu Crist,
That sinful man bedes herst,[5]
Underfong[6] this present,
170　And help this seli[7] innocent
That it mot[8] ycristned be,
For Marie love, thi moder fre!"
　Hye loked up, and bi hir seighe
An asche bi hir, fair and heighe,
Wele ybowed,[9] of michel priis;[1]
The bodi was holow, as mani on is.
Therin sche leyd the child for cold,
In the pel[2] as it was bifold,
And blisced[3] it with al hir might.
180　With that it gan to dawe[4] light;
The foules up and song on bough,
And acre-men yede to the plough.
The maiden turned ogain anon,
And toke the waye hye[5] hadde er gon

*　*　*

9. Prepared, dedicated
1. Went, took herself.
2. Weeping.
3. Prayer.
4. Ms. *he.*
5. Sinful man's prayers hear.
6. Receive.
7. Poor, wretched.
8. May.
9. Branched.
1. Worth.
2. Swaddling blanket, pallet.
3. Blessed.
4. Dawn.
5. Ms. *he.*

Medical Traditions

ARISTOTLE

From The History of Animals (ca. 350 B.C.E.)[†]

Book VII, Part 4

Now among other animals, if a pair of twins happen to be male and female they have as good a chance of surviving as though both had been males or both females; but among mankind very few twins survive if one happen to be a boy and the other a girl.

Of all animals the woman and the mare are most inclined to receive the commerce of the male during pregnancy; while all other animals when they are pregnant avoid the male, save those in which the phenomenon of superfoetation occurs, such as the hare. Unlike that animal, the mare after once conceiving cannot be rendered pregnant again, but brings forth one foal only, at least as a general rule; in the human species cases of superfoetation are rare, but they do happen now and then.

An embryo conceived some considerable time after a previous conception does not come to perfection, but gives rise to pain and causes the destruction of the earlier embryo; and, by the way, a case has been known to occur where owing to this destructive influence no less than twelve embryos conceived by superfoetation have been discharged. But if the second conception take place at a short interval, then the mother bears that which was later conceived, and brings forth the two children like actual twins, as happened, according to the legend, in the case of Iphicles and Hercules. The following also is a striking example: a certain woman, having committed adultery, brought forth the one child resembling her husband and the other resembling the adulterous lover.

The case has also occurred where a woman, being pregnant of twins, has subsequently conceived a third child; and in course of time she brought forth the twins perfect and at full term, but the third a

† From *The Works of Aristotle*, Volume IV: *Historium Animalium*, translated by D'Arcy Wentworth Thompson, ed. J. A. Smith and W. D. Ross (Oxford: Clarendon Press, 1910).

five-months' child; and this last died there and then. And in another case it happened that the woman was first delivered of a seven-months' child, and then of two which were of full term; and of these the first died and the other two survived.

Some also have been known to conceive while about to miscarry, and they have lost the one child and been delivered of the other.

If women while going with child cohabit after the eighth month the child is in most cases born covered over with a slimy fluid. Often also the child is found to be replete with food of which the mother had partaken.

*   *   *

Book VII, Part 6

From deformed parents come deformed children, lame from lame and blind from blind, and, speaking generally, children often inherit anything that is peculiar in their parents and are born with similar marks, such as pimples or scars. Such things have been known to be handed down through three generations; for instance, a certain man had a mark on his arm which his son did not possess, but his grandson had it in the same spot though not very distinct.

Such cases, however, are few; for the children of cripples are mostly sound, and there is no hard and fast rule regarding them. While children mostly resemble their parents or their ancestors, it sometimes happens that no such resemblance is to be traced. But parents may pass on resemblance after several generations, as in the case of the woman in Elis, who committed adultery with a negro; in this case it was not the woman's own daughter but the daughter's child that was a blackamoor.

As a rule the daughters have a tendency to take after the mother, and the boys after the father; but sometimes it is the other way, the boys taking after the mother and the girls after the father. And they may resemble both parents in particular features.

There have been known cases of twins that had no resemblance to one another, but they are alike as a general rule. There was once upon a time a woman who had intercourse with her husband a week after giving birth to a child and she conceived and bore a second child as like the first as any twin. Some women have a tendency to produce children that take after themselves, and others children that take after the husband; and this latter case is like that of the celebrated mare in Pharsalus, that got the name of the Honest Wife.

PLINY THE ELDER

From Natural History (77–79)[†]

*   *   *

When, however, a moderate interval of time separates two concep-
tions, both may be successful, as was seen in the case of Hercules
and his brother Iphicles, and in that of a woman who bore twins of
whom one resembled her husband and the other an adulterer; and
also in that of a serving girl who, as a result of sexual intercourse
on the same day, bore one twin resembling her master and the other
resembling the steward [procurator].

*   *   *

† From *Pliny: Natural History,* Volume II, Books 3–7, translated by H. Rackham (Cam-
bridge, MA: Harvard University Press, 1958), p. 539. Copyright © 1942 by the President
and Fellows of Harvard College. Reprinted by permission of the publishers and the
Trustees of the Loeb Classical Library ®, a registered trademark of the President and
Fellows of Harvard College.

Fable Sources and Analogues: Similar Themes

BABRIUS

From Aesopic Fables†

67. *The Lion's Share*

A wild ass and a lion were partners in the hunt. The lion excelled in valour, the ass in swiftness of foot. When they had made a large killing of animals the lion divided the booty and laid it out in three portions. "Now this first portion," said he, "I shall take myself, because I am king; and I shall take that second one also, as being partner with you on equal terms. As for this third portion, it will make trouble for you, unless you are willing to run away."

Measure yourself: don't get involved in any business or partnership with a man who is more powerful than yourself.

77. *The Fox and the Crow*

A crow, holding in his mouth a piece of cheese, stood perched aloft. A crafty fox who hankered for the cheese deceived the bird with words to this effect: "Sir Crow, thy wings are beautiful, bright and keen thine eye, thy neck a wonder to behold. An eagle's breast thou dost display, and with thy talons over all the beasts thou canst prevail. So great a bird thou art; yet mute, alas, and without utterance." On hearing this flattery the crow's heart was puffed up with conceit, and, dropping the cheese from his mouth, he loudly screamed: "Caw! Caw!" The clever fox pounced on the cheese and tauntingly remarked: "You were not dumb, it seems, you have indeed a voice; you have everything, Sir Crow, except brains."

† From *Babrius and Phaedrus*, ed. and trans. Ben Edwin Perry (Cambridge, MA: Harvard University Press, 1965), pp. 83, 85, 97, 141, 143. Reprinted by permission of the publishers and the Trustees of the Loeb Classical Library. Copyright © 1965 by the President and Fellows of Harvard College. Dated to second century C.E.

108. *The Country Mouse and the City Mouse*

Two mice decided to share their living with each other. One of them lived in the country, the other had his nest in a rich man's pantry. The house-bred mouse first came to dine in the country, when the fields had just begun to blossom with verdure. After nibbling on some meagre and sodden roots of grain mixed together with clods of black soil, he said: "It's the life of a miserable ant that you live here, eating scanty bits of barley meal in the depths of the earth. As for me, I have an abundance of good things, even more than I need. Compared with you, I live in the Horn of Plenty. If you will come with me to my house, you will indulge your appetite as much as you like and leave this ground for the moles to dig up." So he led the toiling country mouse away, having persuaded him to enter a man's house by creeping under the wall. He showed him where there was a lot of barley, where there was a pile of pulse, casks of figs, jars of honey, and baskets full of dates. The country mouse was delighted with it all and went for it eagerly. He was dragging a piece of cheese from a basket when someone suddenly opened the door; whereupon he leapt back in fright and fled into the recess of his narrow hole, squeaking unintelligibly and crowding against his host. He waited a while and then, popping out from within, was about to lay hold of a Camiraean fig;[1] but just then another man entered to get something else, and both mice hid themselves again in their holes. Then said the country mouse: "Farewell to you and such feasts as these; enjoy your wealth and revel all by yourself in superfine banquets. This abundance of yours is full of danger. As for me, I'll not desert the homely clods, under which I munch my barley free of fear."

PHAEDRUS

From The Aesopic Fables of Phaedrus the Freedman of Augustus[†]

Book I

PROLOGUE

Aesop is my source. He invented the substance of these fables, but I have put them into finished form in senarian verse. A double dowry

---

1. Cameiros was a city on the island of Rhodes, and Rhodian figs were considered unusually good.
† From *Babrius and Phaedrus*, ed. and trans. Ben Edwin Perry (Cambridge, MA: Harvard University Press, 1965), pp. 191, 193, 197, 199, 217, 279, 387, 389, 393, 395. Reprinted by permission of the publishers and the Trustees of the Loeb Classical Library. Copyright © 1965 by the President and Fellows of Harvard College. Dated to first century C.E.

comes with this, my little book: it moves to laughter, and by wise counsels guides the conduct of life. Should anyone choose to run it down, because trees too are vocal, not wild beasts alone, let him remember that I speak in jest of things that never happened.

THE WOLF AND THE LAMB

Impelled by thirst, a wolf and a lamb had come to the same brook. Upstream stood the wolf, much lower down the lamb. Then the spoiler, prompted by his wicked gullet, launched a pretext for a quarrel: "Why," said he, "have you roiled the water where I am drinking?" Sore afraid, the woolly one made answer: "Pray, how can I, wolf, be guilty of the thing you charge? The water flows from you downstream to where I drink." Balked by the power of truth, the wolf exclaimed, "Six months ago you cursed me." "Indeed," replied the lamb, "at that time I was not yet born." "Well, I swear, your father cursed me," said the wolf, and, with no more ado, he pounced upon the lamb and tore him, and the lamb died for no just cause.

This fable was composed to fit those persons who invent false charges by which to oppress the innocent.

THE DOG CARRYING A PIECE OF MEAT ACROSS THE RIVER

He who goes after what belongs to another deservedly loses his own.

A dog, while carrying a piece of meat across a river, caught sight of his own image floating in the mirror of the waters and, thinking that it was another prize carried by another dog, decided to snatch it. But his greed was disappointed: he let go the meal that he held in his mouth, and failed besides to grasp the meal for which he strove.

THE COW, THE SHE-GOAT, THE SHEEP, AND THE LION

To go shares with the mighty is never a safe investment. This little fable bears witness to my statement.

A cow, a she-goat, and a sheep, patient sufferer when wronged, went into partnership with a lion in the forest. When they had captured a stag of mighty bulk the lion made four portions and spoke as follows: "I take the first portion by virtue of my title, since I am addressed as king; the second portion you will assign to me because I am a partner; then, since I am superior to you in strength, the third portion will come my way; and it will be too bad for anyone who meddles with the fourth." Thus all the booty was carried off by ruthlessness alone.

THE OLD LION, THE BOAR, THE BULL, AND THE ASS

Anyone who has lost the prestige that he once had becomes in his disastrous state subject to insult even by cowards.

When a lion, worn out by age and bereft of his strength, lay fee-
bly drawing his last breath a wild boar came up with foaming mouth
and murderous tusks and with a thrust avenged an old wrong. Soon
after a bull with angry horns gored the body of his foe. An ass, on
seeing the wild beast maltreated with impunity, gave him a smashing
kick in the face. Then, as he died, the lion said: "I resented the insults
of the brave; but as for you, you disgrace to Nature, when I put up
with you, as now at life's end I must, I seem to die a second death."

THE COCKEREL AND THE PEARL

A cockerel on a dunghill, while looking for something to eat, found a
pearl. "What a fine thing you are," said he, "to be lying in so improper
a place! If only someone who coveted your value had seen this sight
you would long ago have been restored to your original splendour.
But my finding you—since I'm much more interested in food than
in pearls—is of no possible use either to you or to me."
    This tale is for those who do not appreciate me.

Perotti's Appendix

JUNO, VENUS, AND THE HEN
Concerning the lust of women

When Juno was praising her own chastity (*and declaring in the pres-
ence of the gods and goddesses that it was better for a woman to be
joined with one man only*), Venus, just for the fun of it, did not oppose
her, but, by way of showing that there was no other woman like her,
is said to have questioned the hen in the following manner: "Tell me,
please, with how much food can you be satisfied?" The hen replied:
"Whatever you give me will be enough, provided you allow me to
scratch for odd bits with my feet." "Would you give up scratching
for a peck of wheat?" she continued. "Oh certainly, why, that's more
than enough; only do let me scratch." "What will you take then not
to scratch at all?" Then at last the hen confessed her natural
weakness: "Though an entire granary were thrown open for me, I
would scratch just the same." Juno is said to have laughed at the jest-
ing of Venus, because by the hen she branded women in general.

THE WIDOW AND THE SOLDIER
The great inconstancy and lustfulness of women

A certain woman on losing her husband, whom she had loved and
cherished for a number of years, preserved his body in a sepulchre;
and when it appeared that she could not by any means be torn away
from him but was spending her life mourning in the sepulchre, she
acquired the shining reputation of a very chaste wife. Meanwhile

some persons who had plundered the sanctuary of Jupiter paid for
their crime against the divinity by crucifixion; and lest anyone should
take away their remains, soldiers were stationed as guards over the
bodies, adjacent to the monument in which the woman had secluded
herself. Once one of the guards in the middle of the night, being
thirsty, asked for some water from the maidservant, who happened
at that time to be waiting on her mistress as she was going to bed;
for she had been sitting up by lamplight and had prolonged her vigil
to a late hour. The door being opened a bit, the soldier peers inside
and sees a woman of remarkable beauty. His mind is ravished and
at once on fire; gradually there rises within him a lust for the woman,
which he cannot resist. His inventive shrewdness finds a thousand
pretexts for seeing the widow more frequently. Daily association had
its effect upon her. Gradually she became more complaisant to the
stranger; and before long a stronger tie bound her heart to him.
While the guard, more attentive as a lover than as a watchman, was
passing his nights here in the sepulchre, a body was found to be miss-
ing from one of the crosses. Greatly disturbed, the soldier explained
to the lady what had happened. To his surprise the very highly
respected woman said. "There's nothing for you to fear," and she sur-
rendered her husband's body to be fastened on the cross, in order
that he, her lover, might not undergo the punishment for his neglect.
Thus did infamy take by storm the stronghold of fair fame.

GEOFFREY CHAUCER

From The Merchant's Tale (ca. 1390)[†]

* * *

2320	Now lat us turne agayn to Januarie,	
	That in the gardin with his faire May	
	Singeth ful merier° than the papejay,°	*more merrily / parrot*
	"Yow love I best, and shal, and other noon."°	*no one else*
	So longe aboute the aleyes° is he goon°	*garden paths (alleys) / has he walked*
2325	Til he was come agaynes thilke pyrie°	*in front of that very pear tree*
	Wher as° this Damian sitteth ful myrie	*Where*
	An heigh° among the fresshe leves grene.	*On high*
	This fresshe May, that is so bright and shene,°	*fair, beautiful*
	Gan for to syke° and seyde, "Allas, my syde!	*Began to sigh*

† From *The Canterbury Tales: A Norton Critical Edition*, Second Edition, ed. V. A. Kolve
and Glending Olson (New York: Norton, 2005), pp. 209–11. Copyright © 2005, 1989 by
W. W. Norton & Company, Inc. Used by permission of W. W. Norton & Company, Inc.

2330 Now sir," quod she, "for aught that may bityde,°   *whatever may happen*
I moste han of the peres° that I see   *must have (some) of*
    the pears
Or I mot° dye, so sore longeth me°   *must / intensely I long*
To eten° of the smale peres grene.   *eat*
Help, for hir love that is of hevene quene!°   *i.e., the Virgin Mary*
2335 I telle yow wel, a womman in my plyt°   *condition (implying*
May han to fruit so greet an appetyt   *pregnancy)*
That she may dyen but° she of it have."   *unless*
    "Allas," quod he, "that I ne had heer a knave°   *servant*
That coude climbe! Allas, allas," quod he,
2340 "That I am blind!" "Ye, sir, no fors,"° quod she,   *no matter*
"But wolde ye vouchesauf,° for Goddes sake,   *But if you would agree*
The pyrie inwith° your armes for to take   *within*
(For wel I woot° that ye mistruste me),   *know*
Thanne sholde I climbe wel ynogh," quod she,
2345 "So° I my foot mighte sette upon your bak."   *Provided that*
    "Certes," quod he, "theron shal be no lak,°   *i.e., I will not fail*
    to do that
Mighte° I yow helpen with myn herte blood."   *I.e., even if it meant that*
He stoupeth doun, and on his bak she stood,
And caughte hir by a twiste,° and up she gooth—   *grabbed hold of a*
    branch
2350 Ladies, I prey yow that ye be nat wrooth;°   *angry*
I can nat glose;° I am a rude° man—   *gloss over with fine*
    words / rough, plain
And sodeynly anon this Damian
Gan pullen° up the smok, and in he throng.°   *Began to pull / thrust*
And whan that Pluto saugh this grete wrong,
2355 To Januarie he gaf° agayn his sighte   *gave*
And made him see as wel as ever he mighte.
    And whan that he hadde caught his sighte agayn,
Ne was ther never man of thing so fayn.°   *happy*
But on his wyf his thoght was evermo;
2360 Up to the tree he caste his eyen two
And saugh that Damian his wyf had dressed°   *dealt with*
In swich° manere it may nat ben expressed   *such*
But if° I wolde speke uncurteisly.°   *Unless / crudely*
And up he yaf a roring and a cry
2365 As doth the moder° whan the child shal dye.   *mother*
"Out! Help! Allas! Harrow!"° he gan to crye.   *Help*
"O Stronge lady store,° what dostow?"°   *bold, brazen woman /*
    doest thou
    And she answerde, "Sir, what eyleth° yow?   *ails*
Have pacience and reson in your minde.
2370 I have yow holpe° on bothe your eyen blinde.   *helped*

Up° peril of my soule I shal nat lyen: *Upon*
As me was taught, to hele with° your yën   *heal*
Was nothing bet° to make yow to see   *better, more effective*
Than strugle° with a man upon a tree.   *wrestle*
2375 God woot° I dide it in ful good entente."   *knows*
    "Strugle?" quod he. "Ye, algate° in it wente!   *nevertheless*
God yeve° yow bothe on shames deeth° to   *give / a shameful death*
    dyen!
He swyved° thee! I saugh it with myne yën,°   *had sex with / eyes*
And elles° be I hanged by the hals!"°   *Or else / neck*
2380 "Thanne is," quod she, "my medicyne al fals.°   *wrong, useless*
For certeinly, if that ye mighte° see,   *were able to*
Ye wolde nat seyn thise wordes unto me.
Ye han° som glimsing° and no parfit° sighte."   *have / glimpse, fleeting look / perfect*

    "I see," quod he, "as wel as ever I mighte,
2385 Thonked be God, with bothe myne eyen two,
And by my trouthe, me thoughte° he dide   *it seemed to me*
    thee so."
    "Ye maze,° maze, gode sire," quod she.   *are confused, dazed*
"This thank have I for I have maad° yow see.   *made*
Allas," quod she, "that ever I was so kinde!"°   *(with pun on "natural")*
2390 "Now, dame," quod he, "lat al passe out of
    minde.
Com doun, my lief,° and if I have missayd,°   *love / misspoken*
God help me so, as I am yvel apayd.°   *sorry*
But by my fader soule, I wende han seyn°   *thought I saw*
How that this Damian had by thee leyn,°   *i.e., pressed against*
2395 And that thy smok had leyn upon his brest."
    "Ye, sire," quod she, "ye may wene° as yow lest;°   *believe / wish*
But, sire, a man that waketh out of his sleep,
He may nat sodeynly wel taken keep°   *take good notice*
Upon a thing, ne seen it parfitly°   *perfectly*
2400 Til that he be adawed verraily.°   *truly awakened*
Right so a man that longe hath blind y-be
Ne may nat sodeynly so wel y-see
First,° whan his sighte is newe come ageyn,   *At first*
As he that hath a day or two y-seyn.
2405 Til that your sighte y-satled° be a whyle,   *settled*
Ther may ful many a sighte yow bigyle.°   *deceive*
Beth war,° I prey yow, for by hevene° king,   *Be aware / heaven's*
Ful many a man weneth to seen° a thing,   *thinks to have seen*
And it is al another° than it semeth.   *completely other*
2410 He that misconceyveth,° he misdemeth."°   *misapprehends / misjudges*
And with that word she leep° doun fro the tree.   *leaped*

This Januarie, who is glad but he?
He kisseth hir and clippeth° hir ful ofte,   *embraces*
And on hir wombe° he stroketh hir ful softe,   *stomach*
2415 And to his palays° hoom he hath hir lad.°   *palace / led*
Now, gode men, I pray yow to be glad.
Thus endeth heer my tale of Januarie.
God bless us, and his moder Seinte Marie!

The Epilogue

"Ey! Goddes mercy!" seyde our Hoste tho.°   *then*
2420 "Now swich° a wyf I pray God kepe me fro!   *such*
Lo, whiche sleightes° and subtilitees   *what tricks*
In wommen been, for ay° as bisy as bees   *always*
Ben they, us sely° men for to deceyve,   *simple, innocent*
And from a sothe° ever wol they weyve.°   *truth / turn away, avoid*
2425 By this Marchauntes tale it preveth weel.°   *surely proves true*
But doutelees,° as trewe as any steel   *without doubt*
I have a wyf, though that she povre° be;   *poor*
But of hir tonge a labbing° shrewe is she,   *blabbing*
And yet° she hath an heep° of vyces mo.°   *also / heap, great number / more*
2430 Therof no fors°—lat alle swiche thinges go.   *no matter*
But wite ye what?° In conseil° be it seyd,   *do you know what / confidence*

Me reweth sore° I am unto hir teyd.°   *It grieves me painfully / tied*
For and° I sholde rekenen° every vyce   *if / reckon, count up*
Which that she hath, ywis I were to nyce.°   *truly I would be too foolish*
2435 And cause why? It sholde reported be
And told to hir of° somme of this meynee,°   *by / company*
Of° whom it nedeth nat for to declare,   *By*
Sin° wommen connen outen°   *Since / know how to spread*
     swich chaffare.°   *wares, matters*
And eek° my wit suffyseth nat therto   *also*
2440 To tellen al, wherfor my tale is do."°   *done*

PETRONIUS ARBITER

From The Widow of Ephesus[†]

Our efforts at peace seemed to be succeeding. In no time at all, Lichas and I were well on the way to a genuine reconciliation, and Tryphaena was already amorously dumping the dregs of her drink over Giton's head. Eumolpus, meanwhile, his tongue loosened by the wine, was pouring forth a great stream of satire against bald men and branded slaves. Having finally exhausted his chilly wit on this subject, he reverted to verse and improvised the following little elegy on hair:

> Your body's glory's fled, your hair is dead;
> your leaf has perished with the year's.
> On naked brows the shadeless sun beats down:
> Sahara starts above your ears.
>
> O gods above, how cruelly you deceive us:
> the first of all your gifts, the first to leave us.

This effort was immediately followed by a special apostrophe to Giton:

> Unhappy boy, your curls once shone
> more brightly than Apollo's own,
> and Artemis, though wondrous fair,
> combed duller hair.
>
> Now, bald as brass, thy bulbous brain,
> like mushroom cap in pelting rain,
> prinks up, and all thy quondam curls
> are mocked by girls.
>
> But so we die; so death comes on,
> as, even now, thy life has gone,
> and every curl that graced thy head,
> dear lad, lies dead.

I suspect he was on the point of following this doggerel with something even sillier, but before he could open his mouth, Tryphaena's maid snatched Giton away below deck and disguised that poor bald head with one of her mistress' wigs. Then taking a pair of eyebrows

---

[†] From *The Satyricon of Petronius* (dated to first century c.e.), translated by William Arrowsmith (Ann Arbor: University of Michigan Press, 1959), pp. 120–25. Translation copyright © 1959, renewed © 1987 by William Arrowsmith. Used by permission of Dutton Signet, a division of Penguin Group, and by the Estate of William Arrowsmith.

from a tiny case, she deftly fitted them to the vanished hairline, quite restoring the boy to his pristine beauty. Recognizing her true Giton at last, Tryphaena burst into tears of joy and kissed him for the first time with unmistakable warmth. For my part, although overjoyed to see the boy blossom forth in all his old beauty, I felt by contrast, so horribly disfigured and so hideously ugly—even Lichas couldn't bear to look at me—that I covered my face in shame. But the same little maid proved my savior too, and leading me off, covered me with a head of hair quite as splendid as Giton's. In fact, if anything, I acquired rather more than I had lost, for the wig was blonde, and my head fairly shone with a tangled, golden glory . . .

Meanwhile Eumolpus, our spokesman in the hour of danger and the author of our present reconciliation, anxious that our gaiety should not be broken, began, in a sudden moment of silence, to gibe at the fickleness of women, the wonderful ease with which they became infatuated, their readiness to abandon their children for their lovers, and so forth. In fact, he declared, no woman was so chaste or faithful that she couldn't be seduced; sooner or later she would fall head over heels in love with some passing stranger. Nor, he added, was he thinking so much of the old tragedies and the classics of love betrayed as of something that had happened in our own time; in fact, if we were willing to hear, he would be delighted to tell the story. All eyes and ears were promptly turned to our narrator, and he began:
"Once upon a time there was a certain married woman in the city of Ephesus whose fidelity to her husband was so famous that the women from all the neighboring towns and villages used to troop into Ephesus merely to stare at this prodigy. It happened, however, that her husband one day died. Finding the normal custom of following the cortege with hair unbound and beating her breast in public quite inadequate to express her grief, the lady insisted on following the corpse right into the tomb, an underground vault of the Greek type, and there set herself to guard the body, weeping and wailing night and day. Although in her extremes of grief she was clearly courting death from starvation, her parents were utterly unable to persuade her to leave, and even the magistrates, after one last supreme attempt, were rebuffed and driven away. In short, all Ephesus had gone into mourning for this extraordinary woman, all the more since the lady was how passing her fifth consecutive day without once tasting food. Beside the failing woman sat her devoted maid, sharing her mistress' grief and relighting the lamp whenever it flickered out. The whole city could speak, in fact, of nothing else: here at last, all classes alike agreed, was the one true example of conjugal fidelity and love.
"In the meantime, however, the governor of the province gave orders that several thieves should be crucified in a spot close by the

vault where the lady was mourning her dead husband's corpse. So, on the following night, the soldier who had been assigned to keep watch on the crosses so that nobody could remove the thieves' bodies for burial suddenly noticed a light blazing among the tombs and heard the sounds of groaning. And prompted by a natural human curiosity to know who or what was making those sounds, he descended into the vault.

"But at the sight of a strikingly beautiful woman, he stopped short in terror, thinking he must be seeing some ghostly apparition out of hell. Then, observing the corpse and seeing the tears on the lady's face and the scratches her fingernails had gashed in her cheeks, he realized what it was: a widow, in inconsolable grief. Promptly fetching his little supper back down to the tomb, he implored the lady not to persist in her sorrow or break her heart with useless mourning. All men alike, he reminded her, have the same end; the same resting place awaits us all. He used, in short, all those platitudes we use to comfort the suffering and bring them back to life. His consolations, being unwelcome, only exasperated the widow more; more violently than ever she beat her breast, and tearing out her hair by the roots, scattered it over the dead man's body. Undismayed, the soldier repeated his arguments and pressed her to take some food, until the little maid, quite overcome by the smell of the wine, succumbed and stretched out her hand to her tempter. Then, restored by the food and wine, she began herself to assail her mistress' obstinate refusal.

"'How will it help you,' she asked the lady, 'if you faint from hunger? Why should you bury yourself alive, and go down to death before the Fates have called you? What does Vergil say?—

Do you suppose the shades and ashes of the dead
are by such sorrow touched?

No, begin your life afresh. Shake off these woman's scruples; enjoy the light while you can. Look at that corpse of your poor husband: doesn't it tell you more eloquently than any words that you should live?'

"None of us, of course, really dislikes being told that we must eat, that life is to be lived. And the lady was no exception. Weakened by her long days of fasting, her resistance crumbled at last, and she ate the food the soldier offered her as hungrily as the little maid had eaten earlier.

"Well, you know what temptations are normally aroused in a man on a full stomach. So the soldier, mustering all those blandishments by means of which he had persuaded the lady to live, now laid determined siege to her virtue. And chaste though she was, the lady found him singularly attractive and his arguments persuasive. As for the maid, she did all she could to help the soldier's cause, repeating like a refrain the appropriate line of Vergil:

If love is pleasing, lady, yield yourself to love.

To make the matter short, the lady's body soon gave up the struggle; she yielded and our happy warrior enjoyed a total triumph on both counts. That very night their marriage was consummated, and they slept together the second and the third night too, carefully shutting the door of the tomb so that any passing friend or stranger would have thought the lady of famous chastity had at last expired over her dead husband's body.

"As you can perhaps imagine, our soldier was a very happy man, utterly delighted with his lady's ample beauty and that special charm that a secret love confers. Every night, as soon as the sun had set, he bought what few provisions his slender pay permitted and smuggled them down to the tomb. One night, however, the parents of one of the crucified thieves, noticing that the watch was being badly kept, took advantage of our hero's absence to remove their son's body and bury it. The next morning, of course, the soldier was horror-struck to discover one of the bodies missing from its cross, and ran to tell his mistress of the horrible punishment which awaited him for neglecting his duty. In the circumstances, he told her, he would not wait to be tried and sentenced, but would punish himself then and there with his own sword. All he asked of her was that she make room for another corpse and allow the same gloomy tomb to enclose husband and lover together.

"Our lady's heart, however, was no less tender than pure. 'God forbid,' she cried, 'that I should have to see at one and the same time the dead bodies of the only two men I have ever loved. No, better far, I say, to hang the dead than kill the living.' With these words, she gave orders that her husband's body should be taken from its bier and strung up on the empty cross. The soldier followed this good advice, and the next morning the whole city wondered by what miracle the dead man had climbed up on the cross."

*   *   *

Purgatory and the Afterlife

BEDE

From The Ecclesiastical History of the English People[†]

Chapter 12

OF ONE AMONG THE NORTHUMBRIANS, WHO ROSE FROM THE DEAD,
AND RELATED THE THINGS WHICH HE HAD SEEN, SOME EXCITING
TERROR AND OTHERS DELIGHT. [A.D. 696.]

At this time a memorable miracle, and like to those of former days, was wrought in Britain; for, to the end that the living might be saved from the death of the soul, a certain person, who had been some time dead, rose again to life, and related many remarkable things he had seen; some of which I have thought fit here briefly to take notice of. There was a master of a family in that district of the Northumbrians which is called Cuningham, who led a religious life, as did also all that belonged to him. This man fell sick, and his distemper daily increasing, being brought to extremity, he died in the beginning of the night; but in the morning early, he suddenly came to life again, and sat up, upon which all those that sat about the body weeping, fled away in a great fright, only his wife, who loved him best, though in a great consternation and trembling, remained with him. He, comforting her, said, "Fear not, for I am now truly risen from death, and permitted again to live among men; however, I am not to live hereafter as I was wont, but from henceforward after a very different manner." Then rising immediately, he repaired to the oratory of the little town, and continuing in prayer till day, immediately divided all his substance into three parts; one whereof he gave to his wife, another to his children, and the third, belonging to himself, he instantly distributed among the poor. Not long after, he repaired to the monastery of Melrose, which is almost enclosed by

† From *The Ecclesiastical History . . . by the Venerable Bede*, trans. Lionel Cecil Jane, with an introduction by Vida D. Scudder (London: J. M. Dent & Sons, 1910), pp. 241–46.

317

the winding of the river Tweed, and having been shaven, went into a private dwelling, which the abbat had provided, where he continued till the day of his death, in such extraordinary contrition of mind and body, that though his tongue had been silent, his life declared that he had seen many things either to be dreaded or coveted, which others knew nothing of.

Thus he related what he had seen. "He that led me had a shining countenance and a bright garment, and we went on silently, as I thought, towards the north-east. Walking on, we came to a vale of great breadth and depth, but of infinite length; on the left it appeared full of dreadful flames, the other side was no less horrid for violent hail and cold snow flying in all directions; both places were full of men's souls, which seemed by turns to be tossed from one side to the other, as it were by a violent storm; for when the wretches could no longer endure the excess of heat, they leaped into the middle of the cutting cold; and finding no rest there, they leaped back again into the middle of the unquenchable flames. Now whereas an innumerable multitude of deformed spirits were thus alternately tormented far and near, as far as could be seen, without any intermission, I began to think that this perhaps might be hell, of whose intolerable flames I had often heard talk. My guide, who went before me, answered to my thought, saying, 'Do not believe so, for this is not the hell you imagine.'

"When he had conducted me, much frightened with that horrid spectacle, by degrees, to the farther end, on a sudden I saw the place begin to grow dusk and filled with darkness. When I came into it, the darkness, by degrees, grew so thick, that I could see nothing besides it and the shape and garment of him that led me. As we went on through the shades of night, on a sudden there appeared before us frequent globes of black flames, rising as it were out of a great pit, and falling back again into the same. When I had been conducted thither, my leader suddenly vanished, and left me alone in the midst of darkness and this horrid vision, whilst those same globes of fire, without intermission, at one time flew up and at another fell back into the bottom of the abyss; and I observed that all the flames, as they ascended, were full of human souls, which, like sparks flying up with smoke, were sometimes thrown on high, and again, when the vapour of the fire ceased, dropped down into the depth below. Moreover, an insufferable stench came forth with the vapours, and filled all those dark places.

"Having stood there a long time in much dread, not knowing what to do, which way to turn, or what end I might expect, on a sudden I heard behind me the noise of a most hideous and wretched lamentation, and at the same time a loud laughing, as of a rude multitude insulting captured enemies. When that noise, growing plainer, came up to me, I observed a gang of evil spirits dragging the howling and lamenting souls of men into the midst of the darkness, whilst they themselves laughed and rejoiced. Among those men, as I could discern, there was one shorn like a clergyman, a layman, and a woman. The evil spirits that dragged them went down into the midst of the burning pit; and as they went down deeper, I could no longer distinguish between the lamentation of the men and the laughing of the devils, yet I still had a confused sound in my ears. In the meantime, some of the dark spirits ascended from that flaming abyss, and running forward, beset me on all sides, and much perplexed me with their glaring eyes and the stinking fire which proceeded from their mouths and nostrils; and threatened to lay hold on me with burning tongs, which they had in their hands, yet they durst not touch me, though they frightened me. Being thus on all sides enclosed with enemies and darkness, and looking about on every side for assistance, there appeared behind me, on the way that I came, as it were, the brightness of a star shining amidst the darkness; which increased by degrees, and came rapidly towards me: when it drew near, all those evil spirits, that sought to carry me away with their tongs, dispersed and fled.

"He, whose approach put them to flight, was the same that led me before; who, then turning towards the right, began to lead me, as it were, towards the south-east, and having soon brought me out of the darkness, conducted me into an atmosphere of clear light. While he thus led me in open light, I saw a vast wall before us, the length and height of which, in every direction, seemed to be altogether boundless. I began to wonder why we went up to the wall, seeing no door, window, or path through it. When we came to the wall, we were presently, I know not by what means, on the top of it, and within it was a vast and delightful field, so full of fragrant flowers that the odour of its delightful sweetness immediately dispelled the stink of the dark furnace, which had pierced me through and through. So great was the light in this place, that it seemed to exceed the brightness of the day, or the sun in its meridian height. In this field were innumerable assemblies of men in white, and many companies seated together rejoicing. As he led me through the midst of those happy inhabitants, I began to think that this might, perhaps, be the kingdom of heaven, of which I had often heard so much. He answered to my thought, saying, 'This is not the kingdom of heaven, as you imagine.'

"When we had passed those mansions of blessed souls and gone farther on, I discovered before me a much more beautiful light, and therein heard sweet voices of persons singing, and so wonderful a fragrancy proceeded from the place, that the other which I had before thought most delicious, then seemed to me but very indifferent; even as that extraordinary brightness of the flowery field, compared with this, appeared mean and inconsiderable. When I began to hope we should enter that delightful place, my guide on a sudden stood still; and then turning back, led me back by the way we came.

"When we returned to those joyful mansions of the souls in white, he said to me, 'Do you know what all these things are which you have seen?' I answered, I did not; and then he replied, 'That vale you saw so dreadful for consuming flames and cutting cold, is the place in which the souls of those are tried and punished, who, delaying to confess and amend their crimes, at length have recourse to repentance at the point of death, and so depart this life; but nevertheless because they, even at their death, confessed and repented, they shall all be received into the kingdom of heaven at the day of judgment; but many are relieved before the day of judgment, by the prayers, alms, and fasting, of the living, and more especially by masses. That fiery and stinking pit, which you saw, is the mouth of hell, into which whosoever falls shall never be delivered to all eternity. This flowery place, in which you see these most beautiful young people, so bright and merry, is that into which the souls of those are received who depart the body in good works, but who are not so perfect as to deserve to be immediately admitted into the kingdom of heaven; yet they shall all, at the day of judgment, see Christ, and partake of the joys of his kingdom; for whoever are perfect in thought, word and deed, as soon as they depart the body, immediately enter into the kingdom of heaven; in the neighbourhood, whereof that place is, where you heard the sound of sweet singing, with the fragrant odour and bright light. As for you, who are now to return to your body, and live among men again, if you will endeavour nicely to examine your actions, and direct your speech and behaviour in righteousness and simplicity, you shall, after death, have a place or residence among these joyful troops of blessed souls; for when I left you for a while, it was to know how you were to be disposed of.' When he had said this to me, I much abhorred returning to my body, being delighted with the sweetness and beauty of the place I beheld, and with the company of those I saw in it. However, I durst not ask him any questions; but in the meantime, on a sudden, I found myself alive among men."

Now these and other things which this man of God saw, he would not relate to slothful persons and such as lived negligently; but only to those who, being terrified with the dread of torments, or delighted with the hopes of heavenly joys, would make use of his words to advance in piety. In the neighbourhood of his cell lived one Hemgils, a monk, eminent in the priesthood, which he honoured by his good works : he is still living, and leading a solitary life in Ireland, supporting his declining age with coarse bread and cold water. He often went to that man, and asking several questions, heard of him all the particulars of what he had seen when separated from his body; by whose relation we also came to the knowledge of those few particulars which we have briefly set down. He also related his visions to King Alfrid, a man most learned in all respects, and was by him so willingly and attentively heard, that at his request he was admitted into the monastery above-mentioned, and received the monastic tonsure; and the said king, when he happened to be in those parts, very often went to hear him. At that time the religious and humble abbat and priest, Ethelwald, presided over the monastery, and now with worthy conduct possesses the episcopal see of the church of Lindisfarne.

He had a more private place of residence assigned him in that monastery, where he might apply himself to the service of his Creator in continual prayer. And as that place lay on the bank of the river, he was wont often to go into the same to do penance in his body, and many times to dip quite under the water, and to continue saying psalms or prayers in the same as long as he could endure it, standing still sometimes up to the middle, and sometimes to the neck in water; and when he went out from thence ashore, he never took off his cold and frozen garments till they grew warm and dry on his body. And when in the winter the half-broken pieces of ice were swimming about him, which he had himself broken, to make room to stand or dip himself in the river, those who beheld it would say, "It is wonderful, brother Drithelm (for so he was called), that you are able to endure such violent cold;" he simply answered, for he was a man of much simplicity and indifferent wit, "I have seen greater cold." And when they said, "It is strange that you will endure such austerity;" he replied, "I have seen more austerity." Thus he continued, through an indefatigable desire of heavenly bliss, to subdue his aged body with daily fasting, till the day of his being called away; and thus he forwarded the salvation of many by his words and example.

H. OF SALTREY

From Saint Patrick's Purgatory (ca. 1180)[†]

Ninth Torment

But the devils, not yet tired of ill-treating the soldier of Christ, came to him and dragged him towards the south. And suddenly he saw in front of him a horrible flame stinking of foul sulphur which shot up

[†] From Saint Patrick's Purgatory: A Twelfth-Century Tale of a Journey to Another World, trans. Jean-Michel Picard, with an introduction by Yolande de Pontfarcy (Dublin, Ireland: Four Courts Press, 1985), pp. 63–66. Reprinted by permission of the publisher.

as if from a well. It seemed to hurl people of both sexes and all ages, naked and blazing like sparks of fire, high into the air and as the flames lost their driving force, they kept falling back into the well and the fire. As he was getting nearer, the devils said to the knight: 'This well, belching flames, is the entrance to hell. This is our home. And since you have served us up to now, you will stay here with us for ever, because all the people who serve us will stay here with us for ever. And if you once enter here you will perish both in body and soul for all eternity. If however you agree with us, you will be able to return to your home unharmed.' But as he was confident in God's help he despised their promise. The devils then threw themselves into the well, dragging the knight with them. And as he went down deeper he found the well to be wider but he also suffered the pain more intensely. It reached the point of being so intolerable that he almost forgot the name of his Saviour. However, under God's inspiration, he returned to his senses as best he could and shouted out the name of Jesus Christ. Immediately the force of the flame projected him up into the air with the others and when he came down, he stood alone for some time beside the well. While he stood there, having withdrawn from the opening and not knowing which way to turn, other devils who were unknown to him came out of the well. They said to him: 'Why are you standing here? Our companions told you that this was meant to be hell. They were lying. It is our habit always to lie so that we can deceive through lies those we cannot dupe through truth. This is not hell. But now, we will bring you to hell.'

Tenth Torment

So, dragging the knight away with a great and horrible commotion, they arrived at a very wide and stinking river. It was entirely covered with what looked like the flames of a sulphurous fire and it was full of demons. They told him: 'We'll have you know that hell is under this burning river.' A bridge stretched above the river before him. And the demons said to the knight: 'You must cross this bridge. As for us, we will set in motion winds and whirls and throw you into the river from the bridge. And our companions there will capture you and plunge you into hell. However, we want to test you first to see if it is safe for you to cross it.' So, taking hold of his hand, they escorted him onto the bridge. There were three things on this bridge which were most frightening for those who crossed it: first, it was so slippery that, even if it had been very wide, one could scarcely, if at all, get a foothold on it; secondly, it was so narrow and thin that apparently one could barely, if at all, stand or walk on it; thirdly, it stretched so high in the air that even to lift one's gaze to its height seemed horrible. And they said: 'If you would yet agree with us to turn back you will be able to go home, safe even from this dangerous situation.' Thinking to himself of the many dangers from which his most pious Defender had saved him, the faithful soldier of Christ invoked His name and started to advance cautiously on the bridge. As he felt nothing slippery under his feet, he moved forward more firmly, confident in God. And the higher he climbed, the wider he found the bridge. And after a little time, the width of the bridge had increased so much that it would even have taken two carts going in opposite directions. Then, the devils who had led the knight to this point, not having the strength to proceed further, stood at the foot of the bridge as if waiting for him to fall. But when they saw him crossing freely, they shook the air with such a clamour that the horror of it seemed to him more unbearable than any of the pains he had previously endured at their hands. However, realising that they were stationary and had not the power to go further, and remembering his pious Guide, he went on more assuredly. The demons who were running backwards and forwards above the river threw their hooks at him, but he escaped unharmed. Finally, moving forward steadily, he saw that the width of the bridge had increased so much that he could barely look down on the water on either side.

From *The Knight in the Earthly Paradise*

So as the knight went on, now free from all harassment from the devils, he saw in front of him a big wall which rose high in the air. This wall was a wonder and the ornamentation of the masonry was beyond compare. In the wall he saw a closed door adorned with various metals and precious stones, glittering with a wonderful brightness. As he was getting nearer, yet still at a distance of about half a mile, the door opened in front of him and a fragrance pouring from it wafted up to him. It seemed so sweet that, if all the world was turned into spices, it would not surpass the intensity of this sweetness. He gathered so much strength from this sweet fragrance that he thought he would now be able to sustain, without any strain, the tortures he had suffered. And looking inside the door, he saw a land suffused with a very strong light, surpassing the splendour of the sun, and he wished to go inside. Happy is the man for whom such a door opens! And the knight did not fail to understand who had allowed him to arrive there. He was still at some distance when a procession came to meet him with crosses, banners, candles and what looked like branches of golden palms. As far as he could judge, he had never seen a procession so big and so fine on earth. There he saw people of every religious order. He saw that they were arrayed in sacred garments corresponding to their rank: some were dressed as archbishops, others as bishops, others as abbots, canons, monks, priests and the ecclesiastics of all the orders in the holy Church. Also everyone, clerics and lay people alike, seemed to be dressed in the type of clothes in which they had served God in this world. They greeted the knight with great respect and joy and bringing him with them to the harmonious sounds of a chorus unknown on earth, they entered through the door.

*   *   *

TNUGDAL

From The Vision of Tnugdal (1149)[†]

Prologue

To the venerable Lady G . . . , devoted to God and abbess by God's gift, Brother Marcus, her devoted servant: may his service show strength and readiness. * * * [Y]our wisdom has so wished that our pen, although uneducated, should translate the mystery which was shown to Tnugdal, an Irishman, from the vernacular into the Latin language, and that we should send it to you for copying under your vigilance. * * * But since it is not our intention to keep on writing grandiloquent sentences, we shall hasten, with the help of God, to start the little work which has been entrusted to us.

Introduction

BEGINNING OF THE VISION OF AN IRISH KNIGHT WRITTEN FOR THE EDIFICATION OF THE MULTITUDE

Ireland is an island situated at the extremity of the western ocean and stretches out from south to north. It is outstanding for its lakes and rivers, planted with woods, most fertile in cereals, opulent in milk, honey and all kinds of fish and game, lacking in vines but rich in wine. Snakes, frogs, toads and all venomous animals are unknown there, to the extent that its wood, leather thongs, horns and clay are known to triumph over all poisons. It is quite famous for its religious men and women but is also well known for its cruel battles. * * * Armagh is the metropole of the northern Irish, but Cashel is the most eminent see in the south, and there a nobleman was born, called

---

[†]   From *The Vision of Tnugdal*, trans. Jean-Michel Picard, with an introduction by Yolande de Pontfarcy (Dublin, Ireland: Four Courts Press, 1989), pp. 109–15, 123–29. Reprinted by permission of the publisher.

Tnugdal, whose wickedness—or rather the workings of God's mercy on him—are the subject of our little work.

This man was of a young age, of noble lineage, had a happy face and an elegant appearance; he had been brought up in the manner of the court, was carefully dressed, arrogant in spirit and not ill trained in martial arts. But I cannot say this without pain: his confidence in his physical appearance and strength was matched by an equally bad neglect of the eternal salvation of his soul. As he himself confessed with tears on many subsequent occasions, he used to become angry whenever anyone mentioned, even briefly, the salvation of his soul. He did not care about God's Church and did not even want to see Christ's poor. He gave away whatever he had to jesters, players and jugglers. But when divine mercy chose to put an end to so much evil, he was challenged at the appointed time. For, according to the testimony of many inhabitants of the city of Cork who were close to him at the time, he lay dead for a period of three days and three nights, during which he learned bitterly about all the sins he had previously committed with pleasure. His subsequent life bears witness to all the suffering he underwent. Indeed he suffered many kinds of unbelievable and intolerable torments, the order and name of which we have not been loth to write to you, for the sake of strengthening your devotion, just as we learned them from the mouth of the person who saw and suffered them.

* * *

Chapter One

THE DEPARTURE OF THE SOUL

As soon as he had shed the body and knew for sure that it was dead, the soul became frightened, conscious of his own state of sin, and did not know what to do. He wanted to go back to his own body but could not get in; he also wanted to go outside, but he was afraid to go anywhere. And so, this most miserable soul tossed and turned, conscious of his own state of sin and confident of nothing except God's mercy. He behaved this way for quite a long time, crying, wailing and shaking, for he did not know what to do, and then he saw coming towards him a multitude of foul spirits so great that not only did they fill the house and the courtyard where the dead body lay, but one could not see even a single place in all the streets and squares of the city which was not full of them. Yet, as they surrounded this poor soul, they endeavoured not to console him but on the contrary to distress him with these words: 'Let us sing the hymn of death which is due to this wretched soul, who is a child of death and food for the unquenchable fire, friend of darkness and enemy of the light'.

And all turning towards him, they gnashed their teeth at him, and in anger they lacerated their hideous cheeks with their nails, saying: 'Now, wretch, here are the people whom you chose, with whom you will go down to the roasting depths of Hell; feeder of scandal and lover of discord, why not show your arrogance? Why not commit adultery, why not fornicate? Where is your vanity and your vain gaiety? Where is your immoderate laugh? Where is your bravado thanks to which you used to insult many people? Why not wink now with your eyes as you used to do? Why no shuffling with your foot, beckoning with your finger, no evil scheming of your depraved heart?' Terrified by these and similar utterances, the poor soul could do nothing but wail, expecting from all those around him the imminent death he had been threatened with. But He who does not want the death of the sinner, the only One having the power to dispense the cure after death, the almighty Lord, just and merciful, who organises everything according to his own secret judgment, assuaged this misery according to his will.

Chapter Two

THE COMING OF THE ANGEL TO MEET THE SOUL

So, he sent his angel to meet him. When Tnugdal saw him coming from afar like a great shining star, he cast untiring eyes over him, hoping to receive some advice from him. And as he drew near, the angel called him by his own name and greeted him with these words: 'Hail, Tnugdal, how do you fare?' But our unfortunate, seeing the beautiful youth—for he was of beautiful appearance in comparison with the sons of man—and hearing him call his name, burst into tears as much from fear as from joy and broke into these words: 'Alas, my lord and father, I am surrounded by the torments of Hell and have been overtaken by Death's snares'. The angel said to him: 'You have just called me lord and father although you always had me everywhere with you and never found me worthy of such a name'. He answered: 'Lord, where did I ever see you? and where did I ever hear your most sweet voice?'. The angel answered him: 'I have always followed you since your birth, wherever you went, and you never wanted to heed my advice', And, stretching his hand towards one of the foul spirits who insulted him more than the other slanderers, he said: 'Here is the one whose advice you used to trust while you took no notice at all of my wishes. But because God always shows forgiveness in his judgment his undeserved mercy will not fail even you. On the contrary, you will be fortunate and safe because you will suffer few of the many torments you would have suffered had not the mercy of our Redeemer come to your help. So, follow me and take care to

remember whatever I shall show to you, for afterwards you must
return to your body'. * * *

Chapter Seven

THE PUNISHMENT FOR THIEVES AND ROBBERS

Feeling weak as he arose, and trying to steady a tottering step, he
greatly desired to follow but was quite unable to do so, for he was
badly hurt. But the angel of God touched him and comforted him
and leading the way at a brisk pace, he encouraged him to complete
the path he had already mentioned. As they went along, they saw in
the distance a very large and stormy lake, the waves of which pre-
vented those around it from seeing the sky. In the lake there was a
large multitude of bellowing and terrifying beasts which fed only on
the souls they devoured. Across it there was a very long and narrow
bridge which extended for about two miles in length—for such was
the breadth of the lake—and was about the size of a hand in width.
It was longer and narrower than the bridge we mentioned earlier on.
But this plank was inset with very sharp iron nails which pierced
the feet of all who crossed it, so that, as soon as one set foot on it, it
was impossible to escape unhurt. Also, all the beasts gathered
under the bridge to catch their food, that is, those souls who did not
succeed in crossing it. The beasts themselves were so huge that they
could most rightly be compared with big towers. Fire was coming
from their mouths so that onlookers thought the lake itself was boil-
ing. Tnugdal could see on the bridge a soul weeping profusely and
accusing himself of many crimes. He was endeavouring to cross the
bridge overburdened by a heavy load of sheaves of wheat. Although
suffering greatly due to his soles being pierced by the iron nails, he
feared even more falling into the burning lake, where he could see
the beasts with their mouths wide open. When our soul saw the in-
human danger, he said to the angel. 'Alas, lord, if you please, I would
like to know why is this soul straining to go across under such a
weight and also to which souls in particular does this punishment
pertain'. The angel answered him: 'This punishment is particularly
fitting to you and your kind who have committed theft, whether
extensive or petty. But minor offenders do not suffer in the same
way as major ones, unless their petty crime happens to be a sacri-
lege'. The soul said: 'What do you call a sacrilege?' The angel
answered: 'Whoever steals something sacred or from a sacred place
is judged guilty of sacrilege. But even more, those who commit this
crime while in religious orders are judged guilty of a major sin, unless
they reform through penance'. And to this he added: 'Let us hurry
because we must cross the bridge'. The soul said: 'You will indeed

be able to go across by divine power, but I think you will not be able to take me with you'. The angel said: 'I will not go across with you; you will go by yourself. Also, you will not be able to cross unencumbered, for you must drive an untamed cow and deliver it to me safe and sound on the other side of the bridge'. Then the soul, crying and shedding bitter tears, said to the angel: 'Woe is me! Why did God create me if it were only to suffer such torments? And how will I be able to drive anything across when, wretch that I am, I shall hardly be able to stand up on my own in the face of such peril, unless divine mercy comes to my aid?' The angel said: 'Recall to your memory that when you were in the flesh you stole a cow from one of your good friends'. But he said: 'The cow in question, lord, did I not return it to its rightful owner?' The angel said: 'You gave it back, but only when you could no longer avoid doing so. That is why you will not suffer the full torture, because wanting is a lesser wrong than doing, although both are wrong in the eyes of God'. And with these words, turning around to face the soul, he showed him the untamed cow. 'Here is the cow which you must drive across', he said.

So, when the soul saw that he could not avoid the punishment he deserved, he took hold of the cow and, bemoaning his sin, tried to drive it to the bridge with all kinds of threats. The bellowing beasts arrived, expecting their food which they could see standing on the bridge. But when the soul started to walk, the cow did not want to go with him. Why prolong the story? When the soul was standing up, the cow fell and when the cow was standing up, the soul fell and so they went on, now standing and now falling each in turn until they reached the middle of the bridge. When they arrived there, they saw coming towards them the man who was carrying the sheaves of wheat. In mentioning him, I do not refer to those about whom it is said: 'When they came back, they did not come back rejoicing carrying their sheaves'; I refer rather to those whom the Scriptures admonish thus: 'Woe to you who laugh now, for you shall mourn and weep'. For, like them, they came to meet each other mourning and weeping not embracing one another like truth and mercy or justice and peace. For the soul who was carrying the sheaves begged our soul not to take his space on the bridge, and in turn our soul beseeched him with every kind of prayer not to block the way which he had already part completed so laboriously. However, neither of them was able I do not say to turn back but even to look back. And they stood there grieving and, as they stood, they covered the bridge in blood from their bleeding feet. They had been standing there for a long time, crying over the sin of their crimes when, without knowing how, each realised he had passed beyond the other. As our soul reached the other side he saw his angel when he had left behind and who addressed him with these soothing words. 'Welcome to you! Do not

worry about the cow any more, because you have no further obliga-
tions in its regard'. But when he showed him his foot and complained
that he could no longer walk, he answered: 'You must remember that
your feet were quick to shed blood, and this is why ruination and un-
happiness should rightly be on your path, unless the mercy of the
Almighty comes to your rescue'. And after these words he touched
him and the soul was cured; then he started to walk ahead of him.
As the soul was asking: 'Where are we going now?', the angel
answered: 'A most hideous torturer expects your coming. His name
is Phristinus and we will not be able to avoid his lodging house. And
although his house is always full of guests, the host nevertheless still
wants to find more in order to torture them.'

Chapter Eight

THE PUNISHMENT FOR GLUTTONS AND FORNICATORS

So, having gone through dark and barren places, they beheld before
them a house which was open. The house they saw was big, like a
steep mountain so huge was it, and it was round in shape, like an
oven for baking bread. There was a flame coming out of it which
burned every soul it could find for over a thousand paces. Our soul,
who had partially experienced a similar torment, was incapable of
advancing any further. This was why he told the angel who was guid-
ing him: 'What will I do, wretched as I am? Here we draw near to
the gates of death: who will free me?' The angel answered: 'You will
indeed be spared the outside flame, but you shall enter the house it
comes from'. And as they drew closer, they saw executioners with
axes, knives, pruning hooks and twibills, with adzes, augers and very
sharp scythes, with hoes, spades and all the other instruments use-
ful to flay, behead, split or mutilate people. These were standing in
front of the gates amidst the flames, inflicting all the tortures just
described on a multitude of souls. And when the soul saw that the
torments were much greater than those he had already seen, he
said to the angel: 'I beg you my lord, if you please, release me from
just this one torture and I agree to be delivered to all the other tor-
ments which will follow'. The angel said: 'Indeed, this torment is
greater than any you have already seen, but you have yet to see
another one exceeding every kind of torment you could possibly
have seen or thought of. Enter this house of torment, for rabid dogs
are awaiting your arrival inside'. * * * What should I say of what was
inside the house of Phristinus? There was distress and affliction,
pain, moaning and gnashing of teeth. Outside was a slow fire, but
inside there was an enormous blaze. An everlasting and insatiable
appetite for food was present and yet this excess of gluttony could
not be satisfied. Also, the souls were tortured by excruciating pains

in their sexual parts, and furthermore their sexual organs seemed to be rotten with decay and crawling with worms. And it was not only in the organs of lay men and women that the dreadful beasts entered, but—this is more serious and I cannot say it without deep pain—in those of people in holy orders. So, exhausted by tortures coming from all sides, they were totally unable to gather enough strength to endure this pain. No sex, no condition, seemed to be exempt from these wounds, and—I feared to say it but charity itself compels me—even people in monastic garb, both men and women, were among those being tortured. And those who appeared to belong to holier rules were judged worthy of greater punishment.

* * * The soul, full of sadness and bitterness, said to him: 'Lord, why did I suffer so many terrible torments, wretched as I am?' What about what the wise men used to tell us: 'The earth is full of the Lord's mercy'? 'Where is his mercy and his pity?' The angel answered: 'Alas, my child, a great many people have been misled by this sentence, which they did not properly understand. Although God is merciful, He is nevertheless just. Justice repays everyone according to his merits; mercy allows forgiveness of many offences which deserve punishment. As for you, you have indeed suffered those tortures justly according to your merits, but now you will give thanks when you see the torments He has spared you through his mercy. On the other hand, If God pardoned everything, why would man be just? And if he were not terrified of the torments, why would the sinner restrain himself? And why would it be necessary for the penitents to repent if they did not fear God? That is why God, who arranges everything rightly, tempers justice with mercy just as he tempers mercy with justice, so that neither can exist without the other. Although sinners who do not repent are mercifully spared while in the flesh, they nevertheless suffer here according to their merits, following the fitting sentence of justice. And, although temporal comfort is withheld from the just for their misdemeanours while they live justly in the flesh, He mercifully lavishes on them wealth lasting for ever with the angels, once they have shed their body'. * * *

After these words he said: 'Since we have not yet seen all the evil things, it will be useful for you to hurry in order to see those we have not yet seen'. The soul said: 'If we are to come back later to the glory, I beg you to lead me as quickly as possible to the next punishment'.

CRITICISM

Early Criticism

THOMAS WARTON

From The History of English Poetry[†]

In France, no province, or district, seems to have given these [Romantic] fictions [. . .] a more welcome or a more early reception, than the inhabitants of Armorica or Basse Bretagne, now Brittany; for no part of France can boast so great a number of ancient romances. Many poems of high antiquity, composed by the Armorican bards, still remain [. . .]

In the British Museum is a set of old French tales of chivalry in verse, written, as it seems, by the bards of Bretagne. MSS. Harl. 978. 107. "Tristram a Wales" is mentioned, f. 171. b.

⁎ ⁎ ⁎

[Thomas of Chestre] has left a poem entitled Sir LAUNFALE, one of Arthur's knights: who is celebrated with other champions in a set of French metrical tales or romances, written by some Armorican bard, under the name of LANVAL. They are in the British Museum (102–3).

In the mean time, there is reason to believe, that Chaucer himself copied these imageries from the romance of GUIGEMAR, one of the metrical TALES, or LAIS, of Bretagne, translated from the Armorican original into French by Marie, a French poetess, about the thirteenth century: in which the walls of a chamber are painted with Venus, and the *Art of Love* from Ovid (215).

[In Chaucer's Nun's Priest's Tale] the story of the cock and the fox is evidently borrowed from a collection of Esopean and other fables, written by Marie a French poetess, whose LAIS are preserved in MSS. HARL. ut. infr. see f. 139. Beside the absolute resemblance, it appears still more probable that Chaucer copied from Marie, because no such fable is to be found in either the Greek Esop, or in any Latin

† From Thomas Warton, *The History of English Poetry* (London: 1774–81), in *The Reception and Transmission of the Works of Marie de France, 1774–1974*, ed. and intro. Chantal Maréchal, *Medieval Studies*, vol. 23 (Lewiston, NY: The Edwin Mellen Press, 2003), pp. 68–70. Reprinted by permission of The Edwin Mellen Press.

compilations of the dark ages [. . .]. She appears, from passages in her
LAIS, to have understood English. See Chaucer's CANTERB. TALES, vol.
iv, p. 179. I will give her Epilogue to the Fables from MSS. JAMES. viii.
p. 23. Bibl. Bodl. [Twenty lines of the epilogue of the Fables follow].

THOMAS TYRWHITT

From The Canterbury Tales, Vol. 4[†]

[. . .] the name of *Lay* was particularly given to *the French transla-
tions* of certain Poems, originally composed in Armorican Bretagne,
and in the Armorican language. I say *the French translations*, because
Lay, not being (as I can find) an Amorican word, could hardly have
been the name, by which a species of Poetry, not imported from
France, was distinguished by the first composers in Bretagne.

The chief (perhaps the only) collection of these Lais that is now
extant, was translated into French octosyllable verse by a Poetess,
who calls herself *Marie*: the same (without doubt) who made the
translation of *Esope*, quoted by Pasquier [*Recherches* 1. viii. ch. i] and
Fauchet [L. ii. n. 84], and placed by them in the reign of St. Louis,
about the middle of the XIII Century. Both her works have been
preserved together in Ms. *Harl.* 978. in a fair hand, which I see no
reason to judge more recent than the latter end of that Century.

The *Lais* (with which only we are at present concerned) were
addressed by her to some king. Fol. 139.

En le honur de vous, *noble reis*, [. . .].

A few lines after, she names herself.

Oez, Seignurs, ke dit *Marie de France*—

The titles of the Poems in this collection, to the number of twelve,
are recited in the Harleian Catalogue. They are, in general, the names
of the principal persons in the several Stories, and are most of them
evidently Armorican; and I think no one can read the Stories them-
selves without being persuaded, that they were either really trans-
lated from the Armorican language, or at least composed by one who
was well acquainted with that language and country. [. . .].

†   From Thomas Tyrwhitt, *The Canterbury Tales*, Vol. 4 (London: T. Payne, 1775), in *The
    Reception and Transmission of the Works of Marie de France, 1774–1974*, ed. and intro.
    Chantal Maréchal, *Medieval Studies*, vol. 23 (Lewiston, NY: The Edwin Mellen Press,
    2003), pp. 68–70. Reprinted with permission of The Edwin Mellen Press.

ABBÉ GERVAIS DE LA RUE

From Dissertation on the Life and Writings of Mary[†]

[Archaelogia *13, 1800*]

Unfortunately [Marie] has scarcely mentioned any circumstance relating to herself! [. . .]. We are informed by this lady that she was born in France, but she has not mentioned the province that gave her birth, nor the reasons of her going to England. As she appears, however, to have resided in that country at the commencement of the thirteenth century, we may reasonably conclude that she was a native of Normandy. [. . .] (36).

[If we accept this opinion], we must suppose that Mary got her knowledge, both of the Armoric and English languages, in Great Britain. She was, at the same time, equally mistress of the Latin, and from her application to three several languages, we must take it for granted that she possessed a readiness, a capacity, and even a certain rank in life, that afforded time and means to attain them. [. . .] (37).

The first poems of Mary are a collection of Lays, in French verse; forming various histories and gallant adventures of our valient knights [. . .]. These Lays are in the British Museum among the Harleian MSS. No. 978. (38)

[. . .] By treating of love, and the various emotions which it excites; of chivalry, and the acts of valour which beauty inspires in its possessors, she was certain of attuning her lyre to the feelings of the age [. . .] (39).

The second work of our poetess consists of a collection of fables, generally called Aesopian, which she translated into French verse (43–44).

[. . .] her fables are written with all that acuteness of mind, that penetrates into the very inmost recesses of the human heart; and, at the same time, with that beautiful simplicity so peculiar to the ancient romance language.

There are, in the British Museum, three MSS. copies of Mary's fables. The first is in the Cotton library, Vesp. B. XIV; the second in the Harleian, No 4333; and the third in the same collection, No 978. [. . .] (47).

[†] From Abbé Gervais de la Rue, *Dissertation on the Life and Writings of Mary*, in *The Reception and Transmission of the Works of Marie de France, 1774–1974*, ed. and intro. Chantal Maréchal, *Medieval Studies,* vol. 23 (Lewiston, NY: The Edwin Mellen Press, 2003), pp. 70–71. Reprinted with permission of The Edwin Mellen Press.

The third work of Mary consists of a history, or rather a tale, in French verse, of St. Patrick's Purgatory. This performance was originally composed in Latin, by a monk of the abbey of Saltrey, [. . .] (65).

Whether Mary was the author of any other pieces, I have not been able to ascertain: her taste and the extreme facility with which she wrote poetry of the lighter kind, induce a presumption that she was; but I know of none that have come down to us (66–67).

JOSEPH BEDIER

From Les Lais de Marie de France[†]

One can say . . . that with [these Breton *contes*], literature, to speak properly, was born. *Roland* could be sung in a public place, or in the tumult of a feasting hall; but not *Eliduc* or *Perceval*; they were created for contemplative reading. The clamorous jongleur de geste was succeeded by the latinier, who read the Breton tales in "ladies' chambers" where the stained glass windows spilled forth a dim light. Marie created [these tales] with charm, but without great talent. One must say it: her poetic worth is mediocre . . . while possessed of a certain grace, a barrenness of imagination. . . . She recounts the most violent scenes, and the most tender ones, in the same placid tone, without appearing to be moved; which offers a guarantee that these poems must be extremely close to their originals, to the orally performed tales recited by Breton jongleurs; she is too little the artist, too little possessed of imagination, to have added much. She aligns calmly her little octosyllables, of which the dull rhymes seem to have no other meaning than that of a mnemonic process. No splendor in the style, no passion in the recital, nothing but the grace of a very feeble, fragile emotion. But also, no garrulity, no bombast, no empty rhetoric; a language refined and agile, of which even the thinness is not without charm. She stops at the threshold of art. She spills forth a delicate little source of *poesie*, limpid and thin like the fountains where the fairies bathe in her tales.[1] . . . Yes, this literature is suitably feminine . . . (858–59).

[†] From Joseph Bedier, "Les Lais de Marie de France," *Revue des Deux Mondes* 107 (1891), pp. 835–63. Translated by Dorothy Gilbert for this Norton Critical Edition.

1. In none of the *Lais*, or *contes*, presently believed to be by Marie is there an account of fairies bathing in fountains. However, in "Graelent," now thought to be not a source for Marie or written by her, but a conflation of two *Lais*, "Guigamor" and "Lanval," derived from her, a fairy is found bathing in a "fountaine," a word that modern editor and translator Russell Weingartner—in a note on page 80 of *Graelent and Gringamor: Two Breton Lays* (New York and London: Garland, 1985)—tells us means either "fountain" or "pool." The word "fountaine" appears in "Graelent" in lines 219, 222, and 226 (page 12) and in "Gringamor" in lines 422 and 424 (page 62). Weingartner chooses "pool" as the first meaning of the word and uses it in his version. He comments, though, that "this scene in 'Graelent' and the corresponding one in 'Gringamor' are frequently referred to in literary criticism as 'the fountain scene'" [*Editor's note*].

LEO SPITZER

From Marie de France: Poetess of Problem-Märchen[†]

Marie is particularly good at introducing symbols which lead their own life beyond the narrative: they do not merely cling to the plot of a given tale, rather, they seem to escape the plot's shackles and to continue a separate life in our memory, thanks to their sensual and spiritual value. I am not thinking here of relatively primitive symbols such as the two tubs in "Equitan," which we must remember as symbols of error (that is: he who prepares too hot a bath for someone, jumps in himself) because there is no inner relation between the symbolic object (the tubs) and its content (tragic error). Rather, what matters here above all else is the hazelnut-honeysuckle symbol in the center of the lai of "Chievrefueil" the lovers have become human flora, organically growing plant-beings passively enduring their nature's command (such interiorization since the flower maidens of the Roman d'Alexandre!); their law is that they were made for each other—and the music to the lines written on the hazelnut staff (Bele amie, si est de nos . . .) should be quite unnecessary since the plant symbol has until today, until the "Chèvrefeuille" by our contemporary Sandre, spoken movingly and insistently to us. To interpret the passage cf. G. Schoepperle, *Romania* 38, 197 ff.: Nor do I believe, like Foulet, *Zeitschrift* 39, 280 ff., in an earlier letter to which the hazelnut staff alludes; rather, we are dealing here, at least in Marie, with a mutual sign long since agreed upon by the lovers, a sign which is being "developed" before us: *Ce fu la some de l'escrit / Qu'il li avoit mandé et dit* simply means, 'That was the gist of the message." It is peculiar how the sensual-spiritual poetess adds literal explanation to a symbol that speaks (of) itself, how she moreover makes it seem as if the momentary sign were a lasting one—is the particular situation the *lai* describes a condensation of a long series of experiences (something like the relationship between Spanish "Romanze" and epic), or is Marie not yet as competent a, "symbolist" as she is in "Laüstic"? (44)

[†] From Leo Spitzer, "Marie de France: Poetess of Problem–Märchen," *Zeitschrift für romanische philologie* 50 (1930): 29–67. In *The Reception and Transmission of the Works of Marie de France, 1774–1974*, ed. and intro. Chantal Maréchal. Trans. Hans R. Runte. *Medieval Studies*, vol. 28 (Lewiston, NY: The Edwin Mellen Press, 2003), pp. 164, 166. Jill Mann comments, in her note on p. 370 of this volume, that "Despite its age, Spitzer's essay is still one of the finest and most perceptive readings of Marie's art in the Lais."

Modern Criticism

R. HOWARD BLOCH

From The Anonymous Marie de France[†]

* * *

The thesis here presented entails accepting the fact that we will never know Marie from the outside, we will never even be able to disprove what Richard Baum has recently argued with unconvincing rigor, that she is not the author of the three works historically attributed to her. We will never know who the "real Marie" was in the way that we know who Marguerite de Navarre, Jane Austen, Emily Brontë, George Sand, Virginia Woolf, or Marguerite Duras really was, that is to say, in a way that allows us to assign a biography to her with the fantasy, ultimately, of reducing her works to such an elusive category as the person. Marie remains anonymous. Which does not mean that we cannot know her, only that any attempt to deal with the question of her anonymity must proceed internally, from the texts themselves, via an interpretation of the works associated with her.[1] While such a strategy may carry its own burden of sadness, it also brings rewards: "Anonymity," in the phrase of Virginia Woolf, "was a great possession. It gave the early writing an impersonality, a generality. It gave us the ballads; it gave us the songs. It allowed us to know nothing of the writer: and so to concentrate upon his song."[2]

We begin, then, from the premise that the scholar, faced with a mystery so resistant as the identity of France's first woman poet, a mystery that she herself proclaims in the prologue, must renounce the kind of certainty demanded by the positivist philological method that has dominated medieval, if not literary, studies for almost two

---

† From R. Howard Bloch, *The Anonymous Marie de France* (Chicago and London: University of Chicago Press, 2003, 2006), pp. 18–19, 22–29, 36–42, 52–54, 59–60. Reprinted by permission of the the University of Chicago Press.

1. See Marjorie M. Malvern, "Marie de France's Ingenious Uses of the Authorial Voice and Her Singular Contribution to Western Literature," *Tulsa Studies in Women's Literature* 2 (1983): 37.
2. Virginia Woolf, "Anon" and "The Reader: Virginia Woolf's Last Essays," ed. Brenda Silver, *Twentieth Century Literature* 25 (1979): 397.

centuries. Every work of criticism involves some form of risk, a gamble that initial intuitions will be borne out by readings of a more sustained sort; and I am wagering that it is possible to prove from within not only the coherence of Marie's oeuvre but that, far from being the simple, naive, natural, spontaneous, delicate, modest, clear, sincere, comforting, Christian figure she has been portrayed to be, Marie is among the most self-conscious, sophisticated, complicated, obscure, tricky, and disturbing figures of her time—the Joyce of the twelfth century. This is another way of asserting the other half of our assumption at the outset: that Marie was not only a woman but that she was also a poet.

As a poet, Marie was both a disrupter of prevailing cultural values and a founder of new ones. The prologue to the *Lais* is one of those founding texts that appear at a liminal moment in the history of the West. C. S. Lewis claims that there have been very few real moments of historical mutation and that the twelfth century was one; Charles Homer Haskins speaks of the "Renaissance of the twelfth century"; Marc Bloch, of the end of the "first feudal age"; Georges Duby, situating the seismic cultural break a little earlier, proclaims the "watershed years" preceding 1100. All are forms of recognition that something major took place between, say, the First Crusade and the Lateran Council of 1215, something in which it is difficult to place written texts; for writing both reflects a larger cultural shift and is part of such a shift within an essentially oral lay culture that breaks rather suddenly into writing, writing being both the symptom of change and its catalyst.[3] Activities heretofore conducted without it suddenly come to depend upon the written forms that have such a necessary effect upon the perceptual world of those who in increasing numbers beginning around the middle of the 1100s come into contact with literary works composed via writing as opposed to oral performance. Marie de France was acutely aware not only of her role in the preservation of cultural memory but of the transforming effects of writing, and written poetry in particular, upon and within oral tradition. The implications of such a shift for our understanding of literature are developed in the chapters that follow.

*   *   *

The *chanson de geste* presents a multiplicity of events from a single point of view, but at no point is point of view thrown into question. On the contrary, the earliest epic contains a universe of fixed moral categories ("Chrestiens unt dreit, et païens unt tort," "Christians are right, and pagans are wrong"), a universe of externalized and fixed

---

3. See Brian Stock, *The Implications of Literacy: Written Language and Models of Interpretation in the Eleventh and Twelfth Centuries* (Princeton, NJ: Princeton University Press, 1983).

psychological categories ("Roland est preu, et Olivers est sage," "Roland is brave, and Oliver is wise"). This is another way of saying that history moves in only one direction since, in the absence of anything like free will, the individual is merely the vehicle of objective forces outside of his control—in this instance Christian Providence. *Roland* proffers a universe, finally, oriented toward the past, precisely because the powers of interpretation attributed to an individual subject, and therefore his ability to understand a world of increasingly particular realities, are so faintly drawn and because history according to such a paradigm is perceived as a text written once and for all, whose meaning simply will become apparent through time. It is my purpose here to show, on the contrary, that Marie de France not only renders opaque the question of the subject, brings it to our attention as a question, but that the three works attributed to her represent a working out of the issue of the individual in the world in such a way as not only to provide convincing evidence of a unifying obsession, but as also to convince us of her role in the making of a perceptual world, mental structures fundamental to the shaping of social life.

The prologue to the *Lais* suggests a movement past a past-oriented paradigm toward a future-oriented one, for the potential of a subject to interpret his or her world comes to be increasingly synonymous with his or her mastery of it. The prologue opens in the direction of individual free will, and this is the era in which moral philosophy, ethics, even the notions of sin and penance in the discourse of theology and of guilt in that of the law, are, as we shall see in our concluding chapters on the *Espurgatoire*, increasingly subjectivized. Despite her awareness of legal procedure in "Lanval" and despite her concern with political exemplars throughout the *Fables*, it would be difficult to prove that Marie de France functioned as either a jurist or a political theorist alongside the literary jurisconsults she may have encountered in or around the Angevin court. I think it can be shown that her works represent not only expressive symptoms of social change but dynamic forces in the transformation in the High Middle Ages of the nature and practice of legal process, and, in the case of the *Espurgatoire*, a moralization of the social bond and a legalization of the afterlife that can be understood in the specific historical context of the conquest, pacification, and administration of Ireland in the final decades of the reign of Henry II.

The privileging of something on the order of free will opens the question of history as a function of individual agency as opposed to the determinism of an earlier epoch. This amounts to attributing to Marie—as well as to others, but especially to her since she is the most conscious of this freedom—the birth of literature, or what has come to be called the literary. Joseph Bédier sensed this development with respect to the *Lais* as early as 1891: "One can say . . . that with them literature, properly speaking, is born. *Roland* could be sung in a public gathering place, or amidst the tumult of a drinking hall; but not *Eliduc* or *Perceval:* they are made for reflective reading. The noisy jongleur of epic is replaced by the *latinier*, who, in the 'women's chambers' [*chambres des dames*] where stained glass casts a toned down light, reads Breton tales."[4] As we will see repeatedly in the pages that follow, Marie more explicitly than others of her generation—Chrétien, Robert de Boron, or the Tristan poets— initiates literature as the expression within a closed form of a desire residing in the space between a world sensed as individual, interior, and subjective, on the one hand, and the demands of a world sensed as objective and collective, on the other. For while the others present on the level of theme the split between the desire of the individual and the givens of his or her world, a conflict visible in a myriad of motifs from the rivalry of lovers in the lyric, to the lovesickness and quests of romance, no one was more aware than Marie that the thematic expression of this very tension is the stuff of literature as a closed form whose very closure both mediates the space of such a gap and, like all closed systems, itself becomes an object of desire.

Marie's consciousness of the ways literature negotiates between individual and community is, for reasons that will become increasingly clear, equivalent to an integration of the principle not only of difference between the subject and the world, but of difference per se, sexual difference, an integration of the feminine into the wholly masculine world of the epics of the "first feudal age." "Yes, this literature is feminine," writes Bédier, echoing Denis Piramus's assessment some eight centuries earlier:

> E si en aiment mult l'escrit
> E lire le funt, si unt delit,
> E si les funt sovent retreire.
> Les lais solent as dames pleire:
> De joie les oient e de gré,
> Qu'il sunt sulum lur volenté.[5]

And they [counts and barons and knights] greatly love her writing, they have it read aloud, they have them [lays] often told, and they take delight. For lays are used to pleasing ladies: they hear them willingly and in joy, for they suit their taste.

It is, finally, the distinction drawn by a contemporary between the *chanson de geste* and the fabliaux, which appeal to men, and the lais and romances, which appeal to women, that permits us to hold in abeyance the question with which we began. Or, rather, to continue

---

4. Bédier, "Lais," p. 857.
5. Denis Piramus, *Vie de seint Edmund le rei*, v. 43.

to believe for the moment that Marie de France was a woman, not because anything outside of the text makes it so, but because she wrote the *Lais*, to which we turn in our first chapter.

Chapter One. The Word Aventure *and the Adventure of Words*

In the prologue to the *Lais*, which is as close to a vernacular *art poétique* as the High Middle Ages produced, Marie begins with the question of beginnings. She is anxious about origins, about the genesis and genealogy of the tales that she, at the nodal point between past and future, will preserve in memory for generations to come. Having considered the possibility of translating from a Latin, that is to say, a written, source, she thinks instead of "that which she has heard" among the tales told by those "who first sent them into the world":

> Des lais pensai, k'oï aveie;
> Ne dutai pas, bien le saveie,
> Ke pur remembrance les firent
> Des aventures k'il oïrent
> Cil ki primes les comencierent
> E ki avant les enveierent. (v. 33)

> I thought of lais that I had heard and did not doubt, for I knew it full well, that they were composed, by those who first began them and put them into circulation, to perpetuate the memory of adventures they had heard.

As the point of entry to the world of literature, as what Stephen Nichols identifies as "the first explicit canon revision in European history," the prologue raises from the start issues that will dominate not only the *Lais* but the *Fables* and the *Espurgatoire Seint Patriz* as well—issues of memory and transmission; of orality versus writing; of the reception of a work in the mind of others; of the uses to which wisdom from the past will be put; and, finally, of what lies behind the text, the "lais" that in Old French can connote "that which is left behind," here subsumed in the little word *aventure*.[6]

AVENTURE

The word *aventure* is one of the richly plurivalent signifiers of the *Lais* and constitutes a liminal key to the whole. Referring to the brute material out of which the *Lais* are made, the word *aventure* designates that which exists before and beyond the text in the fantasy of an unrecounted, unremembered, chaotic realm of unarticulated

---

6. Stephen G. Nichols, "Marie de France's Commonplaces," *Yale French Studies*, Special Issue (1991): 135. See also Sarah Spence, "Writing in the Vernacular: The *Lais* of Marie de France," in *Texts and the Self in the Twelfth Century*, ed. Sarah Spence (Cambridge: Cambridge University Press, 1996), p. 120.

consciousness, the very opposite of the assemblage—the form and structure—that literature represents. This is why so many of the tales are literally framed by the word *aventure*, which, appearing at either the beginning or the end or both, marks the bounds of where literature begins and ends, sets in relief that which it contains. "Just as it happened, I shall relate to you the story of another lai" ("L'aventure d'un autre lai, / Cum ele avient, vus cunterai" [v. 1])—thus begins "Lanval," in what amounts to a mini-prologue to the lai, whose epilogue reminds the reader that adventure ends when Marie has no more to say: "No one has heard any more about him, nor can I relate any more" ("Nul humme n'en oï plus parler, / Ne jeo n'en sai avant cunter" [v. 645]). "Deus Amanz" commences with a celebrated adventure" that "once took place in Normandy" ("Jadis avint en Normendie / Une aventure mut oïe" [v. 1]) and concludes with attention drawn to the composition of the lai:

> Pur l'aventure des enfaunz
> Ad nun li munz des Deus Amanz.
> Issi avint cum dit vus ai.
> Li Bretun en firent un lai. (v. 241)

Because of what happened to these two young people, the mountain is called the Mountain of the Two Lovers. The events took place just as I have told you, and the Bretons composed a lai about them.

"Now that I have begun to compose lais, I shall not cease my effort but shall relate fully in rhyme the adventures that I know," Marie affirms at the beginning of "Yonec," which ends, like "Deus Amanz," with an explanation of how the lai came into being: "Those who heard this story long afterward composed a lai from it."[7] Finally, in what now seems like somewhat of a formula for beginnings, Marie launches "Laüstic" with the promise that "I shall relate an adventure to you from which the Bretons composed a lai" ("Une aventure vus dirai,/ Dunt li Bretun firent un lai" [v. 1]), and closes no less conventionally:

> Cele aventure fut cuntee,
> Ne pot estre lunges celee.
> Un lai en firent li Bretun:
> Le Laüstic l'apelent hum. (v. 157)

This adventure was related and could not long be concealed. The Bretons composed a lai about it that is called *Laüstic*.

---

7. "Puis que de lais ai commencé, / Ja n'iert par mon travail laisse; / Les aventures que j'en sai / Tut par time les cunterai" (Yónec, v. 1); "Cil qui ceste aventure oïrent / Lunc tens après un lac en firent" (v. 549).

As that which lies outside of the lai, but of which the lai is made, "aventure" refers to an event, an *eventure*, that supposedly happened, a lived experience rooted in the body, the fantasy of the body present to itself, at its outer limits, the imagined wholeness of voice and body joined. "Aventure" refers to the material of the tale, that which lies outside of its formal telling, and also carries the unmistakable resonance of orality. In the beginning of "Equitan" we learn that the Bretons made lais out of the "adventures that they had heard":

> li Bretun.
> Jadis suleient par prüesce,
> Par curteisie e par noblesce,
> Des aventures que oïësent,
> Ki a plusur gent aveneient,
> Fere les lais pur remembrance,
> Que [hum] nes meïst en ubliance. (v. 2)

> In days gone by the valiant, courtly, and noble Bretons composed lais for posterity and thus preserved them from oblivion. These lais were based on adventures they had heard and which had befallen many a person.

Marie hints, moreover, that she has heard one such tale in a manner that leaves little doubt about the fact of oral transmission: "Un ent firent, ceo oi cunter, / Ki ne fet mie a ublïer" (vv. 9–10). "I am minded to recall a lai of which I have heard and shall recount what happened," she states in her own voice in the first line of "Chaitivel," thus revealing, if not an oral source, at least an oral means of transmission of the "aventure"—hearsay ("Un lai dunt jo oï parler") of an adventure to be passed on by means of speech ("L'aventure vus en dirai"). Here we arrive at a second meaning of the term, that is, the "story of an experience," a "tale of adventure," as in Chrétien de Troyes's prologue to *Erec* where he speaks of joining "contes d'aventure" into a "bele conjointure."[8] An "adventure" here constitutes one episode in a larger narrative whole with the specific resonance of orality, of an oral account of an adventure of the type told by Chrétien's itinerant oral poets—jongleurs—as opposed to his own written version that will last, he maintains, as "long as Christianity itself" ("aussi longtemps que la Chrétienté"), the very name "Chrétien" being associated with the permanent preservation of the more fluid, dispersed, oral aventures in written form.

"Aventure" not only refers to the source of a tale, to the past from which the tale comes, and to the tale itself in its present form;

---

8. As Jean Frappier points out, the term "aventure" is used to designate the principle of unity of the *lai*; see "Remarques sur la structure du lai: Essai de définition et de classement," in *La littérature narrative d'imagination, des genres littéraires aux techniques d'expression* (Paris: Universitaires de France, 1961), p. 31.

"aventure"—from the Latin *ad* + *venire*—also relates prospectively to that which will come or happen. It carries the valence of an advent. Within such a future-oriented semantic range, an "aventure" contains its own genealogy, its own expectation for a meaning that is prescribed, predetermined, predestined. It is the equivalent of destiny, as, for example, in the case of Yonec, whose dying father tells his mother of the fate that awaits their unborn son:

> Quant il serat creüz e grant
> E chevalier pruz e vaillant,
> A une feste u ele irra,
> Sun seigneur e lui amerra.
> En une abbeïe vendrunt;
> Par une tumbe k'il verrunt
> Orrunt renoveler sa mort
> E cum il fu ocis a tort.
> Ileoc li baillerat s'espeie.
> L'aventure li seit cuntee
> Cum il fu nez, ki le engendra;
> Asez verrunt k'il en fera. (v. 425)

When he will have grown up and become a worthy and valiant knight, he will go to a feast with her and her husband. They will come to an abbey, and at a tomb they will visit, they will again hear about his death and how he was unjustly killed. There she will give the sword to his son to whom the adventure will be told, how he was born and who his father was. Then they will see what he will do.

Finally, as Erich Koehler observed,[9] "aventure" connotes chance, fortune, risk, and here is where we encounter the other side of the semantic coin: "Beloved," Guigemar exclaims at the end of the tale that bears his name, "how fortunate that I have discovered you like this!" ("Bele," fet il, "queile aventure / Que jo vus ai issi trovee!"). The multiple meanings of "aventure," which on the one hand concretizes, fixes, immobilizes that which is imagined to be beyond language, experience, and the body, also serves as a reminder that no matter how much one tries to pin meaning down, it remains, even in fixed form, uncontrollable, risky, undisciplined, excessive—an intractable "surplus of sense" in Marie's own phrase. And nowhere more uncontrollable, it turns out, than where the word *lai* itself is concerned.

※　※　※

9. See Erich Koehler, *Ideal und Wikrlichkeit in der Höfischen Epik* (Tübingen: Max Niemeyer, 1956), pp. 66–99.

THE OBLIGATION TO SPEAK

Marie de France is an existential writer; and where in the theologized philological tradition of Augustine words may not lead directly to truth, and silence, as in the scene of conversion contained in the *Confessions*, is a prerequisite to the inner perception of a transcendent truth beyond words, she believes in, is committed to, the attempt, despite the odds against it, to produce meaning as seen, first of all, in the obligation to speak:

> Ki Deus a duné escïence
> Et de parler bon' eloquence
> Ne s'en deit taisir ne celer,
> Ainz se deit volunters mustrer.
> Quant uns granz biens est mult oïz,
> Dunc a primes est il fluriz,
> E quant loëz est de plusurs,
> Dunc ad espandues ses flurs. (Prologue, v. 1)

> Anyone who has received from God the gift of knowledge and true eloquence has a duty not to remain silent: rather should one be happy to reveal such talents. When a truly beneficial thing is heard by many people, it then enjoys its first blossom.

In resonance with the Old Testament "In the beginning God created the heaven and the earth" and with the New Testament John "In the beginning was the Word," the prologue to the *Lais* begins with creation and with words. This poetics opens with God's creation of the artist, divinely endowed with "speech" and "eloquence," and with a duty to words. In this Marie is not alone, but shares in one of the potent topoi of the High Middle Ages—the responsibility not to remain silent but to share possession of knowledge. Poets of the second half of the twelfth and the thirteenth centuries, poets who, after all, are beginning to speak at a moment of cultural reawakening, often begin by speaking about speaking.[1]

The metaphorics of flowering knowledge belongs, of course, to biblical tradition, and is also to be found among Latin thinkers both preceding and contemporaneous with Marie. Hugh of Saint-Victor draws upon the Parable of the Talents in his condemnation of those who are capable of learning but choose not to do so contained in the preface to the *Didascalicon:* "Many of this sort, caught up in the affairs and cares of this world beyond what is needful or given over to the vices and sensual indulgences of the body, bury the talent of God in earth, seeking from it neither the fruit of wisdom nor the

---

1. See Anne Paupert, "Les femmes et la parole dans les *Lais* de Marie de France," in *Amour et Merveille: Les 'Lais' de Marie de France*, ed. Jean Dufournet (Paris: Champion, 1995), pp. 169–70.

profit of good work. These, assuredly, are completely detestable."[2] The obligation to teach and speak is writ large across a variety of vernacular genres, where it represents, as in the prologue to the *Lais*, a means of beginning. "He who is wise should not hide but should show his wisdom, for when he passes from this world, he will be remembered forever"—thus begins the classical *Roman de Thèbes* in a manner similar to Benoît de Sainte-Maure's *Roman de Troie*: "Solomon teaches us and says, and one can read it in his writings, that one must not hide his wisdom."[3]

*   *   *

Among the courtly romancers of Marie's generation, Chrétien de Troyes is the most insistent concerning the obligation to speak and the adverse effects of a failure to do so:

> Li vilains dit an son respit
> que tel chose a l'an an despit
> qui molt valt mialz que l'an ne cuide;
> por ce fet bien qui son estuide
> atorne a bien quel que il l'ait;
> car qui son estuide antrelait,
> tost i puet tel chose teisir
> qui molt vandroit puis a pleisir.[4]

The peasant in his proverb says that one might find oneself holding in contempt something that is worth much more than one believes: therefore a man does well to make good use of his learning according to whatever understanding he has, for he who neglects his learning may easily keep silent something that would later give much pleasure.

With the opening of *Erec et Enide*, which some consider alongside the *Lais* to be the first romance, and which is certainly the first Arthurian romance, we are, as in the case of Marie, plunged into the world of literature, by which I mean a self-conscious focus upon the process of writing itself, an awareness of the question of what it means to make literary texts. More precisely, we enter from the start into

2. Hugh of Saint-Victor, *Didascalion*, trans. Jerome Taylor (New York: Columbia University Press, 1968), p. 43; see Brewster Fitz, "The Prologue to the *Lais* of Marie de France and the *Parable of the Talents*: Gloss and Monetary Metaphor," *Modern Language Notes* 90 (1975): 558–64.
3. "Qui sages est nel deit celer, mais pur ceo deit son sen monstrer / que, quant serra del siècle alez, / en seit puis toz jours remembrez" (*Le Roman de Thèbes*, ed. Francine Mora-Lebrun [Paris: Lettres Gothiques, 1995], v. 1); "Salemons nos enseigne et dit, / Et sil lit hon en son escrit, / Que nus ne deit son sens celer" (Benoît de Sainte-Maure, *Le Roman de Troie*, ed. Emmanuèle Baumgartner and Françoise Vielliard [Paris: Lettres Gothiques, 1998], vol. 1).
4. Chrétien de Troyes, *Erec et Enide*, ed. Marie Roques (Paris: Champion, 1963), v. 1. The translation is that of Carleton W. Carroll, *Chrétien de Troyes: Arthurian Romances* (London: Penguin, 1991), p. 37.

literature's questions to itself about language: about the difference between ordinary and poetic language, about intention and reception, about esthetic value, about the social implications of esthetics, in short, the question of origins. Every work is in this sense an awakening, a coming into being of something, a specific, thing. "Li vilains dit an son respit" stands, moreover, as a proverb about the proverbial—that is to say a popular status of language—which goes to the heart of the subject matter of poetry, "tel chose," and to the question of the poet's relation to both authorial agency and meaning. Before the literary "thing" one is faced, in the prologue to *Erec et Enide* as well in that to the *Lais*, with the dilemma of choosing between "leaving off," silence and hiding ("taisir ne celer") for Marie and "easily keeping silent" for Chrétien ("tost i puet tel chose teisir"); or pleasure for Chrétien ("qui molt vandroit puis a pleisir") and a "flowering" and praise for Marie. The rhetorical pressure is, of course, as both Chrétien and Marie acknowledge, on the side of attention: it is better to make something out of nothing, which is potentially the source of pleasure, than to leave nothing alone. As in the case of Pascal's bet, it is better to be safe and stay alert than to "neglect," "leave off," or "antrelait."

In the defense of writing, a *causa scribendi* voiced as the moral obligation in speak, lies one of the deeply obsessive components of Marie's conceptual universe, one that is expressed both personally and collectively, both as a drama of language and as theme: on the one hand, one must speak, and, on the other, one is aware of the perils and pitfalls that speech entails. Where writing is concerned, one must write, convinced that writing may somehow reverse history's degenerative drift, while also aware of writing's fragmenting effects, that writing, finally, might contribute to rather than contain the very loss it appears to restore. This is an opposition that runs throughout the *Lais* and that is manifest from the start in Marie's making of literature a philological project, a project of reclamation in which memory and writing are conceived as means of countering the corrosive consequences of temporal decline.

THE WILL TO REMEMBER

No one is more aware than Marie of the usurious effects of time: the nature of the historical process always involves a loss. Literature as Marie conceives it is a memorial to that loss, representing as it does the various ways in which loss is externalized, figured, mourned, as well as the ways in which it might he recuperated. Here is where *memory* comes into play. Marie is haunted throughout the *Lais*, the *Fables*, and the *Espurgatoire* by the threat of a loss of memory, by the necessity of not forgetting that which is potentially lost because it is literally not articulated, not related, not given via language some more enduring form:[5]

> Des lais pensai, k'oï aveie;
> Ne dutai pas, bien le saveie,
> Ke pur remembrance les firent
> Des aventures k'il oïrent
> Cil ki primes les comencierent
> E ki avant les enveierent.
> Plusurs en ai oï conter,
> Ne[s] voil laisser në oblïer. (v. 33)

I thought of lais that I had heard and did not doubt, for I knew it full well, that they were composed, by those who first began them and put them into circulation, to perpetuate the memory of adventures they had heard. I myself have heard a number of them and do not wish to overlook or neglect them.

This passage seems to refer to an oral event as memory and as being itself remembered, as being that which Marie has "heard tell" about the "adventures" that others have heard, remembered, and recited— "Ke pur remembrance les firent / Des aventures k'il oïrent"—just as she has heard, remembered, and written them down. That which she remembers is, in other words, the memory of a memory, which is not fully recuperated, not really remembered, until it is fixed in writing. The point is consistent with what we find elsewhere: in "Chevrefoil," for example, a lai that is about writing and about the relation of oral to written expression, we read that Tristan was already a writer whose project of remembering is not so different from that of Marie:

> Pur la joie qu'il ot eüe
> De s'amie qu'il ot veüe
> E pur ceo k'il aveit escrit,
> Si cum la reïne l'ot dit,
> Pur les paroles remembrer,
> Tristam, ki bien saveit harper,
> En aveit fet un nuvel lai;
> . . . .
> Dit vus en ai la verité
> Del lai que j'ai ici cunté. (vv. 107, 117)

---

5. "Quant de lais faire m'entremet, / Ne voïl ublïer Bisclavret" ("In my effort to compose lais I do not wish to omit 'Bisclavret'" ["Bisclavret," v. 1]); "De *Bisclavret* fut fet li lais / Pur remembrance a tut dis mais" ("The lai was composed about Bisclavret to be remembered forever more" [v. 316]); "Talent me prist de remembrer / Un lai dunt jo oï parler" ("I am minded to recall a lai of which I have heard tell" ["Chaitivel," v. 1]); "Del aventure de ces treis / Li auncïen Bretun curteis / Firent un lai pur remembrer, / Qu'hum nel deüst pas oblïer" ("From the story of these three the ancient courtly Bretons composed a lai to be remembered" ["Eliduc," v. 1181]).

> On account of the joy he had experienced from the sight of his
> beloved and because of what he had written, Tristam, a skilful
> harpist, in order to record his words (as the queen had said he
> should), used them to create a new lai . . . I have told you the
> truth of the lai I have related here.

The term "remembrance" means, of course, remembering in the
modern sense of the term. But "remembrance" also holds a connota-
tion in Old French that has been lost in modern French except in
the French countryside, where farmers still use it to refer to the
recombination of dispersed lands. "Remembrance" in Marie connotes
a reassembling of that which has been scattered, a recuperation of
that which has been fragmented and lost, an articulation or re-
articulation.[6] And so the obligation to speak, given an ethical cast,
is also an obligation to remember, to heal the wound of dismember-
ment and loss, as Marie herself assimilates moral duty and memory
in the self-characterization at the beginning of "Guigemar"—"Marie /
Ki en sun tens pas ne s'oblie," which means "Marie who does not
neglect her duty or does not forget," but can be stretched to "Marie
who is not forgotten in her time." For remembering is also prospec-
tive: s/he who forgets makes being forgotten. So too, alongside the
obligation to speak, a case can be made for the relationship between
memory and what we have seen to be Marie's fear that her work will
be appropriated by others. As Mary Carruthers argues in her monu-
mental book on memory in the Middle Ages, plagiarism can, in a
tradition heavily dependent on the arts of memory, be conceived as
a failure of memory.[7]

Memory for Marie is not simply a phenomenon of individual con-
sciousness, a question of subjective moral agency, but a cultural
mechanism as well: the memory of the individual is linked to a col-
lective memory, to the commemoration implicit in the dedication
contained in the general prologue:

> En l'honur de vus, nobles reis,
> Ki tant estes pruz e curteis,
> A ki tute joie se encline,
> E en ki quoer tuz biens racine,
> M'entremis de lais assembler,
> Par rime fere e reconter. (v. 43)

In your honor, noble king, you who are so worthy and courtly,
you to whom all joy pays homage and in whose heart all true
virtue has taken root, did I set myself to assemble lais, to com-
pose and to relate them in rhyme.

6 See Milena Mikhaïlova, *Le présent de Marie* (Paris: Diderot, 1996), p. 60.
7. See Mary J. Carruthers, *The Book of Memory: A Study of Memory in Medieval Culture*
   (Cambridge: Cambridge University Press, 1990), p. 218.

Marie's passing on of her material is an act of remembering and literally of "assembling" that which has, in one possible reading, "been left behind—M'entremis de lais assembler." It is a retelling in poetry or rhyme—"Par rime fere e reconter"—of that which has, as we learn in the prologue to "Guigemar," already been told: "Les contes ke jo sai verrais, / Dunt li Bretun unt fait les lais, / Vos conterai assez briefment" ("I shall relate briefly to you stories that I know to be true and from which the Bretons have composed their lais" [vv. 19–21]). In the recounting of that which has already been "counted," Marie inserts herself into a literary genealogy, a genesis of tales. Again, the obligation to speak, the study of the works of preceding generations, and the preservation of the record of the past establish a link, a genealogy, that serves to eradicate a sense of loss and to make whole—that is, to give meaning to—the fragmentary and contingent nature of lived experience, the "adventure."

"GUIGEMAR"

The prologue to the *Lais* contains a virtual program for the writing and reading of medieval literature. France's first woman writer, at over six centuries' remove from Priscian, places herself in the same position to him as the author of the *Institutiones Grammaticae* stands in relation to the ancients; and, indeed, in a position analogous to ours in relation to her. So too Marie poses more generally the problem of the reader before any text; for the project in which she is engaged is not so much a philological as an epistemological undertaking, one that collapses the distinction between historical otherness and the otherness of writing, reading, and interpreting. Just as there can be no access to the past, there is no unmediated access to the text, any text, which, because of the degraded nature of verbal signs according to medieval sign theory, requires interpretation or gloss.

*   *   *

[A]s critics have noted for some time, the *Lais* tend to attract one another in pairs or in groups that can sometimes be defined even in terms of gender pairings—Lanval's feminine fairy benefactor, for instance, set against the dreams of rescue on the part of the imprisoned wives of "Yonec" and "Guigemar."[8] Unlike, say, the romances of Chrétien or the *Tristan* poets, unlike even the *Fables*, where much attention is paid to government and community, or the *Espurgatoire*, where Marie insists upon the spiritual fellowship of the saved and the damned, the couple is the operative social unit within the *Lais*,

---

8. See S. Foster Damon, "Marie de France: Psychologist of Courtly Love," *PMLA* 44 (1929): 968–96; John A. Frey, "Linguistic and Psychological Couplings in the Lays of Marie de France," *Studies in Philology* 61 (1964): 3–18.

where the desire for wholeness is expressed in terms of love as a long-ing for union, a coupling, an appropriate—that is to say, equitable, decent, voluntary—love, which may even involve marriage.

Marriage, however, fails to satisfy the desire for wholeness on the part of a number of Marie's inevitably suffering heroes and hero-ines around the outer edges of these case studies in longing. At an extreme lurk those who, like Guigemar in the beginning, desire noth-ing more than to be beyond desire—autonomous, self-sufficient, entire unto themselves—or those who, as we shall see, confuse wholeness with abundance: Eliduc, who maintains two wives, and the lady of "Chaitivel," who, when it comes to suitors, prefers not to choose and wants to keep them all.

Here we arrive at one of the defining dilemmas of the *Lais*: * * * that is, the constant tension between the recurrent desire to "have it all" and the necessity of choice, which amounts to an analogy between the material of the story, its *aventure*, and the making of narrative. Marie's *Lais* seem, where language is concerned, to per-form that which they recount, to expose the architectonics of their own creation in a way that permits us to erect as a trait of her style, indeed as a productive principle, the fact that almost anything that can be said about the themes of the *Lais*, whether on the level of economics, erotics, or social institutions, can also be said about her conscious concretization of language itself. This is not a ques-tion of interpretation, but, I think, a matter of authorial intent. To repeat, words for Marie are not merely a vehicle, a transparent medium through which we glimpse the portrait of a world that is narratively reclaimed and contained, but a theme—perhaps the theme—of the *Lais* as well as the *Fables* and *Espurgatoire*. For no matter how a particular tale is resolved, whether it ends happily as in the case of "Guigemar," "Lanval," and "Le Fresne," or unhappily as in "Laüstic," "Deus Amanz," "Chaitivel," or "Equitan," or in a mixed manner as in "Yonec" and "Milun," or doesn't end at all as in "Chevrefoil," the tension between a desire for wholeness and a sense of loss both experienced by the characters and thematized in terms of language itself is the inescapable hub around which everything turns. Language is a character, perhaps the main character, capa-ble of eliciting all the emotions connected to the various figures depicted in the *Lais*—trust, love, fear, jealousy, betrayal. For there is no separating Marie's *contes* from their form; rather, there is no separating the themes they contain in language from the thematic performance of language as a constant threat to the wholeness that is the object of all human longing, and, as we shall see in the pages that follow, from language as fatal.

From the beginning Marie's readers have sensed something mel-ancholic in the *Lais* that, as far back as the eighteenth century, conjures geographic associations. The Abbé La Rue, it will be remembered, claims that "the English muse seems to have inspired her. All her subjects are sad and melancholy; she appears to have designed to melt the hearts of her readers, either by the unfortunate situation of her hero, or by some truly afflicting catastrophe."[9] And while there is no reason to believe that the English were any more gloomy in the twelfth or thirteenth century than the French or Anglo-Normans, the pioneering Abbé did sense something operative within Marie's text—that is, the extent to which the geographic sites of the *Lais* are infused with a sadness that seems often to be set in the soil, a sorrow out of which characters and situations seem to grow as if adapting to the depressive ecology of a dolorous natural habitat. The action of "Le Fresne" takes place in the land of "Dol" ("A Dol aveit un bon seignur" [v. 243, see also v. 362]), just as that of "Yonec" is situated on the river "Düelas" ("La cité siet sur Düelas" [v. 15]), both names carrying a sense of sadness, of "deuil" (from Latin *dolus*). The region of "Yonec," of which the old, jealous man is the lord, is called, further, "Carwent" (or "Carüent" in other transcriptions) ("En Bretain[e] maneit jadis / Un riches hum viel e antis, / De Carwent fu avouez" [v. 11]), as if the realm itself, from the Latin *careo, carere*, signified "to be cut off from," "to lack." The lord of the region of "lack" is wanting. The couple lacks progeny ("Unques entre eus n'eurent enfanz" [v. 38]). Most of all, the lady of "Carwent" lacks: she is deprived of the outside world ("Ne fors de cele tur n'eissi, / Ne pur parent ne pur ami," "She did not leave the tower for either family or friend" [v. 39]); of male company ("N'i ot chamberlenc ne huisser / Ki en la chambre osast entrer," "There was neither chamberlain nor doorkeeper who would have dared enter the chamber" [v. 43]); of speech ("Mes ja la dame n'i parlast, / Si la vielle ne comandast," "The lady would never have spoken without the old woman's permission" [v. 35]); finally, she is robbed of her beauty because she lacks desire:

> Mut ert la dame en grant tristur;
> Od lermes, od suspir e plur
> Sa beuté pert en teu mesure
> Cume cele qui n'en ad cure. (v. 45)

The lady was in great distress, and she wept and sighed so much that she lost her beauty, like one who no longer cares.

"Lanval" takes place in the city of "Kardoel" (and in some transcriptions "Cardoel"), an allomorph of both *careo/carere* and *duel/dol*, just

---

9. Of all her commentators, Milena Mikhaïlova is the only one of whom I am aware who links Marie's morbidity not only to the wound but to the sense of dispersion and loss defined as a linguistic drama as well. See *Le présent de Marie* (Paris: Diderot, 1996), p. 60.

as "Laüstic" is situated "En Seint Mallo," which resonates with the *malum/mal* that is its theme. The action of "Les Deus Amanz" occurs in "Neustrie," which, Marie tells is, "we call Normandy" ("Que nus apelum Normendie" [v. 8]); more precisely:

> Une cité fist faire uns reis
> Quë esteit sir des Pistreis;
> Des Pistreins la fist [il] numer
> E Pistre la fist apeler.
> Tuz jurs ad puis duré li nuns;
> Uncore i ad vile e maisuns.
> Nus savum bien de la cuntree,
> Li vals de Pistre est nomee. (v. 13)

A king had a city built which he named after the inhabitants and called Pitres. The name has survived to this day and there is still a town and houses there. We know the area well, for it is called the Valley of Pitres.

The site of the fatal love test of this particular lai is the "vals de Pistre," or the "valley of pity," an unavoidable semantic association with the Old French *pite* meaning "who has pity" or "worthy of pity" and *piteer*, "to have pity," "to pity." Then too, the valley that is in the moral geography of Old French literature linked to sadness is the place to which Lanval, despite the appearance of rescue, repairs at the end of the lai that bears his name—"Avalun," "in the direction of the little valley," "downhill."[1]

* * *

The imprisoned wife, the lady in a tower, is a leitmotif of the *Lais* that cannot be separated from the marital practices of France's nobility at the end of the first feudal age, or from the conflict between lay aristocratic and ecelesiastical models of marriage, or from what I have described elsewhere as a "biopolitics" of lineage.[2] The genea-logical family implied, first of all, the exercise of a certain discipline with respect to marriage, the restriction of unions to the minimum necessary to assure the continuity of the family line. As Georges Duby and others have demonstrated for the regions of Mâcon and the northwest, noble families permitted the establishment of only one or two new households per generation, the rest of the unmarried sons being housed in monasteries and chapters, or simply remaining

---

1. Though her identification of a precise geographical site for the action of "Lanval" may seem overly literal, Elizabeth A. Francis nonetheless affirms the topographic associa-tion of the name and "down the valley" or "downhill." See "Marie de France et son temps," *Romania* 72 (1951); 87–88.
2. See R. Howard Bloch, *Etymologies and Genealogies: A Literary Anthropology of the French Middle Ages* (Chicago: University of Chicago Press, 1983), pp. 70–83.

unattached and disenfranchised.[3] The noble family husbanded its reproductive resources so as to produce sufficient progeny to insure dynastic continuity without a surplus to deplete its wealth through the fragmentation of a patrimony divided among too many sons.

* * *

Thus, if, as we have seen, Marie is concerned about cultural inheritance, about passing on a past that, unarticulated, is lost, the imprisoning old men in her works are themselves anxious about preserving a family line, passing on their property to a male heir. We see in Marie as good a representation of the feudal, aristocratic model of marriage as can be found in Old French literature.

* * *

E. A. FRANCIS

The Trial in *Lanval*[†]

In a recent article in *Romania* (LIX, 351) Professor Hœpffner gave his reasons for tracing in Marie's *lai de Lanval* imitations of the *roman de Thèbes*. * * * [H]e stresses in particular a resemblance between the trial scene in *Lanval* and the trial of Daire le Roux in the *roman de Thèbes*. * * *

* * * Descriptions of trials are not uncommon in twelfth-century literature. Apart from the two quoted by Professor Hœpffner, there is, for example, Béroul's account of Iseut's ordeal and also the frequent theme of the trial of Renart. Yet, if the trial of Lanval is placed in this general context of contemporary fiction, it can be seen to have some characteristics of its own which deserve attention.

A suitable preface to the examination of these characteristics is the description of mediæval legal practice as outlined by Maitland.[1] The materials for discovering record of actual procedure in the twelfth century are scanty, but on the analogy supplied by later

---

3. See Georges Duby, *La société aux XI et XIIe siècles dans la région mâconnaise* (Paris: Armand Colin, 1953), p. 280; "Structures de parenté et noblesse dans la France du Nord au XIe et XIIe siècles," in *Hommes et structures au moyen âge* (Paris: Mouton, 1973), p. 270; "Situation de la noblesse au début du XIIIe siècle," in *Hommes et structures*, p. 344.

† From E. A. Francis, "The Trial in *Lanval*," in *Studies in French Language and Medieval Literature* (Manchester, Eng.: Manchester University Press, 1939), pp. 115–20, 122–24.

1. Cf. Pollock and Maitland, *History of English Law* (Cambridge: Cambridge University Press, 1895).

documents an account of the forms can be pieced together. "Felony in France and elsewhere covered only specifically feudal crimes, breach of feudal faith"—resulting in forfeiture of fief. "An action based on felony . . . has a distinctive procedure and name of its own: it is an Appeal (*appellum*). The active party neither 'complains' nor 'demands'; but he appeals (*appelat*) his adversary."—"In the twelfth century the only mode of bringing a felon to justice has been the appeal: the only mode of meeting the appeal a direct negation and the only mode of proof has been battle."—"The court pronounces a judgment. It awards that one of the two litigants must prove his case by his body in battle; or by oath with the oath helpers, or by the oaths of witnesses. . . . It sets him a task he must attempt." This is the medial judgment. After the medial judgment comes the wager. "The party to whom proof is awarded gives gage and pledge by way of security for fulfilment of the judgment. The doomsmen have declared for law that he must, for example, purge himself with oath helpers; thereupon he 'wages', that is, undertakes to fulfil or to 'make' this 'law'."—"When the parties stand opposite to each other, it then behoves the plaintiff to state his case by his own mouth, or that of his pleader. . . . It is a formal statement bristling with sacramental words, an omission of which would be fatal." It is a statement of the type "X who is here, appeals Y who is there . . . the 'words of felony' will be essential."—"No one is entitled to an answer if he offers nothing but his bare assertion, his *nude parole*. The procedure in the Appeal of Felony is no real exception to this rule. The appellor alleges, and can be called upon to prove; . . . what the plaintiff relies on as support for his word is 'suit'."—"The defendant must speak and as a general rule the only plea that is open to him is a flat denial of all that the plaintiff has said. He must defend all of it, and in this context to defend means to deny. In the past he has been bound to 'defend' the charge with painful accuracy."—"He will probably desire that 'the proof' should be awarded to him rather than to his adversary. He must therefore offer to make good his downright No. When battle has been offered, he must . . . accept the offer. When there has been no offer of battle, he will follow up his defence by the words: 'And this he is ready and willing to defend when and where he ought as the court shall consider.' In the former case the court will award a wager of battle. In the latter case the court will award the defendant some other 'law', to wit, an oath with helpers; he must at once wage this law, that is, find gage and pledges that he will 'make' this law by performing the task that has been set him. The court will fix the number of compurgators that he must produce, and this may in some cases depend upon the number of suitors tendered by the plaintiff."

So much for the fact, now turn to the fiction. (The phrases indicating procedure have been italicised.)[2]

> Lanval *desfent la desenor*
> *Et la honte de son seignor*
> 375 *De mot en mot, si comme il dist,*
> Que la roïne ne requist;
> Mes de ce dont il ot parlé
> Reconnut il la verité,
> De l'amor dont il se vanta;
> 380 Dolent en est, perdue l'a.
> *De ce lor dit qu'il en fera*
> *Quanque la cort esgardera.*
> . . . .
> 390 Et ont *jugié et esgardé*
> *Que Lanval doit avoir un jor,*
> *Mes pleges truist a son seignor*
> *Qu'il atendra son jugement*
> *Et revendra en son present;*
> 395 Si sera la cort esforcie,
> Car n'i ot donc fors la mesnie.
> Au roi revienent li baron
> Si li mostrerent la reson.
> Li rois a *pleges demandez.*
> 400 Lanval fu seus et esgarez;
> N'i avoit parent ne ami.
> Gauvains i vait, qui *l'a plevi,*
> Et tuit si compagnon après.
> Li rois lor dit: *E jel vos les*
> 405 *Seur quanque vos tenez de moi,*
> *Terres et fiez, chascuns par soi.*
> . . . .
> Au jor que cil orent nommé
> Li baron furent assemblé.
> Li rois et la roïne i fu,
> 420 Et li plege ont Lanval rendu.
> Molt furent tuit por lui dolent;
> Je cuit qu'il en i ot tieus cent
> Qui feïssent tot lor pooir
> Por lui sanz plait delivre avoir;

2. For comparison phrases are quoted here, which have been taken from cases in the *Jugements de l'Echiquier de Normandie*, and *Select Pleas of the Crown* (early thirteenth century). "Et Gilebertus appelatus totum defendit de verbo in verbum, etc."—"Episcopus venit et dixit quod veritas fuit—Dies datus est—et dimissus fuit per plegios—Et ideo det vadium—propter defectum garanti sui quem vocaverat quem habere non potuit . . . idem Ricardus erat in misericordia."

425 Il ert reté a molt grant tort.
Li rois demande le *recort*
Selonc le claim et le respons.
Ore est trestot sor les barons.
Il sont au jugement alé;
430 Molt sont pensis et esgaré
Du franc homme d'autre païs,
Qui entre eus ert si entrepris.
Encombrer le vuelent plusor
Por la volenté lor seignor.
435 Ce dist li dus de Cornoaille:[3]
Ja endroit nos n'i avra faille;
Car qui qu'en plort ne qui qu'en chant,
Le droit estuet aler avant!
Li rois parla vers son vassal,
440 *Que je vos oi nomer Lanval;*
De felonnie le reta
Et d'un mesfait l'achoisonna,
D'une amor dont il se vanta,
Et ma dame s'en corrouça.
445 *Nus ne l'apele fors le roi.*
Par cele foi que je vos doi,
Qui bien en vuelt dire le voir,
Ja n'i deüst respons avoir,
Se por ce non qu'a son seignor
450 Doit l'en par tot faire honor.
Un serement l'en gagera,
Et li rois le nos pardonra:
Et s'il puet avoir son garant,
Et s'amie venist avant,
455 *Et ce fust voir qu'il en deïst*
Dont la roïne se marrist,
De ce avra il bien merci
Quant por vilté nel dist de li.
Et s'il ne *puet garant avoir,*
460 Ce li devons faire savoir:
Tot son servise pert du roi,
Et sel doit congeer de soi.

. . . .

---

3. G. B. Adams, describing the trial of the Bishop of Durham for treason, in 1088, raises the question "whether the king was not always represented by some member of the court when he was party to a suit before it". (*Council and Courts in Anglo-Norman England*, [New Haven: Yale University Press, 1926], p. 57, note 32.) Cp. also Maitland (Pollock and Maitland, Vol. 1, p. 156) "At the trial of Becket, though the king was angry and striving to crush one who had become his enemy, he did not venture to pass judgment . . . the duty was delegated . . . to the justiciar, the Earl of Leicester."

Rois, j'ai amé un tien vassal.
Veez le ci! Ce est Lanval!
635 Achoisonnez fu en ta cort:
Ne voil mie qu'a mal li tort
De ce qu'il dist. Ce saches tu
Que la roïne a tort eu:
Onques nul jor ne la requist.
640 De la vantance que il fist,
Se par moi puet estre aquitez,
Par vos barons soit delivrez.

It is evident that the stages in the trial and much of the vocabulary used to describe them are in close agreement with the practice indicated by Maitland. Many of the terms are of course common to other mediæval writers dealing with similar subject-matter, yet if the passages are compared with those used by Béroul and in the *Renart*, it will be found that the *lai* of *Lanval* gives a much greater impression of precision. It is difficult not to infer that many of the phrases are intended to bear a technical value. What, however, is still more noticeable is that, notwithstanding the general resemblance of the whole incident to that in the *roman de Thèbes*, there is much less similarity in terminology than would have been expected, and although the position of Lanval, in the main, is like that of Daire[4], there are differences.

＊　＊　＊

The questions which come before the court in the trial of Lanval are totally different. There is not any problem of whether a vassal has been released from an oath. Nearly all the points in which there is similarity between the two incidents introduce different issues. Although Arthur vaguely threatens hanging and burning, he quite normally refers the case for judgment. The court made up of vassals in the household decide there is a case to be heard, but that it should be for the court with full attendance of vassals to give the "medial judgment". When this court meets, the opposing views current are not that the accused person has powerful kinsfolk[5] (on the contrary as a "foreigner" and landless he lacks the normal sureties) but whether he is liable for judgment at all. Those who think there is a case are those who seek royal favour (presumably those earlier described as maliciously disposed from jealousy of his personal qualities), whereas none of the barons at the trial of Daire is swayed by a wish to please the king. The central problem, whether there should be a case at all, is expounded in the Duke of Cornwall's statement: it turns upon the pronouncement that "Nus ne l'apele fors le rei"

4. [I.e., Daire Le Roux in the *roman de Thèbes*. *Editor's note*.]
5. [As in the *roman de Thèbes*. *Editor's note*.]

and that strictly speaking the case should lapse—except for the fact that a vassal should never take any action which can reflect upon the prestige of his overlord. Lanval's claim of the great beauty of his mistress belittles the queen. The "law" assigned to the defendant is the "waging of an oath" to produce a "warrant". It is in effect to produce the fairy, as either "warranty" or "warrantor". When she does appear, it is not merely her presence, and appearance, which fulfils the task set to the defendant. She makes a formal statement, asserting that Lanval's "denial" is true. This seems to be exactly the function, in many actual instances, of an overlord.[6]

Even assuming Marie was copying the trial of Daire in her *lai*, it appears probable that she was affected also by models of legal procedure of a different kind. It is noticeable how little her legal vocabulary corresponds to that of the *Thèbes* model and how closely to that used by Maitland in description of actual trials. One might venture to think that she may have had knowledge, whether at first or second hand, of cases heard, and that this at least influenced her modification of ideas suggested by the *roman de Thèbes*. * * * The discussions connected with Lanval's trial are proportionate to the importance of the various aspects of the story, which are here linked up together. It is an essential feature of the story, as Marie tells it, that Lanval is a foreigner at the court of Arthur, unrewarded and therefore dishonoured. It may be this very situation which brings about the visitation of the fairy and her gifts, by which Lanval comes under her protection. When he finds himself summoned to appear before the court, all these elements in the situation are again prominent. It is hinted that he need not have recognised the king's justice. Had not the chivalrous Gauvain come forward, he could not even have found sureties. Even the solicitude of Lanval's friends has a practical basis, since death from despair involves them in unpleasant liabilities. It is Lanval's position as an "alien" which adds to the difficulty of settling the matter. The various moments of suspense in the trial are equally distributed between the question of Lanval's uncertain standing at the court, and the question of his power to carry out his appointed ordeal, for two reasons, one (known to himself only) that he has forfeited his claim to the fairy's protection, the other, which concerns the court—doubt of the existence of the fairy. When the fairy does in fact vindicate her existence, and Lanval's innocence, and her own power, it is in a manner to which the prosaic background

---

6. "Aumaricus venit et defendit totum de verbo in verbum, et dicit quod dominus suus Abbas de Westmonasterio habet boscum . . . et inde vocat dominum suum ad warrantum." Also, Adams, *l.c.* p. 163, ". . . the lord's obligations to his tenant. These obligations may be stated in general terms as protection and warranty—protection being broadly interpreted to include not merely military but moral protection, and warranty the protection of the tenant's title against adverse claim."

of the court procedure adds as much fitness as the poetic magic of the ending:

> O li s'en vait en Avalon,
> Ce nos racontent li Breton,
> En un ille qui molt est biaus;
> La fu raviz li damoisiaus.
> Nus hom n'en oi plus parler,
> Ne je n'en sai avant conter.

JILL MANN

From From Aesop to Reynard: Beast Literature in Medieval Britain[†]

Marie de France: The Courtly Fable

It would certainly never have been suspected in modern times that the author of the *Fables* was a woman, if she had not helpfully identified herself in the Epilogue that concludes them.

> Al finement de cest escrit,
> Que en romanz ai treité e dit,
> Me numeral pur remembrance:
> Marie ai num, si sui de France.
> Put cel estre que clerc plusur
> Prendreient sur eus mun labur.
> Ne voil que nul sur li le die!
> E il fet que fol ki sei ublie! (1–8)[1]

---

†   From Jill Mann, *From Aesop to Reynard: Beast Literature in Medieval Britain* (Oxford and New York: Oxford University Press, 2009), pp. 53–58, 62–64, 67–72, 74, 76, 81–82, 83, 92–93, 95, 96–97. Reprinted by permission of the publisher. Notes have been edited when they contain sentences or phrases referring to Mann's material not excerpted in this volume, e.g., her Introduction or Appendix; also, a long note on the date of *The Owl and the Nightingale* (Mann, 149) has been shortened in this volume.

1.   The critical edition of Marie's *Fables* by Karl Warnke is based on London, BL, MS Harley, 978 (English, s.xiii³ᐟ⁴; fols 40r–67v), which also contains the only complete collection of Marie's *Lais* (fols 118r–160r). A full description of Harley 978 is now available in the British Library's Online Manuscripts Catalogue; for a recent discussion of this manuscript, see Pickens, 'Reading Harley 978'. In keeping with the practices current in the late nineteenth century, Warnke introduced extensive changes to the spelling and language of Harley 978 as well as emendations on other grounds (see Jambeck, 'Base Text and Critical Text', and, for a very full discussion of editorial procedure in the editions of Warnke, Otaka, Spiegel, and Brucker, and of the inherent problems in editing the *Fables*, see Trachsler, 'Manuscrits et éditions'). Since I am concerned with the British tradition of beast literature, I cite Harriet Spiegel's edition, which follows Harley 978 more closely (for some reservations concerning this edition, see Trachsler, 'Manuscrits et éditions', pp. 53, n. 42). Occasionally I alter Spiegel's punctuation, or adopt a reading from Warnke's text, placed in angle brackets, which better fits the vocabulary-sets in the *Fables* and so has in my view a claim to authenticity. Square brackets indicate editorial readings in Spiegel's text. I have used Roman numerals for fable numbers instead of Spiegel's arabic numbers, in order to keep clear the distinction between them and line-numbers.

[At the end of this work, which I have composed and put into French, I will name myself, so as to be remembered. My name is Marie, I am from France. It could be that many clerks might take my work as their own. I don't want anyone to say that about it. He who is unmindful of himself acts like a fool!]

The same concern for 'remembrance' is evident at the points where Marie names herself in the *Lais* ('Oëz, seignurs, ke dit Marie, / Ki en sun tens pas ne s'oblie'),[2] in *L'Espurgatoire Saint Patriz* ('Jo, Marie, ai mis en memoire / le livre de l'Espurgatoire / en romanz'),[3] and in the *Vie Seinte Audree* ('Mut par est fol ki se oblie. / Ici escris mon non Marie, / Pur ce ke soie remembree'),[4] and it is not just the repetition of the name, but particularly the repeated appearance of the motif of remembrance that makes it hard to resist the conclusion that all these works are by one and the same author.[5] The use of this characteristic 'signature' indicates that she is above all a self-conscious artist, one who is unwilling to lurk in the obscurity that shrouds the anonymous authors of the Latin *Romulus* collections.[6] Although both the *Romulus-Nilantii* and the *Romulus vulgaris* figure among her sources,[7] the general character of her *Fables* is not pedagogical, but literary, and she clearly wished to have credit for her achievement.

2. *Guigemar*, lines 3–4. I quote the edition of the *Lais* by Jean Rychner; future line references will be given in the body of the text.
3. Ed. de Pontfarcy, lines 2297–9. I have deleted de Pontfarcy's confusing commas after 'mis' and 'memoire'.
4. *Vie Seinte Audree*, ed. Södergård, lines 4618–20. Södergård dates the work to the beginning of the thirteenth century (see p. 55 of his edition). The familiar emphasis on *remembrance*, underlined, as in the *Lais*, by the rhyming of *Marie* and *oblie*, is an important reason for attributing this work to Marie de France. Although not showing the artistic originality of the *Lais* or the *Fables*, the *Vie Seinte Audree* is the work of a skilled poetic craftsman, and is of no lower quality than the *Espurgatoire*. A strong case for seeing Marie de France as its author is made by June Hall McCash, 'La vie seinte Audree'.
5. Common authorship has been vigorously disputed by Richard Baum (*Recherches*), but he spends most of his time trying to prove that the collection of *lais* in Harley 978 are not necessarily the *oeuvre* of a single author, and gives very little attention to the *Fables*. Mickel (*Marie de France*, p. 15) pertinently asks: 'Given the fact that women writers were not exactly commonplace, is it likely that there were four different women all with the name Marie, composing texts in the late twelfth and early thirteenth century?' MacBain ('Anglo-Norman Women Hagiographers', p. 235) has expressed scepticism concerning common authorship of the *Lais* and the *Espurgatoire*, which he thinks rests 'on the basis of little more than the name Marie', but he ignores the repeated motif of remembrance.
6. However, Runte's attempt to show that her use of the first-person pronoun in the pro/epimythia to certain fables is a marker of cases where she is inventing new material is implausible and unconvincing ('Marie de France dans ses Fables').
7. The influence of the *Romulus Nilantii* may have been exerted via an intermediary source or sources.

FABLES AS COURTLY LITERATURE

This literary self-consciousness marks a new development for the fable. It emerges from the schoolroom to claim a place in the courtly literature written 'en romanz'.[8] The way for this transformation is deftly paved by Marie's use of the traditional preamble attributing the fables to the emperor Romulus, who is writing them for his son ('Romulus, ki fu emperere, / A sun fiz escrit': Prol. 12–13). While this allusion to Romulus retains a link with the tradition of 'wisdom-literature' and its traditional format of the father's instruction of his son, or the teacher's instruction of his pupil, in Marie's hands it also serves to establish an aristocratic pedigree for the fable, in which King Alfred ('Li reis Alfrez'), whom she names as her immediate source (Epilogue 16–17), also takes a natural place.[9] The patron and instigator of her work, 'count William, the bravest of any realm', who is 'the flower of chivalry, of learning, and of courtesy',[1] is representative of the audience to whom it is addressed.

* * *

The *Lais* survive in a pitifully small number of manuscripts—the full complement of twelve lais being found in only one.[2] Marie's *Fables*, in contrast, survive in no fewer than twenty-five manuscripts, ranging in date from the thirteenth century to the fifteenth.[3] Many of these manuscripts are large miscellanies containing a wide variety

8. I use 'courtly' in the general sense 'reflecting the values of courtly society', rather than the more specific 'written at the [royal] court'. 'Courtly' literature in this sense could have been produced for any well-born audience (including the convents patronized by aristocratic ladies). Dominica Legge (*Anglo-Norman Literature*, p. 107) says of Marie's *Fables* that they are 'aristocratic, but not courtly, literature', since she 'was writing for a man and not a court personified in a king'.
   Ian Short states flatly that Marie was 'a Continental writer from the Ile-de-France who, like Wace and Benoît before her, worked at the Anglo-Norman court, probably in the 1170s' ('Patrons and Poylglots', p. 240), but he offers no evidence in support of the latter part of this assertion (in surprising contrast to his careful discrimination of fact and conjecture elsewhere in this article).
9. This is highly unlikely to be the real King Alfred; see Lapidge and Mann, 'Reconstructing the Anglo-Latin Aesop', pp. 15–18.
1. 'le cunte Willame, / Le plus vaillant de nul realme' (Epilogue 9–10); 'Ki flurs est de chevalerie, / D'enseignement, de curteisie' (Prol. 31–2).
2. See n. 1 above (p. 362) on Harley 978. The next largest collection is found in Paris, BNF, MS nouv. acq. fr. 1104, which contains nine *lais*; Paris, BNF, MS fr. 2168 contains three, and London, BL, MS Cotton Vespasian B.XIV and Paris, BNF, MS fr. 24432 contain one each. All these manuscripts except the last (which is fourteenth-century) date from the thirteenth century. Fourteenth-century translations of *Le Fresne* and *Lanval* indicate however that knowledge of Marie's *Lais* did not die out in England. Versions in Old Norse and Middle High German also testify to the medieval circulation of the *Lais*.
3. Twenty-four manuscripts are listed, with a description of their provenance, in Keidel, 'The History of French Fable Manuscripts'; twenty-six (including the Nottingham fragment) are listed in Vielliard, 'Sur la tradition manuscrite'.
   In contrast, in modern times Marie's *Fables* have received much less critical attention than her *Lais*. Mickel's book (*Marie de France*) is representative in devoting ninety pages to the *Lais* and only seven to the *Fables*. The only book-length treatment of the *Fables* is Amer, *Ésope au féminin*, which is devoted to an entirely unconvincing attempt to prove that Marie was influenced by the Arabic *Kalila and Dimna* . . . R. Howard Bloch

of literature, clearly intended for enjoyment as much as edification, and some were luxury productions.[4]

The 'courtly' nature of Marie's *Fables* is substantiated by more than their dedication, however; as Hans Robert Jauss has shown, in Marie's hands the fable form is subjected to 'a thoroughgoing feudal interpretation' ('eine durchgängig feudalistische Auslegung').[5] Both the fable narratives and the epimythia following them are saturated with a vocabulary that evokes the feudal world. Whereas the *Romulus Nilantii* will contrast 'the powerful' with 'the powerless', or 'the wicked' with 'the innocent', Marie uses more specific socio-economic terms such as *seignur, vileins, riche hume, povre hume, baruns, produme, franz hume*. These social categorizations are not however independent of a moral taxonomy; on the contrary, they are closely

discusses the *Fables* at some length (*The Anonymous Marie de France*, Chapters 4–6), but as with Amer, his discussions are seriously marred by shaky scholarship (see, for example, the claim on p. 116 that 'the Greek collection attached to the name of Babrius . . . later became known as "the Aesop"', or the erroneous assertion (p. 147), based on mistranslation, that the author of the *Isopet de Chartres* claims to have translated 'the "Avionet"', whereas the reverse is true). Bloch also reveals an inadequate knowledge of Latin beast fable and beast epic. The *Romulus Nilantii*, which represents Marie's most important source, is not even mentioned, while the *Romulus vulgaris* appears only in a footnote; instead, Bloch attempts to determine the distinctive features of Marie's fables by comparing them with the Penguin translation (by Temple and Temple) of Chambry's edition (which is misleadingly referred to on pp. 132 and 134 as 'the original Aesop', . . . with Babrius, and with the *Isopet II de Paris* and the *Isopet de Chartres*, in disregard of the fact that the two Greek texts would have been inaccessible to Marie and the two *Isopets* post-date her. Similarly, Bloch's attempt on p. 187 to link Fable LXI (fox and dove) with 'the institution of the royal peace . . . imposed in France . . . possibly in the very decade of the *Lais* [sic]' ignores the appearance of the peace motif in the earlier versions of this anecdote in both the *Ysengrimus* and the *Roman de Renart*.

4. The *Fables* never appear as the only item in a manuscript, and in only one case do they appear with other fable collections (*Isopet-Avionnet* and the elegiac *Romulus*); on the other hand, they frequently appear alongside fabliaux, *dits*, works by Rutebeuf, Jean Renart, Henri d'Andeli, Jean or Baudouin de de Condé (Vielliard, 'Sur la tradition manuscrite', pp. 389–90). See also Ward, 'Fables for the Court' (on Paris, Arsenal, MS 3142); Trachsler, 'Le recueil Paris, BN fr. 12603'; and Busby, *Codex and Context*, pp. 211–16, 451–4 (on BNF, fr. 19152), 466, 473–80, 526–7, 565, 802–3.

5. See Jauss, *Tierdichtung*, pp. 24–55; quotation on p. 45. Jauss is following the lead given by E. A. Francis, who had drawn attention to the unusually precise relevance of Marie's *Fables* to 'la réalité contemporaine', and who had answered Sudre's praise of the comprehensiveness of the social criticism in her *Fables* with the comment: 'Leur application me paraît moins large et concerne les classes de barons et chevaliers' ('Marie de France et son temps', pp. 80–2, esp. p. 82, n. 1). Jauss's work is ignored by Mary Lou Martin (he does not appear in her Select Bibliography), who in the Introduction to her translation of the *Fables* endorses Sudre's view of their universality: '[The] moral endings address themselves to various levels of society, ranging from peasant to king . . . It is obvious that, in dealing with such a broad range of characters, Marie wishes to portray society on all levels, and not merely the knightly class' (p. 6). It should be stressed, however, that Jauss's case does not concern the range of social classes represented, but rather the 'class-exclusive' nature of the standpoint from which their behaviour is evaluated (pp. 47, 50).

Karen Jambeck ('A Mirror of Princes') has attempted to extend Jauss's view by arguing that Marie's *Fables* are a 'mirror for princes' and proposing parallels with John of Salisbury's *Policraticus*, but these parallels are too general to be convincing. Hans R. Runte's article, 'Marie de France's Courtly Fables', is not as relevant as its title might suggest, since he claims that 'a courtly audience could only have scoffed' at the 'home-spun truisms' of her often 'excruciatingly platitudinous' *Fables* (pp. 454–5); Runte does not refer to Jauss's work, and his own treatment is completely superficial in comparison with it.

intertwined with a system of moral values. On the one hand, the terms *riches hume, produme, seigneur, vilein*, carry moral expectations,[6] while on the other, Marie's moral positives—*lëauté, dreite fei, honur*—find their most natural home in a feudal-chivalric context.

This fusion of social and moral terms is well illustrated in the first two fables of Marie's collection. Jauss has demonstrated the delicate artistry with which Marie reorients the opening fable of the cock and the jewel.[7] In the *Romulus Nilantii* (I.1), the cock envisages the jewel's potential finder as a miser ('aliquis cupidus'); in Marie, the hypothetical finder is 'un riche hume' (I.11). In the Latin version, the cock's rejection emphasizes utility: 'I find nothing useful in you; so I am no use to you, nor you to me' ('nihil invenio utilitatis in te; quapropter nec ego tibi prosum, nec tu michi'). In Marie, the stress is on 'honur': 'Now I have found a jewel here—it will have no honour from me! . . . Since I don't have what I want from you, you will get no honour from me!' ('Ore ai ici gemme trovee—Ja n'iert pur mei honuree! . . . / Quant ma volenté n'ai de tei, / Ja nul honur n'averas de mei!': I.9–10, 15–16). The epimythium, correspondingly, casts the cock as representative of all those, men or women, who do not value 'good and honour' ('Bien e honur': 21). In the *Romulus Nilantii* the natural gulf between the cock and the jewel represents the blindness of a failure in understanding: 'Aesop related this first fable about those who despise wisdom, or whatever good they find' ('Esopus hanc primam fabulam dixit de hiis qui despiciunt sapienciam, vel quodcunque bonum inveniunt'), whereas in Marie it represents an irremediable spiritual coarseness; 'bien' is identified not with material profit, but with an intangible 'honur'. At the same time, as in courtly culture, this intangible honour is manifested in material wealth; whereas in the Latin text the jewel is merely symbolic of good (it has nothing directly in common with *sapientia*), in the French fable its role is not symbolic but *representative*. It is itself part of the accoutrements of the aristocratic life in which 'bien' and 'honur' are realized.

The differentiation between those who have spiritual refinement and those who do not thus coincides in this fable with a differentiation in material wealth and social status. In the Latin fable, the phrase 'aliquis cupidus' denies the human finder any moral superiority to the cock; it is simply that the human definition of 'utility' will differ from the bird's. Marie's fable, in contrast, gives us a strong sense of hierarchy—or rather, of several overlapping hierarchies: natural, social, moral. 'Overlapping' does not mean 'identical', and we should not lose sight of the fact that in the epimythium a moral

---

6. Tobler-Lommatzsch glosses 'riche' adj., as used of persons, as 'rich, powerful', and 'high-ranking, noble, valiant'. The implication of moral nobility is to be borne in mind when I translate *riche hume* as 'rich man' in the quotations from Marie below.

7. Jauss, *Tierdichtung*, pp. 32–3.

hierarchy replaces the natural and social hierarchies which have occupied the corresponding position in the fable. In the immediately following fable of the wolf and the lamb, on the other hand, the natural and social hierarchies run counter to a moral hierarchy. In the *Romulus Nilantii*, the wolf and lamb, while obviously differentiated in respect of brute force, at least address each other as social equals. In Marie's fable, the wolf addresses the lamb as 'tu', while the lamb uses 'vus', and the respectful title 'sire'. And the moral is applied not merely generally, to those who calumniate others in order to seize their property or lives, but specifically to those in a position of authority in society: 'rich lords, sheriffs and judges' ('li riche seignur, / Li vescunte e li jugeür': II.31–2). The social hierarchy here mirrors the natural hierarchy not in terms of an ascending scale of worth, but in terms of an ascending scale of predatory power. * * *

[After setting out the opinions of Jauss and others regarding a feudal hierarchy and feudal values in the ethos of the Fables, Mann develops her complex and sophisticated argument that a number of other social, or societal, attitudes are present as well. She introduces what she calls a "hierarchy of being" (60) that illustrates the "fixity of the natural world" (64), e.g., in Fable #1, of the cock and the jewel, or Fable #74, of the shrew who seeks a wife, aspiring to wed the daughter of the Sun. The Sun, it turns out, is subject to the cloud; the cloud to the wind; wind is withstood by stone; but stone gives way to "the little mouse, who gnaws through the mortar with its teeth" so that the shrew acknowledges that he has come full circle" (64). She also introduces the concepts of *cumpanie* (comradeship), a horizontal pattern (69) in which loyalty (a feudal value, but the only one) is assumed, and of *tricherie,* a betrayal of the former, e.g., in Fable #3, "The Mouse and the Frog"; and the concept of self-reliance and individual survival tactics, as in Fable #21, "The Wolf and the Sow." Below, she contrasts the ethos and perspectives of the Fables and the Lais. —Ed.]

THE ETHOS OF MARIE'S *LAIS*

Self-reliance, suspicion, mistrust of others, self-interest, are thus as much a part of the ethos of the *Fables* as the 'feudal' values of *lëauté* and *honur*. And these traditional fable characteristics at times run directly counter to the values implicit in Marie's *Lais*. Mickel's passing remark that the morality of the *Fables* 'clearly reflects . . . the ethical values found in the *Lais*' needs careful qualification.[8] In this and the following section I shall compare the two works in order to show

---

8. Mickel, *Marie de France*, p. 39.

not only the differences in the values that they express, but also the very different roles played by the animal in each.[9]

Community of theme there may be, but the characteristic stance on the theme is widely divergent. The divergence is evident, for example, in the fable of the naive young fawn (XCII), which makes a contrasting pair with the succeeding fable of the wise young crow, already discussed. Refusing to believe his mother's warnings of the dangerousness of a hunter equipped with bow and arrows, the fawn avers with trusting naivety:

> 'Ne fuirai mie, dici qu'il traie—
> Quel aventure que jeo en aie!'(31–2)
> ['I won't flee until he draws his bow, whatever chance
>   befalls me as a result!']

The key word here is 'aventure' ('chance'). In the *Lais*, the uncalculating—even imprudent—surrender to the issues of chance is a mark of heroic magnanimity. Guigemar, Lanval, Eliduc, commit themselves to their fates with a conscious neglect of consequences—'whether good or bad befall him because of it' ('Turt li a pru u a damage': *Guigemar* 474); 'whether it turns out to be foolish or wise' ('Turt a folie u a saveir': *Lanval* 126); 'whatever is to happen to me' ('Que ke me deivë avenir': *Eliduc* 678)—that merges into the spontaneous flow of *aventures* recorded in the *Lais*. The most powerful image of surrender to this flow of *aventure* is the picture of Guigemar asleep on the rudderless boat that carries him to his destined love; waking to find himself in mid-ocean, he realizes that 'he must endure the chance event' ('Suffrir li estuet l'aventure')—and lies down to sleep again (199).[1] The chivalric hero defines himself, not by martial exploit, but by this willingness to 'adventure himself' (*se metre en aventurel abandun*).[2] In the fable, the fawn's acceptance of 'aventure' is characterized as 'foolish' ('Fous': XCII.34), while it is precisely a sublime indifference to the designation of an action as *folie* or *saveir* that constitutes heroism in the *Lais*.

The difference in ethos means that, although animals have an important role to play in the *Lais*, their associations and significance are quite distinct from those they carry in the *Fables*.[3] The bird that

9. Pickens ('Marie de France et la culture de la cour') has compared the *Fables* and the *Lais*, but his discussion is largely concerned with matters of plot, and he ignores the vocabulary clusters that I shall be dealing with.
1. For discussion of this surrender to 'aventure', see Mann, 'Chaucerian Themes and Style', pp. 144–7.
2. See *Deus Amanz* 169–70 ('le vallet/ Ki en aventure se met'); *Chevrefoil* 19–20 ('puis se mist en abandun/ De mort e de destructïun'). Cf. *Eliduc* 181–4 in Rychner's emended version: 'Ki se mettreit en aventure/ Cume de murir a dreiture/ Bien tost les purreit damagier/ E eus laidir e empeirier.' On this conception of the chivalric hero, see Mann, '"Taking the Adventure"', and 'Sir Gawain and the Romance Hero'.
3. Again *pace* Mickel, who posits a resemblance between the two works in that both are grounded in 'an independent poetic reality in which animals, humans and inanimate objects interact as equals' (*Marie de France*, p. 39).

miraculously turns into a handsome knight in *Yonec* belongs to the
magic world of Ovid's *Metamorphoses* rather than to the sober and
cynical world of the fable. When the white deer speaks to Guige-
mar, the effect is magical and electrifying; the event signals a dra-
matic shift on to another plane of existence. The 'talking animals'
of the fable, in contrast, neither disturb nor excite; calm acceptance
of their linguistic capacities is one of the preconditions of the form.[4]
Above all, in the *Lais* animals are reinstated in a natural context that
allows full play to the reader's emotional responses. It is by means
of these emotional responses that the nightingale in *Laüstic* becomes
a richly concentrated image of the relationship between the two lov-
ers who listen to its song. A married lady falls in love with a knight
who happens to live next door; the only outlet for their feelings is
talking at night from the windows of their adjacent houses. When
her husband asks why she gets up and leaves the bedroom, she replies
that she goes to hear the nightingale singing.

> 'Sire, la dame li respunt,
> Il nen ad joie en cest mund
> Ki n'ot le laüstic chanter.
> Pur ceo me vois ici ester.
> Tant ducement l'i oi la nuit
> Que mut me semble gran deduit;
> Tant m'i delit e tant le voil
> Que jeo ne puis dormir de l'oil.' (83–90)

['Sir,' replies the lady to him, 'there is no joy in this world for
the one who does not listen to the nightingale singing. That is
why I go to stand here. I hear it so sweetly in the night that it
seems to me a great pleasure; I delight in it so much and I
desire it so much that I cannot sleep a wink.']

The nightingale has not been mentioned before this point, although
reference has been made a little earlier to the coming of spring and
the joy ('joie') that the little birds ('oiselet') feel at its arrival (61–2).
The lady's answer to her husband's question fuses this natural surge
of 'joie' with the joy of her love, and makes the nightingale's song a
surrogate for her own desire. The qualities of the nightingale, pouring
out her song in the darkness, and the qualities of the illicit but uncon-
summated love merge into one another, and can be described with
the same range of adjectives: innocent, tender, spontaneous, unforced,
rapturous, but at the same time hidden, unobtrusive, vulnerable,

---

4. Pickens ('Marie de France et la culture de la cour', p. 721) contrasts the animals of the
Fables, who are '"ordinaires", au sens qu'ils sont conventionnels' with the animals of
the *Lais*, who are 'en général extraordinaires, merveilleuses'. However, he concludes
that the *Fables* function only as a kind of originary text, a basis on which the *Lais* can
work a kind of transcendental magic (as the New Testament transforms the Old),
whereas in my view each genre has its own ethos.

and above all *small*. 'Small' is the only one of these adjectives that is applied to the nightingale (121); the rest are left to our intuitive understanding, like our understanding of the lady's unspoken feelings. The smallness of the nightingale shows us how *small* a thing it is that the lady's jealous husband is bent on obliterating, and the contrast between the tiny bird and the grotesquely disproportionate elaboration of 'engin, reis', and 'laçun' ('traps, nets, and snares') he deploys to catch it (94–100) fixes our sympathies with the lovers, who seem as vulnerable and helpless as the bird. When the husband wrings the nightingale's neck in front of his wife, and throws the dead body in her lap, flecking her dress with blood, the shock of this gratuitous violence makes us feel that (as Leo Spitzer says) he has killed not only the nightingale but also something in the lady. The killing of the nightingale destroys the natural 'joie' that unites the animal and human worlds.[5] Seeing that her nightly trysts at the window have been brought to an end, the lady takes the little body ('le cors petit': 121), wraps it in rich cloth and sends it to her lover, who encloses it in a precious reliquary and carries it with him everywhere he goes. It becomes the embodiment of the 'aventure' (134, 147) that has separated them for ever. The identification of the murdered nightingale and the murdered love, both surviving only as treasured memories, is complete. The poem itself is the final act of *remembrance* that enshrines their love.[6] Although no metaphor, since it exists on the plane of the narrative as the human actors do, the nightingale thus carries in its tiny body the whole emotional significance of the *lai*. No animal in the *Fables* is ever given such individual significance or emotional resonance.

In their imaginative perception of the symbolic harmonies between man and animal, the *Lais* are closer in spirit to the bestiaries than to fable. Thus a piece of bestiary lore about the weasel—that it has the power to bring its dead young back to life—becomes the imaginative centre of *Eliduc*.[7]

*   *   *

5. See Spitzer, 'Dichterin von Problem-Märchen', p. 51: 'die rohe Tötung des Tieres—das Halsbrechen, das Hinwerfen des Leichnams—ist ein Mord an der Liebe selbst: er hat nicht nur den Vorwand zu den nächtlichen Stelldicheins der Gattin genommen, er hat in ihr etwas getötet . . . die Nachtigall ist eingeordnet in das Sommertriebleben der Natur—ihre Ermordung ist eine Sünde an der Natur und an ihrer *joie*, indem sie *joie* vernichtet.' Despite its age, Spitzer's essay is still one of the finest and most perceptive readings of Marie's art in the *Lais*.
6. On *remembrance* as the essential role of Marie's poetry ('Dichten heisst für Marie Erinnern'), see Spitzer, 'Dichterin von Problem-Märchen', p. 53.
7. The Second-Family bestiary (*A Medieval Book of Beasts*, ed. Clark, Chapter XLVIII, p. 162) says of weasels 'Dicuntur etiam peritae medicinae, ita ut si forte occisi fuerint eorum fetus, si invenire potuerint redivivos faciant' ('They are said to be skilled in medicine, so that if their young are killed, if they can find them, they will bring them back to life').

This instinctive commitment to self-sacrifice, the passionate immersion of the self in a situation not of the self's making, the willing obliviousness to self-interest, appears elsewhere in the *Lais*. We see it for example when Guigemar's lady decides to drown herself at the spot where his ship sailed away, or when Le Fresne decks out her rival's bridal bed with the rich cloth that is the only clue to her own lost identity. In the world of the *Fables*, there is not a trace of it. The watchword here is the proverb quoted by Marie in her Epilogue: 'il fet que fol ki sei ublie' ('he who forgets himself is foolish': 8).[8] In the fable, self-forgetfulness is conceived in purely practical terms and is associated with the foolish rather than with the sublime.

The differences between the *Fables* and the *Lais*—differences in ethos and in atmosphere—thus run deep; they are not however of such a kind that we are compelled to assume with Baum that the two works are by different authors.[9] For one thing, the division is not complete; each world contains a small gesture towards the other. *Equitan* concludes with a moral on the 'trickster tricked' that is almost identical to the epimythium of fable LXIX (quoted above): 'A man can do another an injury whose ill effects rebound on him' ('Tels purcace le mal d'autrui / Dunt tuz li mals revert sur lui': 309–10).[1] Conversely, fable C reads—rather surprisingly—like a reprise of the 'rudderless boat' motif which dominates *Guigemar*. A 'riches hum' who has a sea journey to make prays to God, first, to bring him safely to his destination, and once arrived, to bring him safely home. Finding himself carried rapidly out to sea, he prays to be brought back to shore, but finds that the harder he prays, the faster the boat sails away from land. Finally gaining wisdom, he asks God to do His will, and instantly finds himself conveyed where he wants to go. Although the patient resignation inculcated here is not on the same plane as the passionate self-sacrifice of the *Lais*, nevertheless such a surrender of the will runs counter to the cynical self-interest we find elsewhere in the *Fables*, and as in the *Lais*, it fuels the dynamic of events with a quasi-magical power. These cases of overlap confirm that the divergences between the *Lais* and the *Fables* result from a shift in genre, rather than in authorship or fundamental point of view. The technique by which Marie impregnates these genres with special meaning, on the other hand, is the same in both works—that is, the repetition of constant vocabulary-sets through a range of different contexts which have an incremental effect on their meaning and associations.[2]

---

8. For the proverbial nature of this saying, see Hassell, *Middle French Proverbs*, F151, and cf. Chaucer's *Troilus and Criseyde* V.97–8.
9. See n. 5, p. 362, above.
1. Since this chapter was drafted, the resemblance between the two passages has been commented on by Pickens, 'Marie de France et la culture de la cour', pp. 714–15.
2. This is a feature that Marie's *Lais* and *Fables* have in common; as far as I can judge, it is not found in the *Espurgatoire* or the *Vie Seinte Audree*.

[Here Mann discusses *cunseil*, "advice," counsel," and thus *trust*, as both a hierarchical principle, as between a lord (or king) and vassal, and a horizontal one, as between lovers or companions, and how that can be betrayed, often by cunning speech, like the frog's in "The Mouse and the Frog" or in Fable #44, "The Woman Who Tricked Her Husband," where the wife convinces her spouse that the evidence of his eyes has nothing like the authority of her observations; he sees his reflection in a tub, but is he in there? Of course not. Mann writes, "Within the collection as a whole, these fables . . . testify to the co-existence of *mençunge* (the lie, lying) and *verité* (the truth) as one of the constant polarities which run through the world of Marie's fables, and thus to the fact that *mençunge* is an ineradicable feature of 'the world as it is'" (91)—Ed.]

[Consider the epimythium of the man and the lion (xxxvii):]

> Par essample hus veut aprendre
> Que nul ne deit nïent entendre
> A *fable, ke est de mençuinge,*
> Ne a peinture, que semble sunge.
> Ceo est a creire dunt hum veit l'ovre,
> Que la verité tut descovre. (XXXVII.59–64; my italics)

[In this exemplum we are taught that no one ought to pay any attention to fables, which are based on lies, nor to painting, which resembles illusion. One should believe what one sees in deeds, which reveal the truth.]

The unexpected element here is the sudden reference to 'fable' and its association with 'mençuinge'. Alongside the 'peinture' which represents illusion in the story, Marie places the fable form of *the story itself.*[3] Like the painting, the fable offers a 'semblance' which is not necessarily guaranteed by truth. The epimythium uncovers the falseness of the very story from which it is derived.

MARIE AS CREATOR OF THE FABLE WORLD

The epimythium to the fable of the lion and the man allows us for a brief moment to 'step into the wings' of the fable, to see it as 'mençuinge' rather than, suspending our disbelief, as a fictional reality. This momentary glimpse behind the scenes encourages the assemblage of other clues which testify to Marie's sense of her own role as puppetmaster, as creator and governor of the fictional world. The first clue of this sort is her use of the English word 'sepande', which,

3. 'Fable' can mean 'lie' in general, but the equation with 'peinture' suggests that the reference is to a structured art-form, and it is hardly possible to avoid associating the word with the fables we are reading.

as Eduard Mall suggested,[4] is a Middle English derivative of the Old English 'scippend', meaning 'creator'. In accordance with this meaning Marie uses the word to indicate a ruling deity in several fables: the fable of the bat (XXIII.34, 39),[5] the fable of the beetle (LXXV.10), and in the fable of the hare and the deer (XCVII.7). But in her case the deity is distinguished from the Christian God by being *female*: 'la sepande'. This use of the feminine article has been a source of bafflement to scholars, who have assumed that Marie perhaps mistook the true meaning of the word. Most of them have, however, failed to appreciate the significance of the fact that she shows a similar independence in substituting a noun of feminine gender in place of the name of the male head of the pagan gods where she found it in her Latin source.[6] Jupiter becomes 'la Destinee' (VI.6, 9; cf. *RN* I. 8; XVIII. 7, 12, 29, 32, 37, 39; cf. *RN* II.1). Juno's name is also dropped, in the fable of the peacock, and she is likewise referred to simply as 'la Destinee' or (in Warnke's edition) 'la deuesse' (XXXI. 5). It has been assumed that these changes are due to a desire to 'Christianize' the fables. If, however, we relate 'la Destinee' and 'la deuesse' to 'la sepande', it looks more like an attempt to 'feminize' them; it looks, that is, as if Marie is projecting *herself* on to the fictional plane of her fables, acknowledging herself as creator and controller of her fictional world. In so doing she initiates a self-reflexive element in the tradition of British beast literature that was to enrich it for a further three hundred years. The delightful picture of Marie as surrogate deity, supplicated by the creatures she has formed, completes our sense of the fable as a playful *mençunge* which does not aim to replace the real world but nevertheless carries the weight of its responsibilities. Like Marie's *Lais*, her *Fables* have a fragile charm whose delicacy the reader must be trusted not to break, and this trust is won by the author's implicit invitation to enter into a world of play.

CONCLUSION

It should by now be clear that Marie's fables are too complex to be characterized simply as an articulation of feudal-chivalric values. If they endorse such virtues as loyalty, honour, truthfulness, companionship, and faithful counsel, they also endorse self-interest,

4. Mall, 'Zur Geschichte der mittelalterlichen Fabelliteratur', pp. 176–9; cf. MED s.v. sheppende. The form 'seppande' is recorded in *The Middle English Physiologus* (ed. Wirtjes, line 313), an East Midland text which was possibly, though not certainly, composed before 1250 (ibid., pp. xxxiv, xl, lii).
5. In Warnke's edition, these lines read 'A lur sepande se clamerent . . . / La sepande lur a juré'. In Harley 978 (and thus in Spiegel's edition), the word used is 'Crïere', but the 'Creator' is still female; see line 40.
6. Harriet Spiegel has commented on Marie's habit of making the gods of her fable world female ('The Woman's Voice', pp. 48–9; cf. Spiegel, 'The Male Animal', p. 113), but she sees this merely as a symptom of a general 'feminine bias' in Marie, rather than a witty dramatization of the female artist's role as creator of an alternative fictional world.

self-reliance, cunning (*engin*), and verbal deception.[7] The hierarchies that structure the animal world shift and reshape themselves; alliances are formed but (for the most part) are quickly dissolved. So, despite the novelty of Marie's 'feudalization' of her fables, taken as a whole, they remain true to the pragmatic, non-systematized nature of the traditional fable. In the *Lais*, the animal represents the instinctive, the spontaneous, the pull of unspoken affinity, sudden miraculous surges of love or pity breaking through socially sanctioned structures. In the *Fables*, in contrast, the animal represents the solid irreducible constants of the world-as-it-is, observed without sentimentality or tenderness. These constants take the form of recurring polarities (as if to show that every truth is countered by its opposite): *leauté* and *felunie, honur* and *hunte, cumpainie* and self-reliance, wisdom and folly, riches and poverty, *mençuinge* and *veire*. The contests between these polarities assume varying configurations: sometimes the *felun* falls into his own traps, sometimes he carries the day, but in either case, the action plays itself out with an inevitability that expresses the traditional 'cold-bloodedness' of fable, its hard-headed recognition of life as an instructive series of miniature triumphs and disasters.

Finally, Marie's fables are also traditional in that they teach the familiar mistrust of words. Yet they also manifest on occasion an enjoyment of verbal ingenuity and the uses to which it can be successfully put. Perhaps, as Jauss suggests, the influence of the beast epic (*Ysengrimus* and the *Roman de Renart*) is making itself felt in this respect. This dual attitude to language culminates in a dual attitude to the fable itself. On the one hand, it aims to have an effect on the real world by mediating serious moral lessons; at the same time, it is a self-conscious lie, manipulated by the female author who is the presiding goddess of its fictional world. The notion that the fable is a lie that conveys truth is an ancient one,[8] but Marie's demonstration of the paradoxical relations between *veir* and *mençunge* gives it a new vividness and force.

*   *   *

The Owl and the Nightingale

The sudden proliferation of beast literature at the turn of the twelfth century in England produced not only Marie's *Fables* and Nigel's *Speculum stultorum*, but also the Middle English debate-poem *The Owl and the Nightingale*. Its date of composition cannot be fixed with

7. *Engin* is also treated as a positive characteristic in twelfth-century romances; see Hanning, *The Individual*, pp. 105–38.
8. See Freytag, 'Die Fabel als Allegorie'.

certainty, but such slender indications as there are point to the reign of Richard I (1189–99) or (less probably) John (1199–1216).[9] Among these indications is the likelihood that the English poet knew Marie's work, since the Nightingale relates a version of the fable of the owl in the hawk's nest which is very those to that found in Marie's *Fables*, and the Owl refers to the story told of the nightingale in her *lai* of *Laüstic*. * * *

THE NIGHTINGALE IN THE LATIN LYRIC TRADITION

The Nightingale's literary history is the fuller of the two, for she was of course a favourite of lyric poets throughout the Middle Ages.[1] In this poetic tradition, it is the image of what we might call the 'natural nightingale' that is to the fore. Since the nightingale is not a biblical bird, and is thus unencumbered with the weight of exegetical reminiscence,[2] the poets were free to present their praise each time in the guise of a spontaneous emotional response to the surpassing beauty of the nightingale's song, poured forth in inexhaustible abundance from beneath her covering of leaves. The impression of immediacy is often created by the use of direct address to the bird: Eugenius of Toledo in the seventh century initiated a tradition that stretches as far as Keats's *Ode* by casting his poem on the nightingale in the second person, beginning with a thrice-iterated 'Vox, philomela tua' (1, 3, 5) and gathering energy until it climaxes in a series of passionate imperatives:

> dic ergo tremulos lingua vibrante susurros
> et suavi liquidum gutture pange melos.
> porrige dulcisonas attentis auribus escas;
> nolo tacere velis, nolo tacere velis. (15–18)[3]

9. See Hume, *The Owl and the Nightingale*, pp. 4–8; Bennett and Smithers (*Early Middle English Verse and Prose*, p. 2) prefer the reign of Richard I. The first piece of evidence is the date of the two manuscripts of the poem, which N. R. Ker placed in the second half of the thirteenth century (*The Owl and the Nightingale Reproduced in Facsimile*, p. ix). The second is the reference to 'King Henri', followed by the pious wish 'Jesus his soule do merci!', at lines 1091–2 of the poem; the natural implication of this is that King Henry II is dead, but King Henry III has not yet come to the throne (since otherwise there would be a need to distinguish the Henry in question). Scholarly attempts to link the poem more closely to particular events of the late twelfth century are generally unconvincing (they are summarized and discussed by Hume, *The Owl and the Nightingale*, pp. 6–8, 67–83; to Hume's survey may be added Coleman, 'Papal Theories of Marriage', but note that Coleman's argument is undermined by an inability to translate Middle English.
1. On the medieval tradition of nightingale poetry, see Hensel, 'Die Vögel', pp. 596–614; Raby, 'Philomena praevia temporis amoeni'; Telfer, 'The Evolution of a Mediaeval Theme'; Ross, 'Rose und Nachtigall' and 'Noch Einmal'; Ochse, 'Zu: Werner Ross' and 'Erwiderung'; Pfeffer, *The Change of Philomel*.
2. As Ochse noted ('Zu: Werner Ross', p. 140).
3. MGH Auct. Ant. XIV, p. 254. Ross ('Rose und Nachtigall', p. 62) asserts that the only rational interpretation of Eugenius's poem is that the nightingale is 'the Christian Muse, embodied in the never-ending hymns of praise of monks', but there is nothing in the text to support this view apart from the conventional doxology that closes it.

[Give forth your warbling notes with quivering tongue, and pour
out liquid melody from your sweet throat. Feed our listening ear
with your sweet sounds—I beg you never to cease, never to cease.]

Eugenius's poem was influential enough to have been imitated two
centuries later by his countryman Paulus Albarus;[4] its echoes are
heard again in the popular nightingale-poem 'Aurea personet lira':

> 9. O tu parva, numquam cessa, canere, avicula! . . .

> 11. Nolo, nolo, ut quiescas temporis ad otia,
> Sed ut letos des concentus tua, volo, ligula
> cuius laude memoreris in regum palatia.[5]

[Little bird, never cease your singing! . . . I beg you, beg you,
never to pause for rest, but to give us joyous harmony from your
little tongue; may it win you praise in the palaces of kings!]

The inclusion of both Eugenius's poem and 'Aurea personet lira' in
the famous eleventh-century manuscript Cambridge University
Library, Gg.5.35, which found a home at St Augustine's, Canterbury,[6]
brings them into an English context.

The poet's direct response to the beauty of the nightingale's song
may occupy the whole of his poem, as it does in the examples men-
tioned so far, or it may resolve itself into secondary responses of a
religious or erotic nature. The latter are probably the more familiar
to us—the nightingale appears in scores of medieval love-poems as
an essential part of a romantic decor[7]—but the Christian response
to the nightingale goes back as far as Paulinus of Nola (353–431).[8]
In Alcuin's poem lamenting the death of a nightingale,[9] the nostalgic

---

4. MGH Poetae III, pp. 126–7.
5. *Carmina Cantabrigiensia*, ed. Strecker, Nr. 10. For other echoes of Eugenius, see
   Strecker's notes. 'Aurea personet lira' has often been attributed to Fulbert of Chartres
   (c. 960–1028), but Strecker thinks this is doubtful (ibid., p. 32).
6. On MS Gg.5.35, see Rigg and Wieland, 'A Canterbury Classbook'. Eugenius's poem is
   in the 'school-book' part of the manuscript (fol. 369v), while 'Aurea personet lira'
   appears in the section of the manuscript containing the lyric collection known as the
   'Cambridge Songs' (fols 432–41, at fol. 434v). On the diffusion of Eugenius's poem in
   the school-text tradition, see Riou, 'Quelques aspects'.
7. See Hensel, 'Die Vögel'.
8. In one of his poems celebrating the feast day of St Felix, Paulinus prays to God to give
   his poetry the eloquence and beauty of the nightingale, 'who, hidden beneath green
   foliage, is accustomed to sweeten country retreats with her varied melodies, and from
   her single tongue to pour forth myriad notes in shifting harmony—a bird whose feath-
   ers are monochrome but who is of rainbow eloquence' ('quae viridi sub fronte lat-
   ens solet avia rural / multimodis mulcere modis linguamque per unam / fundere non
   unas mutato carmine voces, / unicolor plumis ales, sed picta loquellis': ed. Hartel,
   XXIII.29–32).
9. MGH Poetae I, pp. 274–5. The 'nightingale' for whom Alcuin mourns may be a person,
   since animal *cognomina* were much used in his circle; the point made here is however
   unaffected.

commemoration of its song leads him into reflections which antici-
pate the claims of the Nightingale in the Middle English poem to
remind men of the 'blisse of houene riche / Þar euer is song & murȝþe
iliche' (717–18):[1]

> Noctibus in furvis nusquam cessavit ab odis
> Vox veneranda sacris, o decus atque decor.
> Quid mirum, cherubim, seraphim si voce tonantem
> Perpetua laudent, dum tua sic potuit? (11–14)

[In the dark nights your adored voice never ceased from sacred
songs, glorious and beautiful. What wonder is it if cherubim and
seraphim praise the Thunderer with ceaseless voice, when your
voice had such power?]

Yet such reflections preserve the spontaneity of the initial emotional
response, in the sense that the nightingale herself is unaffected by
the meaning the poet finds for her. If she acts as a stimulus to human
thought or emotion, it is because she herself remains innocent of
human concerns; the starting point of Alcuin's meditations is pre-
cisely the contrast between the instinctive nature of the bird's
behaviour and the ratiocinative response which makes it instruc-
tive for humans.

> Hoc natura dedit, naturae et conditor almus,
> Quem tu laudasti vocibus assiduis,
> Ut nos instrueres vino somnoque sepultos,
> Somnigeram mentis rumpere segniciem.
> Quod tu fecisti, rationis et inscia sensus,
> Indice natura nobiliore satis,
> Sensibus hoc omnes, magna et ratione vigentes
> Gessissent aliquod tempus in ore suo. (19–26)[2]

[This, Nature granted, and the benign Creator of Nature, whom
you praised with tireless singing, so that you might teach us,
buried in wine and sleep, to shake off the sleepy lethargy of our
minds. What you did, unendowed with reason or sense, with
Nature as much nobler guide, this all who are blessed with sense
and powerful reason should have done in season, with their own
mouths.]

---

1. 'The bliss of the kingdom of heaven, where there is unending and unchanging music
   and delight'. Quotations from *The Owl and the Nightingale* are from the edition by Neil
   Cartlidge.
2. I have modernized the punctuation by changing colons to commas at the end of lines
   20 and 24.

The parallel between the animal world and the human world depends on its separation; the response created by the nightingale is one from which she is, by its own definition, exempt. The poet speaks to himself, despite the appearance of communication given by the second-person address; the redundancy of the imperatives which needlessly exhort the nightingale to continue singing—that is, to continue to be herself—unmask the dialogue as soliloquy. Traditional motifs emphasize the nightingale's remoteness—hidden by the dark, or by a covering of green leaves—as a poignant contrast to the passionate immediacy of her song.[3] This remoteness throws into relief the subjective nature of the human response, which remains bounded within the human world without seeking to penetrate the intrinsic nature of the nightingale.

The same pattern repeats itself in Marie de France's *Laüstic*, where the subjective response is a romantic rather than a religious one. For the lovers, * * * the nightingale becomes an 'objective correlative' of their love—passionate, yet hidden, miraculously powerful yet at the same time small and vulnerable. But the projection of their emotions on to the nightingale leaves its autonomous being intact; indeed, the serene freedom of the bird is the very condition of its role as a symbol of their yearning. The brutality of the husband, in contrast, expresses itself in his violation of the nightingale's autonomy; annihilating the separation between the animal and the human, he entraps the bird in the world of human guilt, endowing it with responsibility for the significance with which it has been invested.

It is this separation between the subjective human response and the autonomous completeness of the bird that leads me to use the term 'the natural nightingale' for the bird celebrated in lyric. The term does not imply that the poet's affectation of a direct and immediate response is to be taken *au pied de la lettre*, still less that lyric poets were dedicated bird-watchers. The immediate untrammelled response to the nightingale's song is as much a part of literary convention as the repeated motifs and phrases that betray the dependence of these poets on each other. Its importance is simply the implication that the significance of the nightingale is created afresh in the responses of each human hearer, and there is no predetermined 'meaning' for the bird.

This lyric-romantic tradition constitutes the 'literary genealogy' invoked for the Nightingale in the Middle English poem, in so far

---

3. See the quotation from Paulinus, n. 9 above, line 29, the quotation from Alcuin, p. 152 above, line 11, and Eugenius, MGH Auct. Ant. XIV, p. 254, lines 8–10 ('You nourish your tiny brood in the leafy trees; see, the groves ring with your melodious songs, and the foliage of the leafy wood resounds with them'; 'frondibus arboreis pignera parva foves./ cantibus ecce tuis recrepant arbusta canoris,/ consonat ipsa suis frondea silva comis').

as she has one at all. There is no hint of her role in classical myth as the metamorphosed Philomel; nor is there any trace of Pliny's touching story of the nightingale singing so passionately in contest with its peers that it falls dead from the branch.[4] The tradition of religious poetry which makes the nightingale a metaphor for Christ seems to have developed too late to affect this poem.[5] The Owl ignores the Phaedran-Romulan fables in which the nightingale appears and goes instead to the romantic tradition—to *Laüstic*—to find an anecdote characterizing her opponent. It is not only Marie's *lai*, however, that links this Nightingale with the lyric-romantic tradition; other features of the English poem recall its traditional motifs. The richly blossoming hedge on which she perches, for example, replicates the pastoral springtime beauty which is her traditional setting. The oft-repeated comparison between the nightingale's voice and the most melodious musical instruments[6] is likewise echoed by the English poet:

> Bet þuȝte þe dreim þat he were
> Of harpe & pipe þan he nere;
> Bet þuȝte þat he were ishote
> Of harpe & pipe þan of þrote. (21–4)

4. *Natural History*, X.xliii.81–3. The poetic possibilities in this myth are exploited in the *Philomena* (inc. 'Philomena praevia temporis amoeni') of John Pecham, Franciscan friar and archbishop of Canterbury, 1279–92. In John's poem, the nightingale who sings all day until she dies becomes a figure for the Christian soul meditating in the course of the liturgical day on the life and death of Christ. The success of this poem is reflected in the fact that there are three French versions of it. See *Le chant du rous-signeul*, ed. Walberg, and *Rossignol*, ed. Baird and Kane; the third is unedited but is discussed by Okubo ('Le rossignol et le mystère'), who entitles it the *Livret du rossigno-let*. It is likely however that all these poems are too late to have affected *The Owl and the Nightingale*.
5. Despite its title (which seems to refer to the nightingale as the bird of love, since Amor plays a major role in the poem), John of Hoveden's *Philomena* (ed. Blume) mentions the nightingale only briefly (as a figure of Mary in stanza 42 and as a figure of Christ in stanza 824; also in a list of paradoxes describing worldly love in stanza 470). It is given slightly more prominence as a figure of Christ in the Anglo-Norman version of the *Philomena* (*Rossignos*, ed. Hesketh; see lines 1860, 2711, 2969–3012, 3045–52, 3231–78, 3376), but even so it is only one among a large number of recurring metaphors (flowers, jewels, musical instruments, the book, food and drink, etc.). John wrote this Anglo-Norman version of his poem for Queen Eleanor, wife of Henry III, and since she is addressed as 'mother of King Edward', it must have been completed after Henry's death in 1272 and before Eleanor's death in 1291. The examples of Christ as nightingale in French religious poetry which are given by Okubo ('Le rossignol sur la Croix') also date from the late thirteenth century onwards. * * * [T]his tradition is probably too late to find reflection in the English poem.
6. Eugenius of Toledo, MGH Auct. Ant. XIV, p. 254, lines 3–4: 'Your voice, o nightingale, surpasses harps in its music and outdoes wind instruments in its wonderful harmonies' ('vox, philomela, tua citharas in carmine vincit/ et superat miris musica flabra modis'); 'Aurea personet lira', *Carmina Cantabrigiensia*, ed. Strecker, p. 30, stanza 6.1–2: 'The beauty of her voice, clearer than the lyre': ('Vocis eius pulchritudo, clarior quam cith-ara'); stanza 10.1–2: 'no music of the lyre can imitate your notes, which the clear-sounding pipe cannot match' ('Sonos tuos vox non valet imitari lirica,/ quibus nescit consentire fistula clarisona'); p. 31, stanza 12.3: 'the tambourine-player and the sound-ing flutes yield the palm to you' ('cedit tibi timpanistra et sonora tibia').

[The music seemed to come from a harp or pipe more than anything else; it seemed to be produced from a harp or pipe rather than a throat.]

The smallness and drabness of the bird's body, thrown into prominence in the English poem by the Owl's insulting description of her opponent as 'a little sooty ball' ('Þu art dim an of fule howe/ An þinchest a lutel soti clowe./ Þu nart fair, no þu nart strong,/ Ne þu nart þicke, ne þu nart long': 577–80; cf. also 561),[7] is often mentioned in Latin lyric as a striking contrast to the powerfulness and variety of her song.[8]

But this last example already makes clear that if it is the romantic tradition that forms the background to the Nightingale, she is thoroughly de-romanticized in the violent attacks of the Owl. For such de-romanticization the lyric tradition also provides more than one precedent. The best example is the parody of 'Aurea personet lira' (beginning 'Aurea frequenter lingua'), which transforms the passionate entreaties to the nightingale to continue her ceaseless outpourings into equally heartfelt pleas to shut up and give the ears of mortals some rest.[9]

9. O tu parva, cur non cessas clangere, avicula?
Estimas nunc superare omnes arte musica?
Aut quid cum lira contempnis sonora dulciflua? . . .

11. Cessa, cessa fatigando lassata iam bucula,
quia premis dormizantes clam iugiter nausia;
omni ora pro quid canis digna ovans sidera?

12. Misera, infelix illa, tam tenuis viscera,
que nec tumes saciata opima cibaria,
speras cantizando cunctis imperare gracia? . . .

14. Parce vatem iam secura, heiulare tardita,
conticesce, conticesce, ne crepando clangita,
ancxiata vires nollis, locum tuum propera.

7. 'You are drab and dirty in colour and you look like a little sooty ball. You are neither beautiful nor strong, you are neither bulky nor tall.'
8. Paulinus, ed. Hartel, XXIII.32: 'A bird whose feathers are monochrome, but who is of rainbow eloquence' ('unicolor plumis ales, sed picta loquellis'); Alcuin, MGH Poetae I, p. 274, lines 7–8: 'Your colour was despised but your song was not; your voice poured in a flood from your slender throat' ('Spreta colore tamen fueras non spreta canendo,/ Lata sub angusto gutture vox sonuit'); 'Aurea personet lira', Carmina Cantabrigiensia, ed. Strecker, p. 31, stanza 13.1–2: 'Although you appear small in body, yet everyone hears you; you do it all by yourself' ('Quamvis enim videaris corpore premodica,/ tamen te cuncti auscultant, nemo dat iuvamina').
9. The poem is printed in Strecker's edition of the Carmina Cantabrigiensia (Appendix Nr. 1, pp. 111–13). It is found in a Saint-Martial manuscript, of the end of the tenth century. Cf. the Provençal tenso cited by Hensel ('Die Vögel', p. 599), in which Bernard de Ventadour protests that he is through with love, and likes sleep and rest better than listening to the nightingale (Bernard de Ventadour, Chansons d'amour, ed. Lazar, no. 28, stanza 2).

[Will you never stop that racket, overrated little bird?
Do you think your art surpasses all the singing ever heard?
Don't you know that other music is quite frequently
      preferred? . . .

Stop it, stop it, you're a nuisance—surely now you've tired
      your beak?
When I try a little snoozing on the sly, you make me sick.
Must you fill up every moment with pretentious rhetoric?

Wretched, miserable birdlet, with your skinny little chest,
you're not stuffed up like a gander which has feasted on
      the best:
do you hope that through your warbling all will bow to
      your behest? . . .

Have some pity on a poet: please control your nagging tongue;
shut your beak, and let's have silence from that boring
      jangling song.
Save your energies for later: go off home where you
      belong!]]¹

In such a poem we can already hear the voice of the Owl, complain-
ing about the endless monotony of her opponent's song:

> 'Ac þu singest alle longe niȝt
> From eue fort hit is dailiȝt;
> & eure leist þin o song
> So longe so þe niȝt is long;
> & eure croweþ þi wrecche crei
> Þat he ne swikeþ niȝt ne dai.
> Mid þine pipinge þu adunest
> Þas monnes earen, þar þu wunest;
> & makest þine song so unwurþ,
> Þat me ne telþ of þar noȝt wurþ.'   (331–40)

['But you sing all night long, from evening until daylight, and
your unvarying song lasts the whole night through, your
wretched throat continually squawking, never ceasing by night
or day. You batter the ears of men who live around you with your
piping and make your song so cheap that no one thinks any-
thing of it.']

---

1. I quote the somewhat free translation by Fleur Adcock (The Virgin and the Nightin-
    gale, pp. 30–5), since it captures the jaunty metre and rhyme-scheme of the original.

In the shifting subjective responses of the lyric tradition we can see
the fluid outlines which will harden themselves into the implacable
oppositions of the avian debate.

*   *   *

JACQUES LE GOFF

From The Birth of Purgatory[†]

The Church's attitude toward the dead at the beginning of the twelfth
century, so far as we are able to tell from documents of clerical ori-
gin, was this: After the Last Judgment men will be grouped for all
eternity into two classes, the saved and the damned. A man's fate
will be determined essentially by his behavior in life: faith and good
works militate in favor of salvation, impiety and criminal sins con-
sign the soul to Hell. About the period between death and resurrec-
tion Church doctrine had little of a precise nature to say. According
to some writers, after death the deceased would await determination
of their fate by the Last Judgment, either in the grave or in some
dark but neutral region, such as the *sheol* of the Old Testament, which
was not distinguished from the grave. Others, more numerous,
believed that souls would reside in various dwelling places. Of these
the most prominent was the bosom of Abraham, the abode of souls
which, while waiting to be admitted to Heaven in the true sense of
the word, bide their time in a place of refreshment and peace. Most
believed—and this opinion seems to have been favored by ecclesi-
astical authorities—that a final decision was handed down immedi-
ately after death in the case of two categories: first, those who are
entirely good, martyrs and saints, the fully righteous, who go to
Heaven at once and enjoy the ultimate reward, the sight of God, the
beatific vision; and second, those who are entirely bad, who go
directly to Hell. Between the two there were one or two intermedi-
ate categories, depending on which authority we believe. According
to Augustine, those who are not entirely good must undergo a trial
before going to Heaven, and those who are not entirely bad must go
to Hell but while there benefit from some moderation of their tor-
ment. Most of those who believed in the existence of an intermedi-
ate category held that the dead awaiting admission to Heaven would
have to undergo some kind of purgation. Here opinions varied. Some
held that this purification would take place at the moment of the

† From Jacques Le Goff, *The Birth of Purgatory*, trans. Arthur Goldhammer (Chicago:
University of Chicago Press, 1984, 1986), pp. 133–38, 181, 190–201. Reprinted by
permission of the University of Chicago Press.

Last Judgment. But again there were various positions among author-
ities committed to this view. Some argued that all the dead, includ-
ing the righteous, the saints, the martyrs, the apostles, and even Jesus
were required to undergo this trial. For the righteous it would amount
to a mere formality, without consequences, for the godless it would
lead to damnation, and for the almost perfect, to purgation. Others
believed that only those who did not go immediately to Heaven would
be subject to this examination.

What was the nature of this purgation? The overwhelming major-
ity of writers held that it consisted of some sort of fire, largely on
the authority of 1 Corinthians 3:10–15. But some held that there
were various instruments of purgation and spoke of "purgatorial pun-
ishments" (*poenae purgatoriae*). Who was worthy of being subjected
to such examination, which, however painful it might be, was an
assurance of salvation? As we have seen, from the time of Augus-
tine and Gregory the Great, it was believed that the only souls wor-
thy of this "second chance" were those who had only "slight sins" to
expiate or who, having repented, had not had time before dying to
do penance on earth. When did purgation occur? After Augustine it
was generally believed that it would take place in the period between
death and resurrection. But it might extend beyond this period in
one direction or the other. In Augustine's own view, trials endured
here below, earthly tribulations, could be the first stages of purgation.
Others believed that purgation took place at the moment of the Last
Judgment and generally held that the "day" of judgment would last long
enough so that purgation would be more than a mere formality.

Where was this purgation supposed to take place? Here opinions
were not so much varied as ambiguous. Most authors said nothing
in particular on the subject. Some thought that a dwelling place was
set aside to receive souls for this purpose. Gregory the Great sug-
gested in his anecdotes that purgation occurs in the place where the
sin was committed. Authors of imaginary journeys to the other world
were not sure where to locate the purgatorial fire. They were torn
between situating it in the upper regions of Hell, hence in some
sort of underground valley, and placing it, as Bede suggested, on a
mountain.

All in all, there was much hesitation about the nature of this inter-
mediary place. Although almost everyone agreed that some sort of
fire, distinct from the eternal fire of Gehenna, played a role, few tried
to locate that fire, or if they did were quite vague about it. From the
Fathers to the final representatives of the Carolingian Church, the
problem of the hereafter was essentially that of distinguishing
between those who would be saved and go to Heaven and those who
would be damned and sent to Hell. When all is said and done, the
belief that gained the most ground between the fourth and the eleventh

centuries and that helped to prepare the way for the inception of Purgatory was this: that the souls of the dead could be helped by prayer, and more particularly by suffrages. In these the faithful found what they needed both to satisfy their desire to support their relatives and friends beyond the grave and to sustain their own hopes of benefiting in turn from similar assistance. Augustine, a shrewd psychologist and attentive pastor, says as much in *De Cura pro mortuis gerenda*. This belief and its associated practices, which required the intervention of the Church, in particular for the eucharistic sacrifice, and which afforded the Church the benefits of alms and other gifts, helped to tighten its control over the living, who wished to avail themselves of its supposed power to intervene on behalf of the dead.

In this as in so many other areas, the twelfth century accelerated the pace of change. By the century's end Purgatory would exist as a distinct place. In the meantime pokers stirred the smoldering purgatorial fires. Before proceeding with the story, however, a preliminary remark is in order.

Handling twelfth-century sources is a delicate matter. The general growth alluded to above correlates with a marked increase in the number of written documents. Since the sixteenth century, scholars, especially nineteenth- and twentieth-century scholars, have been at pains to publish as many of these documents as possible, and yet many remain unpublished. The documents bear characteristic marks of the period. In order to make sure that a work would be successful, many twelfth-century clerics did not hesitate to attribute it to an illustrious or familiar author. Hence the literature of the twelfth century is rife with apocryphal material. In many cases questions of attribution and authenticity have not been resolved. The then new philosophy of scholasticism has left us many documents that are difficult to attribute to any author, assuming that the word "author" makes sense when speaking of *quaestiones*, *determinationes*, and *reportationes* that were often compilations of notes taken by a pupil of courses given by a master. It was not uncommon for the scribe to mix his own thoughts or the thoughts of other contemporary authors with the authentic words of the master. Finally, we possess few original manuscripts from the period. The manuscripts we do have were written later, between the thirteenth and the fifteenth century. In some cases the scribes have replaced a word of the original text with a word or expression current in their own time, either unconsciously or in the belief that they were thereby doing a good turn—for the men of the Middle Ages were inspired by the quest for eternal, not historical, truth.[1] In this essay I have been unable to resolve certain questions, in part because our knowledge of the Middle Ages is incomplete, but even more because of the very nature of

---

1. See Appendix 2 [of Le Goff] on *purgatorium*. [Le Goff there gives a detailed review of scholarship since 1981 on this subject. —Ed.]

twelfth-century religious literature, whose multifarious eloquence is too subtle for the classificatory grids of present-day history, concerned (and rightly so) mainly with questions of attribution and dating. Nevertheless, I am convinced by my research and textual analyses that Purgatory did not exist before 1170 at the earliest.

Purgatory did not exist, but the number of documents showing an interest in what goes on in the interval between death and the Last Judgment increased rapidly. The expositions may have been disorderly, but this merely reflects the state of work in progress, research under way. What is increasingly evident in these documents is the concern to specify the exact location where purgation occurs.

A Hesitant Author: Honorius Augustodunensis

A typical example of this early confusion may be found in the writings of the mysterious Honorius Augustodunensis, who was probably Irish by birth but who spent most of his religious life at Ratisbon. Honorius, who, according to M. Capuyns, was probably the only medieval disciple of Johannes Scotus Erigena, did indeed have original ideas about the other world. He believed, for one thing, that the other world did not exist "materially." It consisted, rather, of "spiritual places." What is meant here by "spiritual" is ambiguous. It may designate a certain corporeal quality, or it may mean a reality that is purely symbolic, metaphorical. Honorius hesitated between the two. In the *Scala coeli major*, in which he seems to lean toward the completely immaterial interpretation, he hedges by putting forward a theory of the seven hells (of which this world is the second). The degree to which these hells are material or immaterial varies from one to the next.[2] I am particularly interested in two features of

2. See Claude Carozzi, "Structure et fonction de la vision de Tnugdal," in the collection entitled *Faire croire*, soon to be published by the Ecole française de Rome. In my opinion Carozzi exaggerates the importance of a supposed controversy between "materialists" and "immaterialists" in the twelfth century and dates the emergence of Purgatory too early, but his contribution is quite stimulating. Carozzi may be right in thinking that there was in some twelfth-century writers, such as Honorius Augustodunensis, a tendency to see all otherworldly occurrences as *spiritualia*, spiritual phenomena, but this tendency had scarcely any influence on the genesis of Purgatory, a still rather vague notion whose development might at this point have been blocked. When Honorius Augustodunensis has occasion to describe the places in which souls are found in the other world, as he does in the *Elucidarium*, he is forced to concede that in some degree their nature is material, as we shall see. The debate as to whether the fire most frequently indicated as the instrument of purgation was material or spiritual did not last much beyond the first few centuries of the Christian era. The idea that the soul has no body and cannot therefore occupy any material space, put forward by Johannes Scotus Erigena in the ninth century, had little influence, no more than most other teachings of this isolated thinker. See M. Cappuyns, *Jean Scot Erigène. Sa vie, son oeuvre, sa pensée* (Louvain-Paris, 1933). In the first half of the thirteenth century Alexander of Hales expressed the opinion of most theologians, which confirmed the widespread belief: "Sin is not remitted without a double penalty: the remission has no value if there is no suffering on the part of the body" (Non ergo dimittitur peccatum sine duplici poena; non ergo valet relaxati cum nulla sit poena ex parte corporis), *Glossa in IV Libros Sententiarum* 4, dist. 20. No doubt the essential point is to notice that "spiritual" does not mean "disembodied."

Honorius's thought. First of all, he is harshly critical of a spatial conception of spiritual life. In the *Scala coeli major* he says the notion that Hell is underground is purely metaphorical, a way of conjoining the ideas of inferiority, heaviness, and sadness. He concludes with these words: "Every place has length, breadth, and height, but since the soul is deprived of these attributes, it cannot be shut up in any place."[3] The same idea occurs again in his *Liber de cognitione verae vitae*: "But it seems to me the height of absurdity to think that souls and spirits, since they are incorporeal, can be shut up in corporeal places, particularly since any place can be measured by its height, length, and breadth, whereas the spirit, as is well known, is deprived of all these attributes."[4] It seems reasonable to assume that if Honorius's way of thinking had triumphed, Purgatory, essentially defined as a place, would never have been born or would have remained of secondary importance, largely without influence.

Paradoxically, though, in another work, the *Elucidarium*, a treatise summarizing the main truths of the Christian faith, a sort of catechism, Honorius discusses purgatorial fire, and the passage in which he does so played a notable role in the gestation of Purgatory. In book three of this work, a dialogue, Honorius answers questions about the life to come. To a question about heaven he replies that it is not a corporeal place but the spiritual abode of the blessed, situated in the intellectual Heaven where they may contemplate God face to face. His interlocutor asks if this is where the souls of the just are taken. He answers that this is where the souls of the perfect are taken when they leave the body. Who are the perfect? Those who in this life were not content merely to do what was prescribed but attempted more: martyrs, monks, and virgins, for example. The just reside in other dwellings. And who are the just? Those who merely did gracefully what was prescribed. When they die, their souls are taken by angels to the earthly paradise; more precisely, they are transported into spiritual joy, since spirits do not live in corporeal places. There is, moreover, another category of the just known as the "imperfect." Though imperfect they are still inscribed in God's book. Among these, for example, are worthy married couples whose merits are such that they are received into very pleasant dwellings. Many of the imperfect are granted a greater glory even before the day of judgment, thanks to the prayers of saints and the alms of the living; all of them are reunited with the angels after judgment. Among the elect there are also some who are a long way from perfection and who delayed doing penance for their sins. These, like the wicked son who is turned over to a slave to be whipped, are, with the

---

3. *PL* 172.1237–38. Claude Carozzi is probably right to be suspicious of this edition.
4. *PL* 40.1029.

permission of the angels, handed over to demons to be purged. But the demons cannot torment them more than they deserve or than the angels permit.

The questioner next asks how the imperfect may be freed. The master, that is, Honorius, responds that masses, alms, prayers and other pious works are the proper means, particularly if the deceased person has accomplished such works on behalf of others while still alive. Some of the imperfect are set free on the seventh day, others on the ninth, others at the end of a year, still others even longer after being handed over to the demons. Using a mysterious symbolic arithmetic, Honorius then explains how the length of the sentence is determined.

Finally, he is asked a question that bears most directly on our subject:

DISCIPLE: What is purgatorial fire?

MASTER: Some undergo purgation in this life; it may come in the form of physical pain brought by various ills, or physical trials laid down by fasting, vigils, or other activities, or the loss of loved ones or treasured belongings, or pains or illness, or a want of food or clothing, or, finally, a cruel death. But after death purgation takes the form of excessive heat or excessive cold or any other kind of trial, but the least of these trials is greater than the greatest that one can imagine in this life. While they are there, angels sometimes appear to them, or saints in whose honor they did something during their lifetime, bringing air or a sweet fragrance or some other form of relief, until they are set free and allowed to enter into that court from which every taint is banned.

DISCIPLE: In what form do they live there?

MASTER: In the form of the bodies they wore in this world. And it is said of demons that they are given bodies made of air so that they feel their torments.

After explaining, not very clearly, the relations between the body and the soul, Honorius discusses Hell. Actually he thinks, there are two hells. The upper one is the lower portion of the terrestrial world and is replete with torments: unbearable heat, biting cold, hunger, thirst, and various kinds of pain, some having physical causes, such as the pain caused by blows, some having spiritual causes, such as the pain caused by fear or shame. The lower hell is a spiritual place in which there is an inextinguishable fire; there the soul must endure nine special torments: a fire that burns without light, an unbearable cold, immortal worms, serpents, and dragons, a frightful stench, frightening noises such as hammers striking iron, thick darkness, the throng of sinners mingled without distinction, the horrible sight of demons and dragons glimpsed by the flickering light of the flames, the depressing din of wails and insults, and finally shackles of fire that bind all the limbs of the damned.[5]

This text does nothing more than recast the ideas of Augustine, including the idea that purgation begins on earth, with a trifle more insistence on the metaphorical character of the other world, which Augustine too sometimes thought more symbolic than material in nature. And yet Honorius, his imagination no doubt fired by the visionary tales he had read and heard, lets slip images that contradict his ideas. The reason why this text proved influential in the prehistory of purgatory was, I think, even more than the realistic descriptions of Hell, the role accorded to the angels and demons, which follows in the train of Gregory the Great and is more "medieval" than Augustinian.

* * *

Four Monastic Journeys to the Other World

I have selected four twelfth-century journeys to the hereafter, to my mind the most important of any we have, for closer scrutiny. The first of these is worthy of note, I think, because it concerns the vision of a laywoman, the mother of Guibert of Nogent, and an experience of a quite intimate kind. The visions of Alberic of Settefrati and Tnugdal are included for their wealth of detail and also because their authors come from areas that are noted for otherworldly fantasy: southern Italy and Ireland. Finally, Saint Patrick's Purgatory is in a sense the doctrine's literary birth certificate. For our purposes these visions are of interest because they show how the idea of Purgatory as a separate region of the other world made its way into a traditional genre, tentatively at first and later in the form of an image which, despite its hazy outlines, is clear enough. They will also enable us to appreciate the role of the monastic imagination in the inception of Purgatory.

* * *

A similar impression results from reading yet another vision, this one drawn from Ireland, at the opposite end of the world of Benedictine monasticism.[6]

---

5. See Y. Lefèvre, *L'Elucidarium et les Lucidaires* (Paris, 1954).
6. *Visio Tnugdali*, ed. Albrecht Wagner (Erlangen, 1882). I remind the reader of Claude Carozzi's recent study, "Structure et fonction de la vision de Tnugdal," cited previously.

IRELAND: TNUGDAL'S VISION OF AN OTHER WORLD
WITHOUT PURGATORY

Tnugdal's other world—his voyage includes no earthly episode—is somewhat better organized than Alberic's. Like the Cassinian monk, Tnugdal first passes through a series of places in which various categories of sinners are being tormented: murderers, traitors, misers, thieves, abductors, gluttons, and fornicators. The places where they are being punished are of unusual dimensions: deep valleys, a very high mountain, an enormous lake, a huge house. Later on Dante was to give the theme of the mountain a special treatment of his own. Here, the souls on the mountain are subjected alternately to extremes of heat and cold. Darkness and stench are everywhere. Monstrous beasts add to the horror. One of these beasts sits on a frozen lake and devours souls in its fiery gullet, digests them, and then vomits them up (an old Indo-European theme). The souls thus reincarnated have sharply pointed beaks with which they tear at their own bodies. The victims of this beast are fornicators, particularly fornicating monks. In Piranesi-like images Tnugdal sees the souls of gluttons cook like bread in an immense oven. Those who have accumulated sin upon sin are tortured in a valley full of noisy forges by a blacksmith-torturer named Vulcan. Along with the distinctive treatment of various sins and vices, prominence is given to the notion of the quantity of sin. Furthermore—a sign of the times in the justice-smitten twelfth century—the angel makes clear that God is, despite the variety of tortures, nonetheless merciful and, above all, just: "Here each person suffers according to his deserts, in keeping with the verdict of justice."

Then follows a long descent down a steep precipice into the lower regions of Hell, where Tnugdal faces horrors, cold, stench, and darkness greater than anything he has endured previously. He sees a rectangular trench like a cistern from which there emerges a smoky, fetid flame full of demons and souls that resemble sparks, rising for a time, vanishing into nothingness, and falling back into the depths. He then comes to the very gate of Hell and has the privilege to witness, as a living person, what the souls of the damned, plunged in darkness, cannot see, any more than they can see Tnugdal himself. Finally, he sees the prince of darkness himself, a beast larger than all those he has seen previously.

Then the stench and darkness lift and Tnugdal and his angel discover, at the base of a huge wall, a multitude of sad men and women beleaguered by wind and rain. The angel explains that these are the souls of those who are not entirely wicked, who tried to live honorably but who did not dispense their temporal wealth to the poor and who must spend several years out in the rain before being shown the way to a good rest (*requies bona*). Passing through a gate in the wall, Tnugdal and his companion come upon a beautiful, sweet-smelling field, full of flowers and brightly lit, a pleasant place in which crowds of men and women frolic gaily. These are the not entirely good, those worthy of being plucked out of the tortures of Hell but not yet ready to join the saints. In the middle of the field stands the fountain of youth, whose water bestows the gift of eternal life.

At this point in the story we come upon a very curious account of the legendary kings of Ireland—whom Tnugdal evidently considers to have been real historical figures. Those who were wicked have repented, and those who were good were nevertheless guilty of certain sins, and so they are here either in the midst or at the end of a period of expiation. Just as Benedictine patriotism inspired Alberic's vision, so Irish "nationalism" makes its appearance here. This is also another instance of the tradition of the hereafter that we encountered earlier in the vision of Charles the Fat. The existence of a purgatorial place (the word purgatory is not actually uttered here) makes it possible to level moderate criticism at the monarchy, which is both honored and rebuked.

Thus we find kings, Domachus and Conchobar, both extremely cruel and violently hostile to one another, turned gentle, and reconciled in friendship, having repented before they died. Should this be read as a call for unity of the Irish clans? Even more important is the vision of King Cormachus (Cormac), who is seated on a throne in a very beautiful house whose walls, made of gold and silver, have neither doors nor windows but can be penetrated at any point. He is served by paupers and pilgrims, to whom he distributed his property while still alive. After a short while, however, the house becomes dark, all the inhabitants turn sad, the king begins to cry, gets up, and leaves the room. All the souls stand and reach out their hands to heaven, begging God to "have pity on thy servant." Then we see the king plunged into fire up to his navel, his entire body covered with a hair shirt. The angel explains that the king suffers for three hours each day and rests for twenty-one hours. He suffers up to his navel because he was an adulterer and over his entire body because he was responsible for the death of a count who was close to Saint Patrick and because he committed perjury. All his other sins have been forgiven.

At length Tnugdal and the angel reach Paradise, which consists of three regions surrounded by walls. A wall of silver encloses the place reserved for righteous couples; a wall of gold surrounds the place set aside for the martyrs and the chaste, monks and nuns, and defenders and builders of churches; and finally, a wall of precious stones surrounds the virgins and the nine orders of angels, the saint-confessor Ruadan, Saint Patrick, and four (Irish!) bishops. With this final vision Tnugdal's soul returns to his body.

What Tnugdal's vision clearly shows is this: while the geography of the other world is still fragmented, with Hell as such appearing to be unified only because it cannot be visited, three principles are beginning to govern the organization of the various purgatorial places. The first of these principles is geographical: we pass from one area to another, the transition being marked by contrasts of terrain and temperature. The second is moral: those undergoing purgation are distributed among the various places according to the nature of their vices. The third is, properly speaking, religious, not to say theological: men are classified into four categories, namely, the entirely good, who go directly to Paradise after death; the entirely wicked, who are individually judged immediately after death (Tnugdal stresses that the damned "have already been judged") and sent to Hell; the not entirely good; and the not entirely wicked. But Tnugdal is not entirely clear about the last two categories. If we read him literally, it would seem that the souls in these two groups are distinct from the generality of sinners being tortured in the upper region of Hell. In speaking of the not entirely wicked Tnugdal makes no allusion to their having passed through penal places and limits himself to saying that they spend a "few years" in wind and rain, suffering from hunger and thirst. As for the not entirely good, the angel tells Tnugdal that "they have been plucked from the torments of Hell" but are not yet worthy of entering into true Paradise.

Given the date, it is rather suprising, too, that the idea of purgation does not figure in the account (nor is the word mentioned). Tnugdal has made a clumsy attempt to organize a whole range of elements from literary and theological tradition into a vision that he is incapable of unifying. For one thing, he mentions the existence of two Hells, but he is unable to indicate the precise function of the upper Hell. For another, he clearly subscribes to Augustine's theory of the four categories, ranging men on a scale of good and evil from best to worst. But since he does not know what categories to consign to the upper Hell, he has created new regions to accommodate those for whom he has no other place and winds up with something like five regions in his other world. This fivefold division was in fact one of the ways proposed in the twelfth century for solving the problem of how to reshape the other world. The weakest point in Tnugdal's conception (I allow myself to make this value judgment because I believe that the coherence of the system of Purgatory was an important factor in its success with both clergy and the masses in an "age of rationalization") is that Tnugdal does not establish any connection between the places of waiting (and expiation in one degree or another of severity) and the

lower regions of Hell. If he had provided for passage first through the
one and then through the other, he would have given a concrete solu-
tion to the issues raised by Augustine's categorization. He did not do
so probably in part because his conception of space was still confused
but, even more, because his conception of time did not allow a solu-
tion (it bears repeating that space and time cannot be separated). For
Tnugdal, the time of the other world was an eschatological time that
had little or no similarity to time on earth, historical time. Here and
there, it is true, he does slip in references to periods of "a few years" in
the other world, but these periods do not follow one another in any
orderly succession. The time of the other world had not yet been uni-
fied, and a fortiori there was a great gulf between the conceptualiza-
tion of time in this world and time in the next.

DISCOVERY IN IRELAND: "SAINT PATRICK'S PURGATORY"

Although the fourth imaginary voyage, to which we now turn, was
the work of a monk (a Cistercian, however), it introduces into the
usual traditional context certain important novelties. One of
these is of particular importance: Purgatory is named as one of three
regions of the other world. This brief work occupies an essential place
in the history of Purgatory, in whose success it played an important,
if not decisive, role. The work I have in mind is the celebrated *Pur-
gatorium Sancti Patricii*, "Saint Patrick's Purgatory."[7]

7. The *Purgatorium Sancti Patricii* was published twice in the seventeenth century, by
   Messingham in his *Florilegium Insulae Sanctorum* in 1624, which is reproduced in *PL*
   180.975–1004, and by the Jesuit John Colgan in his *Triadis thaumaturgae . . . acta*
   (Louvain, 1647). Modern versions have been provided by S. Eckleben, *Die älteste
   Schilderung vom Fegfeuer des heiligen Patricius* (Halle, 1885); by E. Mall, who gives,
   opposite the text published by Colgan, the manuscript that may be regarded as being
   closest to the original text (MS E VII 59 of Bamberg, from the fourteenth century) and
   variants from a manuscript from the British Museum, Arundel 292 (end of the thir-
   teenth century): "Zur Geschichte der Legende vom Purgatorium des heiligen Patri-
   cius," in *Romanische Forschungen*, ed. K. Vollmoller (1891), vol. 6, pp. 139–97; by
   U. M. van der Zanden, *Etude sur le Purgatoire de saint Patrice* (Amsterdam, 1927), who
   published the text of a manuscript from Utrecht from the fifteenth century, together
   with an appendix consisting of a corrected version of the Arundel 292 manuscript; and
   by Warncke in 1938. I used the Mall edition. The *Purgatorium Sancti Patricii* has fre-
   quently been studied, in both its Latin and vernacular versions (especially English and
   French—with Marie de France's *L'Espurgatoire saint Patriz* in a class by itself). Several of
   these studies, though dated, are still valuable. Most situate the text either in the context
   of age-old beliefs about the other world or in relation to folklore. Though frequently not
   sufficiently critical and nowadays out of date, these studies remain a model of historical
   openmindedness. Among those worth citing are the following: Theodore Wright, *St. Pat-
   rick's Purgatory: An Essay on the Legends of Purgatory, Hell and Paradise, Current During
   the Middle Ages* (London, 1844); Baring-Gould, *Curious Myths of the Middle Ages* (1884,
   reprint ed. Leyden, 1975): "St. Patrick's Purgatory," pp. 230–49; G. P. Krapp, *The Leg-
   end of St. Patrick's Purgatory, Its Later Literary History* (Baltimore, 1900); Philippe de
   Felice, *L'autre monde. Mythes et légendes: le Purgatoire de saint Patrice* (Paris, 1906). The
   study that is considered to be most complete, Shane Leslie's *St. Patrick's Purgatory: A
   Record from History and Literature* (London, 1932), is not the most interesting. V. and E.
   Turner have given a very suggestive anthropological interpretation of the pilgrimage to
   Saint Patrick's Purgatory in modern times, which unfortunately contributes nothing to

The author is a monk named "H" (an initial which Matthew Paris in the thirteenth century expanded for no good reason to Henricus, or Henry) who at the time of writing lived in the Cistercian monastery of Saltrey in Huntingdonshire. He was asked to write the story by a Cistercian abbot, the abbot of Sartis (today Wardon in Bedfordshire). He had first heard the tale from another monk, Gilbert, who was sent to Ireland by Abbot Gervase of the Cistercian monastery of Luda (today Louthpark in Huntingdonshire) to look for a site suitable for the founding of a monastery. Since Gilbert did not speak Gaelic, he took with him the knight Owein as interpreter and bodyguard, and Owein tells him the adventure story in which he figures as the hero in Saint Patrick's Purgatory.

In the preamble to his work H of Saltrey invokes Augustine and especially Gregory the Great to remind his readers how much the living stand to profit from edifying visions and revelations concerning the hereafter. This is particularly true of the various forms of punishment that are called "purgatorial" (*que purgatoria vocatur*), in which those who may have committed sins during their lives but who nevertheless remained righteous are purged and thereby enabled to achieve the eternal life to which they are predestined. The punishments are proportioned to the seriousness of the sins committed and to the degree of goodness or wickedness of the sinners. Corresponding to the range of different sins and punishments is a gradation in the places of punishment, in the subterranean Hell which, according to some, is a dark prison. The places in which the worst tortures are inflicted are at the bottom, and the places of maximum joy are at the top. The middling good and middling bad receive their just deserts in the middle (*media autem bona et mala in medio*). From this it is clear that H of Saltrey has adopted the system of three categories (rather than Augustine's four) and the idea of an intermediary place.

Furthermore, souls receive purgatorial punishment according to their merits, and those souls that God allows to return to their earthly bodies after being punished exhibit marks similar to corporeal marks as reminders, proofs, and warnings.[8]

While Patrick was preaching the Gospel, without much success, to the recalcitrant Irish and seeking to convert them by the fear of Hell and the allure of Paradise, Jesus showed him in a foresaken place a round, dark hole (*fossa*) and told him that if a person animated by

---

our subject: *Image and Pilgrimage in Christian Culture* (Oxford, 1978), chap. 3: "St. Patrick's Purgatory: Religion and Nationalism in an Archaic Pilgrimage," pp. 104–39.

8. In Rome, in the church of the Sacro Cuore del Suffragio, there is a small "museum of Purgatory," which contains a dozen signs (generally burn marks made with a hand, indicating the fire of Purgatory) of the apparition of souls from Purgatory to the living. These occurred at intervals from the end of the eighteenth century to the beginning of the twentieth. The system of Purgatory proved long-lived indeed.

a true spirit of penitence and faith spent a day and a night in this hole, he would be purged of all his sins and would see the tortures of the wicked and the joys of the good. Patrick hastened to build a church beside this hole, installed regular canons in the church, had a wall built around the hole, and entrusted the gate key to the prior of the church. Numerous penitents were supposed to have entered this place since the time of Patrick, who, it is said, ordered that their accounts be recorded. The name given to the place was Purgatory, and since Patrick was the first to have tasted its fruits, it became known as Saint Patrick's Purgatory (*sancti Patricii purgatorium*).[9]

According to custom, those who wished to enter Saint Patrick's Purgatory were required to obtain authorization from the bishop of the diocese, who was supposed to attempt to dissuade them. If he could not do so, he sent the applicant together with his authorization to the prior of the church, who also tried to persuade the person to choose another form of penance with the warning that many had died after passing through the gate. If he too failed, the prior then ordered the candidate to begin his ordeal with two weeks of prayer. At the end of this time the candidate attended a mass, during which he took communion and was exorcised with holy water. He was then taken, in a procession of chanting priests, to Purgatory. The prior opened the gate, reminding the candidate that there were demons about and that many previous visitors had vanished. If the candidate persisted, he was blessed by all the priests and then, making the sign of the cross, passed through the gate into Purgatory. The prior shut the gate behind him. On the following day at the same hour, the procession returned to the hole. If the penitent emerged, he returned to the church and spent another two weeks in prayer. If the gate remained closed, it was assumed that the penitent had died, and the procession withdrew. This was a particular kind of ordeal, or judgment of God, a type that may have been typical of Celtic tradition.

At this point in his account, H of Saltrey skips to his own time (*hiis nostris temporibus*), which he further specifies as the time of King Stephen (1135–54). In the thirteenth century Matthew Paris was even more explicit about the date: without the slightest evidence he says that the adventure of Owein the knight took place in 1153. Heavily weighed down with sins of unspecified nature, Owein, having successfully negotiated the preliminary phases of the ordeal,

---

9. The details about Patrick, who lived in the fifth century, are invented. The older lives of Patrick are silent on the subject. As far as we can tell from the current state of the documentary evidence, Saint Patrick's Purgatory is mentioned for the first time in the new life of the saint written by Jocelyn of Furness between 1180 and 1183. Since the knight Owein is not mentioned there, the 1180–83 period is generally regarded as the terminus a quo for the dating of the *Tractatus* of H of Saltrey.

enters the hole cheerfully and with confidence. He looks upon his undertaking as essentially a knightly adventure, which he confronts by himself, intrepidly [*novam gitur miliciam aggressus miles noster, licet solus, intrepidus tamen*].[1] Advancing through thickening shadows, he comes to a sort of monastery, inhabited by twelve figures clad in white robes, rather like monks. Their leader explains the rules of the trial to him. He is to be surrounded by demons, who will try either to frighten him with the sight of terrible tortures or to seduce him with false words. If he gives in to the fear or the seduction and retraces his steps, he is lost, body and soul. If he feels he is about to give in, he is instructed to invoke the name of Jesus.

At this moment the demons burst in, and from now until the end of his infernal journey they do not leave him for a moment, as he glimpses countless frightening visions by the light of torturing flames and in the midst of fetid odors and shrill cries. From each of the trials he is about to undergo the knight will emerge victorious by invoking the name of Jesus, and after each trial he will refuse to quit and turn back. I shall therefore omit mention of the denouement of each episode. The devils first build a pyre in a room of the house from which his journey begins and attempt to throw him upon it. After passing through a dark desert and being whipped by a cutting wind with an edge as sharp as a sword's he comes to a limitless field in which men and women are lying naked on the earth, to which they are fastened by burning nails through their hands and feet. He then enters a second field in which people of every age, sex, and condition are lying on their backs or their stomachs, preyed upon by fiery dragons, serpents, and toads; a third field in which men and women with burning nails piercing all their limbs are whipped by demons; and finally a fourth field, a real chamber of horrors of the most diverse kinds, where he sees men and women suspended by iron hooks stuck in the sockets of their eyes or in their ears, throats, hands, breasts, or genitals, while others have fallen victim to hell's kitchen and are being baked in ovens, roasted over open fires, or turned on spits—and so on. Next he sees a great wheel of fire, with men fastened to it being spun at high speed through the flames. This is followed by a huge bathhouse, in which a multitude of men and women, young and old alike, are plunged into vats of boiling metals, some completely submerged, others immersed up to their eyelids or lips or necks or chests or navels or knees, while some have only a single hand or foot in the cauldron. Owein then comes to a mountain and to a river of fire flowing in a deep gorge with sheer walls. On the summit a crowd of people is lashed by a violent, glacial wind which blows some of them into the river, from

1. See Erich Köhler, *L'Aventure chevaleresque. Idéal et réalité dans le roman courtois* (Paris, 1974).

which they attempt to escape only to be pushed back in by demons equipped with iron hooks.

Finally, he comes upon a horribly foul black flame escaping from a well, in which innumerable souls rise like sparks and fall back again. The demons accompanying the knight tell him that "this is the gate of Hell, the entrance of Gehenna, the broad highway that leads to death. He who enters here will never leave again, for there is no redemption in Hell. This is the eternal fire prepared for the Devil and his fiends, and you cannot deny being of their number." As he feels himself being caught up and carried down into the well, Owein once more utters the name of God and finds himself at some distance from the pit facing a very broad river of fire traversed by what seems to be an impassable bridge, since it is so high as to induce vertigo, so narrow that it is impossible to set foot on it, and so slippery that it would be impossible in any case to maintain one's footing. In the river below, demons are waiting with iron hooks. Once again Owein invokes the name of Jesus and advances onto the bridge. The further he advances, the wider and more stable the bridge becomes, and half-way across he can no longer see the river to the right or the left. He escapes one last infuriated attempt by the demons and, climbing down from the bridge, finds himself facing a very splendid high wall whose gates, made of pure gold set off by precious gems, give off a delightful odor. He enters and finds himself in a city of marvels.

At the head of a procession are two figures resembling archbishops, who address Owein in the following terms:[2]

> We are going to explain to you the meaning [*rationem*] of what you have seen. This is the earthly Paradise. We have come here because we have expiated our sins—we had not completed our penance on earth prior to death—in the tortures you saw along the way, in which we remained for a more or less lengthy period depending oh the quantity of our sins. All whom you have seen in the various penal places, except those below the mouth of Hell, will come, after their purgation is complete, to the rest in which we find ourselves, and ultimately they will be saved. There is no way for those who are being tortured to know how long they will remain in the penal palaces, because their trials can be alleviated or abridged by means of masses, psalms, prayers, and alms given in their behalf. By the same token, we, who are enjoying this wonderful repose and joy but who have not yet been found worthy to go up to Heaven, will not remain here

---

2. Although I have enclosed the archbishops' story in quotation marks, I have abridged and paraphrased it.

indefinitely; every day some of us move from the earthly Para-
dise to the celestial Paradise.

They then have Owein climb a mountain and from there show him
the gates of the celestial Paradise. A tongue of flame comes down
from these gates and fills them with a delicious sensation. But the
"archbishops" bring Owein back to reality: "You have seen part of
what you wanted to see: the repose of the blessed and the tortures
of sinners. Now you must return by the same path you took to get
here. If from now on you live well in the world, you can be sure that
you will join us after your death, but if you live badly, you have seen
what tortures await you. On your way back you will have nothing
more to fear from the demons, because they will not dare to attack
you, nor from the tortures, for they will not harm you." In tears, the
knight starts back and ultimately rejoins the twelve people he left at
the start, who congratulate him and announce that he has been
purged of his sins. The prior opens the gate a second time and Owein
leaves Saint Patrick's Purgatory to begin a second two-week period
of prayer in the church. Following this he takes the cross and leaves
on a pilgrimage to Jerusalem. When he returns he goes to the king,
his lord, and asks him to designate a religious order in which the
knight may live. This happens to be the time when Gilbert of Luda
is about to depart on his mission. The king offers Owein the chance
to serve as the monk's interpreter. Delighted, the knight accepts
"because in the other world I saw no order in glory as great as the
Cistercian order." They build an abbey, but Owein, as it turns out,
does not want to become either a monk or a lay brother and is con-
tent to remain Gilbert's servant.

For our purposes, the imagery of the other world is not the most
important thing about this story, though that imagery certainly must
have contributed largely to its success. Most of the items traditional
since the *Apocalypse of Paul* are included, and the images prefigure
those to be found in subsequent visions, the *Divine Comedy* in par-
ticular. But the imagery is more the general imagery of Hell than an
imagery peculiar to Purgatory. Certain themes are left out, however,
and their absence here no doubt contributed to the fact that they all
but vanish from later accounts. Cold, for example, has been sup-
planted almost entirely by fire, whereas previously heat and cold had
generally been linked in the penal imagery of the hereafter.

In the vision of Drythelm, for example, the visitor to the other
world first comes to a wide, deep valley whose left slope is engulfed
in terrible flames while its right slope is whipped by a violent snow-
storm. Similarly, Tnugdal, before coming to the lower region of Hell,
encounters "a great mountain traversed by a narrow path, one side

of which is a stinking, sulphurous, smoky fire while the other is wind-whipped ice."

In the sermon attributed to Saint Bernard we read that "those who are in Purgatory awaiting redemption must first be tormented either by the heat of fire or by the rigors of cold."

But the significance of cold as a punishment had for some time not been clearly perceived. The idea of a beneficent *refrigerium* had more or less supplanted it.

In the vision of the Emperor Charles the Fat, the imperial dreamer transported into the infernal beyond hears his father, Louis the German, standing in boiling water up to his thighs, utter the following words: "Have no fear, I know that your soul will return to your body. If God has allowed you to come here, it was so that you might see the sins for which I am undergoing these and the other torments you have seen. I spend one day in this basin of boiling water, but the next day I am transported into that other basin, in which the water is very cool." The author of this text has failed to grasp the original significance of the rite, since the move into the cold water is described as a favor that the emperor owes to the intercession of Saint Peter and Saint Rémi.

In *Saint Patrick's Purgatory* cold figures only in the passage describing the glacial wind that whips the summit of the mountain at the bottom of Purgatory. Fire, which in the twelfth century represented the very place of purgation, has superseded cold. The birth of Purgatory thus sounded the death knell for the concept of *refrigerium* and paved the way for the eventual disappearance of the bosom of Abraham.[3]

Saint Patrick's Purgatory at once met with considerable success. Shane Leslie has written that the work was "one of the best sellers of the Middle ages." Its date of composition is uncertain. It is generally said to have been written around 1190, since its translation into French by the celebrated English [sic] poetess Marie de France presumably cannot have taken place later than the last decade of the twelfth century. In addition, Saint Malachy, who was canonized in 1190, is mentioned in the *Tractatus* in his quality of saint. But other scholars put the date of composition somewhat later, around 1210.[4] While I have tried to situate the time when the word *purgatorium*

3. These images of the other world are still prevalent today among the descendants of the Mayas, the Lacandons of southern Mexico: "The 'sage' Tchank'in Maasch . . . was an inexhaustible source of stories about this realm of shadow in which frozen streams and rivers of fire run side by side." J. Soustelle, *Les Quatre Soleils* (Paris, 1967), p. 52.
4. F. W. Locke, "A New Date for the Composition of the Tractatus de Purgatorio Sancti Patricii," *Speculum*, 1965, pp. 641–46, rejects the traditional date of around 1189 in favor of the 1208–15 period as the time when the *Tractatus* was written. This means that the date of the *Espurgatoire Saint Patriz* must also be pushed ahead by some twenty years. Richard Baum, "Recherches sur les oeuvres attribuées à Marie de France," *Annales Universitatis Saraviensis* 9(1968), has recently argued not only that the

first appeared and to date the decisive change in the representation of the hereafter as precisely as possible, I do not think it is particularly important for our purposes to say that *Saint Patrick's Purgatory* was written in 1210 rather than 1190. The key point, rather, is this: that the new region of the other world took shape in two phases, first in theological-spiritual literature between 1170 and 1180 at the prompting of Parisian masters and Cistercian monks, and then in visionary literature stemming from the 1180–1215 period. In fact, the *Life of Saint Patrick* by Jocelyn of Furness, composed between 1180 and 1183, mentions Saint Patrick's Purgatory but situates it on Mount Cruachin Aigle in Connaught.[5] The real events in the history of beliefs, mentalities, and sensibilities can rarely be dated to the precise day or year. The birth of Purgatory is a phenomenon that we can associate with the turn of the thirteenth century.

By contrast, it is of considerable importance that a description of Purgatory, explicitly mentioned and associated with a specific place on earth, should have appeared around the year 1200. The composition of the *Tractatus* by H of Saltrey must have been roughly contemporaneous with the rise of the legend and the creation of a pilgrimage. Saint Patrick's Purgatory is mentioned again, omitting the story of Owein the knight, in the *Topographia Hibernica* of Giraldus Cambrensis, the first edition of which dates from 1188, but it is not mentioned in the oldest known manuscript and is found only in a marginal note in a thirteenth-century manuscript. Giraldus travelled in Ireland in 1185–86. In chapter 5 of the second part of the *Topographia Hibernica* he describes a lake in Ulster in which there is an island divided into two parts. One of these parts is pleasant and beautiful, with an official church, and renowned as a place frequented by saints. The other, wild and horrible, is abandoned to demons. There are nine holes in the earth. Those who dare to spend the night in one of these holes are seized by evil spirits and must endure horrible tortures in an unspeakable fire until morning, and when they are found are in an almost inanimate state. It is said that if one does penance by undergoing these tortures, infernal punishments can be escaped after death, unless very grave sins are committed in the meantime.[6]

Espurgatoire was later than the last decade of the twelfth century but also that it was not the work of Marie de France. As we shall see later on, Giraldus Cambrensis's *Topographia Hibernica* and Jocelyn of Furness's *Life of Saint Patrick* do not provide decisive information concerning the dating of the *Tractatus*.

5. The *Life of Saint Patrick* by Jocelyn of Furness was published in the seventeenth century in the same collections as H of Saltrey's *Purgatorium*, by Messigham (*Florilegium insulae sanctorum* [Paris, 1624], pp. 1–85) and Colgan (*Triadis thaumaturgae* [Louvain, 1647]). The passage concerning the Purgatory on Mount Cruachan Aigle occurs on page 1027. It has been republished in the *Acta Sanctorum*, entry for March 17, vol. 2, p. 540–80.

6. Giraldus Cambrensis, *Opera*, ed. J. F. Dimock (London, 1867), vol. 5: *Rerum Britannicarum medii aevi scriptores*, pp. 82–83. It was immediately after this passage in the

This island, Station Island, is located in Lough Derg (Red Lake) in County Donegal in the present-day Irish Republic near the border with Northern Ireland. Pilgrims have apparently been making their way to Saint Patrick's Purgatory there ever since the end of the twelfth century. Pope Alexander VI condemned the practice in 1497, but the chapel and the pilgrimage revived in the sixteenth century and have survived several subsequent destructions and interdictions in 1632, 1704, and 1727. Pilgrimages became particularly frequent after 1790 and a large chapel was erected. A huge new church dedicated to Saint Patrick was completed in 1931 and every year some 15,000 pilgrims visit the site between June 1 and August 15.[7]

While Saint Patrick's Purgatory is clearly related to Irish Christianity and the cult of Saint Patrick, it is doubtful whether in the twelfth century it had the same Catholic and Irish nationalist overtones that it acquired subsequently and still carries with it today. Indeed, it seems probable that the pilgrimage was first begun and controlled by English regular clergy.

Following the translation by Marie de France,[8] numerous Latin versions of H of Saltrey's *Tractatus* appeared as well as many

---

manuscript from the first half of the thirteenth century that the words, "This place was called Patrick's Purgatory by the inhabitants," were added, and it is told how Saint Patrick obtained its creation. Cf. C. M. van der Zanden, "Un chapitre intéressant de la *Topographia Hibernica* et le *Tractatus de purgatorio sancti Patricii*," *Neophilologus* (1927). Giraldus Cambrensis seems to have written the *Topographia* at the time when a pentitential pilgrimage—doubtless something in the nature of an ordeal—was shifted from the largest island, Saints' Island, in the northwestern corner of Lough Dergh, to the smaller Station Island, which explains the synthesis in a single island divided between saints and demons.

7. Apart from the very interesting study by V. and E. Turner cited in n. 7, p. 392, above, the available studies of the pilgrimage are either mediocre or summary. Cf. John Seymour, *Saint Patrick's Purgatory. A Mediaeval Pilgrimage in Ireland* (Dundald, 1918); J. Ryan, *New Catholic Encyclopedia* (1967), vol. 11, p. 1039. The fourth chapter of Philippe de Felice's *L'Autre Monde, Mythes et Légendes, Le Purgatoire de saint Patrice* (Paris, 1906), which is entitled "Histoire du Sanctuaire du Lough Derg" is not without interest and concludes with this judicious remark: "The persistence of Saint Patrick's Purgatory over the centuries is a clear, incontrovertible fact, the importance of which deserves to be called to the attention of sociologists." On pp. 9ff., he tells how, together with a cousin, he made his way with some difficulty to Lough Derg and the isle of Purgatory in 1905. In 1913 Cardinal Logue, the primate of Ireland, made the following declaration after visiting Station Island: "I believe that any person who here at Lough Derg completes the traditional pilgrimage, the penitential exercises, the fast, and the prayers that are the equivalent of so many indulgences, and who subsequently dies, will have to suffer very little in the other world" (cited by V. and E. Turner, p. 133). Anne Lombard-Jourdan, who visited Lough Derg and Saint Patrick's Purgatory in 1972, was kind enough to provide me with a copy of the official program, which bears the seal of the local bishop, the bishop of Clogher. During the Middle Ages the length of the penance was reduced from fifteen days to nine days, the nine-day period being more standard with the Church. In more recent times the period was still further reduced, to three days, which is the rule today, but the heart of the pilgrimage is still a trial of twenty-four hours. The 1970 program states that "the Vigil is the principal spiritual exercise of the pilgrimage and means that one goes entirely without sleep for a full twenty-four hours without interruption." An extraordinary continuity of beliefs and practices!

8. *L'Espurgatoire Saint Patriz* by Marie de France was published by Thomas Atkinson Jenkins in Philadelphia in 1894. See L. Foulet, "Marie de France et la Légende du Purgatoire de saint Patgrice," *Romanische Forschungen* 22(1908):599–627.

translations into vernaculars, especially French and English.[9] The Latin version was included by Roger of Wendover in his *Flores Historiarum*, compiled prior to 1231. Matthew Paris, who continued Roger's work in his *Chronica majora*, repeats the story verbatim. That great popularizer of Purgatory, the German Cistercian Caesarius of Heisterbach, who may or may not have known H's *Tractatus*, in any case has this to say in his *Dialogus miraculorum* 12.38: "Let anyone who doubts the existence of Purgatory go to Ireland and enter the Purgatory of Patrick and he will have no further doubts about the punishments of Purgatory." Five authors of the most influential edifying histories of the thirteenth century made use of the *Purgatorium Sancti Patricii*: James of Vitry in his *Historia orientalis* (chap. 92); the two Dominicans Vincent of Beauvais, in the *Speculum historiale* (bk. 20, chaps. 23–24), and Stephen of Bourbon, in his *Tractatus de diversis materiis praedicabilibus* (see below); Humbert of Romans in *De dono timoris*; and Jacobus da Voragine (Jacopo da Varazze) in his celebrated *Golden Legend*, where we read the following passage. "And Saint Patrick learned, by revelation, that this well led to a purgatory, and that those who wished to descend there could expiate their sins and would be dispensed from any Purgatory

---

9. Paul Meyer mentions seven French verse versions of *Saint Patrick's Purgatory* in his *Histoire littéraire de la France*, vol. 33, pp. 371–72, and *Notices et Extraits des manuscrits de la Bibliothèque nationale* (Paris, 1891), vol. 34: Marie de France's version; four anonymous thirteenth-century versions; Beroul's version; the version of Geoffroy de Paris introduced by the Fourth Book of the *Bible des sept états du diable*. One of these was published by Johan Vising, *Le Purgatoire de saint Patrice des manuscrits Harleien 273 et Fonds français 2198* (Göteborg, 1916). The noun "purgatory" is used there several times. For example:

> Par la grant hounte qu'il aveit
> Dist qe mout bonnement irreit
> En purgatoire, qe assez
> Peust espener ses pechiez (vv. 91–94).
> . . . .
> Com celui qe ne velt lesser
> En purgatoire de entrer (vv. 101–2)

There are also several French prose versions. One of these was published by Prosper Tarbe, *Le Purgatoire de saint Patrice. Légende du XIIIe siècle, publiée d'après un manuscrit de la Bibliothèque de Reims* (Reims, 1842). The oldest English versions (thirteenth century) were published by Hortsmann in *Alten Englische Legenden* (Paderborn, 1875), pp. 149–211; Koelbing in *Englische Studien* (Breslau, 1876), vol. 1, pp. 98–121; and L. T. Smith, *Englische Studien* (Breslau, 1886), vol. 9, pp. 3–12.

An edition in Occitan was published at the beginning of the fifteenth century by A. Jeanroy and A. Vignaux, *Raimon de Perlhos. Voyage au purgatoire de saint Patrice, Textes languedociens du XVe siècle* (Toulouse, 1903). This edition also contains Occitanian versions of the vision of Tindal (Tnugdal) and the vision of Saint Paul, which Raymond of Perelhos attributes to himself as he does the voyage to Saint Patrick's Purgatory. All of these texts come from manuscript 894 of the Bibliothèque municipale of Toulouse, illustrating the fifteenth-century taste for visions of the hereafter and Purgatory. In this small group of texts the vision of Tindal (Tnugdal) is converted into a vision of Purgatory. The title (fol. 48) is "Ayssi commensa lo libre de Tindal tractan de las penas de purgatori." On the fortunes of Saint Patrick Purgatory in Spain, see J. Perez de Montalban, *Vida y Purgatorio de San Patricio*, ed. M. G. Profeti (Pisa, 1972).

after their death."[1] Gossouin of Metz speaks of it in his *Image of the World*, of which there are verse versions from 1245 and 1248 and a prose version from 1246.[2] Here is an excerpt from one of the verse versions:*

> In Ireland there is a lake
> Which day and night burns like fire,
> And which is called Saint Patrick's
> Purgatory. And even now
> If someone comes
> Who is not genuinely repentant,
> He is immediately carried away and lost,
> And no one knows what has become of him.
> But if he confesses and is repentant,
> He must suffer many a torment
> And purge himself of his sins.
> The more there are of them, the more he suffers.
> And he who from this place has returned,
> Nothing more pleases him
> In this world, and never again
> Will he know laughter but shall live in tears,
> Moaning about the evils that exist
> And the sins that men commit.[3]

This poem the learned Saint Bonaventure had read either in the original or in a summary, and he discusses it in his commentary on the *Sententiae* of Peter Lombard.[4] Froissart asks a noble Englishman, Sir William Lisle, who traveled in Ireland in 1394, if he has visited "Saint Patrick's Purgatory." Lisle answers in the affirmative and allows that he and a companion even spent a night in the famous hole, to which he refers as a cellar. Both of them slept there and had visions in dreams, and Sir William is convinced that "all that is mere fantasy," exhibiting an incredulity rare for the time.[5]

Dante studied the *Tractatus* of H of Saltrey quite closely. The work's renown did not end with what is traditionally considered the

---

1. (Here translated into English from the French translation of the *Légende dorée* by T. de Wyzewa [Paris, 1920], p. 182. —Trans.) Concerning Stephen of Bourbon and Humbert of Romans, see L. Frati, "Il Purgatorio di S. Patrizio secondo Stefano di Bourbon e Umberto de Romans," in *Giornale storico della letteratura italiana* 8(1886):140–79.

2. The prose version by Gossouin of Metz was published by O. H. Prior, *L'Image du monde de maître Gossouin. Rédaction en prose* (Lausanne-Paris, 1913).

* Here translated literally into English from the slightly modernized French text cited by the author. —Trans.

3. This excerpt from the *Image du monde* by Gossouin of Metz is from the slightly modernized French version of the text given by the Count of Douhet in the *Dictionnaire des légendes du christianisme*, ed. Migne (Paris, 1855), col. 950–1035.

4. Quaracchi edition, vol. 4, p. 526. The great Franciscan master says that this was his source for the legend that Purgatory is found in these regions ("ex quo fabulose ortum est, quod ibi esset purgatorium").

5. Froissart, *Chroniques*, ed. Kervyn de Lettenhove (Brussels, 1871), vol. 15, pp. 145–46.

Middle Ages. Rabelais and Ariosto allude to it. Shakespeare thought that the story was familiar to the spectators of *Hamlet*[6] and Calderon wrote a play on the theme.[7] The vogue for Saint Patrick's Purgatory in both high and popular literature lasted at least until the eighteenth century.[8]

The essential point about both the cult and the *Tractatus* is this: at last there was a description of Purgatory, a place with a name of its own and an other world consisting of three regions (not counting the antechamber of Paradise that Owein visits). Alongside Hell and Heaven, which Owein is not permitted to see, there is Purgatory, in which the hardy knight-penitent travels extensively and which he describes at length. Furthermore, the geography of the next world is fitted into the geography of this one, not by means of a clumsy juxtaposition, as was the case with Alberic of Settefrati, but rather by specifying the precise location on earth of one of Purgatory's mouths. What could be more in keeping with the beliefs and the mentality of an age in whch cartography, taking its hesitant first steps, depicted Paradise (strictly speaking, the earthly Paradise) as contiguous with the world of the living? As the process of "spatialization" of Purgatory went forward, it became more and more necessary to find the mouths, to provide means of access for those living souls allowed to enter from earth. For a long time these mouths remained more or less indistinguishable from the mouths of Hell, and here the image of the "hole" (or shaft or well) took hold. The topography of the mouths of Purgatory centered on caves and caverns. The fact that Saint Patrick's Purgatory, situated in a cavern on an Irish isle, became so popular reinforced the image of Purgatory as a hole.

* * *

6. Shakespeare, *Hamlet*. When the ghost of his father appears to Hamlet (act 1 scene 5), this is what the ghost says:

> I am thy father's spirit
> Doom'd for a certain term to walk the night
> And, for the day, confin'd to fast in fires,
> Till the foul crimes, done in my days of nature,
> Are burnt and purg'd away.

Later, Hamlet's father says that his murder at the hands of his brother was all the more foul because he had no time to confess and do penance before dying. When the ghost has disappeared, Hamlet, without telling Horatio and Marcellus what the ghost has said, invokes Saint Patrick:

> HORATIO: There's no offence, my lord.
> HAMLET: Yes, by Saint Patrick, but there is, Horatio,
> And much offence, too. Touching this vision
> It is an honest ghost.

7. Calderon's *El Purgatorio de San Patricio* was first published in 1636.
8. The Count of Douhet, in his very interesting article, "Saint Patrice, son purgatoire et son voyage," published a version still thought highly of in the eighteenth century. He writes (col. 951): "Of the thousands of versions available, we have chosen a recent one, still popular in the last century, which fully renders the intentions of the Middle Ages."

Selected Bibliography

• Indicates works included or excerpted in this Norton Critical Edition.

BIBLIOGRAPHIES

Burgess, G. S. *Marie de France: An Analytical Bibliography.* London: Grant and Cutler, 1977; Supplement No. 1, 1986; Supplement No. 2, 1997; Supplement No. 3, Tamesis: Suffolk, England, and Rochester: Boydell and Brewer Ltd., 2007.

EDITIONS

Marie de France

Curley, Michel J. *Saint Patrick's Purgatory: A Poem by Marie de France.* Binghamton: Center for Medieval and Early Renaissance Studies, State University of New York, 1993.

Ewert, Alfred. *Marie de France: Lais.* Oxford: Blackwell, 1944. Reissued with an introduction and bibliography by Glyn S. Burgess. Bristol: Bristol Classical Press, 1995.

Rychner, Jean. *Lais de Marie de France.* Paris: Champion, 1966; 2nd ed., 1981.

Spiegel, Harriet. *Marie de France, Fables, edited and translated.* Toronto, Buffalo, and London: University of Toronto Press, 1987. Reprinted by the University of Toronto Press and the Medieval Academy of America, 1994.

Warnke, Karl. *Die Lais der Marie de France.* Halle: Niemeyer, 1885, 2nd ed., 1900, 3rd ed., 1925. Reprint of 3rd ed. Genève: Slatkine, 1974.

———. *Die Fabeln der Marie de France.* Halle: Niemeyer, 1898. Reprint Genève: Slatkine, 1974.

———. *Das Buch vom Espurgatoire S. Patrice de Marie de France und Seine Quelle.* Halle: an der Saale, 1938. Reprint Genève: Slatkine, 1976.

The Owl and the Nightingale

Cartlidge, Neil. *The Owl and the Nightingale: Text and Translation.* Exeter, UK: Exeter University Press, 2001.

Stanley, Eric Gerald. *The Owl and the Nightingale.* London: Thomas Nelson and Sons Ltd. and E. G. Stanley, 1960.

BOOKS

Baum, Richard. *Recherches sur les œuvres attribuées à Marie de France.* Heidelberg: Winter, 1968.

• Bloch, R. Howard. *The Anonymous Marie de France.* Chicago: University of Chicago Press, 2003, 2006.

Bronson, Bertrand Harris. *The Traditional Tunes of the Child Ballads, With Their Texts, According to the Extant Records of England and America.* Four vols. Princeton: Princeton University Press, 1962.

Burns, Jane. *Bodytalk: When Women Speak in Old French Literature.* Philadelphia: University of Pennsylvania Press, 1993.

———. *Courtly Love Undressed: Reading Through Clothes in Medieval French Culture.* Philadelphia: University of Pennsylvania Press, 2002.

Carruthers, Mary. *The Book of Memory: A Study of Memory in Medieval Culture.* Cambridge: Cambridge University Press, 1990.

Child, Francis J. *The English and Scottish Popular Ballads.* Ten vols. Boston and New York: Houghton Mifflin, 1882–98.

Dinshaw, Carolyn and David Wallace, eds. *The Cambridge Companion to Medieval Women's Writing.* Cambridge: Cambridge University Press, 2003. (See especially Roberta L. Krueger, "Marie de France," pp. 172–83.)

Ferrante, Joan M. *To the Glory of Her Sex: Women's Roles in the Composition of Medieval Texts.* Bloomington and Indianapolis: Indiana University Press, 1997.

Gardiner, Eileen. *Visions of Heaven and Hell Before Dante.* New York: Italica Press, 1989.

Holmes, Urban Ticknor, Jr. *Daily Living in the Twelfth Century, Based on the Observations of Alexander Neckham in London and Paris.* Madison: University of Wisconsin Press, 1952.

Kelly, Douglas. *The Art of Medieval French Romance.* Madison: University of Wisconsin Press, 1992.

Kinoshita, Sharon and Peggy McCracken. *Marie de France: A Critical Companion.* Suffolk, England: D. S. Brewer: Boydell and Brewer Ltd., 2012.

Le Goff, Jacques. *The Medieval Imagination.* Trans. Arthur Goldhammer. Chicago and London: University of Chicago Press, 1988.

• ———. *The Birth of Purgatory.* Trans. Arthur Goldhammer. Chicago: University of Chicago Press, 1984, 1986.

• Mann, Jill. *From Aesop to Reynart: Beast Literature in Medieval Britain.* Oxford: Oxford University Press, 2009.

Maréchal, Chantal. *In Quest of Marie de France, a Twelfth-Century Poet.* Lewiston, NY: The Edwin Mellen Press, 1992.

• Maréchal, Chantal, ed. *The Reception and Transmission of the Works of Marie de France, 1774–1974.* Medieval Studies 23. Lewiston, NY: The Edwin Mellen Press, 2003.

McCash, June Hall and Judith Clark Barban, trans. and eds. Foreward by Emanuel J. Mickel. *The Life of Saint Audrey: A Text by Marie de France.* Jefferson, NC, and London: McFarland and Company, Inc., 2006.

Melville, A. D. *Ovid: The Love Poems.* Oxford: Oxford University Press, 1990.

Rothschild, Judith Rice. *Narrative Technique in the Lais of Marie de France: Themes and Variations.* Vol I. Chapel Hill: University of North Carolina Press, 1974.

Sahar, Amer. *Esope au feminin: Marie de France et la politique de l'interculturité.* Atlanta: Rodopi, 1999.

Stone, Brian. *The Owl and the Nightingale; Cleanness; St Erkenwald.* Harmondsworth, England: Penguin, 1971.

• *Studies in French Language and Medieval Literature Presented to Professor Mildred K. Pope.* Manchester, England: Manchester University Press, 1939.

Whalen, Logan E., ed. *A Companion to Marie de France.* Brill's Companions to the Christian Tradition, vol. 27. Leiden and Boston: Brill, 2011.

———. *Marie de France and the Poetics of Memory.* Washington, DC: The Catholic University of America Press, 2008.

ARTICLES

Arden, Heather. "The Lays of Marie de France and Carol Gilligan's Theory of the Psychology of Women." In *In Quest of Marie de France, a Twelfth-Century Poet*, ed. Chantal Maréchal. Lewiston, NY: The Edwin Mellon Press, 1992.

• Bedier, Joseph. "Les Lais de Marie de France." *Revue des Deux Mondes* 107 (1891).

Boyd, Matthew. "The Ancients' Savage Obscurity: The Etymology of Bisclavret." *Notes and Queries*: 2013.

Bruckner, Matilda Tomaryn. "Of Men and Beasts in Bisclavret." *Romanic Review* 82.3 (1991): 251–69.

———. "Speaking Through Animals in Marie de France's *Lais* and *Fables*." In *A Companion to Marie de France*, ed. Logan E. Whalen. Brill's Companions to the Christian Tradition, vol. 27. Leiden and Boston: Brill, 2011.

Finke, Laurie A. and Martin B. Schictman. "Magical Mistress Tour: Patronage, Intellectual Property and the Dissemination of Wealth in the *Lais* of Marie de France." *Signs: Journal of Women in Culture and Society* 25.2 (2000): 479–503.

Foster, Damon S. "Marie de France: Psychologist of Courtly Love." *PMLA* 44 (1959): 968–96.

Freeman, Michelle A. "Marie de France's Poetics of Silence: The Implications for a Feminine Translation." *PMLA* 99 (1984): 860–83.

Jambeck, Karen. "The *Fables* of Marie De France: A Mirror for Princes." In *In Quest of Marie de France, a Twelfth-Century Poet*, ed. Chantal Maréchal. Lewiston, NY: The Edwin Mellen Press, 1997.

Kinoshita, Sharon. "*Cherchez la femme*: Feminist Criticism in Marie de France's *Lai de Lanval*." *Romance Notes* 34.3 (Spring 1994): 263–73.

Krueger, Roberta L. "Beyond Debate: Gender Play in Old French Courtly Fiction." In *Gender in Debate From the Early Middle Ages to the Renaissance*. Ed. Thelma S. Fenster and Clare A. Lees. New York: Palgrave, 2002.

———. "The Wound, the Knot, and the Book: Marie de France and Literary Traditions of Love in the Lais." In *A Companion to Marie de France*, ed. Logan E. Whalen. Brill's Companions to the Christian Tradition, vol. 27. London and Boston: Brill, 2011.

McCash, June Hall. "*La vie seinte Audree*: A Fourth Text by Marie de France?" *Speculum* 77.3 (2002): 744–77.

McCracken, Peggy. "Women and Medicine in Medieval French Narrative." *Exemplaria* 5.2 (1993): 239–62.

Mickel, Emanuel. "Marie de France and the Learned Tradition." In *A Companion to Marie de France*, ed. Logan E. Whalen. Brill's Companions to the Christian Tradition, vol. 27. London and Boston: Brill, 2011.

Painter, Sidney. "To Whom Were Dedicated the Fables of Marie de France?" *Modern Language Notes* 48.6 (1961): 367–69.

Rothschild, Judith Rice. "A Rapprochement between Bisclavret and Lanval." *Speculum* 48.1 (January 1973): 78–88.

———. "Marie de France and the Folktale: Narrative Devices of the Märchen and Her *Lais*." In *In Quest of Marie de France, a Twelfth-Century Poet*, ed. Chantal Maréchal. Lewiston, NY: The Edwin Mellen Press, 1992.

Short, Ian. "Denis Piramus and the Truth of Marie's *Lais*." *Cultura Neolatina* 67 (2007): 319–40.

Spiegel, Harriet. "The Woman's Voice in the Fables of Marie de France." In *In Quest of Marie de France, a Twelfth-Century Poet*, ed. Chantal Maréchal. Lewiston, NY: The Edwin Mellen Press, 1992.

• Spitzer, Leo. "Marie de France: Dichterin von Problem-Märchen." *Zeitschrift für romanische philologe* 50 (1930).